MORE ADVANCE PRAISE FOR
Strong Boy

"Christopher Klein's *Strong Boy* is a well-researched look at a forgotten hero: modern boxing's first heavyweight champion. It's a go-to resource on John L. Sullivan's personal life, his ring career, and the era in which he thrived. For all the talk about 'the man who beat the man,' here's a work that documents the man himself."

—**John Florio,** author of *One Punch from the Promised Land: Leon Spinks, Michael Spinks and the Myth of the Heavyweight Title*

"Sports biography at its best. Rich in period detail, anecdote, and fresh perspective, *Strong Boy* paints both the good and the bad sides of success, as America's growing celebrity culture turned a simple Irish-American gladiator into a national, in fact international hero. A very human story with profound parallels for our sports-obsessed culture today!"

—**Nigel Hamilton,** author of *Biography: A Brief History and The Mantle of Command: FDR at War, 1941–1942*

"This admirable biography has a *Citizen Kane* feel to it: *Strong Boy* both celebrates John L. Sullivan as a sports hero and lights up the pathos of Sullivan the man-child. If he could 'lick any son-of-a bitch in the world,' John L. could out-drink and out-eat all contenders. The first million-dollar man in sports died broke. Christopher Klein does justice to the legend, the man, and the times."

—**Jack Beatty,** author of *The Rascal King: The Life and Times of James Michael Curley, 1874–1958*

STRONG BOY

The Life and Times of John L. Sullivan,
America's First Sports Hero

CHRISTOPHER KLEIN

LYONS PRESS
Guilford, Connecticut
An imprint of Globe Pequot Press

Lyons Press is an imprint of Globe Pequot Press.

Project Editor: Lauren Brancato
Layout Artist: Mary Ballachino

Library of Congress Cataloging-in-Publication Data is available on file.

ISBN 978-0-7627-8152-2

Printed in the United States of America

10 9 8 7 6 5 4 3 2 1

*To the memory of Martin, Krystle, Sean, and Lingzi,
and to the citizens of the greatest city in the world
who remain Boston Strong.*

Contents

Prologue: Rumble on the River

The most wicked men in New York City skimmed along the surface of the Hudson River. With the sun safely tucked beneath the horizon on the night of May 16, 1881, a tug hauled a barge laden with an unsavory cargo of pickpockets, gamblers, swindlers, drinkers, and drifters. Past the waterfront's forest of rocking masts, the motley menagerie crept up the liquid highway on a nefarious moonlight excursion.

As they nervously scanned the river for waterborne police, the four hundred outlaws bathed in the reflected glitter of America's greatest metropolis. On shore and under the yellow glare of Manhattan's gaslights, black-bonneted ladies in pinched corsets and cigar-chomping gentlemen with finely waxed mustaches and silk top hats promenaded to Broadway theaters. Sparkling carriages and hansom cabs rattled over a carpet of cobblestones past the Fifth Avenue palaces of the country's merchant princes. Beneath Delmonico's silver chandeliers and frescoed ceilings, the city's power brokers feasted on oysters and champagne as they peered out at the disembodied arm of the Statue of Liberty lifting its torch above Madison Square Park, a nagging reminder that the pedestal for the copper colossus remained unbuilt.

Behind New York's refined facade throbbed the Gilded Age's tarnished underbelly. Manhattan was an island of "unadulterated deviltry" with infernal-sounding neighborhoods like "Hell's Half Acre" and "Satan's Circus."

No city in the United States offered such an exquisite carnival of depravity. Inside New York's saloons and concert halls, patrons imbibed whiskey while their lascivious eyes drank in the dancing girls who flashed their thighs and sang bawdy tunes. Wealthy men carried published directories of the city's high-end brothels in the vest pockets of their double-breasted suits, but few directions were needed to locate any of the fifteen thousand prostitutes who infested the streets. Roulette wheels clattered inside gambling dens that literally operated in the shadows of police stations polluted with corruption. Crime flourished in a city teeming with disgusting displays of wealth and more appalling exhibitions of poverty.

Manhattan was one enormous red-light district, but there was a particular sin so taboo that it had been exiled from the island of vice—prizefighting. Boxing matches were primal affairs, savage human cock-fights rife with bare-knuckle brawling, wrestling, biting, hair pulling, and eye gouging. In an 1879 championship bout, one slugger even poured turpentine on his hands to blind his opponent.

Prizefighting's brutality repulsed genteel Victorian elites, but not as much as the unscrupulous working-class fans the sport attracted. Boxing was a pillar of urban street culture, a popular pastime with immigrants, particularly the Irish, thirsty for blood and booze. Gambling saturated the sport. Clashes among knife- and pistol-wielding spectators often caused more violence than the gladiators inside the ring.

The savagery, corruption, and gambling endemic to prizefighting roamed so far beyond the bounds of Victorian-era sensibilities that most American jurisdictions outlawed the sport. Government, however, could not legislate away bloodlust. Brawlers and fans engaged in elaborate cat-and-mouse dances with the police and often found refuge in remote locations such as islands, backwoods, and cow pastures.

The scheming matchmakers who had secured the barge that now beat against the current of the Hudson River were sailing the sport into uncharted waters by choosing a battleground that lacked any ground whatsoever. Under the cover of darkness, the tugboat continued to urge the unlit barge upriver. Once they reached the tip of Manhattan at Spuy-ten Duyvil Creek (Dutch for "Spouting Devil"), the men ignited oil-soaked torches, backed by reflectors to prevent their being spotted from shore, and pitched the twenty-four-foot ring on the barge deck.

Despite their best efforts at secrecy, reports filtered back to the Twenty-Second Precinct that a large group of sporting men had slipped away from the pier at the foot of West Forty-Third Street a little after 9 p.m., most likely bound for a nearby island to stage a prizefight. The harbor police received orders to locate the "suspicious barge."

In the hopes of confusing any pursuing lawmen about which jurisdiction they would sully, the fight contingent's tug straddled the watery state line between New York and New Jersey. Finally, ten miles upriver, they halted near the New York suburb of Yonkers, and an anchor struck the murky midstream bed of the Hudson.

In the dimly lit reaches of the ring, a hulking figure with blankets draped over his broad shoulders sat huddled on a campstool. John L. Sullivan shivered lightly as he listened to the Hudson lap against the barge and felt the river roll softly beneath his feet. He breathed in the cool west breezes, fragrant with grass and trees, that dissipated the fumes of whiskey and cigars hovering over the barge.

The twenty-three-year-old boxing phenom from Boston had been the chatter of the heavyweight class. Reportedly blessed with the perfect combination of speed, strength, and stamina, the slugger had dominated every opponent he had faced. New York fight fans risked arrest and paid the steep ticket price of ten dollars to see him—and hopefully watch him get pounded by the city's biggest brute, John Flood.

Outside of his manager, Billy Madden, and his second, Joe Goss, John L. had few friends in the heart of Gotham. The locals gave the scattered Sullivan backers on board 3–1 odds. When the "Boston Strong Boy" shed his blankets and stood stripped to his waist, however, Flood's backers had second thoughts.

Muscular without being muscle-bound, Sullivan was constructed like a pugilistic product of the Industrial Age, a "wonderful engine of destruction" manifest in flesh and blood. The faint torchlight tickled his chiseled biceps and rippled back. It gleamed off his thick chest from which his deep bass voice rumbled. It lit up his enormous shoulder blades, which provided the necessary foundation to support his bull-like neck and bullet-shaped head. His clean-shaven chin glistened like polished granite, although darkness hid in the recesses of a deep dimple.

Sullivan's pristine skin, full set of even teeth, and straight nose belied his profession and visibly testified to the inability of foes to lay a licking on him. His coarse black hair was closely cropped to prevent Flood from grabbing and pulling it during the fight. Even Sullivan's one physical deficiency—his short, stubby legs—aided his quickness and ability to rapidly change positions.

Among the greatest weapons this fighting machine possessed, however, were dark, piercing eyes. Sullivan could say terrible things with his ferocious stare, which often crushed opponents before he ever threw a punch. As he glared beneath his heavy black brows at his foe, those eyes blazed even brighter because John L. knew a clear victory would likely earn him a match with the reigning heavyweight champion, upstate New York's Paddy Ryan, who was aboard the barge. Sullivan hungered so deeply for the title that, as much as he abhorred training, he had spent six weeks—every day since agreeing to the fight—tirelessly working with Madden.

Just north of five feet, ten inches tall, John L. arrived in New York in peak shape at 180 pounds. Flood carried a nearly identical build and had a reputation as a terrific hitter, though he lacked any ring experience. Flood was the toughest thug in the toughest neighborhood in America's toughest city. The brawler had scrapped his way around the notorious Five Points slum, and his gang ruled the rough-and-tumble streets around the Bull's Head horse market in lower Manhattan.

The fearsome "Bull's Head Terror" brought his fellow toughs aboard, and a rumor spread around the floating ring that the gambling gang was prepared to do anything to prevent the loss of their man—and their money. It wasn't uncommon for gamblers, when things were going south for their fighter, to cut the ropes, rush the ring, and prevent the conclusion of a fight. Goss heard that the ruffians even planned to throw Sullivan overboard, giving him a bath rather than taking one themselves. Madden, who began to wonder if he and his fellow Bostonians would make it off the barge alive, warned John L. to stay away from the ropes in case one of Flood's backers tried to gouge his eyes with a cane.

The two sides wrangled over a referee, but Madden and Sullivan successfully held out for Al Smith, a fight-game veteran with a reputation for fair play. The referee shed his coat and announced to the crowd that the contest would be a gloved fight to the finish for a purse of $1,000 under the London Prize Ring Rules, which meant rounds were untimed and lasted until one fighter hit the ground. Then each man had a thirty-second rest period and an additional eight seconds to meet in the center of the ring or forfeit the fight. Having heard the rumors of interference by Flood's supporters, Smith warned them it would be a perfectly square fight under his watch.

The two fighters pulled on leather skin-tight gloves, more to protect their hands than cushion their blows. Through the dim light, John L. noticed that the barge deck sloped away on each side of a crest that ran through the middle of the ring, which meant that both fighters would have to run up the rise to start each round. Sullivan might have considered it symbolic. As the son of working-class Irish-Catholic immigrants, he had been fighting uphill his whole life to earn his welcome in staid Brahmin Boston.

Smith called time at 10:40 p.m. Aware that the police or the crowd could end the fight at any moment, Sullivan uncoiled like a whip out of his corner and dashed up the slope of the barge. He met Flood at the peak, and the two burly sluggers rattled away at close quarters. Sullivan's arms fired like pistons as he pounded his opponent's face and stomach with rights and lefts. John L. drove Flood against the ropes and punctuated his two-minute fistic storm with a big bolt to his foe's stomach.

Behind the lightning flash came the thunderclap as Flood crashed loudly to the deck. The fallen fighter rose and puffed away in his corner as he sat on the bent knee of his second, Dooney Harris.

With the call of time, Sullivan charged from his corner and reached the summit first. The brawlers traded ninety seconds of fireworks in a "most unscientific manner" reported the *New York Herald*. Perspiration cascaded down the fighters' flush faces as they clenched and clawed like a pair of dogs. The second—and the third—ended with John L. throwing Flood to the deck.

Sullivan hammered his opponent's body like a punching bag as Flood's blows lost their bite. John L. felt in control and began to focus his glare outside the ring on the reigning heavyweight champion. Suddenly, panic swept over the barge as another tug approached. The fighters froze in fear. The police may have finally discovered them. But the vessel only carried more fans who wanted to watch the nautical brawl. For the rest of the evening, the New York police remained in the dark, miles down the Hudson.

A groggy, but plucky Flood endured, but by the sixth round could barely see through his swollen eyes. He offered little resistance in the seventh, and as Flood's seconds carried him to his corner, his backers had seen enough. Their man couldn't win, but they could make sure he wouldn't lose. As soon as they pulled their knives, however, referee Smith bellowed, "If anyone breaks into this ring, I'll give the fight to this Boston man."

With the insurrection quelled, Flood wobbled out of his corner for the eighth round. He could barely lift his hands or head. Sullivan lined up his kill shot and unleashed his most powerful weapon—a vicious right to his opponent's jaw. The terrific wallop would have launched Flood into the Hudson had the ropes of the ring not been there. His seconds scraped the "Bull's Head Terror" off the deck and carried him to the corner. Flood couldn't continue.

Smith officially declared the unblemished Sullivan the victor. All eight rounds of the sixteen-minute mauling had ended with Flood sprawled on the deck of the barge.

John L. walked to his opponent's corner, shook hands, and said, "We met as friends, and we part as friends." Sullivan then grabbed a hat, threw in a sawbuck, and circled the boat to collect ninety-eight dollars for the loser.

As he completed his charity work, the rising star who had streaked through the New York night spotted the champion again. His stare kindled, then deepened. John L. growled to Ryan, "I'll get you next!"

CHAPTER ONE

The Strong Boy from Boston

THE AUTUMN WIND THAT BLEW ACROSS IRELAND IN 1845 BORE THE stench of death and the wails of her wretched people. Black spots scorched the country's flowering potato plants. Leaves sagged. Stalks wilted. Potatoes festering underground bled a putrid red-brown mucus.

For the next seven years, a lethal pestilence eviscerated the island's staple crop and plunged an impoverished country, which consumed seven million tons of potatoes a year, into famine.

As the Great Hunger gnawed away at the nation, Ireland's poetic landscape authored tales of the macabre. Barefoot paupers with clothes dripping from their bodies clutched dead infants in their arms as they begged for food. Wild dogs fed on human corpses. In one village, a child suckled at the dried breasts of its dead mother. Ireland's legendary forty shades of green painted the lips of the starving, who fed on tufts of weeds and grass in a futile quest for survival.

Desperate farmers sprinkled their crops with holy water. Hollow figures, with eyes as vacant as their stomachs, bent on their bare knees and scraped their stubble fields with calloused hands searching for one, just one, healthy potato. Typhus, dysentery, and cholera tore through the countryside as horses maintained a constant march carting spent bodies to mass graves.

Centuries of British rule had kept Ireland mired in extreme poverty. In the seventeenth century, Oliver Cromwell exterminated tens of thousands of Irish Catholics and drove hundreds of thousands more to the isolated south and west of their country, an inhospitable land where potatoes were the only practical crop that could flourish on the minuscule plots doled out by wealthy British Protestant landowners. Irish peasants struggled in virtual serfdom, and their desperate plight caused Frederick Douglass, a former slave, to write of his 1845 visit to Ireland, "I see much here to remind me of my former condition."

British laws had deprived Ireland's Catholics of their rights to worship, vote, speak their language, and own land, horses, guns, and swords. Then during the Great Hunger, the British even stripped the Irish of their food as the government continued to export wheat, oats, barley, and other goods from Ireland to England. Charles E. Trevelyan, the British civil servant responsible for the apathetic relief efforts, hesitated to interfere with what he saw as a divine solution to Hibernian overpopulation. "The judgement of God sent the calamity to teach the Irish a lesson." He said, "that calamity must not be too much mitigated."

The Great Hunger struck with particular virulence in County Kerry, a rugged nook in Ireland's southwest where a boy named Michael Sullivan had been born in 1830. The eldest of Johanna and Eugene Sullivan's five children had grown up on the family farm in the townland of Laccabeg, just south of the quaint agrarian village of Abbeydorney and five miles north of the town of Tralee.

Michael Sullivan's father and uncle John lived in adjacent cottages on the family's rectangular plot. The brothers were among Ireland's millions of tenant farmers, although their fifty-two-acre rectangular plot, owned by landlord William Crosbie, was larger than most. When the blight reached County Kerry, it consumed the towns and rural villages surrounding the Sullivan family farm. Due to death, emigration, and the eviction of tenants unable to pay their exorbitant rents, the area around Abbeydorney shed 40 percent of its population between 1841 and 1851. Much the same occurred throughout Ireland. By the time the potato blight abated in 1852, the country with a pre-famine population of eight million had seen one million perish and another two million flee the shipwreck of a country in the largest-single population movement of the nineteenth century.

While most of his family remained in Laccabeg, Michael Sullivan, now in his early twenties, joined the exodus to the United States, Canada, Australia, and England in the early 1850s. When Sullivan needed to choose his new home, he only had to look at a map of Ireland for some guidance. County Kerry's fingered peninsulas pointed straight across the Atlantic Ocean to Boston. Even if Sullivan knew little to nothing about Boston, he could be certain of one thing: It had to be better than the hell that was searing Ireland.

Throughout the Great Hunger, a flotilla of five thousand boats, some of which sailed from Tralee Bay just miles from the Sullivan farm, transported the pitiable castaways from the wasteland to the New World. Most of the Irish boarded minimally converted cargo ships—some had been used in the past to transport slaves from Africa—and the hungry, sick passengers, many of whom spent their last penny for transit, were treated little better than freight.

On a three-thousand-mile journey that lasted at least four weeks, the Irish huddled like livestock in dark, cramped quarters. They choked on fetid air. They were showered by excrement and vomit. They lacked sufficient food and clean water. Each adult was apportioned just eighteen inches of bed space—children half that. Disease and death clung to the rancid vessels like barnacles. Nearly a quarter of the eighty-five thousand passengers who sailed to North America aboard the aptly nicknamed "coffin ships" in 1847 never reached their destinations. Their bodies were wrapped in cloths, weighed down with stones, and tossed overboard without the rites of the Catholic Church to sleep forever on the bed of the cobalt Atlantic.

The Irish were a proud race, but the horror of the Great Hunger broke even their legendary fighting spirit. They arrived in American cities such as Boston numb and traumatized, defeated and demoralized. Although their human and civil rights had been crushed under Britain's iron fist for centuries, these huddled masses did not arrive in America yearning to breathe free; they merely hungered to eat.

Michael Sullivan was one drop of the Irish tide that deluged the shores of Boston in the late 1840s and 1850s. A city of little more than one hundred thousand at the start of the famine saw thirty-seven thousand Irish arrive in 1847 alone. By 1850, the Irish represented more than a quarter of Boston's population.

The destitute, despairing, and diseased immigrants who survived the transatlantic voyage looked forward to transplanting their withered Celtic roots in the fertile American soil, but they quickly encountered old problems—hardship, poverty, and racial and religious discrimination—in their new land.

As ship after ship laden with Irish immigrants landed in New York, Philadelphia, Baltimore, and other American cities, anti-Catholic sentiment swelled. In 1854, a mob seized a marble block gifted by Pope Pius IX for the construction of the Washington Monument and tossed it in the Potomac River. Two years later, opponents of Republican presidential candidate John C. Fremont accused him of being "everything from a Catholic to a cannibal." Rumors of his religious proclivities proved far more damaging than those of feasting on humans.

The anti-Catholic, nativist backlash developed into a political movement that swept into power in the mid-1850s on a platform of "Temperance, Liberty, and Protestantism." The "Know Nothing" movement, so-called because of the semi-secretive nature of its members, found its greatest strength in Massachusetts, where in 1854 it captured all state offices, the entire State Senate, and all but four seats in the House chamber.

The elections proved to the Irish that attitudes in New England were little different than those in Old England. Nowhere was that more true than in Michael Sullivan's new home of Boston. Although their forefathers had kicked out the British in 1776, native Bostonians still considered the "mother country" to be close family.

The Puritans who had founded the city in 1630 sought to cleanse themselves of any vestiges of the Catholic Church, and feelings toward Rome softened little in the ensuing two centuries. The colonial legislature in 1700 banned Catholic priests from entering Massachusetts under the penalty of life imprisonment or even death if they happened to be caught escaping. Every year on Guy Fawkes Day, colonial Boston climaxed its celebration by torching a papal effigy. Even as the city's patriots led the American fight for freedom, Catholics had been excluded. Town leaders in 1772 voted to extend "liberty of conscience" to most Christians, with the exception of "Catholics or Papists" whose doctrines were "subversive of society."

Even in the nineteenth century, as Boston championed the abolitionist cause and prided itself as being the refined, educated "Athens of America," it remained the epicenter of anti-Catholicism. Protestant working-class mobs had burnt Charlestown's Ursuline Convent to the ground in 1834, and priests were banned from visiting Catholic patients in the city hospital until 1859, the same year Boston expelled hundreds of Catholic students for protesting the beating of a ten-year-old boy by his teacher for refusing to recite the Protestant version of the Lord's Prayer.

Sullivan emigrated to "the most class-bound city in America," lorded over by Anglo-Saxon Protestant Yankees ensconced in their stately Beacon Hill brownstones. For generations, the men Oliver Wendell Holmes labeled as "Brahmins" had fiercely protected the "purity of their culture and homogeneity of their blood." Now that the Irish were attempting to inject some green into the city's deep blue bloodstream, the entrenched "codfish aristocracy" sought to defend its social structure from the potato peasants who had invaded their insular enclave. No city forced the famine Irish to fight harder to climb from the bottom of the social ladder than tribal Boston. For years, the Irish remained "a massive lump in the community, undigested, undigestible."

The anti-Irish, anti-Catholic discrimination faced by the famine refugees was not subtle or insidious. It blared in black and white, in shop windows and newspaper classified advertisements. "No Irish person need apply." "Catholics and dogs not allowed."

Irish Americans, many of whom were unskilled and illiterate, competed with free African Americans and the increasingly resentful native-born working class for backbreaking, low-wage jobs. They became the premier source of cheap, exploitable manual labor. They cut canals. They dug trenches for water and sewer pipes. They laid rail lines. They cleaned houses. They slaved in textile mills. They worked as stevedores, stable workers, and blacksmiths. Irish muscle even constructed the new mansions that Boston Brahmins built in streetcar suburbs and the new upscale Back Bay neighborhood to escape them.

By 1850, half of Boston's laborers were Irish, and although his roots were on the farm, Sullivan began his life of manual labor when he arrived in the city. He eventually settled in the city's South End, a neighborhood that experienced an influx of residents after the inauguration of a horse-drawn streetcar line in 1856. It was there that he wed fellow Irish immigrant Catherine Kelly on November 6, 1856, inside St. Patrick's Church, a simple wooden structure on Northampton Street once defended at night by parishioners who feared it might be torched like the Ursuline Convent.

It was a mixed marriage—he from County Kerry, she from County Roscommon. Catherine Kelly, born in 1833, was the second daughter of John and Bridget Kelly. She had grown up 150 miles northeast of Michael on the family farm in the townland of Curramore in the parish of Kiltoom. The Kellys lived less than five miles from the historic city of Athlone, a key strategic town on the River Shannon defended by a six-hundred-year-old castle.

The medieval fortress had offered no defense, however, against the cholera and typhoid fever that pillaged impoverished Athlone and the surrounding townlands during the Great Hunger. By July 1849, nearly three thousand desperate souls flooded the city workhouse, which was built to house only eight hundred paupers. Between 1841 and 1851, Kiltoom shed 25 percent of its population, and by 1855, the Kellys had joined the flight to Boston where two years after their nuptials, Michael and Catherine Sullivan brought a little boy, a strong boy, into the world.

—◦—

The true tales about how folk heroes have entered our earthly realm often become obscured by a mythical haze. Such is the case with John Lawrence Sullivan.

Family records and Sullivan himself dated his birth to October 15, 1858. Church and state, however, disagree. Sullivan's birth certificate lists the date as October 12, 1858, and the Boston Archdiocese records his baptism the following day at St. Joseph's Church.

The whereabouts of his birth are less vague, but often misreported. Michael and Catherine Sullivan lived in a cluster of tenements owned by the heirs of Samuel Salisbury off East Concord Street near the intersection of Washington Street, Boston's main thoroughfare, when they welcomed their first child into the world. The birthplace of John L. is often erroneously listed as Roxbury, a separate town until its annexation by Boston in 1868, but the intersection of East Concord and Washington Streets was inside the border of Boston proper in the city's South End neighborhood.

America was still a young nation at the time of Sullivan's birth. The eldest residents of Boston could probably still recall the raw October day in 1789 when President George Washington, to the pealing of church bells and thunder of artillery, paraded into town atop his white steed over the byway that now bore his name. The country had not yet been torn in two, although historic Faneuil Hall still rang from the October 11 pro-slavery speech delivered by Mississippi senator Jefferson Davis in which he warned the agitating abolitionists from "intermeddling with the affairs of other people."

The Irish influx had transfigured Boston into what Transcendental minister Theodore Parker called "the 'Dublin' of America," and a growing number of those Hibernian immigrants found new homes on newly created land. In the 1840s, as Boston's cramped peninsula reached capacity, the city began to infill the fetid tidal marshes of Boston Harbor and the Charles River to create new residential neighborhoods, such as the South End.

Sullivan grew up in vastly different environs from the hash of houses and crooked lanes that populated centuries-old downtown neighborhoods. He walked the South End's grid of spacious avenues fronted by symmetrical blocks of redbrick brownstones with bow fronts, high stoops, and mansard roofs. Fountains bubbled in shady squares encased in cast-iron fencing. But despite its outward appearance, the South End never fulfilled the elegant promise of its planners. Blocks away from Sullivan's birthplace were piano factories and the malodorous tidewaters of the South Bay lined with warehouses and wharves. Across East Concord Street was the South End Burying Ground, a solidly working-class cemetery that held eleven thousand souls in unmarked graves.

As the Boston Brahmins stayed away from the South End, the Irish moved in during the 1850s and the 1860s. The Catholic Church followed suit. Six months before Sullivan's birth, Jesuits broke ground down the street on Harrison Avenue to build the solid granite Church of the Immaculate Conception and the adjacent brick building that would

become the original home of Boston College, which was founded to edu-
cate the sons of poor Irish immigrants. In 1875, a new Cathedral of the
Holy Cross opened on Washington Street as the epicenter of the newly
created Archdiocese of Boston.

The construction of such imposing buildings signaled to Boston that
the Irish Catholics, in spite of the discrimination they faced, were here to
stay. The white-hot vitriol directed at the Celtic immigrants also cooled
slightly during the Civil War when more than ten thousand Massachusetts Irish demonstrated their loyalty to their new country by enlisting
in the Union cause and fighting with distinction at battlefields such as
Antietam and Gettysburg.*

John L. demonstrated the spirit of the fighting Irish from a very early
age. Catherine reported that her son's already-potent right fist gave his
aunt "as beautiful a black eye as you ever saw" before he even celebrated
his first birthday. Catherine struggled to hold her young child, who "was
as strong as a bear."

Sullivan clearly inherited his brawn, strong features, and build from
his powerful mother, "a model of womanly vigor" who weighed around
180 pounds. Although Michael's brothers and male relatives were burly
men known back in Ireland as the "Big Sullivans," John L.'s father had
not inherited the same traits. Michael was a true featherweight, a wisp of
a man who stood five feet, three inches tall and never topped 130 pounds.
John L. may have been given his mother's looks, but his love of sports,
withering stare, and pugnacious temper came courtesy of his father, who
supported the family on the fifteen dollars a week he earned as a mason
and day laborer. The Sullivans led a frugal, industrial lifestyle, particularly
after the births of Annie in April 1865 and Michael eighteen months later.

While John L. was still a young boy, the Sullivans moved a few blocks
west to Amee Place, a cloistered indentation off Shawmut Avenue just five
houses east of the Roxbury border, where they lived next to extended family.

Sullivan spent his entire youth in the few surrounding blocks of the
South End and the adjoining neighborhood known as the Boston Highlands. He attended a primary school on West Concord Street and then

---

* More than five thousand men with the Sullivan surname fought in the Civil War, including one
thousand who took up arms for the Confederacy.

the Dwight School two blocks over on West Springfield Street, where longtime headmaster Jimmy Page doled out the discipline and was said to be the "first man who ever whipped John L." Like a champion, Sullivan took his beating without a whimper and became a hero to the other boys. John L. was an indifferent student. He enjoyed math, disliked geography. By age thirteen, he was done with his formal schooling.

Sullivan led the life of a typical city boy. He shot marbles and spun tops. On Sunday afternoons, he went to City Point to watch schooners sail in and out of Boston Harbor. He engaged in the occasional boyhood scrap, but he didn't receive many challenges since most boys knew they would be in for a licking. In spite of his superior power, Sullivan was not a neighborhood bully, but he would raise his fists in response to any perceived injustice.

Like many Irish-American boys becoming indoctrinated into American culture, young John L. enjoyed nothing more than baseball. He was an ardent "crank," the nineteenth-century term for a baseball fan, and after the South End Grounds opened in the neighborhood in 1871, the teenaged Sullivan cheered on the Boston Red Stockings. Forerunners of the future Atlanta Braves and baseball's first professional dynasty, the Red Stockings captured four straight titles from 1872 to 1875 before becoming one of the National League's charter members. A quarter-century later, Sullivan could still recite Boston's lineup—which included future Hall of Famers Albert Spalding and brothers George and Harry Wright—and dissect each player's strengths and flaws.

Sullivan regularly played baseball with neighborhood kids on the plot of ground beyond the center field of the South End Grounds. The boys even sneaked out of town on Sunday to play ballgames in violation of the city's puritanical laws. The athletic John L. proved an adroit player. He patrolled first base and the outfield for several semi-professional local nines that barnstormed New England. Sullivan boasted that he turned down a $1,300 contract offer from the Cincinnati Red Stockings to play with them during the 1879 and 1880 seasons, although a sporting newspaper reported years later that the team president could not recall such an offer. John L.'s claims that he enrolled at Boston College for a time also appear to be false since the institution has no records of his matriculation.

Like many Irish mothers of the day, Catherine wanted her son to save souls for a living, and she certainly would have been pleased had he attended Boston College, which groomed boys for the priesthood. Instead, John L. eschewed any notions of a higher calling and, like his father, began to earn a living with his hands.

In his first job, he made four dollars a week during a six-month stint as a plumber's apprentice that came to an end after he engaged in a scrap with a more experienced journeyman. John L. then worked as a tinsmith for eighteen months until he quit after a disagreement with one of his co-workers. Sullivan's job as a "mucker" digging trenches for the city's sewer lines ended after an argument with his boss over the amount of time he was taking off to play baseball ended in blows.

With a work résumé studded with short stints that repeatedly came to a fistic conclusion, it was clear that Sullivan was destined to use his hands for a living—just not in the way his father had.

—◦—

In the 1870s, there wasn't much of a career to be had in professional boxing. Fighters entered the ring only a handful of times in their lives, and purses did not provide living wages for even the leading brawlers. So when John L. wrote in his autobiography that around the age of nineteen he "drifted into the occupation of a boxer," the description was apt.

Much as with Sullivan's birth, the precise details surrounding the advent of his ring career—such as the date and specific identity of his opponent—are murky. The year was 1877, perhaps 1878, when the strapping Sullivan, already weighing nearly two hundred pounds, attended a variety show at Roxbury's Institute Hall, later known as the Dudley Street Opera House. During the evening's entertainment, a young boxer—whose identity has been reported in various accounts as Jack Scannell or Mike Scannell or even as Mike Scanlon by Sullivan himself on occasion—stepped to the footlights in his fighting costume with a challenge: "If there is anybody here who thinks I can't lick him, let him stand up."

Sullivan, who had developed a local reputation as a scrapper, felt the eyes of the audience fall upon him. The crowd urged the reluctant John L. onto the stage. Lacking any fighting gear, he simply shed his coat, rolled up his sleeves, and for the first time in his life slid boxing gloves over his hands. As he stood on the stage expecting to be introduced, Scannell walked up behind him and delivered a big shot to the back of his head.

A furious Sullivan pounced on his smiling opponent. He cocked his mighty right arm and fired his fist against the point of Scannell's grinning jaw. The blow launched Scannell off his feet, knocked him over a piano on the stage, and sent him into the orchestra. The casualties were one unconscious fighter and three shattered fiddles. The boxer sprawled across the string section would not be the last to be felled by Sullivan's titanic right.

Following his impressive stage debut, Sullivan's fistic talent soon caught the attention of two of Boston's leading sporting men—Thomas Earley, a son-in-law of English champion boxer Jem Mace and a fighter who ran a boxing gym on Lagrange Street, and James Keenan, a turfman who owned a sporting house on Portland Street. Earley and Keenan became Sullivan's earliest backers and arranged for him to compete in legal exhibitions around Boston. John L. proved to be a phenom, and by 1879, his incredible displays of power had earned him the simplest of nicknames—"Strong Boy." The nickname soon gained a geographic modifier, first "Highland Strong Boy" and ultimately "Boston Strong Boy."

The *Boston Globe* reported that on March 14, 1879, "the 'strong boy' of Boston Highlands" appeared at the Alhambra Theatre on Hanover Street for a charity benefit for Dan Dwyer, a veteran of both the ring and the Civil War. Benefits, which generally included a slate of gloved exhibitions and other entertainment, were common occurrences in nineteenth-century boxing to raise money for notable fighters. Amid a potpourri of acts that including singing, dancing, and even a rowing machine demonstration, John L. appeared in one of the preliminary exhibitions against veteran John "Cockey" Woods.

The *Globe* reported that the Woods exhibition was actually the second fight of Sullivan's day. In the wee hours of the morning, John L. exchanged blows with Jack Curley of Philadelphia in a prizefight for $250 a side. Sullivan demonstrated that he had stamina as well as power by emerging victorious after seventy-four minutes in the ring. "It is the opinion of the sporting fraternity that Sullivan is the coming man," reported the *Globe*.

Later that year, Sullivan appeared at another Boston benefit for Dwyer inside Revere Hall, but this time he was a big enough name to appear in the main event with the feted fighter. John L. started slowly but soon dictated the action, driving Dwyer to the ropes and putting him on the defensive. In the third round, Sullivan drew blood from Dwyer's nose. He began to pound the honoree with ease, and the master of ceremonies jumped into the ring to prevent the guest of honor from being knocked out.

Sullivan boasted that he never took a formal boxing lesson in his life. "Fighters are born," he once sneered. "A fighter can't be made out of a stiff." He learned his craft by watching other fighters in action and hustling to get spots on fighting programs around New England whenever he could. One trip brought him to the Theatre Comique in Providence, Rhode Island, which hosted weekly fights. He talked the manager into giving him an exhibition slot against local fighter Jack Hogan under the condition that he promised to take it easy on his overmatched opponent.

John L. opened with a rush as Hogan stood waiting with his left hand extended. A moment later, Sullivan found himself in an unfamiliar place—on the ground. Whenever mentioning the episode, John L. would continue to give himself credit for instigating his own knockdown, saying that he simply "ran into Hogan's fist." Angered at the knockdown, however, Sullivan forgot his pledge of leniency and smashed Hogan in the nose, breaking it and sending him flying into the stage wings.

Sullivan's early exhibitions proved that he was constitutionally incapable of holding back. In the ring as outside it, John L. was a vortex of perpetual motion, constantly charging ahead without a moment of retreat. He pounced on his opponents from the start and quickly suffocated the last breathing thoughts of victory that they might be harboring.

"From the first instant of the fight, Sullivan is as fierce, relentless, tireless as a cataract," wrote his friend, the poet John Boyle O'Reilly. "Other boxers begin by sparring; he begins by fighting—and he never ceases to fight. He is as distinct from other boxers as a bull dog is from a spaniel."

John L. employed very little science in the ring. He was an artist— a knockout artist. With a left as lethal as his right, Sullivan's hands were equal-opportunity weapons. When he planted his feet firmly, he concentrated every one of his two hundred pounds onto the knuckles of his fist. He was an expert counter-hitter who paralyzed an opponent's guard with a chopping left before firing a huge right to the neck or jaw of his disarmed foe. Sullivan could even deliver a punch high on an opponent's back "so that it sent a message to the other fellow's heart."

"There's nothing to fighting," he once told a reporter. "Just come out fast from your corner, hit the other fellow as hard as you can and hit him first." That's not to suggest that Sullivan lacked any tactical thoughts or regard for where to land his blows in order to maximize their damage. Through his study of the sport, John L. determined that the jaw was the "most vulnerable part of a man's body." He claimed that after consulting many physicians on the subject, he found "a hard blow on the point of the jaw will render a man unconscious, and at the same time will not effectually weaken him otherwise."

Every time Sullivan stepped into the ring, his confidence grew. Baseball had been his initial sporting passion, but now he was infected with a "fighting fever." Life as a professional baseball player would have offered an easier career path, but that wasn't the occupation into which this "Strong Boy" from Boston "drifted." Perhaps his desired profession had been preordained by his surname anyway. "Sullivan" comes from the Gaelic words meaning "black-eyed one."

The sport that had so captivated this young man from the "Athens of America" sprouted from the ancient Greeks, who incorporated boxing into their Olympic Games in 688 BC. The modern sport began to emerge in early-eighteenth-century England. James Figg, who won the English title in 1719, is considered to be the first in the long line of heavyweight boxing champions that carries down to this day. In Figg's day, however, prizefighters relied on more than just their fists. Combatants wielded swords and cudgels. Kicking, kneeing, hair pulling, wrestling, and gouging were all fair game. Prizefighting in the early 1700s was a brutal pastime. When Figg avenged the only loss in his 270-match career, a bout he had lost to Ned Sutton, he smashed and broke his opponent's knee with his cudgels as Prime Minister Sir Robert Walpole watched from the crowd.

Eventually, the arms permitted in prizefighting were winnowed back to those attached to the fighter's shoulders. In 1743, Figg's protégé and fellow Englishman Jack Broughton drafted the first written rules to govern boxing. He also developed the first boxing gloves, although they were used only for sparring purposes. Prizefights remained bare-knuckle affairs.

The London Prize Ring Rules, based on Broughton's rules, were introduced in 1838 to codify the sport. Under the set of twenty-nine rules, rounds were untimed. They only ended when a fighter was knocked or wrestled to the ground. Although it was illegal to dive to the ground without being legitimately knocked down, fighters constantly abused the rule. After a thirty-second rest time, boxers had eight additional seconds to "come to scratch" by toeing a line drawn in the middle of the ring. The timing rules meant fights commonly lasted for hours and dozens of rounds until one fighter collapsed. Rings were twenty-four feet square with two ropes tied around wooden posts. Biting, eye gouging, kicking, and biting were fouls, but referees did not always scrupulously enforce the rules.

Tom Hyer, whose father was credited with being the first American professional boxer, defeated "Country McCloskey" in a three-hour brawl in 1841 to capture what is considered the first American heavyweight championship. It was during Hyer's decade-long reign that the Irish began to arrive in the United States in the wake of the Great Hunger, transporting with them a passion for boxing. The Irish had a history of fisticuffs based on family grudges, class tensions, and politics. Large groups brawled with sticks in "faction fights" between clans and farmers in markets and fairs, such as the annual Donnybrook Fair on the southern outskirts of Dublin. Irish laborers brought their fistic tradition with them to worksites across America, and the urban Irish underclass saw the sport as an escape valve for their frustrations and a way to once again feel empowered, if only against one man in one ring.

One of the first Irish-American boxing stars was "Yankee" Sullivan, whose real name was James Ambrose. Born in County Cork, Sullivan was a shadowy ruffian and criminal who was transported to the penal colony of Australia by the British. He arrived in America in 1840, and his much-hyped bare-knuckle heavyweight championship bout with Hyer in 1849, which served as a proxy battle between nativists and Irish immigrants, sparked a golden era of boxing in the United States.

During the 1850s, major prizefights bubbled up from barroom squabbles, ethnic tensions, gangland turf wars, and partisan differences. Boxing was closely entwined with politics in antebellum America. Fighters forged close ties with corrupt urban political machines that relied on muscle to help their candidates win elections. New York's Tammany Hall employed a host of fighters, led by John Morrissey, as "shoulder hitters" to protect polling stations and intimidate voters. Morrissey, born in Ireland in 1831, defeated "Yankee" Sullivan for the heavyweight title in 1853 when his opponent joined in a brawl that broke out at ringside during the thirty-seventh round. The following year, the new champion brawled with the notorious William "Bill the Butcher" Poole, the fierce nativist ganglord of the Five Points neighborhood. Poole gouged and bit Morrissey's face as his gang kicked the Irish American until he lost consciousness. Months later, the two men met again inside a Broadway saloon and police intervened, but later that night, Morrissey's friends returned and shot Poole dead.

The last glory days of American boxing peaked when native son John C. Heenan traveled to England in 1860 to fight its reigning champion, Tom Sayers. The bout was declared a draw after the ropes were mysteriously cut in the thirty-seventh round, but Heenan received a hero's welcome when an estimated fifty thousand New Yorkers greeted him on his return to America.

Boxing began a long, steady slide after the firing of the first shots at Fort Sumter in 1861 as "the bellicose spirit of the nation was fully gratified in the awful slaughter of the Civil War." The sport suffered from a lack of captivating and dominant personalities, and from damaged credibility due to a spate of fixed fights. Thugs and gamblers who couldn't use bribes to get their ways relied on brawn to intimidate referees and break up fights. "The prize ring is fast losing its prestige," lamented the *New York Clipper*, one of the sport's strongest advocates, in 1870.

And as the moralizing of the Victorian age became more firmly entrenched, upper classes decried the sport for catering to mankind's basest instincts and animalistic impulses. Ironically, a nation that had witnessed a holocaust during the Civil War and sporadic bloody battles against Native Americans believed the prize ring to be too "brutal."

As a result, prizefighting and bare-knuckle brawling became banned in most jurisdictions, including in Sullivan's home state of Massachusetts under an 1849 statute. In an 1876 case, *Commonwealth v. Colberg*, the Massachusetts Supreme Judicial Court ruled that prizefighting was still illegal even if agreed to by willing participants because "prizefighting, boxing matches, and encounters of that kind serve no useful purpose" and "tend to breaches of the peace." The court declared that boxing, unlike fencing and wrestling, did not foster self-preservation skills.

Boxing's proponents attempted to alter the sport's public image by referring to it as a "craft" in which "professors" gave instruction in the "manly art" and the "science of self-defense." Reformers also saw hope in a new code—the Marquis of Queensberry Rules—that had been introduced in 1867. Although named for John Sholto Douglas, the ninth Marquis of Queensberry and a boxing enthusiast, the rules were chiefly drafted by his Oxford classmate John Graham Chambers, an accomplished oarsman and champion race walker.

The twelve rules called for radical changes to the sport, outlawing wrestling, head-butting, and spiked shoes. Rounds were not open-ended, but strictly timed to three minutes with one-minute rests in between. Boxers sent to the ground had ten seconds to resume fighting or be declared knocked out. And in the most important change, the Marquis of Queensberry Rules mandated the use of gloves, usually between two and eight ounces.

Reformers hoped the new rules would civilize the sport and make it more palatable to authorities and boxing's opponents, and cities such as Boston did start to issue entertainment licenses for limited gloved "exhibitions" in public venues. But at the time John L. Sullivan entered the sport, the London Prize Ring Rules still dominated boxing, and illegal bare-knuckle fighting was still viewed as the only true test for determining championships. Prizefighting remained on the run from the law and mired in corruption. Old-timers looked back fondly on the golden age of Hyer, "Yankee" Sullivan, Morrissey, and Heenan.

Boxing needed a savior to resurrect it.

While John L. Sullivan had made a name for himself in the boxing circles of New England, he had yet to face any championship-level fighters. That changed in 1880.

During the winter, he appeared before a big house at Boston's Howard Athenaeum for a benefit for Mike Donovan, a cagy veteran who had fought for the American middleweight title in 1878 and served as a drummer boy on General William T. Sherman's March to the Sea. Donovan, who had met Sullivan on a previous trip through the city, gave the budding boxer a chance to spar with him in the four-round windup.

When John L. stripped to his fighting togs, Donovan was struck by the youngster's physique. Although he wasn't a giant of a man, Sullivan was a well-proportioned "mass of sinew." He lacked superfluous flesh. His muscular frame was built not just to deliver punishment but to absorb it as well. He was blessed with a deep, barrel chest that always proudly puffed itself out to the world. His neck size was so prodigious that his shirts had to be made to order. In the shadows of a gracefully sweeping black mustache, Sullivan's broad jaw was as solid as the granite chiseled from the quarries of his native New England.

Donovan tried to stare down John L. He gazed into Sullivan's dark eyes, tucked under his furrowed brow, but the youngster didn't blink. He wasn't intimidated by facing a champion fighter before a large audience. As they shook hands, Donovan told Sullivan he would take it easy on him.

"I don't want to hurt my hands on you," Donovan informed his opponent.

"You'll be lucky if I don't break your neck," John L. roared in return.

At the start of the fight, Sullivan rushed Donovan "like a panther." It was the grizzled warrior who became disconcerted. He had never encountered such a combination of speed and power. He never had to engage in "such clever ducking and side-stepping." Try as he might, Donovan couldn't escape John L. A powerful right from Sullivan struck Donovan's back like a baseball bat and knocked the veteran to the floor so hard that the fall broke his nose. As Sullivan looked down at his opponent lying on the stage, he momentarily feared that he had killed him. Donovan made it through to the end, though not before breaking his right wrist in the third round.

Donovan left the ring tired, exhausted, and aware that he "had just fought the coming champion of the prize-ring." Donovan marveled, "He used his right hand as a blacksmith would use a sledge-hammer pounding a piece of iron into shape."

On April 6, Sullivan received his biggest test to date when he put up his dukes against the one-time heavyweight champion of America, the forty-one-year-old warhorse Joe Goss. Eighteen hundred fans filed into Boston's Music Hall for a testimonial to the former champion. The program touted the evening's main event, a three-round exhibition between the Englishman Goss and the "Strong Boy of the Highlands, The Coming Champion of America!"

From the start, John L. showed little respect for his elder, who had first entered the ring before Sullivan was even born. He dictated the action throughout the first round by landing fist after fist on the veteran's face. He easily cross-countered any of the blows from Goss. Then in the second, John L. uncorked a wicked right that laid Goss flat. Earley, who served as master of ceremonies, thought Goss had merely slipped. He helped the Englishman to his feet and then let go. The unsteady Goss "went reeling like a drunken man about the stage." Earley caught him before he fell again and assisted him to his seat as the crowd sent up cheer after cheer "in honor of the Highland boy."

Goss needed extra time between rounds to recover, and Sullivan agreed to take it easy on his opponent in the final round. The exhibition proved to be Sullivan's coming-out party on the national stage. It solidified his position as the rising star of the heavyweight class, and John L. would point to this clash as his first bout of any account.

Goss did not carry any hard feelings from the beat-down, and he and Sullivan became close friends. Such was the tight-knit world of boxing where the underworld nature of the sport forged strange friendships. A fighter who was knocked out one day could be training or seconding their conqueror the next.

Buoyed by Sullivan's performance against the former champion, Earley brought Sullivan with him in May to Erie, Pennsylvania, which was expected to be the battleground for Goss's attempt to regain the vacant bare-knuckle American heavyweight championship against challenger Paddy Ryan, the renowned fighter from near Albany, New York. As with any major title bout, the nation's most prominent sporting men and the boxing "fancy," as fans of the era were called, congregated. Many of them chattered about Sullivan.

John L. caused a stir with a cocky declaration laying claim to the winner. Earley announced that Sullivan stood ready to challenge the victor to a prizefight for $1,000 a side. The lawmen who thronged Erie ended up chasing the heavyweights out of town, and it doesn't appear that Sullivan was present when Ryan ultimately defeated Goss in eighty-six rounds in Colliers Station, West Virginia.

Back in Boston on June 28, John L. met George Rooke, who had fought for the middleweight title in 1878, inside the sweltering Howard Athenaeum. One Boston newspaper noted that "it was plain to be seen that Rooke had been imbibing something stronger than soda water." Sullivan's foe staggered through the motions as John L. knocked him down seven times in the three-round contest before he was carried to his dressing room. Rooke, for his part, blamed the "extreme heat" for his unsteady gait and performance.

Although now in his twenties, John L. remained living in the South End with his parents, siblings, and extended family—two aunts, two cousins, and one uncle—in a two-story wooden frame house at 8 Plympton Court according to the 1880 US Census. Plympton Court would be rechristened Parnell Street that year in honor of Irish nationalist Charles Stewart Parnell. They were nestled on a densely populated block where kids and dogs roamed the streets, and neighbors leaned out of windows to talk to neighbors. Privacy and grass were at a minimum.

Sullivan listed no occupation in the 1880 Census, but boxing was now the center of his life. Money from his exhibitions and semi-professional baseball games was his primary source of income. But if he was to make a living as a fighter and leave manual labor behind, he needed a shot at the new heavyweight champion.

On December 9, Sullivan called out Ryan in print. "I am prepared to make a match to fight any man breathing, for any sum from one thousand dollars to ten thousand dollars," he declared in a letter to the *Cincinnati Enquirer.* "This challenge is especially directed to Paddy Ryan and will remain open for a month if he should not see fit to accept it. Respectfully yours, John L. Sullivan."

There it was, that middle initial. A statement that he wasn't just any "John Sullivan." There were thousands of those, and he was not one to stay in the pack.

To the newspapers, however, he was still a common fighter with a common name. They referred to him as "John Sullivan," "Johnny Sullivan," "Jack Sullivan," and even "Jack L. Sullivan" or "John E. Sullivan." He hadn't quite earned that middle initial yet, but an offer soon came that would help in that quest.

—————

Cincinnati Enquirer reporter John McCormick, who wrote under the pen name Macon, was searching the country for fresh talent. He needed an up-and-coming fighter who would come to his hometown and face Cleveland native John Donaldson, the champion of the West. On a tip, he recruited Sullivan to be Donaldson's foe in return for $150 plus railroad fare and hotel bill.

Donaldson's reputation as a clever fighter had earned him the sobriquet "Professor," but he had also proven to be a big hitter in winning all four of his ring encounters, including a victory earlier in the year in which he knocked out his opponent in less than three minutes.

Sullivan knew a strong performance outside of his backyard would enhance his national name recognition and chances for a shot at Ryan. On December 11, the two fighters took to the stage of Robinson's Opera House for a scheduled four-round exhibition. The audience expected an intriguing contrast between the slugging of Sullivan and the scientific sparring of Donaldson.

The two brawlers were equal in height, but Sullivan had the quickness and weight edge over his 160-pound opponent. He used those assets to his advantage from the start. In the second round, the fans cheered wildly as John L. knocked Donaldson down with such a hard blow "that he almost turned a somersault." In the following round, Sullivan's punishment continued, and at its conclusion, Donaldson came to the footlights, untied his gloves, and said he was through. "I am not in condition, and as this man is in training," he confessed to the astonishment of the crowd, "I refuse to fight him." The crowd didn't want to hear his whining, however, and urged him back into the ring for the final round. Donaldson endured three more minutes of hammering while wishing he hadn't listened to the audience's pleas.

Displeased with his performance, the "Professor" challenged Sullivan to a prizefight for $500 a side. Sullivan accepted and remained in Cincinnati to train.

Prizefighting was illegal under Ohio state law, and when news of the pending contest reached Cincinnati's City Hall, the mayor and police chief vowed to prevent it from taking place. Large numbers of police were placed on special duty on December 24 to keep watch on the Vine Street saloon where the fight organizers were headquartered. The lawmen hoped to divine the secret location of the prizefight scheduled for that day.

Finally, around 8:30 p.m., the patrolmen saw movement. A group of sports jumped into a hired hack and sped up Vine Street. The police gave chase as the carriage began to leave the city behind. The cops figured the bout was planned for some remote backwoods location, a common setting for prizefights, but the hack they were following was actually a decoy arranged by the wily fight organizers who planned to fight right in the middle of Cincinnati.

The fight promoters continued their subterfuge by sending the fighters, reporters from three daily newspapers, and fans in pairs and packs of three on different circuitous routes through the downtown streets. All trails, however, led to the same destination—the rear entrance of the Pacific Garden, a recently shuttered saloon on the northwest corner of Sixth and Vine Streets that had been owned by an Indiana brewing company. The elaborate ruse worked, and all entered unobserved by the police.

On that Christmas Eve night, Sullivan stepped inside the rude abandoned groggery that, much like a manger, was carpeted with straw, sticks, and dirt. By the dim light of a pair of circus flambeaux, broom-wielding men swept a makeshift battleground. Cigarette smoke perfumed the room. All present made sure to remain in a corner of the Pacific Garden where passing pedestrians on Sixth Street could not see them.

From the other side of a canvas wall, John L. heard the din of a freak show—complete with an educated pig, a living skeleton, and wild children of Borneo—entertaining revelers in the Vine Street side of the storefront. The noise from the barrel organ and bass drum was especially loud since the fight organizers had slipped some cash to the showmen to ensure that they played their music with as much gusto as possible to drown out all noise from the prizefight.

Around 10:30 p.m. on the holiest night of the year, Cincinnati's inveterate gamblers and fight fans formed a human ring and prepared to slake their thirst for blood. Donaldson took the only chair inside the place to his corner. Sullivan had to make do sitting on the edge of an old trunk as he stripped, put on his boxing tights, and laced up his gloves.

With the fear of police, organizers did not sell tickets in advance of the fight and decided to collect the prize money at the gate from the fans in attendance, who numbered no more than forty. A hat circled the room, and Sullivan made the first deposit, a twenty-dollar contribution. Donaldson's dodging started before the fight when he couldn't come up with the money for the agreed-upon side bet of $500.

In their roles as Sullivan's seconds, Tom Ryan and Johnny Moran advised and attended to John L. between rounds. The English fighter Dan Crutchley and Abe Smith seconded Donaldson. Referee Patrick Murphy announced the fight was to be under the Marquis of Queensberry Rules, but as one newspaper reported, "really there were no rules about the fight at all."

John L. fixed his vicious stare upon Donaldson and saw that his opponent looked pale and scared. Thoughts of defeat never entered Sullivan's mind. He thought he was invincible. Donaldson probably agreed.

The two undefeated warriors came to the center of the ring for the opening round, which ended with Sullivan tossing Donaldson to the ground. In the second round, the "Professor" grabbed Sullivan by the right leg and attempted to hoist him from his feet. Donaldson had no luck. He spent much of the round running to elude Sullivan's fists and ultimately went to the ground to avoid punishment. John L. finally landed the fight's first big blow in the third round and knocked Donaldson over a trunk.

Donaldson's already lagging confidence waned further, and his guard was fully engaged. He wanted to quit, but his seconds told him to keep fighting. His thoughts were of survival more than victory.

By the sixth round, Sullivan was laughing as Donaldson was carried to his corner by his seconds. In the seventh, Sullivan knocked down the man from Cleveland with two quick rights. His foe fell to the ground without a punch in the next two rounds. After the end of the tenth, Donaldson walked over to Sullivan, said he was satisfied, and shook hands. The fight had lasted ten rounds and a little over twenty minutes. "Donaldson could no more stand the heavy left-hand hits of Sullivan than a stalk of corn could the scythe," reported one newspaper.

Donaldson was so spent that his seconds had to dress him in his street clothes and assist him as he walked uncertainly out of the shuttered bar. John L. took his winnings from the hat and found only fifty-eight dollars, including the twenty he had deposited. His disappointment grew the following day when he spent his Christmas in a Cincinnati police station under arrest for violating the state law against prizefighting, a charge that could carry a ten-year prison sentence.

Four days later, a larger crowd than had seen the fight jammed a Cincinnati courtroom to watch the prosecutor spar with witnesses. The witnesses who took the stand ducked and dodged in the finest tradition of the prize ring.

"Where did this affray take place?" the prosecutor asked the first witness, Thomas Hartshorn.

"What affray?" asked Hartshorn.

"The prizefight between Donaldson and Sullivan."

"Didn't see any prizefight," claimed Hartshorn.

And so it went. Courtroom spectators expecting a legal drama instead were entertained by a farce. Referee Murphy reported that the men were not "fighting" but merely "sparring." Moran, Sullivan's second, said he saw a running match and not a fight. He then claimed he couldn't tell which of the two men he had assisted in the ring. Sullivan's attorney didn't even feel the need to cross-examine witnesses or offer any evidence in his defense.

Judge Wilson dismissed the charges because in his opinion the prosecutors could not prove the encounter was a "prizefight." There had been no evidence presented that money was at stake. According to one newspaper report, the judge, after banging his gavel, adjourned to the local saloon for a spirits-filled sidebar with the prosecutor, witnesses, and fighters. The police chief, annoyed but not surprised at the outcome, said that at least the trial proved there was a corner at Sixth and Vine.

Sullivan had received his baptism into the legal wranglings that came with being a prizefighter. It wouldn't be the last time he saw the inside of a courtroom.

Free from the law, Sullivan sped back to Boston to appear at a scheduled joint exhibition with Goss on January 3, 1881. Fight organizers were surprised by the large crowd that filled the Boston Music Hall "from floor to gallery." The turnout was no doubt bolstered by news of Sullivan's legal battle in Cincinnati.

In a preliminary match, Sullivan sparred with Jack Stewart, the "Champion of Canada." John L. claimed that his overwhelmed opponent fled the stage in the second round and that he assisted the Canadian to his dressing room by planting "a kick where it would be the most assistance." Newspaper accounts, however, have no mention of the incident and report that Stewart was knocked down in the second round but returned for the third while Sullivan played with him "as a cat does with a mouse."

The evening ended with an "altogether uninteresting" spar with Goss, and the two fighters split the $1,300 gate. Sullivan walked away from the Music Hall that evening with something else of value—a new friendship with Billy Madden, who had appeared on the undercard with Patrick "Patsey" Sheppard. Born in London to Irish parents in 1852, Madden was a clever, skillful, and accomplished lightweight. Shortly after emigrating to America, the nineteen-year-old fighter traveled to New Orleans to witness the 1871 heavyweight title bout between Jem Mace and Joe Coburn. He arrived so broke that he walked the twenty miles to the battleground in Bay St. Louis, Mississippi, where he jumped into the ring and defeated Tom Hart in a preliminary bout to receive the $12.50 prize.

A decade later, Madden remained in the fight game while tending bar at Keenan's sporting house. Respected for his boxing knowledge and his scientific form, he quickly became a close confidant of John L. The versatile Madden took on the role of Sullivan's manager and trainer. He helped to mold Sullivan's raw talent and correct his amateur habits. He improved the efficiency of the heavyweight's punches. He corrected his round-arm hitting and perfected his straight hitting. In spite of surrendering three inches and dozens of pounds to John L., Madden proved an adept sparring partner and regularly entered the ring in exhibitions with his protégé.

As Sullivan and Madden began their working partnership, John L. squared off once again with Donovan at a March benefit for Sheppard at the Boston Music Hall. Two thousand fans showed to see the man who had, as one Boston newspaper reported, "force enough to lay low a full-grown Texan steer." Donovan sought to avoid the battering he had taken in their first meeting by employing more dodging tactics. John L. responded with savage blows. The bad blood between the two simmered. Between rounds, Sullivan refused to sit, and his angry opponent barked at him to take a seat. Sullivan's backers showered Donovan with crude remarks. The fight grew so nasty that police broke it up in the third round.

As he continued to improve his craft, Sullivan kept his eyes on Ryan. The pages of the *National Police Gazette* and other newspapers around the country printed Sullivan's regular challenges to fight the reigning heavyweight champion for at least $1,000 a side. Ryan, however, ignored the "Boston Strong Boy."

It wasn't the first time Sullivan had been snubbed by Ryan. John L. still seethed about the time he had appeared at a local exhibition featuring Ryan and Goss. When Goss became hurt during the fight, John L. offered to take his place. Ryan instantly dismissed the young fighter and sneered, "You go get a reputation first."

Sullivan had earned a local reputation and a touch more from his Cincinnati fight, but Madden knew where he needed to take John L. to solidify a truly national reputation—the country's media capital and boxing's mecca, New York City. Madden had introduced Sullivan to the noted wrestler William Muldoon, who was swinging through Boston on a tour. Muldoon was taken by the young heavyweight's "tremendous physical force" and agreed to use his connections with the sport's power brokers to facilitate a trip to New York.

At the end of March 1881, Sullivan arrived in Manhattan with his manager. In short order, he would earn his reputation.

CHAPTER TWO

American Hercules

An urban symphony wafted over New York's teeming sidewalks. Bells jangled from the pushcarts of vendors who peddled everything from apples to suspenders to cigars. Knife-grinders blared bugles to herald their services. Newsboys hawked dailies and extras while hitching rides on horsecars as elevated trains rattled over the tracks. Hack drivers hurled obscenities in a babel of languages as they attempted to thread through the traffic-clogged streets that lacked any signs, any order, any rules, except one: Get out of my way.

If the verbal confrontations bloomed into fisticuffs, so be it. New York was a fight town. Neighborhood gangs scrapped with neighborhood gangs. Club-wielding policemen sparred with young hooligans. Even rival political parties duked it out in Election Day melees. New York's brawling was so incessant that it supported a cottage industry of makeup artists who worked out of storefronts as "black-eye fixers."

The city had "more fighting men and fighting dogs than anywhere else in the world," and both man and beast battled in the hidden backrooms of Gotham's saloons. The seediest dives still staged dogfights and cockfights, although the Society for the Prevention of Cruelty to Animals had largely succeeded in banishing the hideous rat pits. No longer could New Yorkers quench their bloodlust at Kit Burns's Sportsman's Hall where rats freshly harvested from the waterfront were sacrificed against dogs, each other, and even Jack the Rat, Burns's son-in-law, who bit the heads off mice for a dime and off rats for a quarter.

Fight fans, however, still flocked to the more refined Harry Hill's Gentlemen's Sporting Theatre on the northeast corner of Houston and Crosby Streets. "As well-known in New York City as Broadway,"

Manhattan's hottest concert saloon was as much of a must-see for out-of-towners as Central Park and the Metropolitan Museum of Art.

After Hill opened his nightspot in 1854, it quickly became a favorite of the city's sporting men who were drawn by its piano-and-violin ensemble, stage entertainment, and "pretty waiter girls" who danced with patrons and kept the drinks flowing. As Harry Hill's grew in popularity and fame, it consumed neighboring storefronts until it sprawled into "an irregular cluster of two-story buildings."

Hill ran the most reputable den of vice in New York. Placards on the walls loudly announced the prohibition of foul language and misconduct. Hill allowed pickpockets and criminals inside but insisted they ensnare their marks off-premises. The buxom waiter girls could solicit other services from the patrons but only if they were discreet and went elsewhere to finalize their transactions. The proprietor boasted that no one was ever robbed in his "dead respectable place," and the relatively safe environment lured thrill-seeking elites wanting to spend a night "hunting the elephant"—slumming—with the other half.

Harry Hill's stage entertainment included variety acts, dancers, blackface performers, Indian club swingers, fighting dwarfs, wrestlers, and even "grand sacred concerts" on Sunday. But no attraction drew the crowds like boxing. The nightly bouts featured brawlers of all types, even female boxers in knickers and buttoned shoes. Harry Hill's was boxing's premier venue in the sport's premier city.

William Muldoon, who had his first big break at Harry Hill's, knew that Hill offered his venue for free every Thursday to any fighter who wanted to stage a benefit. While Muldoon booked John L. on boxing's biggest stage, Billy Madden and Sullivan dreamt up a sensational novelty act that would have made Hill's landlord, the showman P. T. Barnum, proud. Madden spread the word around New York that John L. would offer fifty dollars to any man who would enter the ring with him and simply remain standing after four rounds under Marquis of Queensberry Rules. It was a supremely democratic challenge, opening the ring to any takers, but also, given its implicit braggadocio that defeating John L. in four rounds was a universal improbability, an extraordinary declaration of the twenty-two-year-old Sullivan's self-confidence.

On the afternoon of March 31, 1881, the red-and-blue glass lantern outside Harry Hill's acted like a beacon attracting the curious fight fans of New York. Eager to see whether anyone would accept the challenge of the "coming man," a cross-section of the city—from derby-wearing sports to Wall Street bankers in top hats—paid twenty-five cents to enter the masculine den. Any interested women could enter for free at the designated side entrance.

The fans ascended the staircase to the upstairs dance hall, flanked on one side by a long counter for ordering drinks and on the other by an elevated platform that protruded into the audience.

As the crowd buzzed, the short, stocky Hill, now in his fifties, waddled onto the stage. The Englishman, who had come to America in 1850 to care for the horse stables of a wealthy sugar magnate across the East River in Queens, was a civic institution. "New York without Harry would be almost like *Uncle Tom's Cabin* without Uncle Tom," said one newspaper. Tongues wagged that Hill had amassed a million-dollar fortune slinging his overpriced drinks—in spite of the hundreds he paid out each week to corrupt cops who allowed his establishment to remain open well beyond its appointed closing time.

"This man, John L. Sullivan, is not afraid to fight any man in the world," Hill called out. "He hereby offers a reward of $50 to any man that will stand before him for four rounds." As the fans scanned the room to see if any takers would come forward, a familiar figure rose and mounted the stage—heavyweight John Mahan, a Jersey City coroner and former cog in "Boss" Tweed's Tammany Hall political machine who fought under the name Steve Taylor. In spite of his unique résumé, the six-foot Irish immigrant was no amateur. He had sparred across the country with the English champion Jem Mace and trained Paddy Ryan for his title fight against Joe Goss.

The sluggers changed into their fighting gear and returned to the stage as the crowd thundered its applause. Sullivan and Taylor slipped on hard gloves and came to scratch on a twenty-foot-square section of the stage. As Hill called time, Sullivan instantly charged and delivered rapid-fire rights and lefts to his opponent's head. Unable to dodge the blows or return fire, Taylor was pressed up against a stage wall until a knock from

John L. sent him to his hands and knees. As soon as Taylor arose, the assault continued. Within seconds, Sullivan thumped him to the wooden stage. By the end of the first round, Taylor had been knocked down a total of three times and fallen to the ground without a blow twice more.

The fans shouted and cheered as the fighters left their corners for the second round. Sullivan's fistic storm howled once more, and the weakened Taylor lacked any power in his feeble shots. John L. quickly deposited his opponent to the stage twice more. Seeing his man was spent, Taylor's second threw up his handkerchief to surrender.

Sullivan's coming-out party in New York was a smash. But before he'd return to Boston, he would encounter a far more powerful foe than Taylor, one who would doggedly chase him for the rest of his career.

—·—

Most of history's great feuds are territorial in origin, and the one between Sullivan and Richard Kyle Fox, the egotistical publisher of the *National Police Gazette* and boxing's powerful kingmaker, was reportedly no different. But it was just a matter of feet, rather than vast swathes of land, that launched their lifelong enmity.

According to boxing lore, Sullivan—surrounded by fawning admirers and empty champagne bottles—was imbibing attention and spirits inside Harry Hill's two nights after pummeling Taylor. The dapper Fox—who cut a dashing figure around Manhattan with his thick handlebar mustache, glistening cufflinks, top hat, and Prince Albert coat draped from his skinny frame—sat at a nearby table. The newspaper tycoon dispatched an emissary with an invitation for John L. to join him. The bullheaded Sullivan, never one for social graces let alone supplication, reportedly barked, "It's no farther from him to me than it is from me to him. If he wants to see John L. Sullivan, he can do the walking." Fox may have been the kingmaker, but Sullivan—still a boxing up-and-comer—thought himself the king.

According to Madden and newspaper accounts, the colorful origin story is likely apocryphal. The more banal tale is that Sullivan and Madden made a pilgrimage to the *National Police Gazette* offices in the days before the Taylor fight to pay their respects to boxing's biggest power broker. Muldoon even sent Sullivan to Brooks Brothers and bought him a new ensemble complete with patent-leather shoes and a cane so that the fighter was properly attired to enter Fox's lair.

Once inside the publisher's lavish office, Sullivan answered Fox's questions with short, gruff retorts as he gnawed his tobacco like a cow masticating its cud. The impertinent young man did not impress the impeccable Fox, but the publisher said he would back Sullivan against Ryan. A few weeks after leaving New York, John L. declared that he had never authorized Fox to make a match on his behalf and declined his backing.

No matter how John L. came to spurn the publisher, the feud between Sullivan and Fox was real—and inevitable. The forces of their personalities were like powerful magnets with the same polarities, so identical that they repelled each other. They were both arrogant, egotistical, self-made products of Irish stock who rose from the working class to make it big in America. They were both relentlessly ambitious and vain self-promoters with the utmost confidence in their abilities to make men submit to their wills, one by the power of the fist, the other by the power of the pen.

Born to Scotch-Irish parents in Belfast, Ireland, in 1846, the teenaged Fox worked as an office boy for the Presbyterian newspaper *Banner of Ulster* before spending a decade at the *Belfast News-Letter*. In 1874, he emigrated from Ireland and arrived in Manhattan with only a few dollars in his pocket and dreams of a new life in America with his wife, Annie. Within days, he landed a job selling advertisements for the *Commercial Bulletin* and soon became business manager for the *National Police Gazette*. When the owners could no longer afford his salary, they sold him the newspaper in 1876 for nothing more than assuming its debts.

The newspaper flourished under Fox's watch. Each week its readers entered a typographical red-light district. The salacious tabloid was as garish as the tint of the pink paper on which Fox had it printed. Each issue was saturated with sensational stories of kidnappings, lynchings, executions, Native American raids, Wild West shootouts, crooked cops, and crookeder politicians. Its advertisements hawked pornographic cabinet photographs, bromides for enhancing "certain parts of the body," and remedies for "weak manhood," "seminal weakness," and "premature debility."

Readers ogled lavish illustrations of flirtatious showgirls, voluptuous vaudeville starlets in stage costumes, and, inevitably, revenge-minded damsels wielding guns, knives, and bullwhips at dastardly villains while revealing a scandalous amount of their bare arms and legs. The newspaper's lurid recipe of sex and crime ensured it a ubiquitous presence in saloons, barbershops, livery stables, hotel lobbies, and any masculine bastion in America.

Fox took pride in lifting Victorian society's hypocritical veil to illuminate the true debauchery of the Gilded Age, but he was no crusader. Like a pig in filth, he wallowed in the illicit and the immoral. Depravity was great for business, and despite his pleas otherwise, he had no interest in seeing it exterminated.

The newspaper tycoon was an entrepreneurial visionary with a flair for showmanship. He foresaw the commercial benefits of recasting almost any human endeavor—no matter how middling or inane—as a competitive enterprise. The newspaper sponsored scores of "championships" for activities such as bridge jumping, steeple climbing, haircutting, and water drinking. Fox personally understood the powerful lure that even a brief flicker of celebrity can have on the anonymous masses. He himself was so smitten with fame that his name and portrait adorned the medals, belts, and trophies awarded to the newspaper's champions.

At a time when few newspapers covered athletic events, Fox also detected the country's burgeoning appetite for sports and its emergence as a pillar of American culture. The Gilded Age was a time for the United States, now a generation removed from the horror of the Civil War, to enjoy itself. Wealthy Americans, flush with time and fortune brought on by the Industrial Age, turned to sports as leisure-time pursuits, while immigrants brought their amusements to their new country.

Sports served as antidotes for the societal ills that afflicted post-war America. Life moved at a velocity never seen before. Rapid advancements in technology and communications compressed notions of time and space. Artificial light unmoored people from their natural circadian rhythms. Doctors reported an epidemic of a new disease—"neurasthenia"—that afflicted nervous, exhausted middle-class men who toiled in sedentary jobs and were overloaded by the constant bustle of modern life.

With industrialization causing Americans to abandon the physically active lifestyles of the farm and frontier, athletic pursuits allowed urbanites to stay fit. Apostles of the Muscular Christianity movement, who established the Young Men's Christian Association in the United States in the 1850s, even saw sports as essential to the development of a healthy "body, mind, and spirit" to properly carry out God's work.

While horse racing continued its antebellum popularity in the decades following the Civil War, by the 1870s, baseball began to emerge as the "national pastime." A rudimentary form of football started to sprout on the campuses of America's prep schools and universities. Another prominent sport that emerged after the Civil War was "pedestrianism," and by the late 1870s, the American "walking mania" was at its height. A Boston newspaper reported in 1879 that "peds" in training could be seen "at all hours of the day." Both men and women competed in long-distance match races and crazy feats of endurance, such as the wildly popular six-day races staged in arenas around the country that would start a minute after midnight on Monday morning and end at midnight the following Saturday, giving the competitors' legs a rest on the seventh day. Top participants in these "go as you please" races could run or walk distances of nearly five hundred miles.

The biggest sporting star at the dawn of the 1880s, however, was an oarsman, Canadian professional sculler Ned Hanlan. His match races with Charles Courtney on the St. Lawrence and Potomac Rivers drew enormous crowds and purses upward of $10,000. In November 1880, one hundred thousand people lined the banks of the River Thames in London to watch him defeat Edward Trickett of Australia to capture the world championship.

While Hanlan was the closest thing to a superstar athlete in the early 1880s, he wasn't American, and rowing's popularity in the United States was largely confined to the Northeast. Still, his races became fodder for the nascent sports columns that began to appear in the American mass media at this time.

Sports coverage had been pioneered by William T. Porter in 1831 when he launched the *Spirit of the Times*. The weekly paper, aimed at society's upper crust, covered theater and athletics. The *New York Clipper,* started by editor Frank Queen in the 1850s, emerged in the 1870s as the country's leading sports authority in large part thanks to reporter Henry Chadwick, the pioneering baseball writer and statistician who created the box score.

Sensing the demand for such content, Fox added sports as a vital ingredient to his newspaper-selling recipe of sex and crime. He introduced a dedicated sporting column in 1879, changed the newspaper's tagline to "The Leading Illustrated Sporting Journal in America," and hired sporting editor William Harding to lead a sports department. The *National Police Gazette* covered billiards, rowing, horse racing, lacrosse, tennis, football, cricket, baseball, and cycling as well as fringe activities such as grand pigeon shooting matches, dog fights, and even a shin-kicking contest in which two men booted each other's lower legs until they were bleeding and "raw as beefsteak." But when the paper's special-edition reporting on the 1880 Goss-Ryan heavyweight championship sold a record four hundred thousand copies, Fox discovered that no sport could sell newspapers like boxing.

For a newspaper already focused on violence, lawlessness, and competitive spectacles, boxing was a natural extension. The *National Police Gazette* quickly became the country's leading chronicler of the ring, and Fox was the sport's self-appointed kingmaker—acting as a middleman in arranging fights, using the newspaper as a mouthpiece to defend the respectability of the sport, and, as with other newspaper-sponsored competitions, issuing championship belts brandishing his likeness. While New York's penal code, which punished those who aided and abetted prizefighting, caused publishers like Queen to distance themselves from boxing, Fox continued to publish challenges from prizefighters and facilitate matches even after several arrests. Driven by its embrace of boxing, the *National Police Gazette* soon eclipsed the *New York Clipper* as the country's primary sporting periodical.

Fox was a powerful enemy for Sullivan to make. If boxing's overlord couldn't control John L., he'd ruin him. And it wouldn't take long for Fox to make his first move.

Seven weeks after knocking out Steve Taylor in Harry Hill's concert saloon, John L. pummeled John Flood on the barge on the Hudson River. The *New York Clipper* branded Sullivan "the most promising Knight of the Fives in America," and his double-barreled performance on New York's big stage firmly positioned him as Paddy Ryan's premier challenger.

On June 13, John L. again entered the ring with Flood, this time on dry land for an exhibition in Manhattan's Clarendon Hall. Before the fight, Sullivan reiterated to the crowd his desire to challenge Ryan to a gloved fight for the heavyweight crown. The wily Fox, however, had someone waiting in the crowd. "Pugilists do not fight for the heavyweight championship with gloves!" yelled *National Police Gazette* business manager James Magowan as old-timers nodded their heads in agreement. Magowan flashed a blank check signed by Fox and told Sullivan he was authorized to fill it out for as much as $10,000 if John L. would fight Ryan with bare knuckles. The fighter refused.

Sullivan had yet to fight with his naked fists, which had been the only way that heavyweight championships had ever been contested. He viewed the London Prize Ring Rules not only as brutal, but not very fan-friendly. "Gentlemen and business men of all vocations cannot afford to give up the time to witness fighting under the London Prize-Ring Rules, for the reason that it takes too long in the first place, and in the second place it is against the law, and every spectator, as well as each participant, is amenable to the law," Sullivan later wrote in his autobiography. From the beginning of his career, John L. saw gloved fighting as the means to reform boxing and increase its popularity, but he also recognized that the newly conceived Marquis of Queensberry Rules—which favored punchers by limiting the ability of fighters to wrestle, fall to the ground to avoid shots, and rest after knockouts—suited his style.

Although gloved fighting could actually be more brutal than bare knuckles—fighters did not restrain their power in fear of harming their hands—Fox taunted Sullivan's manhood. "Old patrons of the ring will be under the impression that the new candidate for the title now held by Paddy Ryan is afraid to fight with bare knuckles," the *National Police Gazette* proclaimed. The champion also accused John L. of fearing the authorities. "Any man who is so ambitious to become champion of

America should not be afraid to take the chances of getting arrested," Ryan scoffed.

As the verbal barbs continued, Billy Madden kept the public pressure on Ryan by taking John L. around the country with his novelty act of challenging all comers to survive his punches for four rounds. In Philadelphia on July 11, amateur Englishman Frederick Crossley took the challenge and lasted barely a minute. John L. quickly drove his tall, burly opponent to the ropes. A big left to the Englishman's nose drew blood, and Crossley cried "Enough!" to the howls of the disappointed crowd. It was left to Madden to spar with Sullivan in order for him to face some true competition.

Following an exhibition with Madden in Trenton, Sullivan returned to Philadelphia ten days later to face another taker, Dan McCarty of Baltimore. The Philadelphia crowd fully expected to see a longer fight this time. They didn't. From the start, Sullivan drove the smaller McCarty across the ring and knocked his opponent to his knees with a left to his face. McCarty regained his footing but seconds later was knocked cold on his back by a Sullivan right. Total time: forty seconds. "Well, I have seen all from Hyer down to the present day, but none could have beaten that young fellow, Sullivan," marveled one fan in the crowd.

The buzz surrounding Sullivan swelled. In Chicago, three thousand fans streamed into McCormick Hall on August 13 to watch the phenom. The crowd choked down a variety program of singing and dancing before indulging in the pugilistic dessert: a match with two-ounce gloves between Sullivan and Captain James Dalton, a tugboat captain on the Great Lakes. For the first two rounds, Dalton, nearly forty pounds lighter than Sullivan, proved himself more than a mere boatman, but John L. knocked out the plucky challenger in the third. Sullivan told the audience that Dalton was the best fighter he had yet faced and awarded him the fifty dollars in appreciation of his effort.

Windy City fight fans were so mesmerized by Sullivan that they recruited him to appear again at a September 3 exhibition arranged by one of the country's leading entertainment and boxing promoters, local sporting man Charles "Parson" Davies. Dalton agreed to a rematch, this time in a friendly spar, and another taker was found, a fighter whom the locals hoped could "retrieve the pugilistic honor of the Northwest." Into the ring before two thousand people inside McCormick Hall stepped Jack Burns, a mountain of a man from Jackson, Michigan, who stood six feet, three inches tall. The imposing Burns appeared to have been constructed to last twelve minutes with Sullivan, but John L. had his opponent sprawled near the footlights within fifteen seconds. Burns arose, but Sullivan quickly brought the "Michigan Giant" down to size with a big punch to the stomach. With Burns doubled over, John L. landed another shot on the point of his opponent's jaw, which sent him into the second row of the orchestra seats. The audience helped the groggy Burns back on the stage. He should have stayed down. Six more blows from John L. finished him.

As word of the punishments being delivered by John L. spread, the line of ambitious fighters who thought they could last four rounds with the "Boston Strong Boy" evaporated. In Kansas City, a dogcatcher named Jacob Gallagher did not show after saying he would accept the offer. Back in Manhattan, two thousand fans filled the New York Aquarium to see Sullivan challenged by an "unknown" put up by saloon owner Owney Geoghegan. When the challenger failed to show, Taylor volunteered to fight. This time Sullivan took it easy on his opponent in a tame set-to. The perturbed crowd gave three cheers for Ryan, and a seething Sullivan upped his challenge to $250 but none of the angry fans stepped forth to the stage.

Nevertheless, Sullivan's traveling show had succeeded in garnering headlines, and his amazing displays of power electrified boxing fans across the country. Ryan may have been the champion of America, but Sullivan had captured the public imagination. The trail of victims left scattered on American stages by John L. earned him the reputation the champion had requested. Now Ryan had to fight.

On the morning of October 5, an enthusiastic crowd crammed the corridors of the six-story *National Police Gazette* offices to witness the signing of the papers to confirm the matchup between Ryan and Sullivan. Fans traveled by train from Albany, Boston, Philadelphia, and cities across the

Northeast just to see a few hands scrawl their names on a paper. Both sides put up $2,500. Fox gladly posted the entire stakes for Ryan, while Madden, James Keenan, and the Cribb Club, an upper-crust boxing organization in Boston, fronted the money for Sullivan. Hill served as the stakeholder.

In spite of Sullivan's preference otherwise, he consented to follow the established tradition and fight with bare knuckles under the London Prize Ring Rules. The title bout was set for February 7, 1882, to take place within one hundred miles of New Orleans, a city known for its moral laxity and the tendency of municipal authorities to turn a blind eye to its anti-prizefighting ordinances.

Ryan, who had ballooned to 230 pounds in the sixteen months since his victory over Goss, would need every day of those four months to return to fighting form. When in shape, the man from rough-and-tumble Troy, New York, was a towering brute. Born in Ireland's County Tipperary three days before St. Patrick's Day in 1851, the "Trojan Giant" was eight when his family immigrated to upstate New York. After working as a lock tender on the Erie Canal, he opened a saloon in Albany. With his bartender's waxy haircut, up-twisted mustache, and amiable personality, Ryan certainly played the part. An accomplished street fighter, the heavyweight champion was actually quite inexperienced in the ring. His championship battle with Goss was his first, and only, voyage into the prize ring.

The out-of-shape champion started work in early December on his quest to shed forty-five pounds under the tutelage of trainer Johnny Roche in the seaside resort of Rockaway Beach, New York. The task was less daunting for Sullivan, who wished to shed only eighteen pounds from his 193-pound frame. In November, he began the trip to New Orleans, hoping to arrive well in advance of the fight in large part to harden his body to the region's notoriously brackish water, which easily disagreed with visitors and could cause crippling abdominal cramps and diarrhea in those who didn't slowly acclimate themselves.

Along with his training entourage—Madden, middleweight Pete McCoy, and lightweight Bob Farrell—Sullivan staged exhibitions in Cincinnati, Cleveland, and Chicago on his voyage south. These exhibitions built interest in the fight and allowed gamblers an opportunity to size up the combatants in person before placing their bets. The Cincinnati sporting public noticed Sullivan's remarkable improvement in just the past eleven months since he last appeared for the Donaldson fight. When Ryan staged an exhibition against the Canadian champion Charley McDonald a few days following Sullivan's appearance, a Cincinnati newspaper reported of the "flabby" champion: "As compared to Sullivan, the general impression seemed to be that he was not his equal."

When John L. arrived in New Orleans in mid-December, he found a city swirling with anticipation of the fight. Even on Christmas Eve, Sullivan managed to draw hundreds for an exhibition, in no small part due to the public interest Fox was stoking with his unprecedented pre-fight hype in the *National Police Gazette*. Each week, the newspaper published profiles and illustrations of the boxers and their trainers, minute details of the fighters' training regimens, reports on their current weights, and expert analyses of their styles.

In early January, Ryan arrived at his training quarters at the Barnes Hotel in Mississippi City, Mississippi. Sullivan, meanwhile, settled in at his training quarters in the coastal village of Bay St. Louis, a popular Mississippi resort about fifty miles east of New Orleans. The town was the playpen of the region's Creole elite. Its elegant villas stretched along a shell road, hugging the Gulf of Mexico like sparkling pearls on a string. The town was quiet in the winter, however, which helped Madden not only to whip Sullivan into form, but to keep his man away from the tempting vices of alcohol and women.

Sullivan abhorred the drudgery and discipline necessary for training, but he relished the seclusion of Bay St. Louis compared with the frenzy of New Orleans. He enjoyed gazing out his window at the Gulf and savored a welcome respite from the bitter Boston winter. Then, less than three weeks before the fight, one knock on his door shattered the serenity of Sullivan's comfortable preparation.

A visitor arrived with a telegram from the Mississippi state capital. As Sullivan read it, dismayed and disappointed, he learned that a bill had been introduced in the state legislature on January 17 to make prizefighting a felony in Mississippi, with pugilists subject to a fine of $1,000 and up to five years in prison. The fighters' seconds could face misdemeanor charges with fines or imprisonment or both.

Paddy Ryan's Mississippi City training ground was to be the likely venue for the hostilities, but now the fate of the fight was in considerable doubt. Within thirty minutes, Madden and Sullivan had packed up their belongings like thieves on the lam and boarded a train to New Orleans.

When Ryan was handed a copy of the *New Orleans Times-Democrat* with the news, he quickly retreated to the Crescent City as well. The champion, who had earned the right to select the fight location by a coin toss, knew that finding a suitable battleground free from judicial interference had just become much more difficult. "Just find a place where we can fight, that is all I ask," Ryan told his camp, "a fair field and no favors, and don't you ignore the other side in the matter."

Ryan moved into a hotel in the West End of New Orleans along the shore of Lake Pontchartrain, while Madden secured new training quarters for Sullivan at Schroeder's Garden in the streetcar suburb of Carrollton. Sullivan's new base, just a thirty-five-minute rail trip away, was convenient to the city center. Too convenient for Sullivan.

Whenever new trainloads of sporting men arrived in New Orleans from points around the country, their first stop was often their man's training quarters to check in on the status of their investments. Like turfmen surveying thoroughbreds in the paddock, men pawed the muscles of the beasts, and women giggled as they touched the boxers' fists. Even local physicians and medical students stopped by to take advantage of the rare opportunity to study such finely tuned anatomical specimens in person.

Almost daily, wild rumors flew throughout New Orleans about the conditions of the two fighters: that Ryan had ruptured a hernia, that Sullivan had broken his arm while pounding a sand bag, that Sullivan had fired Madden, that Sullivan had been arrested. Since the men were considered so evenly matched, even the smallest tidbit of hearsay about the tiniest ailment sent the gamblers into a panic and onto the rails to examine the boxers with their own eyes.

The constant interruptions chafed both men, but Ryan handled it with better grace, putting on a genial face for his visitors, thereby winning him many fans. The surly Sullivan, on the other hand, greeted his unwelcome guests with seething scowls of resentment usually reserved for his ring opponents. The challenger tensed his finely tuned muscles and clenched his teeth whenever he laid eyes on one of his impromptu visitors.

As the days remaining to the fight dwindled, trainloads of fans arrived in New Orleans from as far away as San Francisco, and a prizefighting fever swept through the city. Cotton speculators, instead of haggling over prices, squabbled over betting odds. Thespians incorporated skits about the boxers into their performances to thunderous ovations. Schoolboys brawling on the playground were dubbed "Sullivan" and "Ryan" as their classmates formed a human ring around the combatants.

The "pugs" had become the talk of the nation, too, from boisterous barroom squabbles to surreptitious whispers in church pews. Henry Ward Beecher warned his Brooklyn congregation against betting on the fight, but to little avail. The *New York Times* reported that as much as $200,000 had been wagered on the fight in New York City alone. Even the wispy Irish writer Oscar Wilde expressed interest in the sinewy brutes when he was questioned in Philadelphia during his tour of America. "I'm enthused with this manly gladiatorial encounter. It is Grecian, it is heroic, it is classic," he gushed to a reporter.

Major metropolitan newspapers followed the lead of the *National Police Gazette* in providing an unprecedented level of coverage. The *New York Herald, Chicago Herald,* and *Cincinnati Enquirer* were among the many broadsheets that sent reporters to New Orleans to cover the bout, as did the *New York Sun,* which dispatched future Cuban national hero José Martí to report from the scene. Not since the international match between Englishman Tom Sayers and American John C. Heenan in 1860 had the United States been this enthralled by a title fight.

Finally, in the last few days, the fighters closed their quarters to all but intimate friends and staged last-minute exhibitions with members of their entourages in the theaters of New Orleans, giving gamblers a final chance to judge how the men would perform in actual combat. Sullivan drew eight hundred fans, a larger crowd than Ryan did, but his lackluster sparring performance against Goss, who had arrived in late January to help train the challenger, left some of his uneasy backers asking for odds.

Many handicappers pegged Sullivan as the stronger, quicker man and agreed with Hill's assessment that the challenger was "the most powerful hitter that ever put on a glove." Sullivan had far more ring experience, too, than the champion, but he had never fought with his bare knuckles, a big drawback among many bettors. As the *National Police Gazette* eagerly pointed out, "Fighting with pillows on the hands and contending with nature's weapons unadorned are two different things." Some prognosticators speculated that Ryan's superior wrestling and infighting skills, which were permitted under the London Prize Ring Rules, would thwart Sullivan's rushing style. Prizefights could also be greater tests of endurance than skill, and in that respect, Sullivan was a victim of his own success. Since he dispatched his opponents so quickly, his stamina was untested.

Even though Ryan had not fought in nearly two years, many gamblers put considerable stock in his lone bare-knuckle brawl—the title bout against Goss—believing his eighty-six-round victory proved his pluck, endurance, and ability to take a pounding. His backers, however, dismissed the common measuring stick between the men. Both had fought Goss within weeks of each other in 1880. While Ryan needed nearly an hour-and-a-half to subdue the Englishman, it took Sullivan less than five minutes to knock Goss groggy in a gloved exhibition two months prior. Still, Ryan emerged as the slight favorite in New Orleans the night before the battle.

On the eve of the fight, newspapers speculated where it would be held and whether it would be free of "magisterial interference." When chatter grew that Louisiana was to be the scene of the fisticuffs, Governor Samuel McEnery summoned the organizers of the fight to inform them that the scrum would not take place in his state, not under his watch. That left the planners with less than forty-eight hours to find a new location for the fight. Fortunately for them, the bill introduced in the Mississippi state legislature to ban prizefighting had stalled—partly due to protests from businessmen who didn't want to lose the commerce from fight fans—and there was no chance that it would become law by fight time. It was back to Ryan's original plan. Mississippi had to be the battleground.

Even though newly elected Mississippi governor Robert Lowry called upon county sheriffs and even posses of citizens to stop the fight from soiling his state's turf, too much momentum had built up to do anything to prevent it. The wheels of the hype machine were in full throttle, and in just a few hours so would those of the train out of New Orleans.

―⁓―

Dreams could wait, but the 5 a.m. train would not. Rather than risk oversleeping, the boxing fancy clogged the streets of New Orleans into the wee hours of February 7, 1882.

Mardi Gras was still two weeks away, but a carnival atmosphere gripped the city. A constant parade of nocturnal revelers passed beneath the Crescent City's lacy wrought iron balconies. The saloon doors in the French Quarter rarely stopped swinging as a melody of clinking glasses, hearty laughter, and piano tunes sailed down the cobblestone streets. The air inside the barrooms was thick with cigar smoke and heated arguments about the relative merits of Ryan and Sullivan.

By 4 a.m., fifteen hundred anxious fans thronged underneath the arched roof of the Louisville & Nashville depot at the head of Canal Street. The men jockeyed for position to board the first of the twelve passenger cars so that they could claim the prime vantage spots at the fight—wherever that might be. A few minutes after five in the morning, the train pulled out of New Orleans for a destination unknown to all but a select few.

Sugarcane fields bowed in submission and alligators scurried into the murky swamps as the train thundered across the bayou. Some fans drifted to sleep beneath the brims of their tipped hats. Others continued the night's festivities, sipping flasks of whiskey and spitting tobacco juice on the floor, which formed brown rivers that snaked their ways to the back of the cars. As the dense Louisiana swamps gave way to the sandy Mississippi pinelands, dawn broke and the passengers peering out their dust-caked windows saw no signs of the state militia or armed posses. As each destination along Mississippi's Gulf Coast ticked by—Waveland, Bay St. Louis, Pass Christian—the possible locations for the bout narrowed.

Then, just after 10 a.m., the train stopped and exhaled, letting its merry cargo disembark at the final destination: Mississippi City. The small seaside resort town between Biloxi and Gulfport was in the heart of the old South. Just four miles away, Jefferson Davis sat in his retirement retreat penning books and offering no regrets as he clung to Dixie's glory.

As the passengers poured out of the train, Mississippi City suddenly awoke from its wintertime slumber. The ropes and stakes for the ring were hastily removed from the baggage car, and the fans sprinted to the battleground—the front lawn of the sprawling Barnes Hotel. The upper crust who alit from their private cars intermingled with the ruffian masses rushing to the scene; for at least one moment, they were an egalitarian mob united in their blood thirst.

The fans appeared unconcerned with the Mississippi governor's insistence that the long arm of the law reach out to stop them. Most of them impudently dashed across the grounds of the Harrison County courthouse and jail on the way to the hotel. Even though they didn't know it, their lack of concern was justified. The sheriff, perhaps conveniently, wasn't even in town; he had left for Biloxi to officiate an estate sale.

Rather than greeting the fans with shotguns as the governor had requested, the enterprising citizens of Mississippi City welcomed them with open palms, charging five dollars a head for a chance to watch the fight from their rooftops. Entrepreneurial boys gathered hundreds of beer bottles scattered around the train cars, filled them with water, and sold them to overheated fans on the unseasonably hot day. Few would have begrudged the citizens of the hamlet from cashing in. Until this one February morning, Mississippi City had always come up just short of its chances for renown. In 1841, the town was only one vote shy in the state legislature from becoming home to the University of Mississippi. Then, the federal government reneged on a promise to dredge it a proper harbor. But today would be the day that "Mississippi City" would head newspaper bylines and pass from lips to lips all around the world.

The Barnes Hotel, located where a mighty pine forest met the water's edge, was one of the finest on the Mississippi coast. Since before the Civil War, the grand, two-story inn had been an oasis for a generation of plantation owners, steamboat men, and southern gentility who lazed away summer days on the verandah. Under a canopy of stars on sweltering summer nights, southern belles once danced on the hotel's lush emerald lawn, which the fans hoped would soon turn crimson from the blood of the two warriors.

By 11:30 a.m., workers had pitched the eight stakes and mounted the double line of ropes to erect a twenty-four-foot ring in the shade of towering cedars and great live oaks dripping with gray tendrils of Spanish moss. A second ring was then constructed around it for fans who paid two dollars a head to get as close as possible to the action.

Fans of fewer means but more enterprise dug their fingernails into the trunks of bare magnolia trees and climbed up for a true bird's-eye perch. Looking like oversized crows in their dark suits and bowler hats, the men roosted on bending boughs and wedged themselves between forked limbs. The wealthier fans—well-to-do dandies in stovepipe hats and a handful of corseted women in flowing dresses—gladly surrendered five dollars for the highly coveted vantage on the hotel's verandah.

From their elevated positions, the well-heeled spectators gazed out at the Gulf of Mexico's placid surface, which had been transformed into a sparkling sea of diamonds by the brilliant mid-winter sun. In the distance, a white sailboat glided along the sea's blue canvas and gulls circled the vessels of fishermen rowing out to the catch. It was a beautiful day for barbarity.

As the sun approached its zenith, hopes soared in Boston for her native son. For weeks, the bout had dominated discussions from plush hotel lobbies to gritty waterfront dives. Even Brahmins lolling in their easy chairs in genteel parlors on Beacon Hill conversed about the fight under the thin veneer of decrying the terrible spectacle that had the local untouchables in such a frenzy.

Throughout the morning, hordes of men and boys had carefully navigated the slurry of slush and manure in the crooked downtown lanes to descend upon the head of Washington Street, where Boston's nine daily newspapers were shoehorned into a narrow strip dubbed "Newspaper Row."

The ink-stained rivals, who fiercely competed for the pennies of the newspaper-reading public, posted the latest bulletins outside the windows of their newspaper offices. On this day, a sea of anxious Bostonians craned their necks to get a view of the bulletin boards, waiting for newsboys to climb their ladders and post any news about the location or results of the fight.

By noontime, eager crowds amassed inside Boston's saloons and outside its telegraph offices awaiting the latest bulletins. The teeming mass jammed into Newspaper Row overflowed the sidewalks and spilled onto the streets, snarling the horse-drawn wagons and trolleys of the Metropolitan Railroad Company carrying commuters to the South End and Roxbury, Sullivan's childhood stomping ground. While frustrated coachmen tried to navigate the gridlock, police officers and trolley conductors asked anyone they saw if they heard any news about Sullivan and Ryan.

It wasn't just the rabble who gathered on Newspaper Row. Cabots and Lowells stood shoulder to shoulder with Murphys and Reillys. Even though icy winds blustered down the narrow chasm of Washington Street, the crowd stood there for hours.

The scene in cities around the country was much the same. In New York, while the masses huddled outside newspaper offices in the cold, Fox was firmly ensconced in the warmth of his office, surrounded by the city's leading sporting men who crowded inside to celebrate Ryan's presumptive triumph. An encouraging telegram that Harding, his erstwhile sporting editor, had telegraphed from New Orleans the day before—"Have just left Ryan. I think he is bound to win."—buoyed his spirits.

Uplifted by the rosy assessment, Fox had immediately telegraphed another $1,000 for Ryan to wager with Sullivan before the fight began. The publisher also authorized Harding to announce immediately after Ryan's victory that his paper would back him for $10,000 against any man in the world. The media tycoon passed Harding's telegram among Ryan's supporters, and some of them decided to increase their stake in what clearly looked like a can't-miss investment. Fox brimmed with confidence that today would be the day he would get his revenge against that insolent Sullivan.

━ ⁓

Shortly before 11:45 a.m., a felt cap soared amid the fleecy clouds in the Mississippi sky and landed inside the makeshift ring outside the Barnes Hotel. The restless crowd, recognizing the traditional sign of the challenger's impending arrival, pierced the late-morning air with a chorus of hurrahs. Sullivan—accompanied by his seconds, Madden and Goss, and Arthur Chambers, who as the challenger's umpire would assist in the selection of the referee and watch for rules violations by his opponent—squeezed through the noisy throng, bent down, and snaked between the ropes.

The confident challenger, wrapped to his chin in a blanket, took a seat in one of the corners and unleashed his terrifying scowl. He had stalked Paddy Ryan for the better part of two years, but he'd have to wait a little longer for his title shot. As the minutes ticked by without the appearance of Ryan, the champion's backers showered Sullivan with an endless string of taunts. The fans, pressed up against the ropes, were so close they could sprinkle John L. with the spittle from their angry lips.

While one newspaper reported that Ryan's supporters at ringside outnumbered those of Sullivan by three to one, John L. might have believed the entire crowd was against him during those solitary minutes. The challenger used the stream of invective as kindling to stoke his fire as his blood grew hotter and his glare blazed even fiercer.

"How long will you be there, old man?" an impatient Goss bellowed to Ryan's camp. After the spectators began to call for the champion as well, Ryan emerged at high noon. He threw an old hat into the ring and entered along with his seconds—Roche and Tom Kelly—and his umpire, James Shannon. The fans responded with robust cheers, confirming that the gracious man from upstate New York was the crowd favorite.

The good-natured smile that had won over so many fans was missing from Ryan's visage, however. The champion looked as pale as his white flannel breeches, stockings, and undershirt. The "Trojan Giant" had been ill the night before, and the discomfort from the truss he wore underneath his fighting drawers to protect his hernia didn't help his uneasy disposition. John L. saw the worry in Ryan's eyes.

Goss and Kelly tossed for the corners, and the coin came up in Ryan's favor. The champion chose the shaded corner, forcing the challenger to bake in the sun. As Goss dug his heel into the turf to mark the scratch in the center of the ring where the men would begin each round, the fighters disrobed. Stripped down to his fighting shoes, green stockings, and fighting breeches with green stripes, Sullivan unveiled the results of his tireless work with Madden. "His arms are firm as steel; his chest has dropped all superfluous flesh and is as compact as a rampart," a reporter marveled. John L. had shaved off his bristling mustache and closely cropped his coarse black hair, lest Ryan try to follow the lead of "Gentleman" John Jackson, who hardly lived up to his nickname when he grabbed Daniel Mendoza's long locks with one hand and pummeled him with his other to win the English heavyweight championship in 1795.

John L. walked to the scratch along with Ryan and their seconds. The gladiators came face to face. Sullivan weighed around 180 pounds. Ryan was approximately ten pounds heavier and two inches taller and had a superior wingspan. The thirty-year-old champion, however, couldn't match the youth of Sullivan, more than seven years his junior.

Bettors who had waited to the last possible minute to size up both fighters now chose their man. Sullivan appeared to be in better fighting trim, and the challenger quickly became the 100–80 favorite. Furious fistfuls of cash changed hands as the spectators gambled not only on the victor, but on who would draw first blood and how many rounds the fight would last. Wagers of $100 or $1,000 were common. Ryan added to the betting action by posting the $1,000 that Fox had wired him as a gesture of his faith, and Sullivan quickly covered.

All that remained was the selection of a crowd member as a referee, but negotiations between the two camps dragged on for nearly an hour. The fans shouted out a bevy of possibilities, but unable to settle on one person, a compromise resulted in two referees: Jack Hardy of Vicksburg and Alexander Brewster of New Orleans.

Finally, more than sixty minutes after Sullivan had entered the ring, the two boxers shook hands and toed the scratch. The spikes on their fighting boots dug into the turf. The crowd pressed hard against the ropes and leaned over the rail on the verandah. The sound of two thousand voices generated a roar like a steam engine that echoed off the towering Mississippi pines as the two titans—the champion from Troy and the challenger from the "Athens of America"—doubled-up their clenched, bare fists.

Finally freed after his prolonged wait inside the ring, Sullivan pounced like a caged tiger. He surprised his adversary with a jackhammer left that landed on Ryan's cheek with a sickening fleshy thud. The massive opening salvo tore open a gash on the champion and gave Sullivan first blood. The challenger followed it up with a right fist that rocked Ryan's left jaw, sent him to the turf, and induced winces throughout the crowd.

It had taken all of thirty seconds. Thirty seconds for Sullivan to demonstrate he was the unstoppable force. Thirty seconds to prove his power wasn't diminished by his naked fists. Thirty seconds to prove that a lack of prizefighting experience meant nothing when you had two thunderbolts attached to your arms. Ryan had never been on the receiving end of such hard hits. "When Sullivan struck me, I thought that a telegraph pole had been shoved against me endways," he said after the fight.

As blood spurted down his face, Ryan walked back to his corner to get sponged, but his confidence was shaken. With boyish amusement, Sullivan skipped back to his corner, understanding what most of the fans—and probably Ryan himself—had just discovered: He was the superior man.

Ryan knew his best hope was to claw, wrestle, and bind up Sullivan's fistic firepower. As the second round began, Sullivan landed a few blows to Ryan's head, but the champion fell back upon his wrestling skills, and the spectators erupted as the two giants grappled. Fans flailed their arms, waved their hats, and grew hoarse from shouting encouragements and epithets. The jostling crowd pressed against the bulging ropes of the ring, which served more utility in keeping the spectators outside than the fighters inside.

Ryan hugged Sullivan and then lifted him off the ground with a cross buttock. Although Sullivan was lighter, Ryan found him "as hard to throw as a tree." Both men went to the ground, with Ryan falling heavily on the challenger. Ryan's supporters finally had something to cheer, but the champion was in no mood for celebration.

The fall had caused his truss to slip, and he agonized as it pressed against his intestines. As Ryan sat in his corner, his entourage and fans shouted all sorts of strategy and advice on where to land his punches. But to the champion, the words were likely unintelligible background noise drowned out by the searing pain. The thought of quitting was foremost in his mind, but the fear of disappointing his backers overrode his physical anguish.

Sullivan, angered at being driven to the ground, came out for the third round with the ferocity of one of the hurricanes that regularly tore through this section of the Mississippi coast. Determined not to give Ryan any chance to wrestle, Sullivan unloaded a volley of "rights and lefts like the arms of a windmill with the kick of a mule." The round blurred by, lasting all of four seconds before Ryan hit the ground courtesy of Sullivan's right fist.

After the fifth round, Goss and Madden urged the "Boston Strong Boy" to back off because he had Ryan "done and might kill him." Sullivan had opportunities for body shots but was reluctant to do Ryan irreparable harm. Still, the challenger continued his onslaught with terrific rushes. Ryan could not land any meaningful punches, and his resistance grew increasingly feeble. Worried about protecting his abdomen from any blows, Ryan constantly left his face exposed. The champion hit the ground in the sixth to avoid further punishment and was down on the turf after ten seconds of slugging in the seventh. Sullivan, meanwhile, returned to his corner with a disdainful smile after every round.

As a groggy and exhausted Ryan toed the scratch for the start of the ninth round, his left eye began to swell shut. Sullivan continued to throw blistering haymakers and forced the wounded warrior into the corner. The champion mounted a last counter to get to the middle of the ring, but then Sullivan geared up and threw his favorite punch: a wicked right hook to the left side of the neck, connecting just under Ryan's left ear. The blow made such an awful sound that even those without a direct view knew immediately that Sullivan had unleashed a terrible knockout blow. Ryan crumbled to the ground in a heap, bloodied and broken.

The champion was carried back to his corner in a "pitiful condition." Roche continued to offer encouragement, believing that Sullivan was tiring. "Steady yourself, Ryan, you have got him," the trainer exhorted. But the champion said, "It's no use, Johnny. I am too weak." When he couldn't come to scratch for the tenth round, Kelly sent the sponge aloft in sign of surrender.

The title bout was curt and complete, a savage display rather than a scientific exhibition. "Ryan is lucky to have escaped with his life," said a New Orleans turfman who was in the crowd. "That boy from Boston is liable to kill a man with a blow." The fight lasted only eleven minutes. The final round, which lasted fifty seconds, was actually the longest.

Rather than reveling in his victory, Sullivan's first act as champion was a gracious one, crossing to his opponent's corner to shake hands. Still full of energy, he then hurdled the ropes and sprinted the one hundred yards to his quarters behind the hotel as he laughed every step of the way. The only blood on Sullivan's white skin were splattered droplets that belonged to Ryan. His face was nearly pristine, with the lone battle scar a slight blackening over his left eye from a Ryan head-butt.

The "Trojan Giant," however, had a disfigured nose, a welt on the left side of his neck, a gashed lip, and a cut over his eye. After being carried to his quarters to be examined by a doctor, the ex-champion discovered a further indignity—$300 had been stolen from his vest pocket while Sullivan was stealing his crown.

The fans, sensing they had seen history, stormed the ring to get their hands on any mementoes they could. They smashed Sullivan's stool and carried away the relics like splinters from the True Cross.

While days later Ryan would blame the faulty truss for his undoing, immediately after the fight, he magnanimously acknowledged that he had lost to a superior fighter. "I never faced a man who could begin to hit as hard, and I don't believe there is another man like him in the country," he told a reporter. "One thing is certain, any man that Sullivan can hit he can whip."

The news from the Barnes Hotel cascaded across telegraph wires to cities around the country. Reflecting the quick shift in dynastic succession, saloon owners and barbers around the country tore portraits of Ryan off their walls and replaced them with images of Sullivan.

Sullivan's triumph set off a wild celebration in Boston. An explosion of sound echoed down the masonry canyon of Washington Street as the bulletins were posted on Newspaper Row. Men flung their hats up in the air and gave three hearty cheers to "Sully." Even the proper Bostonians who outwardly decried prizefighting grudgingly admitted their pleasure that the local boy had prevailed. In saloons across the city, happy gamblers immediately worked to divest themselves of their spoils and toasted to the health of "Our Johnny." One drinker, so desperate for a personal connection to the city's new celebrity, openly boasted that Sullivan used to "thump us little fellows at school."

No Bostonians celebrated more than the Irish, who had felt blistered by the red-hot Brahmin scorn since their arrival. Now, one of their own was champion of America. Sullivan instantly became an Irish-American idol, one of the country's first ethnic heroes.

A pall fell over the *National Police Gazette* offices when the news arrived. Under their breaths, the sporting men inside cursed Harding and the other vile newspaper editors who had led their money astray with overly rosy accounts of Ryan's fitness. Fox had lost thousands, but he would recoup his losses—and then some. His subterranean printing presses would rumble for days printing a special eight-page supplement with illustrations and reports from the scene that would sell three hundred thousand copies, twice its normal run.

Fifteen minutes after he had left the ring, Sullivan was back in his street clothes, laughing with his friends and boarding the return train to New Orleans. The intense media attention and fan interest surrounding the championship bout provided a mere glimpse at the future. Newly laid railroad lines had permitted fans and reporters from across the country to witness the event in person, and brand-new telegraph lines instantly transmitted blow-by-blow accounts. With a transportation and communications network stitching the country together and media coverage growing, the modern sports age had begun, and it had found its first athletic god. He had arrived in Mississippi City as John L. Sullivan and departed as an American Hercules.

CHAPTER THREE

The Champion of Champions

Inside Sullivan's quarters at New Orleans's St. James Hotel, wine flowed as freely as Paddy Ryan's blood had hours earlier on the lawn of the Barnes Hotel. Jubilant gamblers toasted to the health of the man who had earned them thousands. Friends plied John L. with glasses of champagne and cigars. Fawning strangers jostled just to shake the hand of the new champion.

The son of Irish tenement farmers suddenly found himself "the most talked-of man in the world." The twenty-three-year-old boxer had departed New Orleans the previous day under a cloak of secrecy luxuriated in his newfound robe of fame, which fit him so perfectly that it must have been tailor made.

A patched-up Ryan graciously accepted an invitation to drop by the celebration. The two men rehashed their encounter and expressed their mutual admiration until the adulation pulled Sullivan away. The abandoned ex-champion sat undisturbed as eyes that sparkled with awe now moved right past him to the newest head that wore the crown.

Two days after his victory, Sullivan and his entourage boarded a train to Chicago. The journey was an unbroken, thousand-mile ovation with cheering crowds waiting at every depot. The throng in Cairo, Illinois, was so thick that it ensnared Pete McCoy and prevented him from re-boarding the train before it puffed out of the station.

Sullivan's arm grew sore from the constant handshakes. His voice turned raspy from the incessant whistle-stop speeches. Luckily for John L., he may have been the most talked-of man in the world, but with photography still not in the mainstream, few could actually recognize him, particularly without his signature mustache. So in his stead posed a burly employee of a Chicago gambling den named "Big Steve," who greeted the crowds and regaled them with flowery orations while the champion puffed on his cigar and watched the ruse in peace.

Sullivan and Billy Madden sparred in exhibitions in Chicago, Detroit, Cleveland, Cincinnati, and Philadelphia before the new champion returned to Harry Hill's in New York City to receive his stakes on March 2. Less than a year after he had caused such a sensation by knocking out Steve Taylor on that very stage, Sullivan stood on the same wooden boards while the stakeholder Hill handed over $4,000.

A week later, John L. returned to Boston and the very spot where a single big right to a fighter named Scannell had launched his boxing odyssey. This time when he mounted the stage of the Dudley Street Opera House, formerly Institute Hall, his friends presented him with a $200 inscribed gold watch and a framed cabinet photograph of himself surrounded by a horseshoe of wax flowers.

Madden told the press that the champion stood "ready to fight any man in the world," and from the hundreds of challenges a day that poured into Sullivan, it appeared as if the feeling was mutual. John L. did not know whom he would fight next, but he was certain of one thing—it would be with gloves. After having Richard K. Fox and other critics challenge his manhood, Sullivan believed his quick dispatch of Ryan also dismissed any remaining questions about his courage and capability to fight with naked fists.

In a March 23 letter to the *Boston Globe*, Sullivan declared, "I will not fight again with the bare knuckles, as I do not wish to put myself in a position amenable to the law." He also told the press, "I have proved that I can fight with my knuckles, and now anyone who wants to tackle me will have to do it my fashion."

Fox, however, would not be superseded by a brazen upstart, champion or not. The London Prize Ring Rules had crowned champions for a century and a half, and only he as the kingmaker would change the hallowed code by which the game was played. Through the pages of the *National Police Gazette*, Fox informed Sullivan of his duty to follow the unbroken line of heavyweight champions dating back to 1719 and defend his title with bare knuckles.

Although he was now the titleholder, Sullivan did not abandon the ploy that had made him so famous as a challenger. He continued to dare any man who thought he could last four rounds with him under Marquis of Queensberry Rules to enter the ring. Madden organized a quick tour with the first stop inside New York's Third Avenue Rink on March 27. Old foe George Rooke accepted the challenge but then refused to fight claiming that the ring was not the proper size. That left Sullivan to engage in light spars with Madden and "lank, green amateur" Joseph Douglass in front of four thousand disappointed fans who came to watch a knockout. John L. finally found a taker for a one-hundred-dollar stake in Rochester, New York, on April 20. Plucky fireman John McDermott lasted until the third round before being finished by the champion.

With the brief tour complete, Sullivan returned to Boston where he threw himself into a new pastime and engaged in some more slugging. This time, though, it wasn't in a ring.

———

When the Irish landed in Boston, they brought their drinking culture in tow. During the height of Irish immigration between 1846 and 1849, the number of licensed liquor dealers in the city increased from 850 to more than 1,200. Puritanical city leaders reacted in 1852 with prohibition laws, which proved so futile that by 1870 Boston had one illegal grog shop for every ninety-seven people. A teenaged John L. started drinking just as Boston repealed prohibition in 1875 and the city's liquor business started to boom with per capita yearly consumption of alcohol more than doubling from eight gallons in 1878 to seventeen gallons in 1898.

Along with gambling and athletics, drinking formed the three-legged stool that supported the male bachelor subculture that nurtured John L. The saloons of Boston quenched an Irish thirst for culture, friendship, and fellowship, and the city's sporting resorts—such as those owned by Sullivan's early backers Thomas Earley and James Keenan—were the champion's stomping grounds. Still, he appeared to be truthful in telling a reporter shortly after the Ryan fight, "Though not a strictly temperance man, I have never gone to excess in drinking."

When he became champion, that all changed.

Free drinks were thrust before him every day, and someone had to down all the toasts raised in his honor. "An ocean would scarcely hold the liquor that was pressed upon me by good fellows," Sullivan said.

The new champion quickly proved that the ring wasn't the only place where he was adroit with two fists. John L. threw himself into his drinking with every fiber of his liver, moving from ale to wine to champagne to rum to whiskey. The drinking often amplified Sullivan's fiery temper and pugnacious proclivities, and when Sullivan tore through town on a bender, he could terrorize policemen, hackmen, and bartenders—not to mention fellow patrons.

Shortly after returning to Boston from Rochester, Sullivan traded blows with a stranger named Charles Robbins in an Eliot Street barroom well after midnight. On April 26, a court found Sullivan guilty of two charges of assault and battery and sentenced him to three months in prison. The champion was released on a $500 bond, appealed the sentence, and ultimately had the charges dropped. In June, Sullivan's drinking again ran him afoul of local law enforcement when he stumbled down Washington Street and blistered a police officer with vile and obscene language. The champion pleaded guilty and paid an eleven-dollar fine, while newspapers wagged their fingers at the "prizefighting bully."

As John L. frequented the courtrooms of Boston, he also courted a new love in his life, Annie Maud Bates Bailey. She had been born a year before Sullivan in the small village of Natick, Rhode Island, and had worked in the nearby cotton mills as a youngster. Annie had married young and lost her husband when she was sixteen. Some reports pegged Annie as a chorus girl or pianist on the stages of Boston. Whatever the case, the widower was—not unlike Sullivan's mother—an attractive, stately brunette of "majestic proportions."

The couple had been introduced by a mutual friend, hackman Albert Stickney. John L. first met Annie after Stickney picked him up at the corner of Shawmut Avenue and Hammond Street, just a couple of blocks from his family house on Parnell Street. The hackman drove them to the Hawthorne House hotel where they drank sherry together. Three days later, they returned to the hotel. This time, according to John L., they "stayed there three hours as man and wife." They were not man and wife yet, however, though their relationship grew serious quickly, and he began to spend time with Annie in Boston and at her family's house in Centerville, Rhode Island.

As the calendar turned toward summer and Sullivan sought to put the bad press of his arrests behind him, the patriotic champion announced that he would host a "grand picnic" in New York City on the Fourth of July, an outing that promised fireworks of a fistic variety.

———

"Walk in and see your country's hero!" cried the gatekeepers as six thousand fans celebrating America's birthday streamed down Sixty-Ninth Street and its neighboring Manhattan thoroughfares toward the East River and Washington Park. Men surrendered their fifty-cent admissions, while women entered for free to see if the grizzled Jimmy Elliott, who had fought on Harry Hill's stage before Sullivan was even born, could last four rounds with the champion and collect $500.

One hundred policemen patrolled Washington Park. They were there not only to maintain order outside the ring, but also inside the ropes. In New York and much of the country, the sport of boxing was operating in a strange purgatory. Much like the Wild West outlaws who were celebrated as folk heroes, boxers during the duplicitous Gilded Age were simultaneously prosecuted and lionized. Prizefights and bare-knuckle brawls were illegal and held in clandestine locations, yet they were quite popular and very much public in that they were covered by newspapers. Limited gloved sparring, on the other hand, was legal in some jurisdictions but not of much interest to fans seeking true competition.

With the sport stuck between public morality and public interest, promoters began to stage "exhibitions of skill," advertised as entertainment for "the lovers of the manly art of self-defense." In these exhibitions, fighters donned gloves and sparred supposedly to demonstrate the science of boxing. However, the veneer disguising these actual ring battles was as thin as the skin-tight gloves fighters pulled over their knuckles. With a barely concealed wink, fighters, fans, and the authorities understood that these exhibitions were in reality serious prizefights.

The police who hovered at ringside during these exhibitions could shut down a fight if they believed that the slugging was becoming too intense or if it appeared that one fighter was on the verge of serious harm. Thus, the lawmen very much played a role in a fight's outcome. They in essence acted as secondary referees who could end a bout. The tolerance for the acceptable level of violence in the ring often fluctuated based on the particular officers assigned to a fight or the moral proclivities of the current municipal officeholders.

The officers maintaining the Washington Park peace and the fans gathered there for Sullivan's grand picnic were pelted by a sharp shower that began just before fight time. The ground melted into a muddy sea around the spectators' feet as Elliott—who happened to have been born in Catherine Sullivan's hometown of Athlone, Ireland—mounted the slick five-foot-high wooden platform and entered the twenty-four-foot ring.

Even in his mid-forties, the hard-edged Elliott maintained the nefarious glint of an impish child. His squinted eyes and wicked scowl always made it appear that he was up to no good—and usually that was the case. Elliott's criminal record rivaled his ring record. After being imprisoned with fellow Irishmen who attacked the British Empire in the quixotic Fenian invasion of Canada in the 1860s, Elliott was convicted of highway robbery and wounding a police officer by a Pennsylvania court in 1870. Politicians sprang him from his sentence early, though, to fight Johnny Dwyer in 1879 for the American heavyweight championship, a bout he lost in twelve rounds.

As the downpour continued, Madden and Sullivan—in blue stockings, green tights, and a white sleeveless undershirt—crawled through the ropes to the cheers of the drenched fans in the park and those watching from the windows and roofs of the neighboring houses. John L. put on hard gloves, chosen by Elliott over soft ones, and prepared to face his opponent, who was ten pounds lighter but three inches taller.

Referee Mike Cleary called time. As the heavens rained down on Elliott, so did Sullivan's blows. The precipitation did nothing to dampen the champion's powder, and he delivered back-to-back strikes that pummeled his challenger to the soggy platform. Elliott, clad in white tights and stockings, arose from the first knockdown with blood trickling from the sides of his mouth, much to the delight of the crowd. The second knockdown blow caused Elliott to scrape against the ropes and one of the wooden posts, painfully stripping a bloody layer of skin from his back.

In the second round, John L. continued to press the fighting and knock Elliott down as both warriors struggled not to slip on the wet platform boards. As the water began to puddle in the ring, blood began to pool in the sinuses of the battered challenger. In the waning seconds of the round, Madden instructed his fighter, "Don't hit him hard now; finish him on the next round." Sullivan didn't listen. He delivered a terrible knockdown blow, and Johnny Roche, who served as Elliott's second as he had for Ryan in Mississippi City, carried his man back to his chair at the call of time. The challenger struggled to breathe as his bleeding continued. Ever the dutiful second, Roche placed his mouth over Elliott's nose, sucked the blood clear, and spat a crimson stream onto the platform.

The groggy Elliott stumbled out of his corner to start the third. After a few passes, John L. unleashed his lethal right to his opponent's neck, a blow that deposited Elliott in the corner "limp and lifeless." It was the same punctuation mark that Roche had witnessed against Ryan five months earlier. Once Elliott came to, Sullivan crossed the ring, shook his challenger's hand, and slipped him fifty dollars.

In the ensuing months, the rakish Elliott continued to challenge Sullivan and flirt with danger. After Chicago authorities blocked a scheduled December 22 rematch with the champion, Elliott had a falling out with Jere Dunn, the sporting man and former prizefighter who arranged the bout. When they ran into each other in a Chicago saloon on March 1, 1883, they drew pistols. Dunn beat Elliott to the trigger and shot him dead. Dunn, who had killed two men earlier in his life, was acquitted after claiming he acted in self-defense.

Fox, meanwhile, continued to hunt Sullivan. After failing to stop John L. with America's reigning champion, Ryan, he imported the man who claimed the championship of England—Joe Collins, alias "Tug Wilson." Much like Elliott, the thirty-five-year-old native of Leicester, England, was not in his prime—if indeed he ever had one. Wilson had first entered the ropes in 1866, and a decade-long hiatus blew a hole in his ring record. His biggest fight was his last, an 1881 draw with the English champion Alf Greenfield that Wilson claimed he was winning when his opponent broke his own arm and had to stop. Sullivan refused a prizefight against Wilson and instead offered him $1,000 and half of the gate if he could stand up for four rounds on July 17 in New York's Madison Square Garden.

"It would take a big stake and a good man ever to put me into training again," Sullivan had said following the Ryan fight. He apparently believed his upcoming fight offered neither because Madden, McCoy, and Bob Farrell could not persuade him to take his preparations seriously. John L. spent the weeks before the fight training in name only while staying with Annie in Centerville. His chiseled physique began to soften. Farrell reported the champion at 215 pounds. Still, John L. had no concerns. He admitted to Madden he knew nothing about his journeyman opponent except one thing: "I can do him with a punch."

If the old Yankee Stadium could become the "House That Ruth Built," then another New York sporting cathedral, Madison Square Garden, could rightfully be known as the "House That Sullivan Built." When William H. Vanderbilt, son of the late Commodore Cornelius Vanderbilt, assumed control of the first incarnation of the "world's most famous arena" in 1879, the building hosted a lineup of masquerade balls, horticultural shows, temperance lectures, revival meetings, and band concerts. P. T. Barnum's Greatest Show on Earth and the new Westminster Kennel Club Dog Show brought in the paying customers, but only for a few weeks a year.

To boost revenue, Vanderbilt decided to host more sporting events at his building across from the northeast corner of Madison Square Park. Wrestling matches and billiard tournaments, however, drew only lukewarm crowds. Six-day pedestrian races attracted fans, but on a nightly basis weren't huge money-makers. Like any New York theater owner, Vanderbilt needed a smash hit with a box-office superstar in the leading role.

He agreed to give boxing—and Sullivan—a chance on his stage. Vanderbilt advertised the appearance of John L. as a "grand international sparring match" to differentiate the legal exhibition from an illegal prize-fight. Yet, the advertisement made no attempt to disguise the fact that Sullivan intended to harm his opponent, rather than demonstrate the science of boxing, as it specifically said the champion would try to "knock him out or stop him in four three minute rounds." Not even Vanderbilt, however, could have envisioned the throng that descended upon Madison Square Garden on the sultry summer evening of July 17. Thousands poured out of the Third Avenue elevated trains and jumped off the Fourth Avenue streetcars as fight time approached. The sweltering swarm with one-dollar tickets in hand pushed, swore, and shoved their ways inside the Fourth Avenue entrance while Manhattan's oligarchs flashed their two-dollar tickets at the entrance on fashionable Madison Avenue. The marketplace laws of supply and demand pleased the army of ticket speculators, who received as much as five dollars a ticket.

Never had so many passed through the gates of the arena. Twelve thousand people boiled inside the oppressive cauldron of Madison Square Garden as at least two thousand disappointed fans pleaded to be allowed inside. Fans flouted convention and divested themselves of their coats, vests, and hats. A stagnant haze of tobacco smoke hovered over the crowd and obscured the views from the building's outer reaches.

What struck reporters was not only the size of the crowd, but also its composition. More than the rabble had been roused by the spectacle. "Hundreds of respectable citizens" turned out as well. "From the highest type of respectability to the lowest grade of depravity, every art, profession, vocation, trade, and crime had its representative," reported one local newspaper.

Fourteen months after Sullivan had absconded from Manhattan in the dead of night to throw his fists against John Flood on a barge full of ruffians, he entered like a gladiator before thousands in a brilliantly lit arena. The enormous, diverse audience testified to the resurgence of boxing and the interest in John L. himself. With Joe Goss and Madden backing him as seconds, the champion, wearing flesh-colored tights and blue stockings, gazed across at Wilson. The five-foot, eight-inch Englishman did not cut an intimidating figure. At 160 pounds, he ceded upward of forty pounds to his opponent. With his average physique and round, doughy face, Wilson "looked like an infant" compared to the champion.

With just twelve minutes to knock out his opponent, Sullivan charged from his corner to start the fight, while Wilson backpedaled. John L. had barely raised his dukes before Wilson hit the Garden floor without much of a strike. The challenger rose slowly with a smile on his face and made sure to use nearly all of his ten allotted seconds. Wilson landed an occasional punch, but he wasn't interested in fighting. Diving was the only sport he exhibited in the Garden. Wilson hit the ground as many as ten times in the opening round, often without any impetus from his opponent. As the first round ended, a smiling Wilson retreated to his corner as his second cooled him with a huge palm-leaf fan. The crowd hissed the "artful dodger," but Fox watched on with a pleased look on his face.

In the second round, the Englishman fell like a wispy feather eight times to the Garden floor while staying down to the count of nine each time. The tactics enraged Sullivan. Knowing every one of his 720 seconds were precious, the champion tried to strike Wilson before he regained his feet. Between rounds, Goss and Madden showered the champion with a sponge as he choked on the cigar smoke and noxious gaslight fumes that swam through the soupy air.

Through the rest of the fight, Wilson never deviated from his strategy. He flopped, hopped, and dropped. He skipped, dodged, and dove. When Sullivan approached, he clenched, hugged, and danced. Although prostrate for most of the twelve minutes, Wilson remained standing in the ring as time was called at the end of the fourth round. The Englishman had failed to land one big blow and by some accounts fell twenty-eight times during the bout, yet he emerged the winner under Sullivan's ground rules.

On Wilson's behalf, Fox posted a $500 forfeit to secure a prizefight with Sullivan, but the Englishman dodged one last time, skipping back to England with his thousands.

To Vanderbilt's joy, the gate money for the Sullivan-Wilson fight topped $16,000. John L. left Madison Square Garden disgusted, but—with his share of the receipts—far richer. He raked in thousands for just four rounds of work with the gloves.

The fight with Wilson also softened opposition to boxing, thanks to the interest it generated among the middle- and upper-class fans. The use of gloves allayed concerns about the sport's brutality, and the backing of a wealthy aristocrat such as Vanderbilt made boxing more socially acceptable.

"The recent glove contests which have taken place in New York bear about the same relation to prizefighting that fencing with foils does to the gladiatorial combat," editorialized the *Boston Globe*. "We see no reason why glove fights should not be encouraged as well as tolerated in these days."

Over the next several years, John L. became a regular draw at Madison Square Garden, both in four-round gloved exhibitions and testimonial benefits. The "new style of fighting" that Sullivan inaugurated with these exhibitions proved to be a sustainable, lucrative source of income that for the first time allowed a fighter not only to achieve fame, but wealth as well.

＊

More money came Sullivan's way in the fall when he, Madden, McCoy, and Farrell joined a traveling variety company managed by theatrical man Harry Sargent. Interspersed with wrestling, club swinging, and variety acts, Sullivan and Madden sparred six nights a week for $500 a night.

The troupe embarked on a planned twenty-week tour of the East and Midwest that took them to many of the same cities being barnstormed by Barnum's Greatest Show on Earth, William "Buffalo Bill" Cody and his Wild West show, and Bob and Charles Ford, who on stage re-enacted their recent shooting of Jesse James, even though they had been criticized by many for shooting the outlaw in the back.

The champion continued to welcome all comers, now for a stake of $500. He found a handful of takers. In Buffalo, he easily defeated young challenger Henry Higgins. In Washington, DC, he knocked blacksmith Jordan Rensler all over the stage "as though he were a man of straw" until the police stopped the fight. In Fort Wayne, Indiana, he knocked 115-pound blacksmith S. P. Stockton out cold. When the challenger came to, he "wanted to know if he fell off a barn."

The real fighting on the tour, though, went on behind the scenes. In Indianapolis, Sullivan broke with Sargent, whom he called a "wind-bag and a fraud," and took over the company's management. Days later in Louisville, the relationship between John L. and Madden severed, apparently over women and money. They argued about one of the company's showgirls, and in Sullivan's mind, his trainer and manager had grown so corrupted by his newfound wealth that he "thinks that he is a Vanderbilt."

Madden quit the tour and boarded a train for New York. For weeks, nothing was heard from him. Then, readers of the *National Police Gazette* learned stunning news about the champion's former right-hand man: Just days after leaving Sullivan's side, Madden had boarded a ship bound for England "to engage a heavyweight to pit against his former favorite." And he did so with Fox's blessing and money.

When Madden arrived in London, he placed an advertisement in a local sporting newspaper announcing that in the days before Christmas he would be hosting a boxing tournament in the city. The winner would receive a prize of forty pounds and be brought to the United States to be matched against Sullivan.

The young fighter who emerged undefeated in a series of elimination fights was Charley Mitchell, a twenty-one-year-old native of Birmingham, England. Although five feet, nine inches tall and 150 pounds, the son of Irish parents feared no man. His pluck allowed him to take on heavyweights, and he once easily defeated an opponent with a ninety-pound advantage. The tart-tongued Englishman matched John L. in self-confidence, and he was a clever boxer. He may have lacked Sullivan's power, but he was fast with his fists, quicker with his feet. Plus, Mitchell was shifty, which served him well in the ring and annoyed his opponents.

While Madden traveled abroad trying to discover boxing's next star, the sport's current champion finally moved out of his parents' house. John L. had resisted Annie's repeated entreaties to propose marriage, but in December, the couple purchased a respectable South End row house and moved in together at 4 Lovering Place across the street from the Boston Female Orphan Asylum. Given that a psychic medium lived next door, the boxer's chosen occupation likely raised few concerns with the neighbors, although Catherine Sullivan, a mother who had hoped John L.

would enter the priesthood, could not have been pleased with her son's unmarried cohabitation arrangement.

Sullivan spent the next few months criss-crossing the Northeast. He sparred with Goss at Harry Hill's on December 15 and returned to Madison Square Garden thirteen days later to spar with veteran heavyweight Joe Coburn—who had just been released from prison for assault with intent to kill a policeman—at a testimonial benefit in his honor. The two fighters made a brief tour through upstate New York and Ontario the following month.

While John L. made regular appearances in New York, Boston fight fans clamored to see their "Strong Boy" in the ring again. When a testimonial benefit was thrown in Sullivan's honor on March 19, 1883, it appeared as if half the city tried to stuff itself inside the sprawling Mechanics' Fair Building to watch. Fifteen thousand people, including politicians and even members of the prestigious Brahmin Somerset Club, packed the hall. Thousands more were turned away. "Never before in the history of the Hub has there been such a turning out of its sporting men," reported a local newspaper. Fans were treated to three appearances by Sullivan—as he sparred with Coburn, Taylor, and Cleary—and a host of other bouts that included McCoy exchanging blows with a rising local boxer named Jake Kilrain.

Sullivan pocketed thousands from the benefit, and he slid a sizable chunk of it across the city's mahogany bar tops in the following month. While the champion caroused around the saloons of Boston, Madden arrived in the United States with his English wonder. Mitchell quickly proved his bona fides to an American audience by whipping Cleary in three rounds in New York as Sullivan watched from the crowd. Soon after, prominent New York sporting man and saloon owner Jimmy Wakely, who now assisted with Sullivan's management, arranged for the champion and Mitchell to meet in mid-May for a four-round gloved "exhibition" at Madison Square Garden. In the weeks before the fight, however, Sullivan's year-long bacchanal finally caught up with him.

On April 24, Sullivan's parents rushed to his bedside on Lovering Place. The ailing champion had suffered a lung hemorrhage and coughed up so much blood that he fainted. He suffered hallucinations and slipped in and out of consciousness. John L. grew so concerned about his condition that he summoned a priest to perform last rites.

The clergyman performed the sacrament and then suggested that Sullivan have a different kind administered as well. As soon as the priest learned that John L. and Annie were living in sin, he instructed the champion to get married. And so, after Sullivan's quick recovery, he stood before Father Joseph Gallagher and quietly wed the Protestant Annie on the first day of May in St. Patrick's Church, the same parish in which his parents were married twenty-seven years before.

With less than two weeks before Sullivan's next big fight, there was no time for a honeymoon, even if one was considered. Before starting his training, John L. defended himself against accusations that his illness was due to "rum and hard knocks." He blamed the episode on a cold and insisted that he had not overdone his drinking while noting that he was limiting himself to four or five glasses of ale a day.

In spite of the illness, Sullivan kept his plans to fight Mitchell. He sequestered himself just outside of Boston to train with Patsey Sheppard, the retired lightweight who had once appeared on an undercard with Billy Madden and now owned the popular Abbey sporting house on Harrison Avenue.

On the evening of May 14, a full house entered Madison Square Garden and proved that the turnout for the Sullivan-Wilson fight the previous summer was no fluke. Once again, the fans represented all classes, "from the plug-ugly and prizefighter to the banker and broker." Every seat was taken. Dry-goods boxes, kegs, and milk cans were hauled onto the floor level for use as makeshift seats.

As Sullivan and Mitchell entered the arena in their fighting costumes, the fans noticed another legendary slugger in uniform at ringside—Captain Alexander "Clubber" Williams. The burly, blunt-spoken New York police officer with a "great bull voice" was there to oversee the "exhibition." Gotham's toughest cop reportedly averaged a fight a day for four years running, although he always brought backup—his trusty nightstick that he wielded with such impunity that it gave rise to his nickname. "There is more law in a policeman's nightstick than in a decision of the Supreme Court," Williams allegedly boasted.

Williams may have been the most crooked cop in the country's most corrupt police force. The protection payments he pocketed from gambling dens, concert saloons, and brothels would pay for diamond rings, gold-headed canes, a small steam yacht, and a seventeen-room mansion in Connecticut. When the "poster boy for graft and excessive force" was transferred in 1876 to the Twenty-Ninth Precinct, a vice-laden district in midtown Manhattan, he reportedly said, "I have been living on rump steak in the Fourth Precinct, I will have some tenderloin now." The name stuck to the notorious Tenderloin District, which shared the same precinct with Madison Square Garden.

Back in the ring, Mitchell appeared poised and confident. The surroundings and his opponent did not overwhelm the boyish-looking brawler, who ceded two inches and at least forty pounds to the champion. One fan noted that the fighters' contrasting physiques resembled those of "an ox and a lamb."

The two sides agreed to the selection of Al Smith, who had officiated Sullivan's barge fight with John Flood, as referee. As soon as Smith called time, Sullivan swung lefts and rights as if he was determined to annihilate Madden's chosen man. Mitchell ducked and dodged, but Sullivan managed to knock him down twice in the opening round. The champion chased the Englishman around the ring.

And then it happened.

As Sullivan charged, the cagy Mitchell crouched and landed a hook clean on Sullivan's chin that sent him backward and down to the floor. The crowd cheered wildly. Newspapers reported Mitchell's shot "was the cleanest knock-down ever seen," but as when Jack Hogan had knocked him down early in his career, Sullivan would offer many explanations as to why he hit the floor, none of them having to do with the prowess of his opponent. "Mitchell hit me when I was off my balance, and my feet crossed so that I was placed so a child might have pushed me over," he said years later. While most fighters have losses that stick with them forever, for a boxer of Sullivan's stature, it was a mere knockdown that would eternally perturb him.

In the immediate aftermath of the knockdown, the enraged champion regained his footing by the count of three. He charged Mitchell "like a bull at a red flag" and battered his opponent on the ropes until the round ended. Sullivan's furious storm of rights and lefts continued to rage in the second round. He trapped Mitchell against the side of the ring and then launched a huge right that knocked the Englishman over the ropes and headfirst into the crowd below. The round ended before Mitchell could return to the ring.

The challenger remained dazed as time was called to start the third round. After Sullivan floored Mitchell several times, he maneuvered the Englishman to the ropes and felled him again. Mitchell clung to the ropes like a lifeline and managed to stagger to his feet before the count of ten. Captain Williams had seen enough, though. The policeman and his famous nightstick jumped on the stage and stopped the battle.

"Let me have one more crack at him," Sullivan begged.

"John, do you want to kill him?" the captain responded.

The two combatants shook hands, and Sullivan left New York with 60 percent of the gate, which by some estimates topped $15,000. Soon after, John L. found a way to make additional thousands without even having to raise a fist.

—⁓—

Following the Mitchell fight, Sullivan began to discover the transcendence of his fame when the owner of the New York Metropolitans professional baseball team inked him to a deal to pitch a game for his American Association squad against a semi-professional team in return for half the gate money. The champion's star now burned so brightly that his fans gladly handed over their money just to bask in his glow.

So on May 28, John L. fulfilled a childhood dream. He pulled a white flannel uniform over his burly arms, donned a white pillbox hat, and took to the field of the Polo Grounds. More than four thousand fans paid fifty cents to watch the exhibition game. The crowd included scores of wide-eyed boys and flirtatious women—fans who likely wouldn't join the normally testosterone-laden fight crowds.

"His breadth of shoulder, thick legs, and expansive rump distinguished him from every other player in the field," noted a reporter. While

John L. looked good in his uniform, his pitching didn't make anyone forget the great hurlers of the day such as Albert Spalding or Charley "Old Hoss" Radbourn. He uncorked three wild pitches, committed four errors, and surrendered hit after hit. Still, his squad won 20–15 and he did hit a double, albeit with the other pitcher lobbing the ball to him. Most important to Sullivan, he walked away with around $1,200.

Three days later, he suited up to pitch for another American Association squad, the Philadelphia Athletics, against a semi-professional team. The results were much better as he held the opposition to a pair of runs in a 15–2 rout.

As Sullivan barnstormed the country throughout his career, baseball club owners continued to hire him as a sideshow to boost attendance. Fans also came through the gates to see him umpire semi-professional and amateur baseball games. (Few players argued balls and strikes in the games John L. worked.) Sullivan's employment by baseball club owners proved an economic stimulus for local taprooms. He made it a rule to pump all money he earned as a player or an umpire back into the local economy.

Sullivan still enjoyed attending games at the South End Grounds whenever he could. Before games, Boston left fielder Joe Hornung threw baseballs as hard as he could at the champion standing on home plate. John L. hardly flinched as he let the baseballs bounce off his prodigious chest. Disbelieving onlookers made Sullivan lift his shirt to prove that he wasn't hiding a board underneath his vest.

The story straddles the border of legend, and the surest sign of Sullivan's growing celebrity was the proliferation of myths surrounding him. Newspapers printed stories that he posed as a Quaker student at an Ivy League university—in some accounts Harvard, others Princeton—and pummeled a roomful of blue bloods to break up a campus hazing ring. Rumors spread that he could crush a silver dollar in his hand or pound nails with his fists and pull them out with his teeth. (Legends persist that Sullivan's ankle-length fighting tights inspired the name for "long johns" underwear.)

Like many folk heroes, tales of Sullivan's feats of strength, many of them perpetuated by John L. himself, took on Bunyanesque proportions. He bragged that he once single-handedly lifted a derailed horsecar on

Washington Street and placed it back on the rails after six men failed in the task. With every telling, though, the number of men who couldn't lift the car seemed to mount—six, then eight, then ten.

Sullivan's sense of humor gave rise to one of the rumors that clung to him. One day when walking through Manhattan trailed by the usual caravan of youngsters, a boy asked him what he drank to be so strong. "Blood, my son. Nothing but blood." The wide-eyed youths flocked to the waterfront slaughterhouses to down quarts of beef blood, and the legend grew that Sullivan drank cow's blood or pig's blood.

Anyone acquainted with John L., however, knew he preferred his liquids distilled. As Sullivan's bank account increased, his taste for alcohol deepened. In June, he arrived in New Haven, Connecticut, for a scheduled exhibition and spent the entire day sleeping off a terrible hangover before turning in an uninspired performance with Steve Taylor.

Then, just weeks into his marriage came reports that a drunken John L. was bringing his work home. New York and Boston newspapers printed stories that an inebriated Sullivan had smashed furniture and struck his wife in a fit of anger. Some accounts circulated that he had also abused his sister, now married to County Roscommon native James Lennon.

Both women publicly disavowed the reported abuse. "My husband has always treated me kindly," Annie Sullivan told a newspaper, "and I regret extremely that such falsehoods should be made public." She also told the press, "His great misfortune is that he has a heart too big for his body, and is so lavish in entertaining his friends that he sometimes oversteps the bounds of prudence in his habits of sociability and is then a little morose and surly."

Annie, however, was only putting on the public front expected of a dutiful nineteenth-century wife. She had noticed a change in John L. since their marriage. He was chronically inebriated, and he hurled swear words— and sometimes objects—at his wife when returning home after drinking away the night. Given the ugliness of the truth about their hero, it's little wonder that Sullivan's fans chose to traffic in the world of mythology.

⚬⚬⚬

While John L. continued to earn money at an unprecedented rate for a fighter, he wasn't the only one profiting from the boxing revival. Business was also good for Fox and the *National Police Gazette*, which in early 1883 moved into a new headquarters overlooking Franklin Square and the entrance ramp to the Brooklyn Bridge. Fine furniture, polished hardwoods, and ornate chandeliers decorated the well-appointed quarters. The newspaper invited readers to come and view its collection of sports trophies, memorabilia, and pictures, including a life-size portrait of Sullivan in ring costume.

The *National Police Gazette* publisher naturally spared no ink in heaping praise on his "veritable palace of journalism, unequalled by any newspaper establishment in New York." Fox's massive ego towered over the seven-story building. A stone head of a fox lorded over the entrance, and the proprietor's name was plastered on the side of the building. Fox's initials adorned the cast-iron fire escape railings along with images of boxers, wrestlers, baseball players, and pedestrians.

Fox's office had a bird's-eye view of New York's grandest gala celebration since the completion of the Erie Canal when the Brooklyn Bridge opened on May 24, 1883. He could gaze down from his office as President Chester A. Arthur, New York governor Grover Cleveland, and a seventy-five-piece band led a procession of seven thousand lucky ticket-holders across the bridge.

The reception that Fox threw to celebrate the wedding of two of America's largest cities—New York City and Brooklyn, which remained independent until 1898—devolved into a wild affair. More than a thousand sporting men, politicians, and businessmen overran Fox's lavish new quarters. By the time police arrived at noontime to break up the party, revelers had already devoured an entire barbecued ox, downed 108 bottles of Blue Grass whiskey in the religious editor's office, and started to smash Fox's ornate furniture modeled after pieces in the Louvre.

While Fox may have risen to the top of the media industry, he remained stymied in his efforts to dethrone Sullivan. He literally searched to the far ends of the earth to find someone, anyone to match against John L. In the fall of 1882, he dispatched a message to New Zealand, where the former English champion Jem Mace was on an exhibition tour. Perhaps naively seeking to turn back time, the publisher asked the fifty-one-year-old Mace to come to New York to fight Sullivan. The former champion initially agreed but apparently thought better of it because he was not alone when he arrived in America.

With him was a "new wonder" whom he had discovered—towering Herbert Slade. The thirty-two-year-old New Zealander was the son of an Irish whaler and a Maori mother. Slade reportedly had an undefeated record in his homeland, and Mace telegrammed Fox that the six-foot, one-inch fighter was the "coming man." Sight unseen, Fox agreed to match his "unknown" for the championship of the world. Once again, Sullivan only consented to a four-round gloved fight, scheduled for Madison Square Garden on August 6.

Fox organized a combination that toured the country with Mace and Slade in the first half of 1883. To some, the bronze-skinned brute was as much of a curiosity as a freak show performer or dime museum exhibit. The press called him the "half-breed" as if he were some dog. MR. MACE AND HIS GIANT announced the headline of a *New York Times* article that read as if the white man had brought a feral beast back from a savage land.

Meanwhile, Sullivan's indulgences had caused his weight to balloon to 230 pounds. He worked with Goss and McCoy in the weeks before the fight to shed the superfluous flesh at their training quarters south of Boston in a cottage overlooking picturesque Scituate Harbor.

As a rainstorm tore through New York on the evening of August 6, ten thousand fight fans splashed through the Manhattan puddles to see the much-hyped Slade face the well-known champ. The pre-fight chatter built the Maori up to be such a leviathan that his appearance would inevitably disappoint. While long-limbed, Slade was not overly muscular. He was tall, yet only bested Sullivan by three inches, and they both weighed just north of two hundred pounds.

As Captain Williams watched from beneath the elevated platform holding the ring, Sullivan and Slade engaged in combat. It took little time for Sullivan to establish his superiority. The champion "resembled a drummer beating a drum" in the way he pounded his opponent's body and face. The challenger, on the other hand, appeared slow and clumsy. He "sparred like an automaton." As a big left felled Slade, waves of applause rippled through the arena. Slade regained his footing, but Sullivan gave him no time to breathe. The champion smashed the New Zealander through the ropes, off the platform, and headfirst into the crowd. By the time the challenger was helped back into the ring, the opening round was complete.

John L. walloped Slade all around the ring in the second round. He bullied the New Zealander to the ropes with a barrage of rights and lefts. Slade tried to run away. Sullivan pursued. Much like the Ford brothers did to Jesse James, John L. pumped shots into the fighter's back. The lefts and rights sent Slade through the ropes and off the stage once more.

By the third round, the listless challenger could only stagger around the ring, barely able to raise his right guard. John L. pinned him against the ropes again and knocked him down with a thunderbolt. Slade toppled "like an ox knocked down with a butcher's axe," reported the *National Police Gazette.* Blood oozed from his ears, mouth, and nose. As Sullivan hovered, the wobbly fighter was assisted to his quivering feet. Williams, however, mounted the platform and ordered a stop to the fight in the name of the law, not that there was much of a fight to stop. The receipts, of which the victor took 65 percent, were estimated as high as $15,000.

Only hours after he bathed himself in the applause of thousands of clapping hands in Madison Square Garden, Sullivan boarded a train to rush back to Boston. The following night, he would launch another enterprise to capitalize on his growing fame.

———

As the sun began to fade on August 7, a sea of human heads swelled beneath a sign outside 714 Washington Street that simply declared in big gilt letters: JOHN L. SULLIVAN. Mounted police tried in vain to chisel a passageway through the horde for vehicles to pass. Inside, the champion prepared for the grand opening of his new saloon. Backers such as Earley, friends such as Goss, and foes such as Ryan all owned drinking establishments, so running a grog shop was a natural side business for a fighter.

Sullivan spared no expense in the creation of his "Mahogany Palace." He spent $20,000 to convert the storefront into a "gorgeous temple of Bacchus" and then dropped another $5,000 to stock it.

When the doors opened at 7 p.m., a "mass of swearing, perspiring men" pushed, jostled, and squeezed inside. The aroma of tobacco and fresh paint wafted through the watering hole as the men besieged the long mahogany bar. So many feet populated the ornamental brass rail that it broke away and fell to the floor. Six bartenders kept the liquor flowing and piled the mounting volume of silver and cash notes on the shelf behind them. As customers gazed at the fighting scenes adorning the walls, they hoisted their bar glasses etched with the champion's initials.

Sullivan's brother, Michael, manned the cigar stand and his friend Frank Moran managed the establishment. Inside a private reception room in the front of the saloon, John L. drank and swapped tales with a few lucky sporting men. Sullivan's deep guffaws periodically rumbled through the barroom.

The saloon took in $2,900 on the opening night alone, and John L. recouped his initial investment in the saloon in just the first ten days. Over the long run, though, John L. proved much more adept at guzzling booze than slinging it. He drank or gave away too much of the stock. The charitable champion would not deny a drink to a customer who lacked money. And even for a congenital drinker such as Sullivan, the good manners required of a proprietor taxed his liver. "One man comes in and asks me to drink champagne, another beer, a third whiskey, and a fourth brandy," he explained to a reporter.

Much as he had eighteen months before at the St. James Hotel on his first night as champion, Sullivan spent his first night as a saloon owner quaffing spirits and imbibing the fawning adulation of his fans. In the year and a half since he left New Orleans, however, Sullivan had transcended mere notoriety to achieve superstardom.

He had earned an unheard of income in the tens of thousands of dollars. He had broken new ground for a boxer and reinvigorated the sport with his gloved exhibitions at Madison Square Garden. He had discovered that a fighter could make money by simply appearing on a baseball diamond or inside a saloon. Not only did the American public now know of "John L. Sullivan," there was also no misunderstanding about whom someone was talking about when they simply mentioned "John L."

Now, as Sullivan held court in his gilded refreshment parlor, he prepared to embark on an even more ambitious endeavor, one that would carry his fame to every corner of the Union.

CHAPTER FOUR

America Takes Its Best Shot

THE CITY OF BOSTON WANTED ONE LAST GLIMPSE OF HER CHAMPION. Hordes of Sullivan's fans stood outside of his saloon on the evening of September 26, 1883. Heads craned and tilted as they attempted to steal a passing glance of their hero through the open doorway. Inside, a ceaseless flow of well-wishers shook the champion's hand and offered their farewells.

John L. never liked goodbyes and so would have been happy when the time finally arrived to leave, to swim through the dense ocean of humanity that lapped up to the door of his liquor palace, and to alight in a waiting carriage for the Boston and Providence Railroad depot. Sullivan had departed from the Park Square train station on many journeys before, but no champion had ever set out on such an ambitious adventure as the one he was about to undertake.

For the next eight months, Sullivan would circle America. He would travel to Appalachian coal towns, to Pacific coastal cities, to Wild West boomtowns, to Texas cow towns, to southern crossroads, and to scores of places from sea to shining sea. He would head west crossing northern states and territories, swing down the West Coast, and then travel east through the southern states. He would visit twenty-six of the country's thirty-eight states. He would travel to six American territories—Arizona, Montana, New Mexico, Utah, Washington, and Wyoming—in addition to the District of Columbia and British Columbia.

Along the way, John L. would spar with the world's top professional fighters in upward of two hundred boxing exhibitions in nearly 150 different locales. And as Sullivan swaggered—and staggered—across the United

States, he would reprise his signature challenge daring any man to last four rounds in the ring with him under Marquis of Queensberry Rules.

John L. was leaving Boston to challenge America to a fight.

Sullivan's transcontinental "knocking out" tour was gloriously American in its audacity and concept. Its democratic appeal was undeniable: Any amateur could take a shot at glory by taking a punch from the best fighter in the world. It also celebrated the rugged individual, the self-made man who stood on his own two feet.

The challenge was furthermore a statement of supreme self-confidence from a man who supposedly bellowed his own declaration of independence: "My name is John L. Sullivan, and I can lick any son-of-a-bitch alive!"

The epic barnstorm dwarfed the size of any of the champion's previous exhibition tours. Off-days were few, holidays nonexistent. Not one, but two shows were scheduled on Christmas.

Al Smith, the referee for Sullivan's fights with John Flood and Charley Mitchell, is generally given credit for conceiving of the grand boxing road trip. The man known as the "Prince of Sportsmen" managed the overall logistics and aligned the galaxy of stars that accompanied the champion. Smith had earned the respect and trust of John L., perhaps because he was a scrappy fighter in his younger days and an imposing figure at six feet, two inches tall.

The "Great John L. Sullivan Combination" compiled by Smith included lightweights Pete McCoy and Mike Gillespie and a pair of heavyweights already vanquished by Sullivan—Steve Taylor and the man who had just been steamrolled by the champion, Herbert Slade. In addition to being a fighter of similar stature to Sullivan, the "half-breed" was still a curious specimen to nineteenth-century America and a valuable sideshow draw for Smith's traveling fight circus. Suspicious minds, though, believed the New Zealander joined the combination with the ulterior motive of studying Sullivan's style and gaining face-to-face experience for a future title bout.

Sullivan's friend Frank Moran was brought along officially to be the master of ceremonies, but his more critical—and difficult—job was to keep the "Big Fellow" out of trouble. Jake Munzinger was hired as the treasurer. Advance agent Hugh Coyle, who once worked for Forepaugh's circus, traveled ahead of the combination, oftentimes with Smith, to arrange logistics and generate publicity.

Coyle plastered cities with big posters containing Sullivan's image surrounded by those of his victims, including Slade and Mitchell. In a blank corner of the poster was a question: WHO'S NEXT? Newspaper advertisements, which assured readers that large police forces would be present and that special attention would be given to "ladies and their escorts," itemized the names of Sullivan's previous conquests, which couldn't have pleased all the combination members since Taylor was the first victim on the list and Slade the last. Fans who saw the advertising could have been forgiven if they began to view Taylor and Slade as pillaged trophy pieces being paraded into town by the conquering hero.

Sullivan announced to the press that a ninth person would join the traveling party—Annie. She had accompanied the champion on tour the prior year, so she understood the hectic schedules and constant travel that was awaiting. What she may not have known yet was that she was in the early stages of pregnancy with their first child.

Before leaving Boston, Sullivan pledged that he had stopped his out-of-control drinking and swore that his lips hadn't tasted a drop of alcohol in weeks. "I have given up the flowing bowl. That may seem queer, as I keep a saloon; but 'tis so," he insisted to a reporter. "A man in my position cannot drink and stand up in the ring." John L. would prove himself wrong spectacularly as America watched.

⚊⚊

The "knocking out" tour opened in Baltimore on September 28 before thirty-five hundred eager fight fans who filled Kernan's Theatre. No one challenged the champ for a $250 stake on opening night, but there was a "flutter of excitement" that palpitated through the audience when Sullivan and Slade took to the ring to spar and re-enact scenes from their Madison Square Garden encounter, which was still fresh in the minds of the boxing fancy.

The combination rotated partners in four-round gloved sparring exhibitions. Taylor and Slade served as Sullivan's primary sparring partners.

The two lightweights squared off with each other and Taylor. Audience members could challenge the other fighters as well as Sullivan, albeit for smaller stakes, and John L. would pass smaller challengers over to Slade and McCoy to fight. When cries started to develop months into the tour, however, that Sullivan was doing it to dodge opponents, he made sure to personally deliver the whippings. Smith, who told the press he expected each of his fighters to abstain from alcohol during the tour, wanted two things from his boxers: "temperance and good shows."

After opening in Baltimore, it was on to Virginia with stops in Richmond, Petersburg, and Norfolk. Following two shows in the nation's capital, it was off to Pennsylvania. The locales started to tick by day after day—Harrisburg, Reading, Lancaster. Then the combination pulled into Pottsville where Smith's expectation of temperance from the boxers, if it hadn't been previously breached in the tour's first two weeks, was dashed.

Newspapers reported that after the evening's performance at the Academy of Music, the combination went on a spree through the town's saloons. After midnight, the fighters decided to discard abstinence altogether and stop by a "disreputable resort in Railroad Street." (Whether Sullivan joined in the brothel visit with Annie traveling along is questionable.) The police raided the whorehouse in the early morning hours and arrested the proprietress and four women. The sluggers escaped and left for Wilkes-Barre.

Two days later, the combination arrived in Scranton, where a last-minute venue change had forced the show outdoors at the city's horse-racing track. When the fighters arrived, they were "much disgusted" at the muddy surroundings and the meager attendance. With skies threatening, Sullivan and the others didn't even bother getting out of the carriages. They drove around the track and kept on galloping to their downtown hotel.

A burly mob of incensed miners and ironworkers rushed the money collectors to repossess their fifty-cent admissions. They wrestled for the money boxes and tossed them around like footballs until the besieged ticket manager fled on horseback with the gate receipts while being pelted with sticks and stones. The mob then came upon Sullivan at a downtown barbershop. They hissed, hooted, and hollered. They kicked and beat the policemen who tried to break up the crowd. Sullivan escaped out a rear door and barricaded himself in the safety of his hotel until the mob dispersed after midnight.

John L. finally encountered his first challenger in McKeesport, Pennsylvania, on October 17. Local slugger James McCoy looked like the consummate tough guy. Tattoos of snakes, flowers, and a wide-mouthed dragon plastered his broad chest. The 160-pound challenger's looks proved deceiving, however, as he stepped forward to compete for the $500 prize now being offered. (By the end of the tour, it would rise to a $1,000 offer.) After McCoy opened with a weak blow, the champion needed only a right and a left. And then it was over. The challenger was down and out. It had taken mere seconds. "I never thought any man could hit as hard as he does," McCoy said afterward. "But I can say what few men can, that I fought with the champion of the world."

And that's precisely why the "knocking out" tour generated unprecedented publicity in newspapers around the country, both for Sullivan and the entire sport of boxing. Not only was the best fighter in the world bringing the sport to the masses, he was letting the masses get in the ring with him!

Although Sullivan's title wasn't at stake in these challenge fights, his reputation and his de facto designation as the world's toughest man was at risk each and every night. Plus, Sullivan—big hitter taking on inexperienced amateurs—had to be mindful not to cause irreparable harm to his opponents.

The tour rolled on into the Midwest. The cities started to blur. Youngstown. Steubenville. Terre Haute. In East St. Louis, Illinois, an overflow crowd greeted the combination on November 3 along with local bruiser Jim Miles, who challenged the champion. The fighter known as "The Gypsy" weighed only 135 pounds, and Sullivan's first blow sent him to the ground. The champion floored Miles as many as nine more times before a Sullivan shot under the chin knocked the challenger off the stage and ended the fight at the one-minute mark.

The next day in St. Louis, Sullivan was knocked hard, but not in a ring. He suited up to take to the baseball diamond with the St. Louis Browns, who recently had completed their 1883 season with a second-place finish in the American Association. Browns owner Chris Von der

Ahe paid the champion $1,000 and a percentage of the gate to appear in an exhibition. Five thousand fans watched as Sullivan hurled five lackluster innings for a squad of Browns and semi-professional players in a 15–3 loss. After the game, fans thronged Sullivan. He barely made it to the dressing room and then escaped the crowd by dashing away through a rear exit with Slade sprinting alongside.

Although Missouri law prohibited public sparring and boxing exhibitions, the combination staged two nights of shows at the People's Theatre in St. Louis. The authorities permitted the shows to go on, but they arrested Taylor and Sullivan as they were preparing to leave the city. Both fighters posted bonds to appear in court in December, but they ultimately chose to forfeit them instead of abandoning tour dates to return.

The combination moved north along the Mississippi River. Quincy. Keokuk. Burlington. In Chicago, Sullivan as usual drew enormous audiences, a crowd of nine thousand one night. The combination pulled in nearly $20,000 in two nights. Milwaukee. Fond-du-Lac. Oshkosh. In St. Paul, Minnesota, in late November, Sullivan finally faced an opponent who could match him pound for pound. As soon as time was called, Sullivan stretched out his arm, and six-foot railroad engineer Morris Hefey, who weighed 195 pounds, "fell on the stage as if struck by an axe." The challenger rose, but as soon as he was within arm's reach of the champion, he was down again. The fight took thirty seconds. "If you want to know what it is to be struck by lightning," the challenger said afterward, "just face Sullivan one second."

Into Iowa. McGregor. Dubuque. Clinton. In Davenport on December 4, blacksmith Mike Sheehan, the "strongest man in Iowa," told his family that he was going to face off with the champion. Sheehan's frantic wife visited Sullivan before the fight and beseeched him not to fight her husband, but not for the reason the champion suspected. "We've got five small children, and I don't want them to have a murderer for a father. If you get into a fight with him, he'll surely kill you," she warned the champion.

John L. took his chances, entered the ring, and started with a smash to the nose of the stunned challenger. Sheehan's surprise turned to rage. He charged at Sullivan. A big clout on the jaw by the champion sent his foe spinning to the back of the stage, and the challenger decided he had

had enough of his foray into the ring. Sullivan sent Sheehan away with one hundred dollars for being game.

Muscatine. Omaha. Topeka. The combination rattled through Iowa, Nebraska, and Kansas. As they passed into Colorado, they began their long ascent into the Rocky Mountains. On Christmas Eve, Sullivan and his entourage took the stage in Central City, Colorado, a mountain mining town founded in 1859 during the Pike's Peak Gold Rush.

John L. had arrived in the West for the first time.

While some of the gold and silver rushes had slowed, the wars with Native Americans had ebbed, and the frontier had begun to close, the Wild West element still endured in the states and territories beyond the Rockies. Seemingly as soon as "Sullivan's Sluggers" set foot in the West, an outlaw aura and a feral element attached itself to the fighters. They became wild men having wild times in a wild land.

———

Sullivan's unprecedented transcontinental tour and his traverse of the West would not have been possible without one of the technological marvels of the age—the railroad. Only fourteen years had slipped by since the driving of the Golden Spike married the Union Pacific to the Central Pacific and bonded the nation's railway system together. In the decade between 1870 and 1880, railway mileage in the United States almost doubled from nearly fifty thousand to over eighty-seven thousand. In the West, however, mileage more than tripled.

The railroads were powerful symbols of the industrial might of Gilded Age America. "The old nations of the earth creep on at a snail's pace; The Republic thunders past with the rush of the express," wrote steel magnate Andrew Carnegie of the raw energy that stoked the United States in the 1880s. That same rough fire of youth burned inside Sullivan and propelled him like a "living locomotive going at full speed."

In fact, perhaps no American has so embodied his times like John L. The United States was the fastest-growing country in the world. Its population would soon eclipse that of Great Britain, and it was on its way to becoming the world's leading industrial superpower. The country pulsated with the infusion of new immigrants, new industry, and new inventions— telephones, electric lights—that were transforming daily life.

Both Sullivan and the upstart United States in the 1880s were young and virile, proud and cocky, crude and pugnacious. A boxer always represents power in its most visceral sense, and John L. symbolized an ascendant America that was flexing its economic muscles on the world stage. The champion exuded a rough masculinity that appealed to the growing numbers who feared that life in an increasingly urbanized United States was becoming less rugged, more sedentary. Chiseled body types—rather than lean, wiry physiques—were en vogue. And at a time when the increasingly popular theory of social Darwinism emphasized the survival of the fittest, there was no place in America where that could be so clearly demonstrated than inside a boxing ring.

Even Sullivan's hard-charging ring style captured the spirit of 1880s America. When the champion met former president Ulysses S. Grant in the lobby of Manhattan's Fifth Avenue Hotel, the grizzled general told John L., "Your style of fighting, Mr. Sullivan, proves the idea I tried to put into operation during the Civil War—that is to carry the battle to the enemy and fight all the time."

John L. attacked almost every endeavor he undertook with that same combative attitude. "I believe in having a little fight in most everything except funerals," Sullivan liked to say. "Anything that ain't got some fight in it is like a funeral, and I don't like funerals."

That legendary spirit of the fighting Irish that was made flesh in Sullivan transformed him into a hero for tens of thousands of sons and daughters of the Emerald Isle who had felt emasculated in the wake of the Great Hunger. To Irish Americans who had believed themselves powerless under the thumb of the British, slighted in their new homeland, and traumatized by the horrific famine, here came one of their own who exuded strength, who didn't lack confidence, and who didn't suffer from a lack of pride. His self-belief was an elixir for a people who had suffered from malignant shame.

Irish Americans sought respect. Sullivan earned it with his fists. Paddy Ryan had as well. He had been an Irish-American heavyweight champion—one born in Ireland no less—but Sullivan had a force of personality that Ryan never did, one that made him an idol.

Working-class Irish Americans thought of the champion as one of them, just another Irish bloke scrapping to earn a living with his hands.

(He had been one of them, too, in his early years working as a laborer.) The champion's rough hands and broad back matched those of tens of thousands of Irish. They could easily relate to Sullivan's line of business more so than those of Irish-American pedestrian star Daniel O'Leary or baseball star Mike "King" Kelly.

Certainly not all Irish Americans took pride in Sullivan. Many middle-class, lace-curtain Irish viewed the sport as barbaric. *Donahoe's Magazine* denounced boxing as "human butchery" supported chiefly by a "worthless, gambling class of lodgers" who patronized saloons, poolrooms, and other "gilded haunts." These Celts feared the sport fed the stereotype of the "ignorant, drunken, belligerent, and pugnacious Irish buffoon."

On the "knocking out" tour, Sullivan traveled to the outposts where the Irish labored in twelve-, fourteen-, and sixteen-hour shifts: mining towns, lumber camps, and steel mill cities along railroad lines that were built by calloused Celtic hands. Boxing was ingrained in the culture of these locales. In railway camps and mining towns, bare-knuckle bouts were regular pastimes on Sundays, the only off-day during the week. Even Wyatt Earp, the famed gunman and US marshal, had begun refereeing railway camp fights in 1868 at the age of twenty and became a regular on the Sunday mining camp circuit.

When the Irish idol and a group of pugilistic stars came to town, it sometimes merited a reception as if the president himself had arrived. In Leadville, Colorado, the combination found the entire town draped in bunting. A big banner read JOHN L. SULLIVAN IS LEADVILLE'S GUEST. Business came to a stop in the town. Irish Americans flocked to see their idol and to, at least for a few hours, blow off some steam. Once the combination left for the next town and the sound of the train whistle faded in the distance, life returned to its back-breaking normalcy.

While there were occasional reports of rowdiness by the fighters in the "Great John L. Sullivan Combination," such as in Pottsville, for the most part they appear to have been well behaved in its first few months. Whether it was the outlaw element that persisted in the western states and territories or whether the fighters were beginning to chafe at the travel and each others' constant presence, reports of drunkenness and brawling began to appear with increasing frequency.

On Christmas Day in Denver, Sullivan almost killed Gillespie while playing around with a double-barreled shotgun he was told was unloaded. The champion picked up the gun, pointed it at Gillespie's head, and pulled the trigger. The barrel was empty, so it didn't fire. Then John L. tried the other barrel. He aimed it at a table, pulled the trigger, and blew it to splinters. Had he reversed the order, Gillespie would have been a dead man.

Two days later, the fighters moved on to Leadville, a mining boomtown that had recently sprouted out of nowhere when silver was discovered in 1876. Four years later, it was a city of forty thousand people. Among those seeking their fortunes in Leadville were four thousand first- and second-generation Irish Americans.

The combination devoted four nights to Leadville, the same amount of time it had spent in Chicago. On the second night in town, Sullivan drank heavily during the day and staggered through his performance. Backstage, he stumbled into McCoy. The two fighters exchanged words and then Sullivan slapped McCoy, who responded by picking up a chair and smashing it over the champion's bullet head. McCoy bolted to the other side of the room as John L. seized a lighted kerosene lamp and hurled it at his fellow fighter. McCoy dodged the projectile, which had been extinguished in mid-flight. Sullivan told a marshal who tried to break up the fray to get out of the way. "If you come near me I will put a bullet through you," the lawman warned as he drew a revolver. The altercation quieted down, and Sullivan was taken to his hotel. He missed the following night's performance. "To tell the plain unvarnished truth, Mr. Sullivan's conduct here has not been such to elevate him very much in the eyes of Leadville people," the local newspaper reported.

Then it was back on the rails. Cheyenne. Laramie City. Ogden. After swinging through Utah, the combination came to Butte, Montana, another Irish stronghold. Many of its miners had emigrated from the Beara Peninsula in Ireland's southwest when the copper mines shuttered there.

The Irish miners came out in force to watch Sullivan face challenger Fred Robinson, a burly miner with a bushy red beard. The champion had spent much of the day drinking and was well lubricated by fight time. Fearing the looks of the challenger, Moran attempted to get Sullivan to take the miner seriously. "Got a red beard, has he?" the inebriated champion quipped. "That'll stop the blood when I get at him." When told his opponent was a strapping man, John L. remained unconcerned. "The bigger he is, the harder the fall," he said. The champion wobbled into the ring against Robinson, who entered in his cowhide boots. Once the match started and the miner struck the champion on the jaw, Sullivan snapped to. Within a minute, he had Robinson knocked out.

Some critics charged that the challengers brought on stage during the "knocking out" tour were setups, men gladly willing to take a dive for a small fee. Others spread rumors that Sullivan had a mallet-wielding employee on stage behind a curtain who could deliver a well-timed strike to a challenger's head if he began to give John L. trouble.

Sullivan had numerous flaws, but dishonesty wasn't one of them. In a corrupt country and a crooked sport, John L. was a straight shooter. He never took a dive. He never participated in a setup. Sullivan attributed part of his popularity to always fighting on the level. "Boxing as well as all other sports, is an honest man's game," he said. "The public has no use for a faker in anything, but less in boxing than in anything I know of."

For most of Sullivan's opponents on the tour, however, a knock with a mallet would have been superfluous. One ferocious stare and a guttural snarl usually sufficed to win the match. More than the parade of amateurs, it was the bottle that posed the greatest challenge to Sullivan staying upright in the ring as he traveled on from Montana.

Salt Lake City. Virginia City. Sacramento. In Astoria, Oregon, on February 1, 1884, Sullivan faced an enormous Frenchman, topping over three hundred pounds, who was a fisherman on the Columbia River. The challenger's trainers went through elaborate preparations, rubbing him with oil and wrapping four yards of blue flannel around his stomach. It was all for naught. Sullivan led with a left to the forehead that knocked down the giant. The fisherman returned to an upright position, and then Sullivan crossed with a right that knocked him cold for fifteen minutes.

Six days later, the combination crossed the border for a quick two-night appearance in Victoria, Canada. The capital of British Columbia was already abuzz because of the presence of oarsman Ned Hanlan, the country's most popular athlete. Schools had been closed so that children could watch a rowing exhibition starring the Canadian idol. That evening Sullivan and Gillespie attended a banquet in the genial Hanlan's honor before his departure to Australia.

Sullivan had been tippling earlier in the day, and the free drinks at the banquet worked him into "a state of beastly intoxication." After dinner, the diminutive mayor asked all to rise and drink to the health of Queen Victoria. To many Irish Americans with long memories and strong ties to their homeland, the British monarch remained the "Famine Queen." Gillespie rose. Sullivan grabbed his collar and threw him back into the seat.

"Is it possible that any of our guests refuse to stand and drink to the health of her most gracious majesty?" asked the dignitary.

"To hell with the Queen! Come on, Gillespie," barked Sullivan as he grabbed the fighter, put on his topcoat, and "withdrew in high dudgeon." John L. explained that he "hadn't been brought up to seeing Irishmen drinking to the health of English monarchs."

Insulting the head of state wasn't proper diplomacy anywhere in Canada, but especially not in her namesake city. The president of the banquet declared to the local newspaper that he was due $1,000 since he knocked Sullivan out of the supper room in one round.

As Sullivan's behavior grew more boorish, the famous man started to grow infamous. Towns that rolled out the welcome mat for John L. began to slam the door behind him as he left. "That Sullivan, the slugger, leaves an unsavory reputation behind him wherever he goes," a Victoria newspaper editorialized in disdain. The *Seattle Chronicle* celebrated Sullivan's departure and expressed a pious hope that "he will never again turn his erratic footsteps" toward their city. One newspaper reported of Sullivan, "Bets are even that he will not leave the coast alive."

———

"Sullivan's Sluggers" left a trail of broken bottles and fighters littered across America as they staggered into San Francisco on February 18. They were scheduled for a badly needed travel break. An extended stay of three weeks was planned while Sullivan prepared to put on the gloves for an actual prizefight.

Two of the eight people accompanying Sullivan across the country, however, did not stay in San Francisco for long. Annie Sullivan had finally had enough of the grueling travel and the loutish behavior of the father of her unborn child. Now noticeably pregnant in her last trimester, Annie returned to Boston with $6,000 in her pocket.

Slade had become fed up as well. His relationship with Sullivan had been fraying, and he wasn't happy with the amount of money he was being paid. In San Francisco, he announced he was quitting. John L. did not take kindly to the decision and tracked him down at a local sporting palace.

The two heavyweights argued. Then Sullivan gave Slade a head-butt that bloodied his nose. By the time police were called to the scene, Slade was lying on top of the liquor-laden champion and pinning him to the sawdust-coated floor. After police removed the Maori, Sullivan remained motionless "suffering from an overdose of whiskey." Slade and the officer helped John L. to his unsteady feet. He swayed out the door and was poured into a carriage back to the hotel. "If the present state of affairs lasts much longer, it is very doubtful if any of the Eastern sluggers will reach home again," reported a local newspaper.

Hugh Coyle had the unenviable job of refuting the regular news flashes about the misbehavior of the combination. The advance man said the reports were much exaggerated, but acknowledged that "the men occasionally went in for having a good time."

Apparently, the boys were having a great time in San Francisco. Once Annie left, Sullivan's drinking and behavior grew even more oafish. At one performance in San Francisco, Sullivan took to the stage with "a scab across the instep of his nose." Gillespie came out for his bout with a "dark shadow cast by his lower eyelid." It didn't take long for the audience to connect the dots. On another night, McCoy, who gained liquid muscles when he drank, challenged one of the world's mightiest wrestlers, Clarence Whistler, to a brawl in a San Francisco barroom. McCoy was thrown to the ground so heavily by the "Kansas Demon" that it rattled every bottle behind the bar and he crumbled to the floor "a palpitating and quivering mass of insensible humanity."

The drinking and infighting grew so out of control that fans really had no reason to pay for admission to the shows because they might be able to watch more violent punches being thrown by the combination in some saloon afterward. Everywhere that Sullivan and the combination went, a barroom fight seemed to follow.

Sullivan's odious behavior did little to engender support for his upcoming four-round prizefight, Marquis of Queensberry Rules, with George Robinson of the local Olympic Club. John L. had inked a deal for a rematch with Paddy Ryan in San Francisco, but the former champion backed out, reportedly to please his mother, who was concerned her boy might be killed or maimed for life. A week after John L. arrived in the city, an agreement was reached to pit Sullivan against the local fighter Robinson, who was to receive a fatter prize if he could last the four rounds with Sullivan.

The bad press surrounding the champion did not dampen the interest in the March 6 fight among San Franciscans, perhaps because one-third of the city was Irish-born or the children of Irish immigrants. Fifteen thousand people turned out to the Mechanics' Pavilion to witness the bout. Thousands more were turned away. Sullivan, who was still greeted with great cheers, had done little training in preparation and was at least thirty-five pounds heavier than his opponent. Old acquaintance William Muldoon, who happened to be in San Francisco at the time, served as Sullivan's timekeeper.

Before the fight could begin, authorities confiscated the three-ounce gloves that were to be used by the men and made them wear eight-ounce versions instead. Not that the size of the gloves mattered much for Robinson. He didn't intend on using them. The affair was more farce than fight. Robinson had cribbed Tug Wilson's playbook and immediately fell to the platform floor the first time he was tapped by Sullivan. The challenger did the same thing when Sullivan charged a second time. Robinson fell eight times in round one alone. He escaped physical punishment, but not the verbal barbs of the hometown fans, who pelted him with hoots and hisses for his cowardice.

Sullivan puffed between rounds. Even though he had been in a ring nearly every day, he suffered from a lack of conditioning. As the fight progressed, Robinson's delegation grew more excited and even offered money to bettors. The diving continued in the third. The challenger used "every trick and device" as he continued to fall. By some accounts, Robinson went to the ground dozens of times. Finally, in the fourth round, he was called for fouls for falling without being hit, and the fight was given to Sullivan.

The following day, there was an unscheduled sequel as Robinson and a friend entered a bar at Baldwin's Hotel where Taylor and other members of the combination were partaking of the goods. Taylor fired a contemptuous remark at Robinson. The words escalated until Taylor nailed the other man with a shot under his ear, and much as the night before, Robinson hit the ground. A wild brawl ensued until they were separated. As a result of the incident, the Olympic Club voted unanimously to expel Robinson.

Following their lengthy layover in San Francisco, the combination returned to their travels, the party now two short from when they had started in Baltimore. While there would be a new face to take Slade's place shortly, there would be no change in Sullivan's spree across America.

—◆—

Headed south to Los Angeles and then turning back toward the East, the combination spent March traveling through the Southwest. San Bernardino. Tucson. Tombstone. In Deming, New Mexico, Sullivan's entourage found him in a drunken slumber on a hotel lobby bench only an hour before fight time with an unknown challenger. They deluged him with buckets of water to no avail. Sullivan napped through introductions, but at the call of time, he leapt forward and downed his opponent with one blow and returned to the dressing room to go to sleep.

Waco. Austin. San Antonio. When Sullivan arrived in Galveston, Texas, on April 10, an imposing fighter was awaiting. Al Marx, a powerful cotton baler, was considered the champion of Texas. Smith was concerned given Sullivan's hard drinking that he was not in condition to face "such a powerful giant who towered over him and outweighed him probably forty pounds or more." Although Smith knew that Sullivan had not failed to put out his man "drunk or sober," he feared it would be different with Marx.

Sure enough, John L. was under the influence again, and the Tremont Opera House was packed with Marx's friends and family, who thought that he not only would last four rounds, but whip John L. as well. The challenger wanted to send an early statement. Just after shaking hands, he nailed Sullivan in the jaw. The Texas giant gained confidence after landing several hard blows on Sullivan in the first two rounds, and he was convinced John L. had met his match.

When Sullivan came out in the third round, however, the "cowboy pugilist" noticed a change in the champion's eyes. John L. glared "like a wild animal." Then Sullivan launched an "uppercut that lifted the giant almost off the floor" which was followed by a left smash to the jaw. Marx sank "down like a bag of oats." Sullivan lifted him up and then cracked him over the footlights and into the orchestra pit, which broke two chairs, three violins, and a bass drum. Once again, Sullivan's fists had caused the premature demise of some musical instruments. The Texan was unconscious for ten minutes before he came to, while Moran reached into the gate receipts to scrounge for twenty-four dollars to pay for the destroyed drum.

The next stop was New Orleans. John L. made his first return visit since he had left there in 1882 as the newly crowned champion. Waiting for the combination was Slade's replacement, and another fallen foe of Sullivan's, Mike Donovan. The veteran had been working as a boxing instructor in New York and worked off some ring rust as he battled with the combination on a nightly basis.

Mobile. Savannah. Chattanooga. On April 26 in Nashville, twenty-year-old Enos Phillips took the champion's challenge. The 150-pounder lasted all of two minutes. The champion would have an even easier time of it two nights later in Memphis when bricklayer William Fleming took the stage. At the opening signal, Sullivan charged. He feinted with his left and struck a blow on the lower part of Fleming's left jaw that knocked him unconscious for fifteen minutes. Total time of the bout: two seconds. Fleming was lifted over the ropes and helped out of the building to his home.

When he came to, he asked, "When do me and Sullivan go on?"

"You've been on," he was told.

"Did I lick him?" the oblivious bricklayer asked.

As the tour wound down, McCoy left early in the first days of May for a prizefight against Duncan McDonald in Butte, and heavyweight Florrie Barnett was brought in by Smith as his replacement. On May 7, the combination returned to St. Louis, the city where Taylor and Sullivan had been arrested on their earlier visit. This time the police permitted the combination to perform, but they barred Sullivan from issuing his challenge to all comers.

While in St. Louis, Sullivan crossed paths with another great entertainer who was barnstorming the country: William Cody, who had recently launched his new "Buffalo Bill's Wild West" show. Cody invited the combination to come to his performance at the fairgrounds, and they sat in the judges' stand with dignitaries including Gen. William Tecumseh Sherman, the man under whom Donovan had served as a drummer boy in the Civil War. Sullivan and other members of the combination occupied the famed Deadwood coach driven by "Buffalo Bill" through the rifle shots and war cries of a mock battle with Native Americans. After Cody hosted Sullivan at a barbecue, the two rode back to St. Louis in the front seat of a four-in-hand coach to ovations all along the route.

On May 23, "Sullivan's Sluggers," with the exception of Gillespie, who had amicably parted ways with Sullivan in Detroit, pulled into Toledo, Ohio. Nearly eight months after they had started in Baltimore, the combination had reached their final stop on an epic journey, and Sullivan reportedly tore through the town to put a fitting exclamation point on his spree across the continent. John L. showed up drunk for the first exhibition and "made the motions." The second show was cancelled but not before the champion made a "consummate ass of himself" around the city, according to a Toledo newspaper. He hurled abusive language at the staff of his hotel. At the local baseball stadium, he made "vile and vulgar insinuations against the ladies present." The police finally ordered the company to board the next train out of the city.

In spite of Sullivan's loutish behavior, the tour had been a success, and somehow, through all the debauchery, everyone in the combination made it through without any permanent damage. According to some accounts, thirty-nine men had stepped into the ring seeking to go four rounds with the champion. Thirty-nine men failed. Many of those amateurs were inexperienced stiffs, but they included some credible local toughs. Accounts of the financial receipts from the tour vary. Sullivan estimated that the combination netted $187,000 and had $42,000 in expenses. Moran reported the troupe earned $110,000 outside of expenses. Sullivan himself likely pocketed tens of thousands of dollars, and his earnings probably approached or surpassed the $50,000 salary earned by President Chester A. Arthur that year. He made enough money to send $5,000 home to his mother for a present and for newspapers to roll their editorial eyes in horror: "In this day brawn evidently holds first place over brain," lamented one newspaper.

While the exact size of his financial windfall may not be known, it's certain that Sullivan did earn an incredible level of superstardom by traversing the continent. John L. pointed to the tour as a seminal moment in his career. "I have always believed that what popularity I have today is due to that triumphal tour," Sullivan said after his fighting days were done. Sullivan proved to be a drawing card around America due to both his prowess in the ring and his personal magnetism. He was more than just a boxer. He was an entertainer with a flair for show business.

The novel tour made Sullivan one of the most "seen" people in the entire country. Certainly, more eyes gazed upon him than even the president of the United States, and the audiences he drew around the country rivaled those of Barnum and "Buffalo Bill." Thanks to the "knocking out" tour, Sullivan became the most famous athlete in the United States—and one of the most famous Americans in any walk of life.

Celebrities are made by being seen, and through his travels, John L. had become an American celebrity of the highest order. Through railroads and newspapers, he was able to reach hundreds of thousands of people across America, something that wasn't possible just years before.

The American publicity machine and celebrity culture was beginning to crank, and John L. knew how to pull the levers. He rarely turned down a request for an interview, and he was good copy. Whatever Sullivan did, it would be interesting and entertaining. In addition, images of stars were being conveyed by photography. Newspaper illustrations made it even easier for the public to make connections to famous figures now that people could see what they looked like.

Sullivan lived his life in a public spotlight that shined more brilliantly on him than on anyone else in the country. His tumultuous life outside the ring was considered fair game and fresh fodder for big-city newspapers engaged in heated circulation wars. John L., like generations of athletes to follow, thought that the light pointed at him by the press burned too harshly at times. "My excesses have always been exaggerated," he said. "I am almost as much in the public eye as the President of the United States and one drink is magnified into a hundred." John L. had it wrong, however. He lived a life much more in the public eye than the president, but he was resigned to the downside of fame. "If the President can stand it, I suppose I must. I am public property, and the press is free to say of me what it pleases."

The American people literally wanted a piece of John L. A New York dentist who pulled one of Sullivan's teeth kept it and had it engraved. Sullivan's barber Billy Hogarty sold the champion's shorn hair for a dollar a lock to girls who wanted to snap it into a locket.

Most of the United States, however, was content to hold a cabinet photograph or a trading card of the champion, printed by tobacco companies such as Allen & Ginter. Sullivan also lent his name as a pitch man for boxing gloves and beef broth.

Even people who crossed Sullivan's orbit became defined by him, rather than by their own achievements, something the champion's former schoolmaster, Jimmy Page, lamented: "I shall go down to posterity, not on account of fifty years of continuous service in one school, but because I happened to be the teacher of John L. Sullivan."

John L.'s celebrity gave rise to vaudeville songs and marching tunes. The Forepaugh circus began to feature a performing elephant named "John L. Sullivan." The pugilistic pachyderm wore a boxing glove on the end of its trunk and fought its trainer in the ring. He scored numerous knockouts. He stood on his hind legs in the ring and challenged all comers.

While Sullivan was touring through the South in April, a farce comedy written by Charles H. Hoyt called *A Rag Baby* opened at Tony Pastor's Fourteenth Street Theatre in Manhattan. One of the leading characters, "Old Sport," was a drugstore clerk and boxing fan with the dream of one day meeting Sullivan. When a customer mentioned he had shaken the hand of John L., Old Sport couldn't stop shaking the young man's hand because if the clerk couldn't achieve his dream, the next best thing was to "grasp the hand that grasped the hand of Sullivan."

The line quickly became a cultural catchphrase. In retellings, it morphed to "let me shake the hand that shook the hand of Sullivan," which became the title of a popular song of the 1880s. And wherever John L. traveled, an outstretched arm always reached in his direction.

On May 26, Sullivan quietly slipped back to Boston. He didn't even tell his family or friends of his travel plans. Still, it was impossible for the "Boston Strong Boy" to pass unnoticed in his hometown. A group of eight men, including a city councilman, waited on the platform to greet his train. They climbed into hacks at the station, but the minute the horses began to trot away, a trailing crowd of one hundred fans "gathered as if by magic" and started to run through the city streets to Sullivan's saloon.

By the time John L. pulled up to his Washington Street barroom, eight months to the day after he had left it, his adoring public had already packed it full. They couldn't wait to shake his hand.

CHAPTER FIVE

Battles with Brawlers and Bottles

WHEN THE BACK-SLAPPING AND THE HAND-SHAKING INSIDE HIS SALOON finally abated, Sullivan headed home to his brick row house on Lovering Place for the first time in eight months. The only sign that the building belonged to America's first sports superstar was the name SULLIVAN elegantly etched on a silver plate mounted near the door.

John L. had not seen Annie since February, when she left his side in San Francisco to return to Boston. Inside the house awaited not only his wife, but the couple's new child.

While John L. had been trading blows with Al Marx in Galveston, Texas, on April 10, 1884, Annie had given birth to a baby boy, John Lawrence Sullivan Jr. Newspapers reported the young slugger weighed an appropriately hefty eleven pounds. Protestant Annie fulfilled her pledge to raise her child Catholic by having the boy baptized two days later on Easter Sunday. Uncle Michael Sullivan was the child's godfather, Aunt Annie Lennon the godmother.

John Jr. had stomach problems as a baby but grew into a healthy and rugged toddler. The press reported that he possessed his father's temper—"He gets mad quick and is quick over it"—and his phenomenal strength. The champion's son was said to have lifted a coal bucket off the floor when he was just nine months old.

Inside the Lovering Place home, the young boy was constantly surrounded by extended family. The champion's brother, Michael, had a room of his own, and much to the consternation of John L., Annie's brothers Henry and William often stayed for weeks at a time. "When I married my wife I thought I was marrying her alone, but I soon found out that I married the whole state of Rhode Island," Sullivan groused.

While Annie Durgin, a longtime acquaintance of Annie, worked for the family as a servant, the Sullivans did not live in palatial surroundings like the Brahmin lairs on Beacon Hill or in the Back Bay that were fitted with brass fixtures, mahogany paneling, and paintings of clipper ships cutting through foaming waves. Since he had become champion, John L. had earned an income surpassed by few others in Boston, but he had burned through it at a rate that outpaced most of the city as well.

A small fortune went up in smoke and down the hatch as Sullivan conspicuously consumed cigars and champagne. Given public attitudes toward his profession, Sullivan desperately sought acceptance as a gentleman, and he spent lavishly on tailored clothes, gold chains, and diamond pins. "Don't I know how to dress myself as well as any gentleman?" he asked one reporter. "I'll bet them there pants cost as much as Vanderbilt's, and I get my jewelry at Tiffany's," he boasted. Sullivan cut a dashing figure around Boston with his silk top hat, Prince Albert coat, and gold-headed cane, but his preference for tight-fitting pants and bright colors deviated from the uniform of the Yankee gentleman in his staid city.

While John L. spent freely on some of the finer things in life, he also gave much of his fortune away. Sullivan was known as a soft touch who rarely turned down friends or even strangers in need. Heavy imbibers always knew to tail the champion because he often set up drinks for the entire house. Before embarking on the city sidewalks, John L. made sure his pockets brimmed with pennies, nickels, and dimes. As he jingled down the street, the champion loved to scatter coins like a farmer sprinkling feed to his chickens and watch the children flock to the riches. "We are going to be a long time dead," Sullivan said about his easy attitude toward money, "and only a few of us know how to enjoy life as it goes."

Sullivan fueled his spending and charity habits with regular ring appearances, and with the "knocking out" tour now complete, the twenty-five-year-old champion found no shortage of suitors among the challengers who had put their title aspirations on hold. Fighters clamored loudly for a shot at Sullivan, but former foe Charley Mitchell was among the most vociferous. Since their battle in Madison Square Garden, the cocky Englishman had been rewriting history by proclaiming that the American authorities stopped the fight when he was on the verge of winning in a desperate attempt to protect their fellow countryman.

Before Sullivan had arrived back in Boston at the conclusion of his "knocking out" tour, he met Mitchell in New York to make arrangements for a fight. In response to the challenger's extended hand, John L. snapped, "I'll shake hands with you after I have licked you for what you said during my absence." The men were separated, and an agreement was reached for them to meet again inside Madison Square Garden for a four-round match, Marquis of Queensberry Rules, on June 30. The winner would leave New York with two-thirds of the gate.

Although John L. had spent most of the prior year in a ring, he finished the "knocking out" tour out of shape. Sullivan was sometimes in—but mostly out of—sobriety, and his burgeoning alcoholic proclivities would lead to the lowest point of his career.

Sullivan spent June training with Joe Goss and Pete McCoy in Boston for the rematch with Mitchell. Then, four days before the fight, the champion received a surprising message from his manager, Al Smith: The fight was off. Billy Madden, now Mitchell's manager, had informed Smith that the Englishman had taken ill with malarial fever while training in Pleasure Bay, New Jersey.

Freed from the incentive to train, Sullivan let his drinking rip before an even more surprising message came from Smith two days later. Mitchell's fever had broken. The fight was back on. Sullivan, however, was mid-bender and felt the need to see it through. A well-marinated John L. boarded the train to New York the night before the fight and tried to continue his spree on the ride south. When McCoy discovered Sullivan with a bottle of brandy in his hands, he grabbed it and threw it out the window. Hours later, McCoy watched as John L. emerged from his sleeping car with yet another brandy bottle, which McCoy also heaved out of the train.

Hours before the fight, the air around Madison Square Garden grew thick with the cries of hoarse ticket speculators and rumors about the champion's sodden condition. Steep admission prices—two dollars for tickets and twenty-five dollars for boxes—dampened attendance from the prior year's Mitchell-Sullivan fight, but a large crowd still streamed into the arena to watch Sullivan's first serious challenge since he had defeated Herbert Slade in the Garden nearly a year ago.

The fans patiently sat through the preliminary bouts, watched by hawk-eyed copper Clubber Williams, who would deliver a scolding to any overeager fighters with a simple rap of his signature nightstick on the elevated wooden platform. Then the crowd waited. As the minutes passed, the whispered grumbles of restless spectators cascaded into angry shouts.

Finally, a burly figure in a black suit stumbled into the arena from the Madison Avenue entrance. Even the fans sitting in the outer reaches of the cavernous arena could immediately tell that the champion had been boozing, but those close to the ring could read it on Sullivan's swollen, blotchy face and his eyelids that drooped at half-mast beneath a mangle of violently tousled hair.

The rum-soaked Sullivan, trailed by Mitchell in a light gray tweed suit, reached the ring after a prolonged stagger. He humbly removed his hat like a schoolchild knowing he was about to break bad news and receive a severe reprimand. Master of ceremonies Bill O'Brien raised his hand to silence the hisses of the unhappy fans. He then announced that Sullivan was sick—and with a doctor's note to prove it!

The champion clung to the ropes as he swayed like a boat seeking its footing on the chop of the ocean. The deep bass voice of the man who whispered like other men shouted was barely audible as he mumbled: "I can't spar. I'm sick. People say I'm drunk, but I ain't drunk. I'm dead sick, an' I've a doctor here'll prove it." The crowd hooted and jeered.

Mitchell then yelled out to the crowd. "Gentlemen, I'm not in a fit state to spar myself. I've been sick with malaria, but I came here to spar and I'm willing to go on. But it wouldn't be fair as I'm feeling pretty good myself and Mr. Sullivan is really ill. All I can say is that I'm willing to spar." The crowd gave three cheers for the plucky Englishman as he left the stage.

Hisses, groans, and catcalls accompanied Sullivan out the doors of Madison Square Garden. Disbelieving fans lingered inside the arena for a half-hour afterward until management extinguished the gaslights.

The roasting continued as the pathetic John L. wobbled back to his hotel room. Indignant fans spit out curses through the streets of Manhattan, and if not for the presence of Williams and his nightstick, there might have been violence. "This is the first time I ever disappointed an audience in my life," he muttered to a reporter, apparently forgetting his cancellation the prior month at the end of the "knocking out" tour and a spree through Toledo. Sullivan kept blaming his condition on a fever and insisting he wasn't drunk—usually the surest sign that someone is under the influence. "If I took a glass of water they would say it was gin," John L. complained.

To the fans, it was one thing for John L. to be drunk on his own time. Now he was soused on theirs—and it cost them money. When Madison Square Garden management discovered that counterfeit tickets had circulated for the fight, it decided not to refund money because it was impossible to tell who held legitimate tickets. Sullivan and Mitchell still received the $8,000 gate, although the champion told Smith to give his share to charity.

Smith reported later that Sullivan had been drinking freely during the afternoon of the fight and had secured a doctor's certificate excusing him from the bout many hours in advance. Sullivan's manager had urged John L. to personally address the thousands of disappointed fans, which turned out to be disastrous advice. Smith was disgusted at Sullivan's behavior; the champion blamed his manager for telling him the fight was off and putting him in an embarrassing situation. The incident severed the business relationship between the men.

Irate fight fans thought they were being scammed, and they knew that John L. was not being forthcoming by hiding behind the excuse of sickness. It was a rare stain on his honest reputation. One New York newspaper speculated that the incident would be the "death blow of exhibitions of that nature in this city." Indeed, Sullivan would receive much greater scrutiny from New York authorities for his subsequent appearances in the city, and the farce blunted the momentum that the fight game had achieved during his championship reign.

An Irish-American newspaperman once editorialized, "There are moments in every man's life, I don't care who he is, when he wishes he were John L. Sullivan, if only for half an hour." On the evening of June 30, 1884, however, no one wanted to be in Sullivan's shoes—not even for thirty minutes.

A young, muscular Sullivan poses around the time he captured the heavyweight championship in 1882. LIBRARY OF CONGRESS

Portrait of Sullivan as a twelve-year-old boy growing up in Boston's South End.
YALE COLLECTION OF WESTERN AMERICANA, BEINECKE RARE BOOK AND MANUSCRIPT LIBRARY

An illustration of Sullivan's 1880 defeat of John Donaldson in Cincinnati, which helped to establish John L. as boxing's rising star. CLAY MOYLE, FROM *JOHN L. SULLIVAN, CHAMPION PUGILIST OF THE WORLD* (1882)

Harry Hill ran the premier sporting resort in New York City, a venue that launched the careers of many fighters, including Sullivan's. *THE PORTRAIT GALLERY OF PUGILISTS OF AMERICA AND THEIR CONTEMPORARIES* (1894)

John Flood, the "Bull's Head Terror," fought Sullivan in 1881 aboard a barge towed up the Hudson River in New York to elude authorities. *THE PORTRAIT GALLERY OF PUGILISTS OF AMERICA AND THEIR CONTEMPORARIES* (1894)

Staying a step ahead of the authorities, Sullivan fought John Flood, the "Bull's Head Terror," aboard a barge towed up the Hudson River in 1881. CLAY MOYLE, FROM *JOHN L. SULLIVAN, CHAMPION PUGILIST OF THE WORLD* (1882)

Paddy Ryan reigned as heavyweight champion until he met Sullivan in 1882 in Mississippi City, Mississippi. *THE PORTRAIT GALLERY OF PUGILISTS OF AMERICA AND THEIR CONTEMPORARIES* (1894)

Fans watch from the verandah of the Barnes Hotel and even perch in trees to see Sullivan defeat Paddy Ryan for the heavyweight championship on February 7, 1882, in Mississippi City, Mississippi. TRACY CALLIS, BOXING HISTORIAN

Portrait of a twenty-three-year-old Sullivan taken a day after defeating Paddy Ryan in 1882 for the heavyweight title. YALE COLLECTION OF WESTERN AMERICANA, BEINECKE RARE BOOK AND MANUSCRIPT LIBRARY

Richard K. Fox, publisher of the *National Police Gazette,* spent years and tens of thousands of dollars trying to dethrone Sullivan from his championship reign. STEVE VANCE

Richard K. Fox recruited Herbert Slade, "The Maori," all the way from New Zealand to challenge Sullivan in 1883.
THE PORTRAIT GALLERY OF PUGILISTS OF AMERICA AND THEIR CONTEMPORARIES (1894)

Sullivan flanked by training partners Pete McCoy (left) and Joe Goss (right) prior to his 1883 bout with Herbert Slade. LIBRARY OF CONGRESS

An 1883 Currier & Ives lithograph depicts the "champion pugilist of the world."

Sullivan lent his endorsement to Liston's Extract of Beef, which he used "as a beverage and as a muscle and health producing food," in this 1885 advertisement.

An 1887 lithograph of Sullivan. LIBRARY OF CONGRESS

Sullivan's fans raised thousands of dollars to purchase a gold and diamond-studded championship belt that was presented to John L. in 1887. *THE PORTRAIT GALLERY OF PUGILISTS OF AMERICA AND THEIR CONTEMPORARIES* (1894)

Sullivan, America's king of the ring, met with the Prince of Wales in London on December 9, 1887, and sparred three rounds before the future King Edward VII. CLAY MOYLE, FROM *THE MODERN GLADIATOR, BEING AN ACCOUNT OF THE EXPLOITS AND EXPERIENCES OF THE WORLD'S GREATEST FIGHTER, JOHN LAWRENCE SULLIVAN* (1889)

Jack Ashton toured America, Australia, and the British Isles with Sullivan as his sparring partner. *THE PORTRAIT GALLERY OF PUGILISTS OF AMERICA AND THEIR CONTEMPORARIES* (1894)

A souvenir copy of the colors worn by Sullivan in his 1888 fight against Charley Mitchell in Chantilly, France. DON SCOTT, *BOXING COLLECTORS' NEWS*

The bombastic British fighter Charley Mitchell was a constant thorn in Sullivan's side, particularly in a thirty-nine-round draw in France in 1888. *THE PORTRAIT GALLERY OF PUGILISTS OF AMERICA AND THEIR CONTEMPORARIES* (1894)

Sullivan's drinking delivered a body blow to his public image, but even that didn't—or couldn't—get him to change his habits. He spent the summer in a near-constant state of inebriation. If he wasn't a flat-out alcoholic by now, he was well down the path.

On August 13, he stepped back in the ring for the first time since the disgrace at Madison Square Garden. John L. received thunderous applause from three thousand hometown fans at a testimonial benefit for councilman Tom Denney at Boston's New England Institute Fair Building. He sparred three rounds with Denney, Steve Taylor, and Dominick McCaffrey. The *National Police Gazette* reported, though, that John L. plainly showed the effects of drinking again and had been on a spree after attending a wake a day or two prior.

Annie had hoped that the arrival of the baby would temper her husband's drinking and loutish behavior. It didn't. In fact, it grew even worse. John L. frequently stayed out to 3 a.m. and came home intoxicated three or four times a week. Sometimes he had to be carried upstairs by Annie's brothers. He struck his wife on several occasions. While even in Sullivan's most inebriated and enraged states he never did anything to harm his son, Annie grew afraid that he might accidentally injure John Jr. while striking her.

Fearing for their safety, Annie left Boston with John Jr. and fled to her brother's house in Centerville, Rhode Island. A drunken John L. stormed the cottage and demanded to see his son. When Annie refused to let him into the bedroom, Sullivan struck his wife and knocked her over a trunk. The couple reconciled, but eventually, the abuse resumed its pattern. Finally, in early December, Annie left John L. for good. She took John Jr. to Rhode Island and never returned to Boston.

As Sullivan's marriage crumbled, he forged a relationship with a new manager, Pat Sheedy. The Chicago gambler, said to bear an uncanny resemblance to Thomas Edison, had been born in Ireland and emigrated with his family to America when he was seven years old. Even as a schoolboy, he excelled at gambling. When forced to make a living for himself after the deaths of his parents, he turned to card games, first in Boston, then New York, before opening a sporting house in Chicago. Sheedy brought a hustler's mentality to his management of Sullivan, but unlike the more humble Madden and Smith, Sheedy possessed a sizable ego and wanted to be a star as well. In newspaper advertisements, the name of "P.F. Sheedy" was exceeded in size by only that of Sullivan himself.

Sullivan's new manager realized that a first step in the champion's rehabilitation was a return to Madison Square Garden. He arranged for John L. to fight "Professor" John Laflin in a four-round Marquis of Queensberry exhibition at the arena on November 10.

John L. trained once again with Patsey Sheppard and completed his preparations in the days before the fight at the Monico Villa in the far northern part of Manhattan. It appeared that the champion still retained his popularity in New York. For days leading up to the fight, fans made the uptown pilgrimage by wagon, foot, streetcar, and elevated railway. Sullivan's fans waited for hours just to see him return from his walk. Dozens of ladies sent their cards to Sullivan's room, "some begging him to appear in the parlor, while others wished 'just to see the fine fellow.'" All entreaties received a polite, but firm refusal.

On fight night, Sullivan stepped back into Madison Square Garden. This time he was sober. John L. appeared in good form as he had dropped upward of thirty pounds with Sheppard. He was back to his fighting weight, just short of two hundred pounds. His opponent—the finely tuned, six-foot, two-inch-tall Laflin—was a few pounds heavier.

John L. was the clear favorite. Although advertised as thirty-six years old, Laflin was a forty-two-year-old journeyman with a meager ring record, though he had faced the champion before. The two fighters had sparred the year before at a Madison Square Garden benefit for Midwest flood victims.

Laflin looked scared as the men shook hands before a crowd of five thousand fans that included Edison. (No word if Edison met his doppelganger, Sheedy.) From the start, Sullivan pounced on his prey. Laflin threw his arms around John L. to tie him up. The challenger clung like a dance partner as the champion dragged him around the ring. After Sullivan was finally able to extricate himself, he knocked his foe with a vicious blow that propelled him into the corner and showered the fans with drops of blood. He quickly shot another right hand that sent Laflin to his knees.

Laflin's second helped his fighter to his feet in violation of the Marquis of Queensberry Rules. The referee, however, did not want to end the fight on a foul, particularly with the debacle of Sullivan's last appearance in the arena fresh in the minds of all.

The next two rounds unfolded in much the same manner. Sullivan floored Laflin numerous times, as the challenger tried to drape himself around his opponent in a bid to survive. Sullivan held Laflin's arms down just so that he could throw a punch.

Both men began to labor as the fourth and final round started. They clutched and puffed. Blood and sweat rolled down Laflin's face. Sullivan threw his foe to the ground, another violation of the Queensberry Rules that wasn't called. Laflin rose and Sullivan landed quick blows in succession. John L. pressed his opponent to the ropes. Then a big shot knocked Laflin into a corner "with such force that his body seemed to rebound and his head rung on the timbers as though it were cracked." Laflin was carried helpless to his corner as the referee awarded the fight to Sullivan, who walked away with the $7,500 in receipts.

The workmanlike performance was solid, but not one of Sullivan's best. And he had little time to recover because he was due back at Madison Square Garden in just one week's time to face Richard K. Fox's latest pet—Alf Greenfield, who laid claim to being champion of England. The thirty-one-year-old from Birmingham, England, had little ring experience, but he had defeated Jack Burke, the "Irish Lad," in the final of a tournament organized by Jem Mace the year before. Fox paid for Greenfield's transit to the United States and offered to match him against Sullivan for $5,000 and the title. John L. agreed only to a four-round gloved contest, which was scheduled for November 17.

Before fight day arrived, however, Sullivan and Fox would find themselves in a very strange position—fighting on the same side.

As Sullivan and Greenfield prepared for their tilt in Madison Square Garden, New York mayor Franklin Edson grew increasingly concerned about the thinly veiled "exhibitions" that had become regular occurrences in his city. The hard, bloody hits delivered by Sullivan in his bout against

Laflin only served to highlight once again the barely concealed flouting of state law concerning prizefighting.

With the next Sullivan exhibition just days away, Edson sent a letter to the police board outlining his view of the fight: "I believe that such exhibitions are disgraceful to the city in the higher degree, demoralizing to young men, and in their tendency leading to disrespect of law and order." He wanted the men arrested along with their backers for intending to commit a misdemeanor by indulging in, or abetting, a prizefight. The police rounded up Sullivan, Greenfield, Fox, and Sheedy, and on the morning of November 17, the scheduled date of the fight, they appeared in the Supreme Court Chambers.

For the first time, Fox and Sullivan fought on the same side of the battle. The champion—dressed in blue pilot coat, checked trousers, and a white flannel shirt with a blue ribbon—assured the court that the bout would be "simply a scientific exhibition of the manly art of self-defense." He denied having any animosity against Greenfield. "In fact I rather like him," he said.

When Greenfield was asked if he had any enmity toward Sullivan, he shook his head and exclaimed, "Lord bless you, no!" Sheedy testified that John L. would receive 65 percent of the gate, a slice that would not change based on the result.

After hearing the testimony, Justice George Barrett ruled that it was difficult to determine the nature of the fight in advance. Given that the fixed percentages meant that technically there was no prize for winning, there could be no intention to stage a prizefight. He released the men and turned it over to the police to intervene if the fighting became too hard.

The managers decided to postpone the sparring match until the following night. The change in the fight date and the legal cloud hovering over the bout squelched attendance. "Scores of vacant boxes" and "an acre of empty benches" greeted the fighters inside Madison Square Garden. So did more than one hundred patrolmen determined to keep watch on the two boxers. Police Chief George Washington Walling and Inspector Thomas Thorne joined Captain Williams in his usual post at ringside.

As the fighters came together in the ring, Sullivan loomed over Greenfield, who stood at best five feet, nine inches tall and weighed around 160 pounds. With the court appearance and police presence front of mind, both fighters opened the bout with light jabs. Then Greenfield surprised Sullivan with a heavy right to his ear. The challenger landed another right to the champion's jaw. In close quarters, he landed a left on Sullivan's nose and a right to his eye. Sullivan was taking hits, albeit not heavy ones, and he landed few big blows of his own. The crowd gave the fighters plenty of applause at the end of the opening round.

At the start of the second round, John L. displayed more life. He delivered sledgehammer blows with both hands to the Englishman's head and neck. Sullivan caught Greenfield over the left eye and cut it open as if it had been slashed with a knife. The champion then noticed blood dripping on his gloves, drizzling from a cut behind his ear. Sullivan forced Greenfield against the ropes and had him trapped. He hit the challenger with a powerful right, then a big left. A right. A left. Sullivan's intent was clear. It wasn't to exhibit the manly art anymore but to destroy his opponent.

At that point, the law entered the ring. Williams jumped onto the platform and pushed the fighters apart. It was announced that Sullivan had won—and that the fighters were under arrest.

Williams escorted Sullivan and Greenfield across the floor of the arena and toward the dressing rooms. A hail-like snow and the jeers of one thousand jostling fans pelted Williams as he paraded the "captured gladiators" across Twenty-Seventh Street and up three blocks on Broadway to the police station. The crowd cheered the fighters as they were brought inside for booking. Harry Hill made bail for Sullivan; Fox did the same for Greenfield. As the bail bonds were drawn up, a newsman asked the surly Sullivan what he thought of the evening's course of events. "What the f--- do you think I think?" he shot back.

A large crowd stuffed the courthouse on December 17 when the boxers came before Justice Barrett once again. Sullivan, clad in a heavy pea jacket and a pair of deep blue trousers, swaggered into the courtroom with a silk hat resting on his arm and diamonds sparkling from his cravat. Peter Mitchell represented Sullivan, while Fox enlisted the prestigious Howe and Hummel law firm to defend Greenfield.

After both men entered pleas of not guilty, Walling testified that the bout was anything but scientific and that he ordered the match stopped.

When Thorne and Williams took the stand, however, they undercut their police chief. Thorne said he did not see passion demonstrated by the fighters. Williams admitted he had seen more blood and harder blows in bouts organized by the Police Athletic Association. The jury pawed the blood-stained gloves, and then the fighters took the stand. They kept up their same line of testimony from a month before. They claimed that they did not intend to harm each other and that the bout was "only an exhibition."

After just eight minutes, the jury returned. The fighters stood. Sullivan pierced the foreman with his stare as he delivered the verdict.

"Not guilty!"

It was a legal victory for Fox, but once again, he had failed in his quest to dethrone the champion. John L. began to come to terms with Fox's obsession and even appreciate the upside. After all, the publisher kept Sullivan in the limelight and earned him tens of thousands of dollars.

The string of failed fighters fronted by Fox became public fodder and gave birth to a chorus song that was first performed at Tony Pastor's Music Hall in New York and then spread through the country: "The Fox may go to England / And the Fox may go to France / But to beat John L., he can go to Hell / And then he won't have a chance."

— ⋅ —

Back in Boston after beating the charges in New York, Sullivan continued his drinking ways. Just before New Year's, the champion caroused through the city with his friend and barber Billy Hogarty. John L. drove a pair of hired horses and pulled in front of Yeaton's saloon on Washington Street.

As Hogarty went inside, Sullivan remained at the reins, making the horses uneasy. They jerked and tipped over the sleigh, which sent John L. into a fury. He kicked one of the horses three times under the ribs with his right foot and then for good measure punched the other equine in the face. The champion continued his physical abuse inside the saloon. He struck head waitress Rose Booth over the head with his wet, heavy sealskin glove. Then he kicked her as she fled to the kitchen and struck her between the eyes with his big right hand.

Newspaper reports of the incident swirled as Sullivan traveled to Brooklyn, where he opened a weeklong appearance at the Academy of

Music in which he sparred with Mike Donovan during a scene in the stage play *Lottery of Life*. John L. denied the reports in a letter to Fox in which he said he had merely "tapped the waiter-girl with the wet driving gloves" and "left the place on the best of terms." The forgiving audiences in Brooklyn gave three cheers for the champion on opening night.

Sullivan apparently settled with the waitress out of court, but a payoff was not possible for the other assault victims—the horse team. The Society for the Prevention of Cruelty to Animals was granted a warrant for Sullivan's arrest, and at the end of January 1885, he was found guilty and fined $115.07 for "fast driving and unnecessary cruelty in beating a horse."

The champion's egregious behavior began to hamper his box-office appeal, particularly among the upper classes he had drawn into arenas. "John Lawrence Sullivan is losing his popularity as a pugilist," noted the *Boston Herald* after a January 12 bout with Greenfield at the city's Institute Hall drew only two thousand fans. (Two years before, an overflow crowd of fifteen thousand had come to watch "Our John.") The newspaper in particular noticed the "absence of the Beacon Hill and Commonwealth Avenue admirers."

A week after his tame four-round victory over Greenfield in Boston, Sullivan returned to Madison Square Garden for a rematch with Paddy Ryan. In the ensuing two months since his arrest inside the arena, New York had inaugurated a new mayor, William Grace. A native of County Cork and the first Irish Catholic to lead the city, Grace was determined not to show any favoritism toward a current and former Irish-American heavyweight champion. He ordered the police to stop the bout at the slightest sign of violence. (The following year, Grace would order raids on leading concert saloons, including Harry Hill's, that resulted in their closure.)

Three police surgeons were on hand "to give expert medical testimony in case of an arrest." Thorne watched from the side of the platform with a club in his hand and a wad of chewing tobacco plugged in his cheek. Williams earnestly briefed both men as their trainers rubbed them down.

A large crowd of ten thousand had turned out. "The great floor was thronged from end to end, and tier after tier of silver-headed walking sticks, opera hats, white shirt fronts, and evening ulsters rose to the eaves of the gallery," reported the *New York Times*.

Sullivan led with gentle sparring as Ryan backpedaled. Then Ryan rushed suddenly and caught Sullivan by surprise. Ryan landed blows to Sullivan's face and "an ugly light came into the champion's eyes, and he threw discretion to the wind." He broke down Ryan's guard and landed a big blow.

The moment he saw the blast, Thorne crawled through the ropes and seized Ryan by the feet. Williams bounded behind and separated the two warriors as the crowd howled in disgust. The bout lasted a little over a minute, if that. Sullivan and Ryan could console themselves, however, with their splits of $11,000 for a brief night's work.

The fight would be Sullivan's last inside the building that he put on the American sporting map. The changing political winds would close the ring to him, and the arena would be torn down in 1887 to give way to a second, more glorious incarnation of Madison Square Garden.

Sheedy lined up John L. to fight McCaffrey on April 2 in Philadelphia, but a court blocked the fight and ordered the men arrested for conspiring to stage a prizefight. They were both released on $5,000 bail. In addition to the legal roadblocks in New York and Philadelphia, Boston toughened its requirements for the granting of boxing exhibition licenses. Moral reformers were gaining the upper hand against pugilism, and fight activity in eastern cities slowed significantly. The sport was in retreat again.*

Around this time, Sullivan severed his relationship with Sheedy. The champion said that his manager was seeking too much money. For his part, Sheedy said the belligerent Sullivan would die with his boots on.

Details about another of Sullivan's breakups, however, would soon be revealed and shock his hometown.

On May 27, the attention of Boston was focused on the Supreme Court of Suffolk County and the case that had the gossip flying all around the city:

---

* Sullivan even ran afoul of the law trying to play baseball. He was arrested in Cleveland on September 14 for the high crime of taking to the baseball diamond on a Sunday.

Annie Sullivan vs. John L. Sullivan. Annie had stunned the city in February by filing for divorce. Even though their marriage had been irreparably damaged, John L. himself may have been surprised when handed a copy of the libel inside a storefront on the corner of Washington and Pine Streets.

According to Annie's written statement, she claimed to have always been true to their marriage vows. She asserted that the same could not be said of her husband, whom she said was also guilty of extreme cruelty. She itemized specific dates on which he beat, bruised, and threatened to kill her. Annie asserted "cruel and abusive treatment and gross and confirmed habits of intoxication." She asked for custody of John Jr. and the attachment of $20,000 of real and personal property to support her and her son. Fearing for her safety, Annie sought and was granted a restraining order.

Annie took the stand on the first day of the trial and detailed her husband's frequent intoxication and abuse before an audience of celebrity-chasers and curious citizens eager to listen to the airing of the couple's private affairs. Dressed in a close-fitting black dress and yellow silk gloves with a black half-veil shading her eyes, she told the court that the first instances of physical abuse occurred in 1883 during the transcontinental tour. Annie testified that she needed to get Herbert Slade to protect her after her drunken husband chased her out of a hotel in Leadville, Colorado, and threatened to kill her. She said he threw a glass at her in the dining-room car of a train passing through Montana.

The famous Sullivan stare was not to be found as John L. gave only occasional glances in his wife's direction. He sat beside his lawyer and gently stroked his mustache. Periodically, he chewed on a toothpick.

On cross-examination, Annie made some curious claims on the stand. She asserted that she had never partaken of any intoxicating beverages in her whole life. She also declined to say whether she had lived with John L. before their marriage. When the champion took the stand, however, he had no such qualms. He even discussed their first romantic encounter. Sullivan said his wife was jealous and constantly accusing him of cheating on their vows. He claimed she had never told him of her previous marriage and that she had thrown bottles and books at him.

The champion ducked and dodged on the stand. He admitted striking a horse but never knocking him down. He parsed words: "I have been intoxicated, but I never was drunk." When asked about the Mitchell fiasco, he denied he was ever unfit for a match through his intoxication—and he had a doctor's bill for fifty-eight dollars to prove it.

Family and friends called to the stand closed ranks in their testimonies. The judge took their comments under consideration and ruled against Annie's petition for divorce. He said that it had not been proved that Sullivan had been a "gross and confirmed drunkard" nor engaged in the cruel acts.

The couple remained permanently separated. John L. turned the Lovering Place house and its furniture over to Annie, but she remained in Rhode Island and rented out the house until she ultimately sold it. John L. moved to 7 Carver Street, and in the fall of 1885, he paid nearly $3,500 to purchase 26 Sawyer Street, a nine-room house around the corner from his parents' Parnell Street residence. He gave the house to his parents, but they didn't want to leave their longtime home, so they used it as a rental property.

While the rings in the East were closing to him, Sullivan continued to find a welcome reception in Chicago, where he fought Jack Burke in a scheduled five-round bout on June 13. Twelve thousand fans—and hundreds of police officers and Pinkerton detectives—roamed the Chicago Driving Park, which was dressed up in bunting for the affair. Shortly after 6 p.m., the crowd rose as the strands of "See the Conquering Hero Comes" played and Sullivan entered the ring to lusty cheers. Between his drinking and court appearances, Sullivan had little time to indulge in training in the lead-up to the battle. Plus, he entered the ring with two painful boils the size of large cherries on the back of his neck.

After the police examined the gloves, the fighters shook hands. Sullivan carried at least forty more pounds than the five-foot, eight-inch "Irish Lad." Despite his nickname, Burke was actually a Jewish fighter born and raised in England who joined many non-Irish boxers in adopting Hibernian personas to assist them in landing spots on fight cards.

The two men felt out each other cautiously at the open. They exchanged blows, clinches, and rushes. On the challenger's first hit, he opened the two boils on Sullivan and broke them. The furious champion rushed his foe and "went at him like a madman." He threw Burke to the floor.

Both men landed solid blows in between clinches. A police lieutenant at ringside shook his cane over the ropes as a warning to Sullivan when he grew a little too boisterous in his slugging. In the fourth, a heavy body blow felled Burke. The challenger rose and was soon under attack again and down on the floor a second time. By mistake, time was called to end the round earlier than it should have concluded. The men took their seats for a moment before they were brought back out and Sullivan continued to punish Burke.

After the fifth round, the referee awarded the match to Sullivan, who did not have clear superiority but had "done the better fighting." Burke had proven to be a very competitive fighter, the rare opponent to go the distance with the champion. Within months, another boxer would give Sullivan an even bigger scare.

On August 29, thousands of excited fight fans boarded the streetcars of Cincinnati for Chester Park, the city's premier entertainment district. Harness racing, Cincinnati Red Stockings baseball, and even chariot races usually lured the city's sporting public to Chester Park, but on this day, the draw was the biggest sporting event ever staged in the city.

After being blocked by the law in Philadelphia, Sullivan and Dominick McCaffrey were scheduled to enter the ring together, finally—not that authorities hadn't tried to impede in Cincinnati, too. The day before the bout, Sullivan was arrested at the behest of the Law and Order League under a municipal statute that authorized citizens to call upon a constable to nab principals of a planned prizefight. The champion posted $1,000 bail, and McCaffrey went into hiding when he heard of the arrest. The morning of the fight, the judge ruled that a bout with gloves was not a prizefight and could continue.

McCaffrey had fought well and delivered a bloody nose to Sullivan when the men had appeared in the ring together the year before at Tom Denney's benefit in Boston, so the champion knew it would be a tough matchup. He put in the necessary work training in Maine and arrived in Cincinnati only ten pounds over his preferred fighting weight. He even had gone several days without a drink, which had become such an anomaly by this point that it drew national headlines. SULLIVAN IS SOBER, an amazed *New York Times* declared upon the champion's arrival in Cincinnati.

The matchup was historic—considered by many to be the first heavyweight title bout in the United States under the Marquis of Queensberry Rules—and even by the standards of 1880s boxing, the encounter proved bizarre.

The fighters emerged in late afternoon, scaled a raised platform erected in front of the racetrack's grandstand, and slipped on three-ounce gloves. Sullivan was the heavy favorite, but McCaffrey had proven his credentials by whipping Mitchell in four rounds at Madison Square Garden the prior October. John L. had the decided height and weight advantage over the twenty-one-year-old challenger from Pittsburgh, who weighed less than 170 pounds and stood five feet, nine inches tall at best. McCaffrey had a big right, but his biggest asset was speed. And he planned to use it to keep his distance for two rounds before engaging Sullivan.

From the start, McCaffrey displayed his great quickness. Sullivan struggled to catch him in order to hit him. The champion grew frustrated at the "Tug Wilson tactics" as he chased the challenger around the ring. "Why the hell don't you force the fighting?" he roared.

The champion resigned himself to force more of the fighting himself in the second round. A huge uppercut that caught McCaffrey square on the jaw made the challenger even more wary of engagement. He continued to either dodge or bind up the champion in close quarters so that he would be out of range of taking a risky blow. Sullivan felled McCaffrey with a blow to the neck in the third round. The timekeeper, perhaps unfamiliar with the still-new Marquis of Queensberry Rules, called time to end the round a minute too early, which erroneously gave the dazed McCaffrey a full minute between rounds to recover from the big shot.

First blood was awarded to Sullivan in the fourth after he cut McCaffrey on the left cheek with a right-handed swing. He bloodied the challenger's lower lip with a left hook. Like a shark picking up the sanguinary scent, Sullivan rushed McCaffrey to the ropes. He pounded away as the timekeeper announced the end of the round.

McCaffrey looked exhausted at the end of the fourth round. His loud rooting section, which included five hundred pistol-packing ironworkers from Pittsburgh, grew discouraged. Their man, however, gained a second wind in the fifth before Sullivan landed a short punch that decked his opponent. As the August heat wilted the champion, Sullivan grew more cautious and limited his rushes. Both men went down heavily with Sullivan on top during the round.

At the end of the sixth round, Sullivan thought the fight was over. The written agreement between the boxers called for the fight to be "six rounds or to a finish." Sullivan took that "or to a finish" to mean the fight would end if a knockout occurred before the end of the sixth round. McCaffrey thought it meant they would fight all night until there was a victor.

The challenger yelled at the champion to come out for the seventh frame, and John L. obliged. McCaffrey dominated the round at long range with punches to the face and stomach, and at the end of the round, Sullivan took off his gloves and announced, "I've done enough fighting here today."

McCaffrey begged for the bout to continue. Sullivan's umpire and seconds approached referee Billy Tate and demanded a decision. While many in the crowd believed McCaffrey the better man and that the fight should continue, the referee declared Sullivan the winner. Brawls erupted at ringside. Rival fans fired shots in the air. McCaffrey's brother, who had served as his bottle-holder, drew a pistol on Arthur Chambers, one of Sullivan's seconds. The ring platform collapsed. Chaos reigned.

In the confusion, John L. fled Chester Park, while McCaffrey's supporters lifted their man on their shoulders. The confused ending took on new life when Tate was found that evening at a local saloon, still apparently mulling over the final result. He said that he "had merely expressed his opinion that Sullivan had had the better of the match." The referee told fans that Sullivan was ahead on points at the end of the sixth round, but he announced that he had not yet made an official decision.

The next day, Tate returned to his home in Toledo, while fight fans made a pilgrimage to his door to learn if the referee had yet divined a winner. Tate said because he hadn't seen the written agreement, he couldn't "in consequence render a decision." He received telegrammed word from the stakeholder that while the agreement originally called for points to determine the winner in case no knockout was achieved, Sullivan had excised any reference to points in the document. The stakeholder also informed the referee that Sullivan had already received the winner's share. After two days of agonized contemplation, Tate apparently latched on to this convenience and declared Sullivan the winner.

By that point, there wasn't much of a winner's purse remaining. Most of the $6,000 had been distributed by the champion among the saloons of Cincinnati. While Sullivan left Cincinnati with little money in his pocket, he departed as the winner of what some have called "the first heavyweight title fight of the modern era."

———

By 1886, the novelty of the Washington Street saloon had worn out for Sullivan. He sold his share to his brother but maintained an interest in the bar business by partnering with William Bennett to open a corner saloon in Manhattan. At the same time, another avenue of fame and fortune outside of the ring opened to Sullivan when he joined the Lester and Allen Minstrel Show for the 1885–1886 theatrical season. Between September 1885 and May 1886, he earned $500 a week to mimic the poses of famous ancient and modern sculptures.

Wrestler William Muldoon had already found success in living statuary, and Sullivan took lessons with a Boston Theatre ballet-master to learn the craft. Covered with powder to make it appear as if he was constructed of the palest marble, Sullivan replicated Greek and Roman statues such as *Ajax Defying the Lightning, Hercules at Rest,* and *Dying Gladiator* as soft music and lighting re-created the aura of a museum. Sullivan's teacher praised him for being "steady as the marble statues which adorn the Louvre."

Lester and Allen's advertising in particular targeted ladies, who may not have been apt to attend a boxing match but who would want to see an 1880s archetype of masculinity and male beauty in the flesh. The champion, however, was starting to lose the chiseled form of a Greek god as he ballooned to 237 pounds.

By the end of 1885, he also had a new woman in his life. Annie Livingston was a showgirl with a traveling burlesque company who was billed in advertisements as a "charming vocalist and actress." Like Sullivan's wife and mother, his mistress was another well-proportioned, voluptuous woman—a statuesque blonde beauty.

The woman born Anna Nailor received her first break at Boston's Howard Athenaeum, which was managed by Frederick Anderson, a former candy manufacturer who gave up the confectionery business to enter the theatrical world. Nailor and Anderson fell in love, married, and had a daughter, Eva. The marriage broke apart, however, and the couple separated around 1884, with Eva living with her paternal grandparents.

According to some reports, John L. first met the woman whose stage name was Annie Livingston as a schoolgirl at the age of ten and fell out of touch until they crossed paths again at the Howard Athenaeum in 1885. Whether the backstory is true or not, it seems likely that sometime after both Sullivan and Livingston separated from their spouses, they found their lives intersecting as they traveled around the country in their respective companies.

Annie Livingston proved just as powerless as Annie Sullivan in curtailing the champion's drinking, and Sullivan's abhorrent drunken behavior reared itself again on January 3, 1886, on a stop in New York. Outside the Gilsey House, he reportedly struck newsboy Tommy Lee with a heavy umbrella after he asked the scowling champion if he wanted to buy a copy of the Sunday *Daily News*.

Even Sullivan's hometown newspapers could not excuse his behavior anymore. He had struck horses, he had struck his wife, and now he had struck a newsboy. The newspapers were also quick to point out that the twelve-year-old victim, who was scared to press charges, was so "sickly and inoffensive" that he actually passed for nine or ten.

After the completion of the theatrical season in the spring, Sullivan was due to return to the ring and meet "Nonpareil" Jack Dempsey (not to be confused with the twentieth-century champion Jack Dempsey) at the LeGrande Skating Rink in Chicago on May 31. There was great anticipation in the matchup of two of the world's premier fighters. Advanced ticket sales were brisk. But once again, the law stepped in and prevented the fight from taking place.

With even the normally reliable city of Chicago having shuttered its doors to him, Sullivan reunited with Sheedy, who worked to arrange a six-round bout with Frank Herald, the "Nicetown Slasher," somewhere around New York City. After local authorities thwarted several proposed battlegrounds, Herald decided to leave New York for Pittsburgh. Sullivan caught word that the challenger planned to spread the news that a fearful John L. had personally informed the authorities of the pending fight to sabotage it and prevent him from taking a beating. Right after Herald boarded the 6 p.m. train to Pittsburgh, Sullivan boarded the 7 p.m. express and tailed him to the Steel City.

After arriving with Sheedy and his entourage in Pittsburgh on the morning of September 18, arrangements were made for the fighters to meet across the river in Allegheny City that night. In spite of the hasty arrangement, thirteen hundred fans entered the Coliseum Rink.

The familiar Sullivan fire blazed in his eyes. Sullivan jumped to scratch and led with a hard left to the nose of the twenty-four-year-old Herald. Sullivan pounded viciously at close quarters. A heavy left on the point of the jaw brought Herald down. Herald rose. Sullivan delivered another left to the jaw. Herald fell again. The challenger tried to slide away from Sullivan and dance around the ring. Sullivan forced Herald over the ropes after desperate infighting. The brawlers' attendants pulled them apart and took them to their corners.

In the second round, Sullivan brought a "vicious smile" with him to scratch. John L. pounded the challenger on the head, to the face, and on the neck until Herald slid away and landed a clean blow under the champion's eye. The surprised Sullivan staggered. He gathered himself. He unleashed an uppercut under Herald's chin for a clean knockdown. Herald rose in a flash. They clinched. Herald slipped and fell. With Sullivan sufficiently whipping his man, the police broke in to separate the fighters. Referee Johnny Newell declared Sullivan the victor.

Finding himself continually stymied by authorities in engaging ring opponents, Sullivan discovered an exhibition tour, in spite of its travel, more financially attractive. Sheedy organized another combination and another tour, one that wouldn't match the ambition of the grand transcontinental "knocking out" tour, but a lengthy trip nonetheless. The combination was made up of a changing cast of characters that included Steve Taylor, Joe Lannan, Duncan McDonald, Jimmy Carroll, Patsy Kerrigan, and George LaBlanche, "the Marine."

The combination opened in Racine, Wisconsin, in October and then headed west. John L. found himself back in familiar whistle-stops from the transcontinental "knocking out" tour, mining towns like Butte and Leadville. Sullivan found some doors now shuttered to him—the police chief in Seattle allowed the combination to give speeches but not fight—but others remained open. Even Victoria, Canada, where John L. had blasphemed the British monarch, welcomed him back.

Livingston may have accompanied Sullivan on the tour. The champion checked into a Milwaukee hotel in late October with a woman he registered as his "wife." In spite of press reports that Sullivan and his wife had "amicably settled their differences," the woman was not Annie Sullivan.

She was back in Rhode Island caring for a very sick child. Not yet three years old, John Jr. had been a healthy toddler. He had suddenly taken ill during an epidemic of diphtheria, however. After several days of sickness, the young boy passed away on October 28, 1886.

Annie was greatly bereaved. "He was all I had, and it seemed cruel to take him from me," Annie said later, a year after the boy's death.

Annie wrote her husband and told him the awful news. The diphtheria had come on so suddenly that Sullivan probably didn't even know that his son had taken ill. Annie asked him to pay for a headstone. He wrote back and told her that he wouldn't contribute a single penny unless she came back to live with him. Annie wrote back saying that she would never have anything more to do with him. That was the last they communicated directly. "He has plenty of money to spend on wine and on other women," an incredulous Annie told the *National Police Gazette,* "but he can't provide a stone for his own child's grave."

John L. did not leave the road to attend his boy's funeral. The minister at the service asked the bereaved to "voice a prayer for the happiness of the absent father." There is no record if John L. ever visited his son's grave in Rhode Island, over which was eventually placed a tombstone etched with LITTLE JOHNNIE and MAMA'S DARLING. Annie would be buried beside her boy in 1917.

In San Francisco on November 13, Sullivan faced Paddy Ryan for the third time. Unexpectedly, Ryan landed the first big punch of the fight, a right on Sullivan's right cheek. Yells of "Good for Paddy!" came from the crowd. They traded savage blows with Ryan leading. The pace was so furious in the opening minute that Ryan started to labor. Sullivan then rushed his foe. They clinched and were separated at the call of time.

In the second round, Ryan tried to force the fighting again, but he was much less effective. He continued to tire. Sullivan started to force the action. He downed Ryan with a body blow and repeated it twice more. Ryan clinched in a desperate attempt to prolong the bout.

He made it into the third round. Sullivan was the fresher of the two although both showed "signs of heavy punishment." A big right to Ryan's jaw spun him down. The "Trojan Giant" staggered to his feet and received another right to the jaw. He then lay on the stage motionless as the police rushed in. Sullivan cradled his opponent in his arms and carried him to his corner "while the cheering of the crowd made the rafters ring."

The front-page illustration on the *National Police Gazette* depicted Sullivan as a Christlike figure holding a fallen Ryan in his arms as he tenderly sponged him down. JOHN L. SULLIVAN THE INVINCIBLE, read the headline.

Two days later, the adulation continued as Sullivan picked up extra cash umpiring a California League baseball game in Oakland. His presence created such a frenzy that thousands in the overflow crowd spilled onto the only space left—the playing field—preventing players from taking their positions. The game could not proceed until Sullivan was escorted around the field by the police and then left the ballpark.

As the calendar turned to winter and the tour continued, Sullivan ended up in Minneapolis on a seasonably bitter January 18, 1887, to fight Patsy Cardiff in a six-round bout before ten thousand spectators. Sullivan had not put in much training, but the twenty-four-year-old Cardiff had toned himself to 185 pounds. The six-footer had notably knocked out English middleweight Jem Goode in 1884 and defeated former Sullivan foes Captain James Dalton, George Rooke, and "Professor" John Donaldson. He had also fought Charley Mitchell to a draw. Still, few gave the challenger a shot against the bulging 230-pound champion.

Sullivan opened the fight with his signature rush. Cardiff dodged and countered with a left to the body. When John L. rushed a second time and swung his big right, Cardiff extended his right arm and ducked. The full force of Sullivan's arm collided with his challenger's forehead. The sickening pain trembled down John L.'s arm, and he tried his best to mask his suffering.

For the rest of the fight, Sullivan lacked his normal aggression. His arm swelled terribly. Cardiff began to force the fight but could not take advantage of his injured foe with the dangling arm. The fight grew "cautious and tiresome." The crowd began to hiss. Cardiff was easily able to dodge any shots fired by Sullivan the rest of the night. At the end of six rounds, backers of both men believed their fighters had won, but after a long consultation, the referee declared the champion the victor. If a more adept fighter had been in the ring with Sullivan, however, John L. would not have emerged victorious.

John L. was rushed to his hotel in excruciating pain. His arm had swollen to double its normal size. Two surgeons examined the champion and found the radius bone broken. After they set the arm, the champion stayed with the tour through the Dakota Territory and to Winnipeg, Canada, although he couldn't fight.

The pain persisted, however, and John L. visited a trusted surgeon in New York who said the arm needed to be re-set. The surgeon summoned his two sons and told them to hold the champion's biceps and forearm. The doctor took grasp of the champion as if he was one of Sullivan's thousands of adoring fans who clamored to shake his hand. He gave a sudden wrenching yank and re-broke the arm. Sullivan's arm was locked in a plaster cast for five weeks.

Sullivan finally returned to the ring at the end of March in Hoboken, New Jersey, for a brief tour of the East with Taylor, LaBlanche, Lannan, Carroll, and James McKeon that concluded in Hartford, Connecticut, on July 4.

When the tour swung through Washington, DC, on April 4, Sullivan attended one of the public receptions that President Grover Cleveland held at the White House three times a week. Sheedy introduced the champion to the president and tactlessly told the portly commander-in-chief,

"If you should wish any suggestions in the way of exercise he'd be just the man to give them. I know he would cure you of any unhealthiness arising from want of exercise."

The presence of Sullivan, dressed in an elegant black suit, drew more excitement from his fellow citizens than the president. Why not? He was the bigger celebrity. The press wrote that THE PRESIDENT MEETS JOHN L. SULLIVAN rather than vice versa. The three hundred citizens who left the White House that day were more apt to brag that while they had met the president, they had just "shook the hand that shook the hand of Sullivan."

Fox had searched the world to unearth a fighter who could defeat John L. Now he was convinced that he had discovered the next heavyweight champion right in Sullivan's backyard.

Jake Kilrain had grown up in the working-class suburb of Somerville, just four miles from Sullivan's neighborhood in the South End. Born John Joseph Killion in the Greenpoint section of Brooklyn, the fighter was called Kilrain by boyhood friends and the name stuck.

Not only did the two heavyweights share a geographic proximity, their biographies were similar as well. Kilrain, born just four months after Sullivan, was also the son of Irish immigrants. He first learned to fight as a teenager working in the mills near Boston, and he fought his first professional bout at age nineteen.

Kilrain's ring record was sterling. He had risen through the ranks of the Boston boxing scene about a year behind Sullivan and conquered some of the same fighters vanquished by the champion—Dan Dwyer, Greenfield, and Herald among them. He fought both Mitchell and Burke to draws in 1884. After Kilrain knocked out Lannan in the eleventh round of a bout inside a Watertown, Massachusetts, hotel in March 1887, it appeared he was the first challenger in line to get a shot at the champion.

In May, Fox on behalf of Kilrain posted a certified check for $1,000 with the *New York Clipper* to make a match with Sullivan. The publisher was led to believe that he had a verbal agreement with the champion. But citing his injured arm, Sullivan never posted his forfeit for the match and refused to acknowledge that there was an agreement.

The furious Fox declared that the champion had forfeited his title, although the *Police Gazette* claimed it acted "dispassionately and judicially" in its decision. The publisher said his motivation was not spite, but patriotism, because Sullivan was not responding to the boastful challenges of Englishman Jem Smith. "Anxious that the slur upon his country be repelled," Fox felt someone needed to fight for America's honor, and if Sullivan wouldn't do it, then Kilrain would.

Fox matched Kilrain with the English titleholder Smith for the championship of the world and sent the American overseas to square off with the Englishman. Before Kilrain departed, Fox fired one more shot across the bow of the USS *Sullivan*. On June 4, 1887, inside Kernan's Monumental Theatre in Baltimore, where Sullivan's "knocking out" tour launched, *National Police Gazette* sporting editor William Harding, on Fox's behalf, presented Kilrain with the *Police Gazette* diamond belt representing the championship of America.

John L. sneered and called the belt a mere "dog collar." The *National Police Gazette* replied that if they were going to manufacture a dog collar for Sullivan, it would read, "The inmate of this collar is the private and exclusive property of Pat Sheedy. Everybody else is requested to let him alone."

Fox commissioned a four-verse song about Kilrain, which was sung by Irish-American vocal queen Maggie Cline, and he praised the modest new champion: "Hail to the most straightforward and the most unassuming champion the world ever had."

The same could not be said of Sullivan, particularly during the last three tumultuous years. His drinking raged. He grew violent when intoxicated. He was gaining weight. He no longer had his son. His marriage existed only in the eyes of the law. Now, in the eyes of some, he was no longer champion. And he needed money.

Even on this latest exhibition tour, Sheedy increasingly struggled to obtain entertainment licenses. America was becoming an increasingly difficult place for a boxer to work. Sheedy cast his eyes to fertile, virgin territory where he wouldn't have such obstacles—Europe.

CHAPTER SIX

The King and the Prince

IT HAS BEEN TRUE OF BOSTON SINCE THE PURITANS GRAZED THEIR cows and hanged their suspected witches in the Common: Nothing can unite the city like an insult from a New Yorker, particularly an egotistical Gotham newspaper publisher. Incensed at Richard K. Fox's presentation of the *Police Gazette* championship belt to Jake Kilrain, proud Bostonians, at the behest of Sullivan's manager, Pat Sheedy, pooled their money to bestow an even more glorious piece of pugilistic jewelry upon their "Strong Boy."

Nearly four hundred diamonds, each weighing between one-half and three karats, studded the Tiffany-crafted marvel. Gold pins resembling the ropes and posts of a boxing ring linked eight smaller plates of sixteen-karat gold to a central plaque with the enormous inscription:

> PRESENTED TO THE
> CHAMPION OF CHAMPIONS
> JOHN L. SULLIVAN
> BY THE
> CITIZENS OF THE UNITED STATES
> JULY 4, 1887.

Sullivan's name shimmered in a dazzling diamond array. On the central plaque, American, British, and Irish flags flanked a solid gold American eagle with its wings spread, while the smaller plates bore the images of Sullivan in evening wear and ring costume, Irish harps, and the Stars and Stripes. The ostentatious hardware cost $10,000, more than thirty times the average yearly income of a Massachusetts citizen at the time.

In spite of the patriotic date etched on the belt, the presentation ceremony did not occur until August 8 when four thousand people filled the Boston Theatre from pit to dome for an affair as studded as the forty-four-inch championship belt. Residents of every caste—from proper Bostonians in evening dress in the orchestra boxes to the rabble who choked the galleries—united to honor John L.

Four decades after Irish Catholics began to flood to Boston in the wake of the Great Hunger, the coronation ceremony inside the city's grandest theater confirmed that they had finally made the city a place of their own. Mayor Hugh O'Brien, who had been sworn in as the city's first Irish-American leader in 1885, sat in a place of honor. Nearly every politician in Boston attended rather than risk a Celtic electoral backlash by snubbing the city's greatest Irish hero.

With no little irony, Boston prepared to lavish a prizefighter at the same time it banned his line of work. City law prohibited sparring exhibitions, but Sheedy successfully lobbied the mayor and the entire board of aldermen to permit bouts just at the ceremony.

That an "open law-breaker" and a "drunken champion bruiser" would be publicly crowned in the presence of civic dignitaries chafed segments of Boston's old order, who took it as an affront to the "culture, piety, and decency of the Hub." Surely, the entire affair would have ruffled the starched collars of the city's Puritan forebears, their "City Upon a Hill" sacrilegiously worshipping a ring idol and bestowing upon him an offering of gold and diamonds.

Sullivan ran late for his own affair, which gave rise to obvious speculation about the cause. The "howling rowdies" in the gallery freely, and loudly, shared their theories with the rest of the audience, which prompted Sheedy to scurry to center stage. Shaking his fist, he warned the disorderly patrons, "You fellers want to remember that Mr. Sullivan and myself are gentlemen with gentlemen, but among toughs we're kings."

The admonishment simmered the gallery, and John L. soon arrived. Once the sparring exhibitions were complete, the theater's green curtain lifted to reveal Sullivan in a fine dress coat and shimmering silk tie. To the strains of "Hail to the Chief," councilman William Benjamin Franklin Whall escorted the champ to the center of the stage as the crowd cheered, clapped, and stomped the floor. The audience showered Sullivan with huzzahs as Sheedy and the councilman buckled the belt around his waist.

The audience howled for a speech from the champion, who appeared uneasy with the pomp and circumstance. Poet John Boyle O'Reilly had fashioned an address that John L. memorized line by line, but once on stage, the champion's mind blanked. Forced to abandon the scripted oration, Sullivan delivered an impromptu speech of thanksgiving so well received that O'Reilly came up to him afterward and asked, "Why the devil did you get me to write that speech for you when you could make a better speech yourself?" The program closed with Sullivan donning his fighting shirt and trunks—but not his new belt—for an exhibition with Mike Donovan.

The public celebration for John L. orchestrated by his manager was a tremendous success. Only a few weeks after Sheedy's presentation of jewels to Sullivan, however, their professional marriage would come to an abrupt end.

Following the lackluster performance of their last exhibition tour of the United States, Sheedy and Sullivan decided to sow fertile ground in a foreign land—the British Isles. As his manager began preparations, John L. enjoyed the waning days of summer with friends at Nantasket Beach, the seaside resort south of Boston, where he squeezed in a "two-weeks drunk at the Ocean House."

At the end of August, Sheedy asked Sullivan for a brief pious interlude to his carousing. He arranged for his man to meet Steve Taylor in an exhibition at the Nantasket Beach Skating Rink to raise money for construction of a new Catholic church. A big crowd turned out to see Sullivan and the undercard between George LaBlanche and Patsy Kerrigan, and the benefit raised $1,500. In spite of the evening's divine cause, however, John L. arrived obviously inebriated. Sheedy finally lost patience with Sullivan's drinking. The livid manager took to the platform and said, "The next bout is supposed to be the most important one of the evening. But I decline to introduce the contestants." Sheedy stormed off the stage and never spoke to Sullivan again. And with that, John L. had torn through another manager.

The publicity-hungry Sheedy took his complaints about Sullivan's drinking and diligence to the press, and the champion responded with a verbal volley of his own. Sullivan groused about his former manager's tendency "to make the leader of the band play second fiddle." John L. also claimed that at Sheedy's request he had remained temperate for a year, but that there was only so much a man in his profession could do. "Is it in the nature of a boxer—pugilist, if you will—to keep away from allurements of sociability?" he asked. "You cannot by any process known to a living being make a monk or a hermit out of a prominent pugilist."

With the trip abroad still looming, Sullivan scrambled to find a new manager. He hired Harry Phillips, a well-to-do Montreal sporting man, and gave his new manager his pro forma pledge to avoid even a drop of alcohol while under his care. Phillips brought aboard as an advance man and press agent his close friend Ed Holske, a Boston gymnasium owner who had toured England as a champion pedestrian in the 1870s. It was a potentially combustible hire given that Sullivan loathed Holske, who had regularly roasted the champion in his *Boston Police News* column until his recent firing, a dismissal that drove Holske's wife to show up at the newspaper office and whip his old boss with a cowhide.

As Sullivan prepared to leave for the exhibition tour through Ireland, Scotland, and England, Kilrain began his own tour across Britain with Charley Mitchell in the lead-up to the fight with the English heavyweight champion, Jem Smith. John L. was eager to follow close behind to prove to the British public "who the real champion is," but he also had pound signs in his eyes, imagining a big potential payday from his popular traveling show and a matchup with either Smith or Kilrain. Before Sullivan's departure, his friends gathered at Billy Hogarty's Dover Street barbershop and presented him with a gold-headed cane and an umbrella for England's notoriously damp climate, both of which were made by Shreve, Crump & Low and valued at $1,100 each.

As the sun rose on October 27, the steamship *Cephalonia* prepared to sail from the Cunard wharf in East Boston with the champ in tow. But as the embarkation time came and went, Sullivan could not be found and the steamer remained in port. About an hour later, John L. finally arrived from across the harbor on one of two tugs carrying his family, hundreds of friends, and two brass bands. Sullivan climbed on board the *Cephalonia* with his new championship belt. After tearful goodbyes, the mighty whistle blew, cannons fired, and the ship cast off its lines. Sailing with the champion were Phillips and his wife, sparring partner Jack Ashton (who had lost an eight-round decision to Kilrain in 1886), his personal friend and financial expert Jack Barnett, and a woman the press reported to be his "wife" and passenger lists recorded as "Annie Sullivan."

The champion's female traveling companion was not, in fact, his lawfully wedded wife. She was Annie Livingston and the reason for his delayed arrival aboard the *Cephalonia*. Sullivan had quietly planned to bring mistress Annie, who had vacationed with him in Nantasket, but word had leaked out to his wife in Rhode Island. John L. had heard that the real Annie Sullivan might board the ship to stop them, so he sent Livingston ahead and planned to arrive at the last minute. Until the steamer finally left the dock, the nervous Sullivan craned his neck in every direction, looking for any sign of his wife. Other than an uncomfortable question from one of Annie Sullivan's acquaintances who happened to be boarding—"Where is your other wife?"—John L. shoved off to England without further incident, although a *New York Herald* reporter noted that Livingston, "who appeared to take a great interest in the champion pugilist," was aboard.

As the two tugs escorted the *Cephalonia* across Boston Harbor, the pale steeple of the Old North Church and the gold dome of the Massachusetts State House shrank in the distance. Sullivan's father stood atop the pilothouse of one tug, holding the colors his son had won in battle with Paddy Ryan while they flapped in the breeze. As the steamer passed Boston Light at the harbor's edge, the *Cephalonia* left its nautical escort—and America—behind. Sullivan, his voice choking, shouted, "Goodbye, boys! Goodbye!" His friends and family took off their hats and gave one final cheer as Sullivan's parents cried softly. The strains of "Auld Lang Syne" faded along with the New England coast. Old England lay ahead.

With the British Empire at its zenith and her monarch, Queen Victoria, celebrating her fiftieth year on the throne, the world's mightiest superpower opened its arms to America's greatest superstar as the

Cephalonia arrived in Liverpool on November 6. A specially chartered tug with two hundred sporting men aboard, including former challenger Alf Greenfield, greeted the ship as it sailed down the River Mersey and approached port. "Every British pugilist who was out of jail thronged to the water side to welcome his great exemplar," reported one British newspaper.

In spite of the warm reception, British authorities denied entrance to an important member of Sullivan's traveling company: his bejeweled championship belt. Denying requests that the belt be allowed to enter the country duty-free since the champion had firm plans, at least in his mind, to return to America with the hardware and the title still firmly in his grasp, British customs officials imposed a prohibitive duty of more than one hundred pounds (then equivalent to $600).* Rather than pay the exorbitant duty, Sullivan left the diamond belt in the Queen's bonded warehouse to await his sail home.

Although prizefighting was as illegal in England as it was in the United States, the "Great John L." learned instantly that his popularity had crossed the Atlantic with him. Thousands of voices cheered Sullivan as he disembarked, and he had to push through the crush just to get to his quarters at the Grand Hotel. The next day, a "cheering multitude" chased his open carriage to the railway station where he boarded a train to London. At Edgehill, Crewe, Rugby, and stops throughout the English countryside, scores of excited townspeople greeted him. In some cases, they scaled the roof of Sullivan's train in frantic attempts to shake his hand.

As the train eased into London, it appeared that nearly every inhabitant of the world's largest city had descended upon Euston Station. A crowd estimated as high as twelve thousand waved their handkerchiefs, hats, and walking sticks in the air. Fans cried out, "Welcome, John!" and "Bravo, Sullivan!" Men and boys scaled lampposts for a better view. Hands were thrust at Sullivan from every direction, and one newspaper noted he "ran a fair risk of having his arm shaken off." The two hundred policemen were powerless to fight back the human tide that swallowed them whole.

------

* Sullivan could take solace in the fact that the British government only imposed a tax of seven pounds, seven shillings on Fox's "dog collar" when Kilrain attempted to enter the country with the *Police Gazette* belt.

Fearing for their safety, Sullivan and his party tried to take refuge in a nearby coach, but as fans followed him inside, the bottom collapsed under the weight and sent everyone to the cobblestones.

Once safely ensconced in his carriage, Sullivan rode to the offices of the *Sportsman*, London's popular sporting newspaper, with the crowd trailing in a triumphal procession worthy of a royal. As the throng clogged traffic on Fleet Street, Sullivan leaned out of a window and delivered a brief thank-you.

England's enthusiasm for boxing had been stoked by Kilrain's arrival and his pending matchup with Smith, but Sullivan's appearance elevated the fistic fever to unprecedented heights. The Sullivan mania that swept England—the reception that one newspaper lamented could not be drawn by a "prince, statesman, peer, philosopher, poet, preacher, or artist"—led to prolonged hand-wringing among high society who tut-tutted the spectacle created by a mere prizefighter.

The fact that Sullivan and another American celebrity then touring England, "Buffalo Bill," were setting the British public agog was not lost back in America. For months, William Cody's Wild West show had packed in audiences across Britain. A command performance even drew Queen Victoria, who bowed at the presentation of the Stars and Stripes, marking the first time a British monarch had saluted the flag of its former colony. During one performance in the midst of the queen's Golden Jubilee celebrations, "Buffalo Bill" drove the Prince of Wales and kings of Denmark, Greece, Belgium, and Saxony in his Deadwood coach as they attempted to escape a simulated Indian attack.

Life magazine spoofed the British reaction in a two-page drawing entitled "The Triumph of the West," which depicted a royal procession passing by Queen Victoria's box. Preceded by three noblemen in robes, "Buffalo Bill," cowboy hat on his head and rifle strapped across his chest, rode on horseback as the parade stepped on top of a Union Jack strewn on the ground. Towering behind "Buffalo Bill," a bare-chested Sullivan rode atop a grand royal carriage being driven by the Prince of Wales and pulled by a nobleman, barrister, and professor as ballerinas danced alongside.

Manager Harry Phillips tried to capitalize on the frenzy by charging double the regular prices for Sullivan's exhibitions, which resulted in less than a full house for his first London appearance on November 9 at St. James's Hall. John L. first walked on stage in evening dress and spoke to the audience, as did Smith. Then Sullivan, wearing a Stars-and-Stripes handkerchief festooned with shamrocks and Irish harps around his waist, sparred four rounds with Ashton while the Marquis of Queensberry himself watched from the audience. Londoners marveled at the speed and power of Sullivan's blows. The evening was an "enthusiastic success," according to one reviewer, who noted that it surpassed Kilrain's "exceedingly tame and disappointing" opening exhibition.

The *Sportsman* ran a special supplement devoted to Sullivan, and the London sporting dailies devoted one or two columns to "Slugger Sullivan" in each issue as he left for a barnstorming tour of England. Posters in city after city heralded the arrival of the "Famous Fistic Marvel," the "American Cyclone," and the "champion of the world." A company of professional and amateur British fighters including Sam Blakelock joined Sullivan and Ashton. Reprising the popular act from America, Phillips, on Sullivan's behalf, offered one hundred pounds to any man who could last four rounds with the champion. Ebullient crowds thronged John L. at every stop, and the working class and Irish immigrants filled the coffers in cities such as Leicester and Manchester. Nearly twenty thousand turned out for a two-night stay at Bingley Hall in Birmingham where Sullivan sparred with Greenfield.

John L. returned to London at the end of November to open a twelve-night set on the great central stage of the Royal Aquarium, a huge entertainment complex steps from Westminster Abbey that included theaters in addition to its tanks of sea creatures. The eclectic acts that appeared with John L. included Professor Roche and his pack of fifteen wild Russian wolves, Madame Josephine's garden of living statuary, and La Belle Fatma Ben-Eny, the beauty of Tunis. The young women who sold flowers and gloves at the Aquarium's stalls grew so smitten with Sullivan that they abandoned their wares to sneak a look at him whenever he appeared on stage.

The charms, style, and looks of the woman referred to in the British press as "Mrs. J.L. Sullivan" attracted notice, as well. "British crowds are marveling that such perfect types, physically, of the two sexes should happen to be united as man and wife," one American newspaper reported, before adding, "They are at a loss to understand, too, how it is that the couple now live in such delightful connubial harmony when less than a year ago a suit for divorce was on." The *National Police Gazette* was only too happy to expose the true identity of the champion's traveling companion in a full-page article, and the reports of the British fawning over "Mrs. Sullivan" only further angered the real Mrs. Sullivan in Centerville, Rhode Island. Even friends of hers who had read the newspaper thought she had reconciled with her husband and traveled to England at his side. If Annie Sullivan hoped that Victorian England, with its strict public morals, would rebuke John L. for openly parading his mistress through their country, however, the news that soon emanated from the palace of Queen Victoria herself would not please her.

A few weeks after their arrival in England, Ed Holske received a royal request for Sullivan and Ashton to spar at a private exhibition before His Royal Highness, the Prince of Wales, and a party of noblemen. The prince was a member of the "fancy" who followed pugilism, and Sullivan's well-publicized arrival in London would have attracted his attention.

Despite their disparate upbringings and vocations, the prince and Sullivan were remarkably kindred spirits. Both men had enormous hedonistic appetites. Under different circumstances, the boxer who brought his mistress abroad might have compared notes with the playboy prince whose affairs included the actress Lillie Langtry and Winston Churchill's mother, Jennie. The corpulent heir to the throne ate twelve-course dinners and was on his way to a forty-eight-inch waist. Nicknamed "Edward the Caresser," he grew so rotund that he required a specially designed "siege d'amour" to support himself on his regular visits to Le Chabanais, one of the finest bordellos in Paris, where he was also known to soak with prostitutes in a champagne-filled bathtub. (That no doubt would have struck John L. as a waste of champagne.) If thoughts of disappointing Queen Victoria didn't restrain the prince from indulging his pleasures, the morals of the age named for his puritanical mother did nothing to stop him either.

On December 9, the king of the ring rode in a carriage through London to hold court with the prince. Around noon, his coach pulled up at St. James Barracks on Cleveland Row. Sullivan brought along Arthur Brisbane, a young London correspondent for the *New York Sun* who was covering John L.'s foreign adventures. The reporter had been hired by Charles A. Dana's newspaper at age nineteen and received his big break when he was called upon to record the names of prominent fans at one of Sullivan's earlier fights in America after fellow reporters arrived too drunk for the assignment. The fighter took a liking to the newspaper man and broke him the news of the pending royal audience, a huge scoop in a competitive business as brutal as the one in the ring. Brisbane, though, did not have a proper invitation, and the event was to be off-limits to the press. A royal equerry halted the newspaper reporter and told Sullivan that guests were not allowed. But flashing his common touch, loyalty, and keen sense of currying favor with the press, John L. said, "Well, if you don't let that guy in, there will be no show. I won't go, so you can tell the prince what you like." The equerry quickly admitted Brisbane, who agreed to write an account only for the American press.

Before meeting the prince, Sullivan dined on salmon and cuts of beef with the officers of the elite Grenadier, Coldstream, and Scots Guards. The aristocratic audience included Lord Randolph Churchill, father of thirteen-year-old Winston, who would someday become prime minister. Talk focused on the old days of championship prizefights, and the men drank in silence to the memories of American John C. Heenan and Englishman Tom Sayers, who had fought so memorably in 1860 in what some considered the first world heavyweight championship bout.

When word of the prince's arrival came, Sullivan was led to the gymnasium in the nearby London Fencing Club. As he walked in, he saw the forty-six-year-old prince with his perfectly trimmed brown beard standing in front of an open-wood fireplace smoking a cigarette. He was dressed in terra cotta gloves with black stitching, a cutaway black coat, and gray trousers. The varnish on the prince's solid walking boots reflected the rays of the gaslight, and he grasped a slender black bamboo cane with a silver head. The equerry presented the demure Sullivan to the future king, who held out his hand and removed his hat. The men exchanged a hearty handshake, and Sullivan told the prince that outside of Smith, he was the man he most wanted to meet in coming to England. According to the *Manchester Guardian*, they talked briefly of the royal's trip to the United States before the Civil War and a sparring match the prince had fought—yes, fought—in Detroit. Today, the prince was just a spectator, and during the preliminary bouts, Sullivan sat next to him and analyzed the uppercuts, hard rights, and other punches being thrown by the boxers.

The regal surroundings were a jarring departure from the more familiar pugilistic underworld settings of saloons and barges. Blue silk covered the ropes of the twenty- by twenty-four-foot ring, and fencing foils, masks, and boxing gloves festooned the gymnasium walls. The British brawlers who performed for the forty members of high society gathered inside the club included Smith, Greenfield, and Blakelock. The exhibition offered the prince a pleasant break from his royal duties, which in the past week had included opening five fairs and three bazaars, laying two cornerstones, and attending seven funerals by proxy.

After the rest of the fighters displayed their skills before Britain's highest-ranking boxing fan, Phillips stood before the royal audience to introduce Ashton and "the champion of the world." In a nod to their Irish heritages, both men wore emerald tights festooned with harps and sewn-on medallions of famous Irishmen dating back to the ancient Celtic king Brian Boru. Sullivan and Ashton exchanged blows for three rounds and reportedly offered such a spirited slugging for the prince's enjoyment that the rounds were cut short for Ashton's benefit. At the end of the bout, the prince pounded his cane on the floor, applauded, and smiled. "I never saw anything like him in the world," he raved to Phillips. "He's a marvel of a man, altogether out of the ordinary." The prince also couldn't help but notice "the strength of his eye."

After the spar, the future king offered John L. his congratulations and commented on the hard knocks the men delivered to each other. He then departed in a hansom cab to Marlborough House where he was due to taste a culinary novelty prepared by a celebrated cordon bleu from Paris.

Thanks in part to the presence of the *New York Sun*'s Brisbane, news of the supposedly private exhibition quickly reached the United States and reverberated back to England. The prince's royal reception for the purveyors of a sport illegal in his domain rankled the upper crusts of English society and reportedly infuriated Queen Victoria. Preachers denounced the pugilistic audience from their pulpits. The Reverend Hugh Price Hughes told his congregation that "no man has a right to call himself an English gentleman who would shake hands with John L. Sullivan." According to one newspaper account, "those who organized the show all declare that had the Prince known that the slightest publicity was to be given to his visit he would never have entered the building." If true, the blowback introduced the royal to the new era of celebrity personified by John L. Anything and everything that occurred in the realm of America's superstar king would be consumed by the public.

The American press took great glee in writing up accounts of the summit between the self-made fellow and the gentleman to the palace born. Writers were practically giddy in inventing dialogue that demonstrated how "Sullivan indulged in a free and easy style of speech when addressing the Prince." Ever the democratic man of the people, Sullivan reportedly greeted the prince as he would one of his old-time drinking buddies: "I'm proud to meet you. I have often heard of you." The papers reported that he concluded just as informally as he began: "If you ever come to Boston, be sure and look me up."

The reports of Sullivan's folksy language to the prince circulating in the American press caused a scandal. British newspapers even shot down the truly outrageous reports circulating through the country that the prince took his hat off to speak to Sullivan. The accounts of the champion's conduct with the prince did nothing to ingratiate him with Britain's blue bloods, but it added to his mythic lore with the working classes in America and abroad.

Of course, John L. himself perpetuated some of these exaggerated reports of the royal meeting through the simple way he described their encounter. He called the prince "a nice, sociable fellow with splendid manners" and "the sort of a man you like to meet anywhere, and at any time, and introduce your family to."

Although the meeting between Sullivan and the heir apparent was brief, John L. forever talked about the prince, particularly following his ascension to the throne as King Edward VII after the death of his mother in 1901, as "his good friend." He hardly missed a chance to steer a conversation to the subject of his royal audience. And he would keep up the colloquialisms in his references to "King Ed," one time writing of their meeting, "I shook his flipper and wished him well."

The day after meeting the prince and playing before a packed house at the Royal Aquarium, John L. and his combination left London by train for Ireland. More than three decades after Sullivan's parents had fled the Emerald Isle, the proud country continued to struggle under British rule. The British House of Commons had the prior year defeated a Home Rule bill championed by nationalists such as Charles Stewart Parnell to allow Irish self-government.

Peasants in rural counties still lived in extreme wretchedness. The "Land War" plagued Ireland's hinterlands as tenant farmers rebelled against the economic system that had oppressed them for generations. After ostracizing Charles Boycott, the land agent of an absentee landlord, in 1880, the Irish took to "Boycotting" other land agents, landlords, and even tenants who moved into farms where previous residents had been evicted. In some cases, the civil unrest exploded in violence. Nationalists murdered English landlords and tenant farmers who refused to honor rent strikes, and just months before Sullivan's arrival, police had killed three Irish Land League protestors in County Cork in what became known as the "Mitchelstown Massacre."

The heavy British hand squashed free speech and a free press. Just days before the arrival of John L., a fellow Sullivan—Timothy Daniel Sullivan—was locked up in Tullamore Jail for publishing proceedings of suppressed branches of the Irish Land League in his newspaper. This Home Rule leader wasn't just any old Sullivan at the time of his sentencing; he was the Lord Mayor of Dublin.

The boxer who waved the banner of liberty in America naturally believed that Ireland should be free from British rule and sympathized with the Irish rebels. "If you owned a house and farm and planted things and had your family depending on you," he said, "and some bigger fellow came along and chased you out, you'd always be ready to fight him, wouldn't you?" (In spite of his opposition to the British rule in Ireland, Sullivan would never blame his friend King Edward VII after his ascension to the throne for the state of affairs: "There are a whole lot of things he would like to do, but his hands are tied by Parliament, just like the president's are tied by Congress.")

Sullivan's weeklong trip to Ireland offered his brethren a particularly welcome break from the bitter news that dominated their lives. At least for seven days, they had something to cheer. After crossing the Irish Sea from Wales by mail steamer, John L. arrived on December 11 in the land of the Sullivans and the Kellys. Fifteen thousand Irishmen besieged John L. at the docks near Dublin as he set foot on his ancestral homeland for the first time. Two brass bands struck up "See the Conquering Hero Comes" and "The Wearing of the Green." After arriving at his quarters at Dublin's Grosvenor Hotel, Sullivan addressed the crowd from his drawing room window and tossed verbal bouquets to the land "he was proud to call his own."

The evening after his arrival, Sullivan took to the stage of Leinster Hall where he earned a loud roar of approval after giving a brief speech in which he expressed his solidarity with the Irish struggle for independence. He then refereed a series of amateur bouts before stripping and sparring with Ashton for four rounds.

The next morning, he left for Waterford and along the way visited sacred ground for the fighting Irish, Donnelly's Hollow. Before thousands of his countrymen sitting on the grassy slopes of that natural amphitheater in 1815, Irish boxer Dan Donnelly had struck a symbolic blow against the Crown when he defeated Englishman George Cooper. The victory transformed Donnelly into such an Irish folk hero that decades after his death, his mummified right arm was placed on display in a small County Kildare pub. During his visit, Sullivan literally followed in Donnelly's footsteps, which were preserved in the hollow as islands of bare patches in a lush ocean of meadow grass.

After sparring with Ashton in Waterford, John L. traveled to Cork where he took a brief sightseeing detour to kiss the Blarney Stone—as if he needed the gift of gab. That night, a brave Corkman, Frank Creedon, stepped forward before a sold-out audience to take up Sullivan's knockout challenge. Seeing the twenty-three-year-old, who gave away three inches and many more pounds, Sullivan refused to fight. "Why the man is not in my class," he barked as he sent out another member of the company to dispatch with the young butter market porter. Impressed by Creedon's fortitude, however, John L. presented him with a gold medal and congratulations for his bravery.

After a performance in Limerick, the traveling boxing show returned to Dublin for a final performance at Leinster Hall. Sullivan then completed his tour of Ireland in Belfast, the birthplace of his newspaper nemesis, Fox. Sullivan might have felt his rival's hand somehow at work in a disappointing turnout, attributed to a lack of promotion, despite the local newspaper's description of it as "the local sporting event of the year."

Although the proud son of Erin did not have an opportunity to visit the homesteads of his mother or father on the whirlwind trip, his week in Ireland was a success. Sullivan said he earned more money in one week in Ireland than in his entire time in England, and he left with a suitcase of souvenirs bestowed upon him during his travels, including seventeen blackthorn sticks, four jugs of whiskey, and one Irish tweed suit.

By the time Sullivan arrived in Scotland, news had arrived that Kilrain and Smith had fought an incredible battle, a 106-round draw that lasted nearly three hours until darkness settled in. The marathon bout on a French island in the middle of the River Seine was called "the greatest battle ever fought in a prize ring" by the *National Police Gazette*. Although the *Gazette* said that "every spectator of the fray, including all the Englishmen present" declared their man Kilrain the emphatic winner and thus champion of the world, the inconclusive result further clouded the picture as to who might be Sullivan's next opponent. John L. told crowds throughout his trip that he had come to England to meet the best fighter they had, and he understood that to be Smith. Now, that wasn't so clear, and Sullivan's path forward brought him back to the "bombastic sprinter" who continued to torment him daily in the British press.

Charley Mitchell was the undisputed champion of getting under Sullivan's skin. His boxing style gave Sullivan fits, but his spew of bluster needled him to no end. The English fighter knew how to play the media game, and he delivered the braggadocio that made good copy, something Sullivan could understand even if he didn't like it. Mitchell could boast of knocking down Sullivan in their 1883 encounter, and the drunken fiasco at Madison Square Garden the following year still haunted John L. The champion had come to England targeting two big dogs—Smith and Kilrain—but the pesky Mitchell got his attention by incessantly nipping at his heels every day in the newspapers and questioning his manhood. Ultimately, Mitchell's big mouth earned him a title shot.

Sullivan and Mitchell met on November 29, 1887, to sign articles of agreement for a bare-knuckle title fight under the London Prize Ring Rules within one thousand miles of London. The purse would be five hundred pounds (approximately $2,500) a side, which each side deposited with Harry Bull, a notorious gambler and hotelier better known as "Chippy" Norton. The drag-out negotiating session took nearly as long as the Kilrain-Smith epic and almost featured the same hand-to-hand fighting. Mitchell disputed every article, according to Sullivan, and insisted that he would only fight in a twenty-four-foot ring, not the smaller sixteen-foot enclosure that John L. preferred. Tired of Mitchell's chirping, Sullivan finally agreed to the larger ring, even though the additional real estate would provide his fleet opponent with a significant advantage. "You'll find even that too small to skulk in when the day comes," the champion warned. Mitchell, however, continued to taunt the American until Sullivan offered to knock him out on the spot. The Englishman just smiled as the sporting men hurried Sullivan away.

In the days before Christmas, Sullivan's combination toured through Glasgow, Dundee, and Edinburgh. In the new year, they appeared in Cardiff where William Samuels of Swansea, the Welsh champion, became the only challenger during Sullivan's tour of the British Isles to slug it out with the champ. John L. toyed with his opponent for two rounds before easily dispatching him in the third.

By the time Sullivan's tour closed in Portsmouth on January 10, 1888, he had appeared in fifty-one exhibitions and earned an impressive five thousand pounds. With the tour complete, John L. turned his attention to pounds of a different variety—those abbreviated "lb."—as he began to train for the title bout with Mitchell. Sullivan headquartered himself in Windsor, a town quite familiar to his pal, the Prince of Wales. The champion ran the roads in the shadows of Windsor Castle and took daily walks through her majesty's park. The *National Police Gazette* depicted Queen Victoria watching from her coach as the big fellow ran through the streets of Windsor, and the champ claimed the monarch peeked out the castle windows to watch him at work, but there's nothing to suggest the royal viewing actually occurred.

Amid rumors that Sullivan had another falling out with one of his managers, Phillips traveled to the European mainland to visit his horse stables, but Norton, Holske, Ashton, Barnett, Blakelock, and George McDonald remained with Sullivan to train. Sullivan had not been in top shape when he left Boston weighing over 225 pounds, and the hectic tour did not lend itself to a strict training regiment. By mid-February, Holske reported that Sullivan had slimmed to 210 pounds, and he hoped to be 196 in time for the fight.

Mitchell made his camp at a country home near London where he trained with Kilrain, who was worried about the sketchy characters in John L.'s entourage. "I think he is afraid to fight fair and has the gang to break [it] up," he wrote to a friend. Norton, who Kilrain called "the worst man in England," was a particular concern because he was suspected of breaking up a fight between Smith and Greenfield in 1886.

In late February, Mitchell won a coin flip and set March 10 as the date and France, as it had been for Kilrain and Smith, the location for the bout. Betting in London ran heavily to Sullivan as he departed the city a few days in advance of the clash. Like warriors had done for centuries of European history, Sullivan crossed the English Channel girding himself for a fight.

A bright, balmy morning dawned on Amiens, France, on March 10, and the entourages rose early and left by train to the secret fight location after breakfast. Mitchell, having shaken the seasickness from a rocky ride across the channel, laughed and bantered with his father-in-law and adviser, George Washington "Pony" Moore, a former circus and minstrel show performer. Sullivan, however, appeared quiet as he prepared for his first fight in more than a year and his first bare-knuckle bout since

1882. After departing the train at Creil, an eight-vehicle procession arrived at the chosen spot some thirty miles north of Paris on the estate of Baron Alphonse Rothschild near Chantilly. Apparently without the baron's knowledge, the ring was pitched a half-mile from his white Italian marble summer residence behind an empty barn sheltered from view by trees. The venue couldn't have been any more different from the scene of the contestants' first match, inside the grand athletic palace of Madison Square Garden before ten thousand fans. The crowd for this secretive, outdoor bare-fisted affair, by contrast, barely topped three dozen and included some of the world's worst criminals.

In Sullivan's corner, he had a one-time drinking companion, William O'Brien. Although he looked respectable in his stovepipe hat and elegant blue coat with velvet collar, O'Brien lived a double life in the underworld as the dangerous Billy Porter, "one of the most celebrated cracksmen and bank burglars in America." Porter had cut his teeth on pickpocketing and graduated to banks and jewelry stores. He had shot a criminal rival dead in a Manhattan saloon a few years back and was over in Europe "on business." With both hands in his overcoat pockets, Porter sauntered over to Moore and flashed the barrels of two revolvers along with a threat. "Tell the Manchester men in your corner not to take any chances on me," he growled as a warning against anyone interfering with the bout.

The champion entered the ring first, and Mitchell followed about five minutes later. The clean-shaven Sullivan, with his hair cropped to stubble, wore his colors—a square American flag adorned with an Irish golden harp, shamrocks, his initials, and an American eagle holding a scroll with the motto "May He Always Be Champion"—around his waist. Mitchell had won the toss for corners and selected the side with his back to the sun and the wind. John L. held up a five-hundred-pound note as a side bet, which the challenger declined. Phillips had returned to Sullivan's side, but serving as his seconds were Ashton and McDonald, whose father had assisted Heenan in the legendary fight with Sayers. Kilrain and the English boxer Jack Baldock seconded Mitchell, which made for strange bedfellows since Baldock had attempted to gouge Kilrain's eyes when he served as Smith's second ten weeks earlier. Charley Rowell served as the umpire for Mitchell, and Sullivan, in a last-minute switch, chose Barnett as his umpire rather than Holske, whom he still didn't trust. The decision left the advance man seething. George Angle, who worked at the London Stock Exchange, was selected as the referee.

Under ominous skies, the two men, stripped to the waist, toed the scratch and dug their spikes into the turf a little before 1 p.m. Sullivan weighed just over two hundred pounds, while Mitchell barely cracked 160. The champion had the distinct weight, height, and power advantage, but his challenger had one big edge enhanced by the twenty-four-foot ring: speed.

After some cautious, long sparring to open the first round, the champion connected with a heavy blow on Mitchell's left jaw. The challenger returned with a light body blow, and then Sullivan employed his usual style. He rushed Mitchell. And as during their first encounter in New York five years prior, a knockdown ended the first round. Unlike at the Garden bout, though, this time Mitchell hit the ground first after absorbing a heavy right hand to the head. In the second, John L. again pounced. He rushed Mitchell into a corner and rained heavy blows on his chest. After a brief escape, the challenger found himself cornered again and then down on the soggy grass after a right hand to his head.

Mitchell now realized it was futile to try to match Sullivan's style and outslug him. Beginning with the third round, he sought to stay away from Sullivan's big right long enough to wear down John L. The challenger began to walk and run around the ring with Sullivan following him. As the rounds progressed, so did the whirl of the Englishman's legs. Mitchell ended the fifth round by plunging to the turf to avoid John L.'s massive right, which earned him a caution from the referee. The challenger did manage to land periodic head shots, and Sullivan started to tire from running after him. The affair now drew a small group of curious locals, although the Frenchmen quickly expressed their Gallic disgust at the fisticuffs and agreed among themselves that it was an "idiotic exhibition."

After each round when Sullivan returned to his corner, Blakelock bent down on all fours and transfigured himself into the champion's stool. If being a human chair wasn't bad enough, Blakelock had bet all his savings that Sullivan would win in less than half an hour, and he grew increasingly concerned as the minutes ticked away. After the fight eclipsed thirty minutes, he was despondent, and although Brisbane wrote that "his heart was not in the work," he continued to crouch in the mud to give his man a breather.

In the seventh, as Sullivan launched a heavy right, Mitchell put up his left elbow. John L.'s upper arm struck his opponent's elbow hard. Sullivan's arm dropped to his side. The contorted look on his face signaled to his corner that something was wrong. He continued to press on through the pain as his arm swelled to twice its normal size, but his powerful right weakened.

With his lighter weight and the bigger ring, Mitchell began to move easily out of the way of Sullivan's rushes. The fight fell into a tedious pattern where Mitchell danced around the ring, threw a punch or two, and ultimately hit the grass to end the round to be carried back to his corner by Baldock and Kilrain. Sullivan, of course, was never one to shift strategies. He knew no other way of fighting, so there was no strategy to which he could switch. He grew increasingly frustrated, at one point reportedly snapping, "Fight like a gentleman, you son of a bitch, if you can." Mitchell wisely refused to engage Sullivan at close quarters, and John L. couldn't comprehend why. The affair started to resemble a pedestrian race more than a heavyweight bout as Mitchell beat a circular path resembling a sheep run around his opponent.

And then in the fourteenth round, the rains came. Sheets of water lashed the fighters' bare skin and further slickened the already greasy footing. Soon, the ring turned into a quagmire more suited to the animals in the nearby stables, and the pace of the fight mired as well. Between rounds, the rains blew toward Sullivan's corner and incessantly strafed the champion's face and body. By the twenty-second round, Sullivan's teeth started to chatter, and his skin turned blue. The champion, who had never fought so deep into a bout, breathed hard. Mitchell appeared to be getting stronger in comparison. The challenger ran his mouth as much as his legs, and his constant dialogue annoyed Sullivan to no end. In the twenty-fifth, Mitchell drew blood with a left to Sullivan's mouth, causing his lip to swell. With variable weather more suited to England, the rain stopped, and the sun suddenly cracked through the clouds in the twenty-sixth round.

When Mitchell flagged, Baldock ducked his head through the rope and delivered a verbal prop to his man: "Think of your wife, Charley! Think of your little babies at home crying." The missive re-energized Mitchell, and less than a minute later, he accidentally spiked Sullivan as his steel nails drove into John L.'s instep.

The rain returned in the thirtieth round. The mud had now become ankle-deep, and the fighters moved in suspended animation, as did the rounds. The thirty-first round took more than twenty minutes. The thirty-second lasted nearly a half-hour. The thirty-fourth round clocked in at fourteen minutes. With Sullivan's arm hurt, his fists battered, and his body convulsed by shivers, it became clear that he couldn't win. But could Mitchell? The challenger began to charge. He delivered a left on Sullivan's right eye in the twelve-minute thirty-fifth round. In the next round, he delivered walloping rights and stomach blows with only feeble rejoinders offered from the champion. The men wrestled each other to the mud. Mitchell's eye started to swell shut.

By the thirty-eighth round, the men were "out on their feet." Three times, the exhausted fighters agreed to break to the corners to clean the mud off their shoes. They leaned on the ropes just to keep their legs from buckling, and they stood in the middle of the ring just to catch their breaths. Darkness loomed as the thirty-four-minute round came to a close. The fight had turned into a filibuster.

With the gloaming nestling into the French countryside, the return of the showers, and the fight transformed into a stalemate, the minds of everyone present turned to a draw. But how that draw occurred would become the subject of great debate and controversy. Most initial accounts reported that Baldock suggested a draw after thirty-nine rounds and that Sullivan's corner accepted. However, the whispers soon grew louder in the following weeks and months that Phillips had flashed a wad of cash at Baldock to bribe him into accepting the draw.

However it transpired, three hours and eleven minutes after Sullivan and Mitchell toed the scratch, it was over. The draw elicited vastly differ-ent reactions from the fighters and their entourages. Sullivan appeared as glum as the weather, and Blakelock pounded his head in despair. A slight smile, however, cracked Holske's face. In the other corner, Moore threw his arms around Mitchell's neck and kissed him while Kilrain laughed and taunted Sullivan. The champion blamed the big ring, the weather, and his injury for the end result. "The most surprised man is Sullivan," Brisbane wrote, "and the next most astonished man is Mitchell." Once again, John L. left the ring with an unsatisfactory result against Mitchell, and the trip to France would soon become even more of a fiasco.

The spent gladiators, their entourages, and the spectators piled into their carriages and began the return trip to Creil. A mile up the road, however, a shadowy figure with a colorful cape flowing behind him galloped quickly in their direction. Suddenly, three mounted gendarmes with sabers drawn surrounded the procession and ordered the coachmen to stop. One of Porter's friends bolted for the woods but stopped when a policeman fired his pistol. Another gendarme pointed his gun at Baldock's head.

Through the pouring rain, ten officers escorted the coaches on an hour-long journey to the gendarmerie in the town of Senlis. It was quite a different procession from the joyous parades Sullivan had grown accustomed to in England. At the police station, the sergeant asked which of the men were the combatants. No one responded, but the answer was as clear as Mitchell's discolored left eye and Sullivan's swollen lip.

The gendarmes handcuffed the boxers and released everyone else after taking their names. The jailer took away the fighters' silk handkerchiefs "to prevent their hanging themselves"—though that was rather unlikely—and threw the men into a slimy cell so damp that water ran down the stone walls. Sullivan's sparse accommodations included a filthy plank bed with an army blanket nearly as saturated as the sodden turf on which they had fought. The surroundings did nothing for Sullivan's chills. He tried to appeal to his jailers, but as he recounted later, "they pelted me with parleyvoos I couldn't understand." Initially, Mitchell was just as frosty to Sullivan in their shared jail cell, but eventually, the Englishman took pity on his foe. As Sullivan's chills worsened, Mitchell convinced the gendarmes to provide them both with some brandy.

After their night in the French country jail, the men appeared before a magistrate and posted a bail equivalent to $1,600 to appear in court the following morning. That money now gone, so too were Sullivan and

Mitchell. After they enjoyed a champagne breakfast together with their entourages at the Hotel du Grand Cerf, they boarded a train to Paris and started back to London. In their absence, the French court sentenced the fighters to a fine of two hundred francs and six days' imprisonment. The experience strengthened Sullivan's vow to never fight with his bare fists again.

Meanwhile, back in Boston, Sullivan's fellow citizens once again congregated in front of the bulletin boards on Newspaper Row when they heard that the fight had begun. They expected the result to be a mere formality; betting in Boston was extremely light because few takers for Mitchell could be found. Then, the flash crossed the Atlantic with news of the draw. Disbelief and anger swept through the city. "Sullivan is drunk," said one fan. "It is a lie," added another. John L.'s brother, Michael, doubted the veracity of the report, as well. "No Charley Mitchell can have any show with our John." Hours later, however, the confirming cable arrived from Holske. Michael Sullivan knew who was to blame: Livingston. "She is playing him for a fool, and he has completely lost his head for her," he said. "Poor John! I am sorry for him. He has brought disgrace upon himself and upon his family." Hogarty told a reporter, "This is a cold day for us." Two days later, the weather truly grew frigid as the massive Blizzard of 1888 buried Boston and much of the East Coast along with news of Sullivan's defeat.

Fox, naturally, expressed his satisfaction when hearing about the draw. "It is just as I thought. Sullivan was overconfident and did not half train." Annie Sullivan also rejoiced at the news from Chantilly and only wished that "Mitchell had killed him." Sheedy could hardly hide his schadenfreude, telling a reporter, "Well, he was always kicking about playing second fiddle to me. Now he has been playing first fiddle and he's broken the fiddle."

Before returning home, Sullivan performed at two farewell benefits in Liverpool with Jem Mace. When Sullivan, who had shorn his famous handlebar mustache for the Mitchell fight, appeared, "the audience became uproarious." The crowd shouted that the clean-shaven man was an impostor and that they were being hoodwinked. Mace insisted to his countrymen that his opponent really was Sullivan, but they didn't believe it until John L. himself could finally be heard to offer the explanation for the removal of his whiskers.

Sullivan was viewed as a changed man in his hometown, too. Bostonians no longer saw him as invincible. Less than two weeks after the fight, the Washington Street vendors discounted the price of their cabinet-size photographs of Sullivan from fifty cents to five cents. Boston was selling its "Strong Boy" on the short.

—✦—

While a band played "When Johnny Comes Marching Home," Sullivan waved an American flag to hundreds of well-wishers as he departed Liverpool on April 12 with his championship belt back in tow. The voyage home was tempestuous, but it had nothing to do with the seas. The maelstrom of Sullivan and Livingston terrorized the fourteen hundred passengers aboard the *Catalonia*. The trouble all began in Liverpool when the ship officers refused to allow Sullivan's friends to board to say goodbye. Once the steamer set sail, John L. went on an ocean-bound spree. On one occasion, the steward fended off an attack by breaking a soda siphon bottle over the champion's head, and on another, the chief engineer threatened to turn a hot water hose on him. Sullivan struck a storekeeper in the back and bloodied a fellow passenger who accidentally stepped on his toes. One day, he passed out on deck, and the rocking waves caused him to roll under a lifeboat, which he struck with his head upon waking up. As he rampaged for liquor, stewards hid under tables with the lights off. His behavior was so out of control that the captain threatened to put him in irons.

Sullivan and Livingston drank and fought constantly. Throwing anything they could find at each other—even glasses and shoes—the ruckus from their room kept the passengers awake at all hours. Reverend William Manley, a missionary assigned the room next to the quarreling couple, must have wondered what he had done to anger God. Sullivan cursed the clergyman's wife and threatened to "swipe her damned brats out of existence" if she did not keep her four children out of his way. Most of Sullivan's entourage had returned weeks before, so it was left to poor Sylvie Gookin, a championship sculler from South Boston and a friend of the Sullivan family, to play the peacemaker and offer his constant apologies to his fellow passengers.

The press savaged Sullivan's loutish behavior and questioned his fans. "A greater disgrace to his native island and to his adopted city it would be hard to conceive of," thundered one New York newspaper. "We tell the Irishmen of America that they cannot expect to have the honor of our people so long as they honor, or fail to denounce, such men who are their shame and disgrace."

Sullivan had earned about $25,000 since he left Boston, but Mitchell's crafty strategy of eluding the "Strong Boy" rather than engaging in a slugfest exposed his vulnerabilities and offered a playbook for future opponents to employ. The draw raised questions about whether John L. had paid off his opponent to avoid defeat and whether he had lost his grasp on the heavyweight title. "It is impossible to understand how Sullivan can recover from the injury to his reputation," Brisbane wrote after the Mitchell fight. The *Boston Globe* declared his fighting days "finished." The *National Police Gazette* even depicted an angry Columbia, personifying the United States, casting the unworthy Sullivan away as she hands a banner to Kilrain to uphold the honor of the Stars and Stripes. (Never mind that both men returned to America with draws against English fighters.)

Sullivan's behavior on the voyage home renewed familiar concerns about the limits of his self-control, but also raised questions about the limits of his adulation by the American sporting public. The hits he received in the press were worse than any delivered by Mitchell, and soon, he would be locked in a fight for his life that made the draw in France pale in comparison.

CHAPTER SEVEN

The Epic Brawl

JOHN TAYLOR, *BOSTON GLOBE* SPORTING EDITOR, BOBBED UP AND DOWN as Boston Harbor undulated beneath his fish-scented dory. His swollen hands ached as he gripped the oars for another heave through the water. As daylight broke on April 24, 1888, Taylor tried to shake off the restless night he had spent on one of the rugged harbor islands with the blinking eye of Boston Light his only companion. He was full of shivers and yawns, but the enterprising Taylor would do anything for a scoop.

For two days, he had plied the harbor searching for any sign of the *Catalonia* and her famous passenger. All of Boston, which had finally recovered from the shocking result of the Charley Mitchell fight, had fixed its gaze eastward anticipating the return of its "Strong Boy" from his six-month trip abroad, and Taylor wanted to be the first to welcome him home.

Shortly after dawn, Taylor squinted through his eyeglass and spotted a twisted ribbon of black smoke cresting over the horizon. Soon, he saw the spars and smokestacks of the *Catalonia*. As Taylor rowed toward the mighty steamship, a familiar figure on the hurricane deck emerged from the sea spray. The unmistakable hulk of the "Big Fellow" appeared, although he looked a little heftier, a little more haggard, and a little grayer than when he left Boston six months ago.

Taylor's patience was rewarded with an exclusive. John L. griped that Mitchell had fouled him forty times, and he said the spike marks on his legs and feet would prove it. "I had to fight an Englishman, an English referee, and an English press, which never treated me squarely," he complained. Sullivan told Taylor he was glad to be back in his homeland, and he challenged Jake Kilrain to fight in a sixteen-foot ring for $10,000 a side.

Word of the ship's sighting raced through the saloons on Portland and Lagrange Streets where Boston's sporting men kept vigil. Hacks rushed Sullivan's fans to Commercial Wharf where their chartered tugboats, festooned with flags and bunting, awaited. Before everyone could arrive, however, Harry Phillips ordered the boats into the harbor. As Phillips's tug approached the steamer and whistled a greeting, the cheering passengers waved their hats and handkerchiefs. Before a ladder could be positioned, Sullivan climbed the rail of the steamer, leapt onto the tug, and embraced his father, Phillips, and old friends such as Mike Clarke and Billy Hogarty. The passengers aboard the *Catalonia,* no doubt happy to finally rid themselves of the boorish prizefighter, joined in the festivities. A brass band aboard the tug struck up "When Johnny Comes Marching Home" as they closed in on the busy waterfront.

Newsboys began to hawk the second edition of the *Globe* featuring Taylor's exclusive interview as the champ set foot on American soil. The joyous scene at the wharf, where two thousand people serenaded Sullivan with music and cheers, demonstrated that Bostonians still swelled with pride for the man they embraced as "Our John." There was no sign of Annie Sullivan, who had threatened to greet her husband and his mistress in a carriage donned by a banner declaring: THIS IS MRS. JOHN L. SULLIVAN NO. 1. THE OTHER CAN FOLLOW AFTER. Michael Sullivan looked in wonder at the open arms that Boston threw around his son, a reception he never encountered after his transatlantic voyage from Ireland decades ago. "I am glad to get back to Boston, for there is no place in the wide world like it," the younger Sullivan had told Taylor. "This is God's country."

The night after Sullivan's return, his friends hosted a grand banquet in his honor at the Quincy House. They lit cigars, dined on oysters and striped bass, and raised their champagne glasses to toast the long life of the champion, who continued to claim victory against Mitchell. "Any fair man who saw the match will say I won the fight forty times over," he told his true believers. Ed Holske, still smarting from Sullivan's last-minute snub at Chantilly, grit his teeth and proposed three cheers.

Within days, however, Holske turned Judas in a letter to the *Boston Herald.* Sullivan's advance man asserted that he indeed had bribed Jack Baldock to accept a draw in France. Holske claimed that he could tell by the tenth round that Sullivan could not win because of his "injured arm and the inclemency of the weather" and that a few rounds later he had sent a dispatch to Mitchell's corner offering the payout, "preferring that method to a disgraceful proceeding by breaking into the ring and 'gouging' the affair." Mitchell's second refused at first, but as Sullivan weakened, the price eventually climbed to an acceptable 250 pounds, which Holske claimed Phillips helped to bankroll.

Sullivan's manager initially denied the report, but years later admitted that he had indeed bribed Baldock, but without the champion's knowledge. Sullivan, always suspicious of that "dirty backcapper" Holske, fumed. "I did not expect anything different from Holske," he told a reporter. "Anything he says is not worth answering."

Sullivan's enemies, Richard K. Fox in particular, reveled in the story. Although the *National Police Gazette* claimed that not even Sullivan's worst enemy would "accuse John L. of cowardice," that's exactly what it did. While acknowledging there was an "absence of any substantiating evidence," Fox's pink paper asserted that Sullivan "never manifested the courage or back bone of a fighter" and showed his "true colors" by selling out.

Two weeks after appearing at a benefit for Joe Lannan, the champion returned to the ring at Boston's Music Hall during a welcome-home "monster testimonial" that included Lannan, Steve Taylor, Pete McCoy, and Ike Weir, the "Belfast Spider." Fans could view Sullivan's colors and fighting shoes from the Mitchell fight, and "Boston's fistic pride" promised to spar with Ashton in the same costumes they wore in front of the Prince of Wales.

Bizarre drama, both on stage and off, overtook the entire evening. Backstage, Sullivan and Phillips fought over the receipts, estimated at $3,000. Sullivan's manager claimed the fighter owed him money from the European trip—including the cash Phillips used to bribe Baldock according to some reports—so he attached the proceeds from the full house to cover the debts.

Then, once the testimonial started, the veteran black fighter George Godfrey was unexpectedly summoned from the audience. As "Old Chocolate" walked to the stage to great applause, the master of ceremonies said, "I have been authorized to offer you a money consideration to spar John L. Sullivan a friendly bout this evening." The champion, who had never fought a black man, may have been the most surprised man in the house. While John L. said he would be happy to spar with the black man, and any man for that matter, he then found a way to change the subject at hand with a stunning announcement. Sullivan fingered Phillips as the man responsible for summoning Godfrey to the stage and then told the audience that he and his manager "are done and have quit." Even to an audience used to Sullivan's constant managerial changes, this public breakup was a first.

With thoughts of a bout with Godfrey now overshadowed, the black fighter returned to his seat, and Sullivan finished the night sparring with Lannan and Ashton. "This benefit is not for me, but for Phillips," Sullivan told a reporter afterward. "I don't get a cent of the receipts."

New Yorkers also arranged a testimonial benefit for John L., but the June 6 event at the Brooklyn Academy of Music turned into a "disastrous fiasco." The audience was thin, and Sullivan was fat. The champion puffed so hard in his three-round exhibition with Mike Donovan that the rounds had to be shortened to one minute. Even with that concession, Donovan did most of the work and all the leading. SULLIVAN'S GLORY IS GONE, declared the *New York World*.

Sullivan's ring career had stalled. The press began to view him as a has-been and no longer above the boards given the controversial aftermath of the Mitchell fight. Sullivan was rudderless, and his interest in fighting waned so much that he soon entered a ring of an entirely different kind.

In the spring of 1888, Sullivan decided to follow in the footsteps of another showman, P. T. Barnum, when he purchased a one-third interest in the John B. Doris Circus. That summer, John L. toured with acrobats, clowns, jugglers, and performing dogs, and he and Ashton sparred at each performance. John L. even demonstrated his versatility as a performer by bringing a white stallion into the ring and leading it through a series of show tricks he had taught the horse.

From the start, though, the circus struggled financially to pay its performers and even buy bran for its steeds. Sullivan hoped a hometown stop and his debut as a ringmaster would revive its fortune. In mid-July, the circus pitched its big top on the corner of Dover Street and Harrison Avenue in Boston's South End, just blocks from Sullivan's birthplace. The opening day and night were a smash, drawing three thousand people. A Boston newspaper even proudly reported that John L. was "perfectly sober." The magic quickly waned, however, and soon the performances averaged crowds of just fifty. Sullivan imbibed heavily at his old neighborhood joints and mustered only lackluster performances against Ashton, even drawing hisses from his hometown fans. By the end of July, the circus had folded up its tent.

The financial collapse of the circus simply freed up more time for Sullivan to drink. On August 11 with Hogarty at his side, Sullivan was arrested for drunk driving after recklessly charging his horses around the neighborhood of Brighton and smashing into another coach. Sullivan pleaded guilty, paid a five-dollar fine, and then boozed the rest of the summer at Nantasket Beach.

Newspapers reported John L. was in training with Ike Weir for a possible match with Kilrain, but the only thing the champion was taking seriously was his partying. He indulged in cigars and steaks. His drinking ballooned his weight to 230 pounds. And he managed to get himself grazed by a bullet.

Likely aided by alcohol, Sullivan agreed to hold a quarter between his thumb and forefinger to test the marksmanship of Dan Murphy, proprietor of the Clarendon House. Murphy walked ten paces, fired, and missed. The bullet tore off flesh from Sullivan's thumb and finger, but he was lucky it wasn't any more serious. TWO IDIOTS, screamed one newspaper headline, which was particularly appropriate given that Murphy had shot Weir's fingers the week before attempting the same stunt.

Sullivan's constant inebriation also broke up his affair with Annie Livingston. She begged him to cut back, but the champion told her to go to hell. Livingston decided to resume her stage career, and she turned to Phillips to arrange a variety company with her as the star. For seventy-five dollars a week, Livingston would be billed as "Mrs. John L. Sullivan."

In September, Sullivan moved his base camp for seaside debauchery to a cottage north of Boston at Crescent Beach in Revere. There, the drinking finally took its toll, and serious illness struck John L. In his autobiography, Sullivan ticked off his litany of symptoms: "typhoid fever, gastric fever, inflammation of the bowels, heart trouble, and liver complaint all combined." Rumors spread that his sickness came as a result of injuries from the Mitchell fight in March or from swimming in unsanitary water at Nantasket, and John L. even fingered the filthy conditions of the circus. The true cause, however, was as clear as a bottle of gin. The ocean of alcohol that had coursed through Sullivan's body for years finally shut it down.

Sullivan's temperature skyrocketed. The coating of his stomach nearly disintegrated, and he could barely eat. His weight plummeted. Breathless bulletins flashed from Sullivan's sick chamber to Boston every few hours with his latest condition. The city's mood rose and fell in direct correlation to the degrees on his thermometer. On September 19, rumors of Sullivan's death even circulated through the Hub, which led the *New York Times* to declare in a headline: SULLIVAN NOT DEAD. Reporters rushed to the cottage to see for themselves that the champion had not expired.

The illness brought Livingston back to Sullivan's side and cancelled her theatrical plans. Her anger melted away as she nursed him back to health. When John L. reluctantly confessed to a visiting priest that Annie was his mistress, the clergyman exhorted him to cast her away, but Sullivan would not listen, even at the risk of eternal perdition. "Annie Livingston has been a true friend to me in time of trouble," he told the clergyman. "She has stuck to me when others who were nearer gave me the cold shoulder. She has nursed me kindly for the last three weeks, and I don't propose to go back on her now."

Sullivan disposed of his doctors at the same frequency as his managers, but the fifth one finally stuck. His weight plummeted to 160 pounds, but he slowly began to recover and managed to keep down milk, soda, and beef extract along with his medicine. The champion's thirtieth birthday approached, and he was determined to spend it at his family home on Parnell Street. The doctor warned that moving locations would be "suicide," but Sullivan told the doctor that if he had to die, it would be there and not at some seaside cottage. Propped up in a carriage, John L.

returned to Boston and continued to convalesce. He spent nine weeks in bed, and incipient paralysis kept him on crutches another six.

Friends feared that John L. would never be the same again after the ordeal, and the champion said he was indeed a changed man. A shaken Sullivan had contemplated his mortality as he laid in bed for weeks, listening to the breaking waves mark the seconds of his existence. "I have made up my mind that in thirty years of life I have had about fun enough," he told a reporter. John L. believed he had been given a second chance on life and vowed that he would experience it completely sober. "Not even the most seductive beverage concocted by the god Bacchus will ever tempt me to break my resolution never to drink again," he pledged.

Even with John L. lying on a sickbed, Fox, like a fighter seeing blood, kept up his unrelenting crusade to smash the champion's dynastic dominance. Kilrain had returned to America in "splendid physical condition," and the *National Police Gazette* publisher, seeing how Mitchell had browbeaten an unprepared Sullivan into the ring in Europe, was determined to bait the weakened champion into a fight with Kilrain. He asserted that it was time for "John L. to put up or shut up."

The clamor for a fight grew, and on December 7, Sullivan penned his answer on the letterhead of the *New York Illustrated News*. He challenged Kilrain to a title fight under the London Prize Ring Rules and, making no mistake as to how he viewed himself, signed it "John L. Sullivan, Champion of the World." A month later, on January 7, 1889, with worries about interference by American authorities, Sullivan and Jack Barnett slipped across the Canadian border and traveled to Toronto to sign the articles of agreement with Kilrain's representatives. The two men agreed to fight for the largest purse ever offered, $10,000 a side, along with the *Police Gazette* belt and the title of champion of the world on July 8, 1889, within two hundred miles of New Orleans. In spite of his repeated pledges not to fight with naked fists again, Sullivan agreed to return to the ring and leave his gloves behind.

Sullivan, who had only weeks before regained enough strength to walk without crutches, had only six months to regain his fighting trim. However, he showed little concern for the enormous task that awaited. Even after Sullivan's terrible sickness and his vow of sobriety, the bottle lured him back, and the epic benders reappeared as soon as he returned to Boston.

The champion's friends and Livingston pleaded with John L. to control himself, but to no avail. The press reported in January that Livingston even blackened his eye with a right-hand punch after he refused to leave a Harrison Avenue saloon. The man charged with his training, Jack Hayes, hardly laid down the law. The training regimen developed by Hayes included some bag punching, a daily twelve-mile walk around Boston, a rubdown at Sylvie Gookin's house, and a three-hour nap followed by stops at the South End saloons owned by Tom Hagerty and Mike Clarke.

After seven weeks of lushing through Boston saloons, in March Sullivan took his drinking to New York City. One night on a rampage through the bars on Sixth Avenue, the surly Sullivan even found himself in the crosshairs of Jere Dunn, the gangster who had slain Jimmy Elliott, before his friends rushed him out the doors and eventually onto a train to Connecticut where for days he continued his "lively drunk" in Bridgeport and New Haven.

Sullivan's lackadaisical training spooked his financial backers— Charley Johnston of Brooklyn, Jimmy Wakely of New York, and *New York Illustrated News* proprietor Frederick Willetts. The champion's backers summoned John L. to the *New York Illustrated News* offices and chided his behavior. Sullivan, however, said the reports of his dissipation were overblown. "I'm no saint, but I'm not half as bad as I'm painted," he said. While John L. was correct that the media could overstate his drinking, his waistline was testimony to his habit.

Sullivan was forty pounds overweight, still recovering from a serious illness, and more than two years removed from his last victory, over Paddy Ryan in San Francisco. John L. only had vague plans to start his real training. Unless an iron hand could be found to guide Sullivan, his championship reign teetered on the edge.

⚫⚫⚫

Johnston, Wakely, and Willetts required someone familiar with Sullivan, someone who couldn't be physically intimidated by the champion, and someone not awed by his fame. The conditions severely narrowed their pool of potential trainers. When middleweight champion "Nonpareil"

Jack Dempsey proved unavailable, Sullivan's backers found their man in reigning Greco-Roman wrestling champion William Muldoon.

The "Iron Duke of Wrestling" had known John L. since his earliest days in the ring, and the pair toured together as living statuary performers with Lester and Allen Minstrels in 1885. The two athletes shared a mutual antipathy for Fox and had led parallel careers. Muldoon received his launch on the stage of Harry Hill's a few years prior to Sullivan's, and like John L., he had ruled his sport for nearly a decade. Muldoon was a famous sportsman in his own right—his image graced tobacco cards and he drew large audiences on exhibition tours—but like all other athletes of the 1880s, his star paled in comparison to Sullivan's supernova.

The challenge of putting America's most fearsome fighting machine back in working order intrigued Muldoon, a health fanatic and Muscular Christianity disciple. He knew that the publicity generated from restoring the superstar's luster could springboard his next career as a training and physical fitness guru. With the fight little more than two months away, Muldoon had scant time to get the out-of-shape brawler into fighting trim, but he had such faith in his training program that he accepted the task with no up-front money. The wrestler would only receive his fee—a sizable chunk of the $20,000 purse—if John L. won the fight. Muldoon may have had supreme belief in his methods, but success ultimately depended on a true wildcard: Sullivan's discipline.

Muldoon possessed the perfect training ground to sequester a fighter easily tempted by the vices of city life—his home and seventy-acre family farm in the small western New York village of Belfast. The hamlet sixty-five miles southwest of Buffalo started as a lumber town, but it morphed into farm country once the timber had been harvested. The town boomed in the years following the Great Hunger when large numbers of Irish immigrants arrived to hand-cut the Genesee Valley Canal, which opened between Rochester and Belfast in the 1850s and eventually linked the Allegheny River with the Erie Canal. The farming village had been a major stop on the Underground Railroad, but once the canal closed in 1878, its population shrank.

Like Sullivan, Belfast's heyday appeared to have passed by the time the champion arrived with Muldoon on May 11, 1889. When John L. stepped off the train, he entered a pastoral paradise. He breathed in the fresh air and listened to the rushing waters of the Genesee River that bisected the rolling hills. A coach carried the champion down the main drag, which sported only a couple of saloons, and pulled up on a dirt road in front of Muldoon's spotless-white, two-story frame house, which he called the "Champion Rest," surrounded by verandahs and shaded by towering trees. The refined interior included vases of freshly cut roses, Muldoon's pet parrots, and lace curtains that dimmed the sunlight. The neighbors— St. Patrick's Church and two cemeteries—were certainly quiet.

A pastoral paradise it may have been, but to the city boy from Boston, bucolic Belfast was the dreariest place on Earth. "I wouldn't live here if they gave me the whole country," Sullivan muttered. Belfast had once been called Podunk, and John L. thought the moniker still applied. His isolation eased, however, with the arrival of his brother, Michael, Jack Barnett, and Mike Cleary, an experienced middleweight who would serve as the champion's sparring partner.

Muldoon and Sullivan, both sons of Irish immigrants, shared power-ful personalities in addition to their builds. The "Iron Duke" possessed an iron will; in an 1881 match with Clarence Whistler, he lasted for seven hours before the match ended in a draw. As with John L., braggado-cio coursed through the veins of Muldoon, who claimed to have fought in the Civil War although no records of service can be found and the 1852 birthday recorded in the family Bible means he would have been too young to enlist.

In spite of their similarities, however, the two men had vastly differ-ent world views. John L. still retained the working-class ethos from his urban upbringing, but Muldoon exuded a patrician air in spite of having grown up on a farm. The "Solid Man" also viewed his body as a temple and eschewed alcohol and tobacco, while his pugilistic counterpart gloriously indulged his hedonistic urges. The biggest sticking point between the two men, though, was simply control. John L. loathed training and hated to be managed, and Muldoon was a stern taskmaster.

Inevitably, the pair clashed early and often. Like a petulant child with a new babysitter, Sullivan tried to test his trainer's authority. "During my training with Muldoon we had a little misunderstanding, but after a day we were led to bury the hatchet," John L. wrote in his autobiography. The champion's brief account apparently understated the lasting tension between the two men. At least once a week, Barnett urged Johnston or Arthur Lumley, who founded the *New York Illustrated News* in 1888 and assisted with the champion's management, to come to Belfast at once because of the animosity between Sullivan and Muldoon. Barnett and Cleary, who had a particular knack of getting John L. to laugh, constantly played peacemakers between the two egos.

Sullivan told the press he intended to take "a bit of rest" upon his arrival in Belfast. Muldoon had other ideas. He imposed a strict fitness regime not only to shed Sullivan's fat but also to build back his muscle. The denizens of the farm assisted their master in keeping Sullivan on task. Muldoon's cows and canaries stirred loudly every day at 5 a.m., which ensured that Sullivan arose at daybreak. After the champion took a brief walk, he received a rubdown with a mixture of ammonia, camphor, and alcohol and ate a breakfast of oatmeal. Then John L., even on the warmest of summer days, put on a heavy knit sweater, a suit of heavy corduroy, and a pair of gloves to alternate between running and walking over twelve miles of dusty roads that ribboned over the hills of nearby Black Creek, Angelica, and Caneadea.

After a lunch of meat and bread, the champion entered the makeshift training quarters that Muldoon had fashioned inside his pair of whitewashed barns. In the stall next to his prized horses, Muldoon had suspended from one of the barn beams a huge sandbag for punching. A large white wrestling mat blanketed the creaky wooden floor of an upstairs room in which a collection of dumbbells and Indian clubs stood in the corner and a chest expander was mounted on the wall. While Sullivan sparred, jumped rope, and tossed a football stuffed with twelve pounds of hair, Muldoon's rigorous regimen included chores foreign to a city boy— chopping wood, milking cows, and plowing fields. For supper, the champion dined on cold meat and stale bread and was permitted the occasional glass of ale.

"Muldoon may know how to train a wrestler," Sullivan grumbled after his first few days in Belfast, "but he doesn't know much about training a fighter." His trainer's wrestling expertise, however, was extremely valuable for a prizefighter preparing for a bout under the London Prize Ring Rules. The men spent hours on the grappling mat as Muldoon trained Sullivan in many of the wrestling holds and tricks that would be legal in the fight with Kilrain.

The trainer tried to sweat the alcohol out of his pupil and keep him so busy that he wouldn't have time—or energy—to drink and carouse. Not that Sullivan reportedly didn't try. *Cincinnati Commercial Gazette* sports editor Ban Johnson, future founder of baseball's American League and one of the few newsmen permitted inside the camp, reported tagging along while a drunken Sullivan rampaged through the village, knocking on the doors of darkened houses searching for tumblers of gin.

Still, stories of Sullivan's drinking in Belfast have clearly been overblown. The tales of John L. dismantling a bar and throwing it onto Main Street after being denied a drink as well as Muldoon wrestling him into submission and chaining him like an animal inside a training barn to dry him out are almost certainly folklore. But while Muldoon may not have physically humbled Sullivan in the privacy of his barns in Belfast, he did so in full public view.

———

Just two weeks after John L. arrived in Belfast, Muldoon took his fighter on a weeklong exhibition tour in which Sullivan not only sparred three rounds with Cleary but wrestled his trainer. The combination opened in Detroit and then traveled to Cincinnati, Philadelphia, and New York. John L. held his own on the mat. Sullivan and Muldoon grappled for nearly half an hour in Cincinnati on May 28, but their Decoration Day matinee two days later at a baseball stadium outside of Philadelphia was a titanic battle between the two alpha males.

Sullivan took the first round in two minutes by forcing Muldoon's shoulders to the ground. In the second round, the "wrestling gladiator" dropped the "pugilistic gladiator" in three minutes. After the men exchanged handshakes before the tie-breaking round, Muldoon grabbed the winded Sullivan's head and shook it violently. John L., his face and ears bright red, broke loose, tripped Muldoon, and threw him on his side. The "Solid Man" then lifted the "Boston Strong Boy" from his feet and threw him forcefully on his back. "The fall seemed heavy enough to shake the earth," reported one newspaper. The teacher had schooled the student, and the pupil was none too happy. Sullivan cocked his arm to punch Muldoon, but before he could swing, some of the two thousand fans flooded the ring and mobbed the two gladiators.

Shortly thereafter, a natural deluge—one that resulted in the disastrous Johnstown Flood on May 31—washed out railroad bridges in upstate New York and slowed the combination's return to the training ground, which cost them several valuable days. Once back, John L. became woven into the fabric of Belfast, and the villagers abandoned their initial misgivings of becoming a magnet for "roughs, toughs, and plug uglies." Townspeople began to tag along on the champion's roadwork, and local boys found work as Muldoon's messengers and errand-runners. The men in the training camp amused themselves by offering the boys small purses for boxing and wrestling bouts. In mid-June, Sullivan and Cleary even gave a lively sparring exhibition to raise $126.90 for the local fire department.

Muldoon, however, had no patience for his curious neighbors who rapped on the door of Champion Rest asking to see the champ. He turned them away with a curt reminder that he did not run a hotel nor a roadhouse. The trainer barred most visitors, even Livingston, from the camp, but he couldn't turn away one of the most famous women in the United States when she came knocking.

Like Sullivan, Elizabeth Cochrane was an American pioneer and celebrity. Known to the public by her pen name, Nellie Bly, the young reporter had started her journalism career writing about fashion, flowers, and art for the *Pittsburgh Dispatch,* but she chafed at being pigeonholed to write what were perceived as female-interest stories. Bly quickly became a journalistic sensation in October 1887 by feigning insanity to expose conditions inside the mental asylum on New York City's Blackwell's Island (now Roosevelt Island) for Joseph Pulitzer's *New York World.* She found her voice by going undercover to probe everything from police misconduct to the baby-buying trade. Now one of America's premier investigative journalists journeyed to Belfast to plumb the mind of its biggest sports superstar.

The champion had never been interviewed by a woman before, and he behaved more like a bashful schoolboy than a growling prizefighter. In her blunt, yet soft way, Bly asked John L. about everything from his bathing habits to his earnings. Even Sullivan's biggest fans learned that he always dreamt of running a hotel in New York and never took a cold bath because "it chills the blood." The journalist wasn't afraid to use her femininity to charm her subject, such as unsuccessfully trying to wrap both her hands around his biceps. As Bly left, Sullivan confessed, "I have given you more than I ever gave any reporter in my life."

The dispatch of Bly to upstate New York reflected the intense journalistic interest in the coming fight, which was building to a crescendo. The *National Police Gazette* and the upstart *New York Illustrated News*, in particular, used Sullivan and Kilrain as proxies in their ink-stained battle. Arthur Lumley had founded the *New York Illustrated News* after working for Fox for the better part of a decade, and the newspaper not only backed Sullivan financially, it employed Fox's nemesis in a literary role as a "sporting editor."

The *New York Illustrated News* offered its readers copies of Sullivan's colors, which featured a portrait of the muscular, mustachioed fighter with his arms crossed with an American flag, a sprig of shamrock, and an Irish golden harp. The *National Police Gazette* produced the colors for Kilrain that featured his bare-chested portrait along with the shields and flags of the United States and Ireland.

Fox portrayed the coming battle as a morality play between the alcoholic, wife-beating brute and the devoted family man, a humble fighter who led a clean life and possessed an even cleaner liver. Fox's newspaper printed illustrations of Kilrain petting dogs and lacing up gloves with his young daughter for some playful sparring. The *National Police Gazette* even informed its readers that Kilrain had established bank accounts for his children and taken out life insurance for his wife in case he should be injured or killed during the fight.

Kilrain earned more public goodwill when he sparred with Mitchell at a June 13 Madison Square Garden benefit for the Johnstown Flood victims. The crowd had hoped to see Sullivan as well, but the champion's former manager Pat Sheedy, who acted as master of ceremonies, read a telegram stating that the backers of John L. did not want him leaving his training quarters. The announcement drew a chorus of hisses, and the public relations fallout increased in the following days as newspapers reported that Sullivan had fought with Muldoon, dispatched a bartender from his post at a Belfast hotel, and helped himself to the liquor.

Still, public opinion remained in the champion's corner. Dynastic reigns in sports, particularly ones as long as Sullivan's, are by nature polarizing. They inspire both admiration and loathing among fans. However, there is nothing sports fans love to see more than for a king to topple from his throne and then claw his way back on top. John L. had now become an underdog figure, an object of sympathy trying to overcome age, sickness, doubters, and foibles.

The eager public finally saw the results of Sullivan's seven weeks of hard work when he departed Belfast on July 1 to venture south. When Johnston joined the entourage outside Rochester, he immediately grabbed the fighter's midsection to feel how much fat remained and was pleased with the state of his investment. "I was never in better health in my life," the champion later told a reporter in Cincinnati. "My appetite is excellent, my wind good, and I feel as strong, if not stronger, than I ever did in my life." John L. even boasted of skipping rope more than a thousand times in a row without a miss as proof of his stamina.

The journey to New Orleans very much echoed the one Sullivan had experienced seven years ago prior to capturing the heavyweight championship. Well-wishers awaited him at station after station. The reception was very familiar, but so was the looming threat that awaited him down south.

Robert Lowry vowed not to be ignored again. The Mississippi governor still smarted from his impotence in preventing the bare-knuckle fight between Sullivan and Paddy Ryan in Mississippi City in 1882. Now in the summer of 1889, rumors flew that for a second time John L. would raise his naked fists in his jurisdiction, and Lowry once again decreed that the bout would not occur on his soil. This time, however, Lowry no longer had to rely solely on the moral outrage of his citizens. He had the force of law behind him.

In the weeks following the Sullivan-Ryan championship fight, Mississippi had enacted a law banning prizefighting. Combatants now faced fines of up to $1,000 and prison time of up to one year. By 1889, all thirty-eight states in the Union had outlawed the sport.

On July 2, Lowry issued a proclamation calling on his lawmen to prevent the prizefight and offering a $250 bounty per head for the apprehension of two pugilists. The governors of Louisiana, Texas, Arkansas, Alabama, and even Nebraska joined Lowry in pledging to enforce the laws of their states and prevent the fight.

Out of necessity, the fight's promoters, New Orleans sporting men Bud Renaud and Pat Duffy, kept tight-lipped about the bout's secret location. When the promoters heard that Lowry ordered the sheriff in Meridian, Mississippi, to arrest the champion and his party when the train stopped there en route to New Orleans, they stopped Sullivan's train in Alabama before it crossed the state line and placed John L. aboard a special engine and coach that sped straight through Mississippi without stopping.

Sullivan arrived safely in New Orleans on the Fourth of July. The Crescent City always reveled in the sordid and the unseemly, and the illicit aura surrounding the prizefight only heightened the excitement for it. John L. lodged at Mrs. Green's private boardinghouse on Rampart Street and worked out at the Young Men's Gymnastic Club (now the New Orleans Athletic Club, where a plaster cast of Sullivan's right arm still hangs on the wall).

Muldoon took extraordinary measures to ensure Sullivan remained in top form during his few days in New Orleans. The trainer personally prepared meals to prevent tampering and even brought hermetically sealed caskets of well water from his Belfast farm to prevent sickness. He posted a guard outside the boardinghouse to protect Sullivan's privacy, prevent any foul play by gamblers, and deny any delivery of liquor to his fighter.

The added protection also turned out to be necessary to fend off the numerous female admirers who schemed to have "personal interviews" with the champion. One young woman offered Johnston $500 if she could spend an hour with Sullivan, and a nineteen-year-old girl bribed the fighter's regular cook to take her place until Muldoon discovered the ruse. The trainer's thwarting of the women of New Orleans was just as well since, as one newspaper informed its readers, "John himself preferred to postpone lovemaking until after the fight."

Two days after Sullivan's arrival, Kilrain stepped off the train from Baltimore to a loud ovation. Among those greeting the fighter was a "short, chunky man," the famed Dodge City gunslinger William Barclay "Bat" Masterson. The Wild West icon of the penny press not only had twenty-two men "in his book of lives," he was a noted member of the boxing fancy. Masterson's old acquaintance "Pony" Moore, Mitchell's father-in-law, had summoned him to serve as Kilrain's bodyguard. Crowds lined Royal Street as the challenger rode to his quarters at the Southern Athletic Club.

Fox's deep pockets brought Mike Donovan into the Kilrain camp, and he accompanied the challenger to New Orleans. The fight veteran immediately noticed that the domineering Mitchell "ordered Kilrain around like a lackey." The Southern Athletic Club members noted the fighter's submissive behavior as well and wondered whether such a passive personality in such an aggressive line of work had the fortitude to stand tall against the champion. The sporting men and reporters who congregated inside the lobby at the St. Charles Hotel chattered that Kilrain appeared ill at ease, and the betting momentum moved in Sullivan's direction.

As the fight day of July 8 approached, Governor Lowry maneuvered his militia like a military general seeking to repel the invasion of enemy forces. Mississippi's chief executive stationed his troops—including the Jefferson Davis Rifles, the Vicksburg Rifles, the Scranton Guards, and the Bay St. Louis Rifles—along the major rail lines leading into the state from Louisiana. He ordered the soldiers to do anything, short of tearing up the tracks, to prevent the passage of the trains bearing the fighters and spectators.

On the afternoon of July 7, the fighters and their attendants received a wild sendoff at the Queen and Crescent Yards. Sullivan already wore his game face. His piercing eyes shot a contemptuous look at Donovan, who was so amazed at the champion's conditioning that all thoughts of a Kilrain victory vanished from his mind.

As John L. and the challenger boarded two separate passenger cars, which were linked by a baggage car that could be used for exercise en route, their final destination remained unknown. Renaud pledged to his friend the Louisiana attorney general that his state would not be the location.

But if the fight was not to come off in Louisiana, then where? Within hours the mystery would be solved.

———

Hours after leaving New Orleans, the train bearing the fistic cargo halted among the tall pines three miles from Hattiesburg, Mississippi. Sullivan and Kilrain disembarked in the unincorporated lumber town of Richburg, a hamlet of nine hundred people that consisted chiefly of a sawmill, a school, a church, and a general store that carried everything from diaper pins to caskets. As secret locations go, this one was barely on the map.

The village bore the name of its founder and still chief citizen, Col. Charles W. Rich. The lumber baron, sporting man, and future mayor of Hattiesburg had offered the fight promoters the use of his thirty thousand acres of pine forest. A few dozen laborers hastily cleared the soaring pines that surrounded a level spot previously used as a baseball diamond on a small hilltop. They constructed an outdoor arena with tiers of bleachers on three sides of the ring, which consisted of eight towering posts and two manila ropes. The workers stripped nearby pines of their lower limbs and built a picket fence to prevent freeloaders from viewing the fight.

They labored into the night by the flicker of pine torchlights, which bathed Rich's house in an orange glow. Inside, Kilrain, plagued by mosquitoes and nerves, spent a restless night. Two hundred yards away, the champion slept soundly inside the home of Rich's foreman, J. W. Smith.

One hundred miles southwest in New Orleans, thousands of fight fans spent the early morning of Monday, July 8, in the dark, literally and figuratively, as they waited to board trains to the mystery location. Fans paid handsomely for their tickets—general admission seats cost ten dollars, and ringside seats ran fifteen dollars. Scalpers stalking New Orleans received as much as forty dollars for the ducats.

A swarm of dark suits and bowler hats descended upon the first of two trains to the fighting ground, which was due to leave at 1 a.m. Hot, sweaty passengers stuffed the seats and aisles inside the twelve coaches, while freeloaders clung to the roof, sides, and even axles of the train cars like barnacles. The small band of off-duty policemen hired by the fight promoters to handle security was vastly outnumbered. Their efforts to extricate the hundreds of stowaways were fruitless, and amid fears that passengers might fall off their precarious perches, the train crawled out of New Orleans an hour behind schedule.

The promoters, however, were not about to watch their coffers sucked dry by the human leeches stuck to the train. Twice they ordered the train to stop, and security guards fired their six-shooters over the heads of the scroungers as passengers inside dropped to the floor at the sounds of the shots. Even the gunfire failed to shoo the entire flock of deadbeats.

Fiery embers, choking soot, and swarms of bugs pelted the exterior riders as they lurched across the steaming bayous. As the train crossed the Mississippi border near Nicholson, they spotted the militiamen's flickering campfires. A troop of twenty-five guardsmen waved signal lights and ordered the train to stop. Much like prizefighting fans had been doing for decades, however, the conductor simply ignored the law and chugged his iron horse encrusted with outlaws down the tracks, scattering the lawmen in his wake. The momentum for a Sullivan-Kilrain fight had grown steadily for two years and was now simply unstoppable.

A few hours after the dawn, the first train finally arrived in Richburg. Within the hour, the second fourteen-coach special chugged into view. Fans who had journeyed the entire way on top of the train emerged covered head to toe in the grimy soot that had been belched by the engine.

The fans, some carrying campstools under their arms, bolted from the idling train and sprinted the half-mile uphill to the battleground to join the locals who had already arrived by foot and horseback. When they arrived at the ring, they found a local attempting to extract another two dollars for entrance to the makeshift arena. The fans, who had understood that they had purchased combination tickets, rose as one, easily swallowed up the ticket taker, and breached the exterior picket fence. In short order, the bleachers bore the weight of about two thousand fans. Another seven hundred watched from standing-room-only areas.

Sullivan awoke fresh after a good night's sleep and ate breakfast around 9 a.m. About an hour later, he stepped out the cottage door and tried to catch his breath in the suffocating heat. This was Richburg's day in the sun—literally. Even at this early hour, the temperature already edged toward triple digits. In spite of the swelter, Sullivan wrapped himself in a Turkish bath rug fashioned into a coat for the short buggy ride to the ring.

A few minutes before 10 a.m., John L. pushed his way forward toward the ring as the crowd parted. He heard a great yell rise from the crowd and knew at that moment that Kilrain had climbed inside the ropes with his seconds, Mitchell and Donovan. Trailing about one hundred yards behind, John L. soon heard the fans chanting, "Sullivan! Sullivan!" He looked up to see the excited fans exchanging bets. When he reached the ropes, the champion sailed his hat into the ring and entered with his old swagger along with his seconds, Muldoon and Cleary. He took an American flag attached to a stake from Cleary's hand and dipped it three times to the tumultuous approval of the fans. John L. leaned back in his chair, stretched his arms over the ropes, and fixed his glare of disdain upon the challenger.

Back in the Mississippi capital, Governor Lowry received reports that Sullivan had once again successfully infringed upon his territory to stage a prizefight. He ordered the Marion County sheriff, W. J. Cowart, to stop the fight. The diminutive lawman barely cracked the five-foot mark, and he looked even smaller underneath his large sheriff's hat as he stepped into the ring with two huge revolvers stuck into his belt and a deer gun strapped to his back for good measure.

The human arsenal of a sheriff was severely outgunned. The crowd, in the spirit of ensuring "fair play," packed as much heat as the Mississippi sun. Nearly every hip pocket held a revolver. Masterson, who served as Kilrain's timer, naturally had a weapon, and even Mitchell toted two pistols.

The sheriff lifted his hand for order, sputtered an introduction, and called upon all present to desist in their illicit behavior and disperse in the name of the sovereign state of Mississippi. The fans hissed and booed as Renaud stepped between the ropes, talked briefly with the sheriff, and then slipped him $250. Cowart left the ring and took a seat to enjoy the combat with the rest of the crowd.

With the legal disclaimer concluded, John L. shed his heavy covering to reveal the wondrous results of his seven weeks in Belfast. Sullivan's physique amazed the fans, who murmured that Muldoon must be a miracle worker. The 207-pound champion still wasn't the chiseled figure he had been at age twenty-four—a small layer of fat lingered around his midsection—but it was the fittest he had appeared in years.

Even with all of the work done by Muldoon and Sullivan, the 190-pound Kilrain was the leaner man, although a little too thin to the liking of some of his backers. The challenger wore black tights and fighting boots, while Sullivan sported green tights, calf-high flesh-colored stockings, and black fighting boots. A makeshift belt of the Stars and Stripes encircled his waist, and a large plaster protected his stomach and back. Both men were clean shaven with their hair closely cropped.

With few nearby trees remaining and the sun approaching the sky's zenith, there was no shade in which to take cover. Locals did a brisk business ladling warm, acrid well water from their old tin pails at five cents a dip. The challenger naturally chose the corner with the sun at his back after winning the toss. The two camps also settled upon John Fitzpatrick of New Orleans, who would be elected mayor of that city in 1892, as the referee. Fitzpatrick had limited knowledge of the London Prize Ring Rules and reportedly had $700 riding on Sullivan, but all vouched for his honesty.

As New Orleans photographer Thomas Pye readied his camera to document the fight from atop a wooden stand, reporters gathered on the east side of the ring with pads and pens in hand. The promoters did not establish a dedicated telegraph line to the fight, lest it give away the bout's secret location, which meant that the rest of the country would receive no updates about the progress of the fight. It also ensured that once the fight ended the newsmen would engage in a mad scramble to get back to New Orleans to wire the result back to their editors.

William Harding, sporting editor of the *National Police Gazette*, handed Kilrain $1,000 on behalf of Fox. The challenger walked over to the champion's corner and formally offered his side bet. "Hey, Johnston, got one thousand dollars there?" Sullivan then spoke with his Brooklyn backer. Quickly, the champ had his cash to cover the bet.

After the referee received the side bets, the fighters walked to the middle of the ring and crossed hands. They appeared nearly evenly matched in height and age, with Sullivan just four months older. The crowd of nearly three thousand rumbled with anticipation and last-minute wagers.

Finally, after years of battling with ink in the newspaper, the two titans came face to face to battle for the championship of the world. The opportunity had arrived for Kilrain to prove worthy of the *Police Gazette* belt and the title of "champion of America" that Fox had bestowed upon him. For Sullivan, the time had come to disprove the doubters.

This was John L.'s chance to demonstrate that he still had the power and stamina to conquer the heavyweight class. This was his occasion to prove that the gray wisps in his hair did not mean he was too ancient to rule the ring. This was his moment to erase the memory of his draw with Mitchell and complete the resurrection of a career that had been plagued by alcohol, sickness, a broken arm, and boredom over the past two years.

Around 10:15 a.m., Fitzpatrick looked at one man then the other and asked, "Are you ready?"

The crowd—nearly all men and all white—craned their necks and leaned on each other's shoulders as they peeked through the sea of straw and derby hats. The fighters' seconds and attendants knelt down at ringside and leaned on the ropes to peer in the enclosure.

The fighters came toe to toe and dug their spikes into the turf as the referee roared, "Time!"

For an instant, the two fighters eyed each other. They circled like tomcats in an alley. Then Kilrain darted at Sullivan, who dodged and fired a wayward shot at his opponent's jaw. Jake pounced, grabbed John L. by the shoulders, and threw him to the ground with a back-heel maneuver that gave the first fall to Kilrain. The challenger's backers howled with joy and opened their palms to receive their winnings from the bets taken on the first fall. The first round had lasted no more than fifteen seconds.

Sullivan roared as he went to his corner, "So you want to wrestle, do you? Well, I'll give you enough of that." He came to scratch for the second round in a rage and threw Kilrain down hard with a wrestling maneuver that would have pleased Muldoon.

The third round featured some of the hardest slugging of the entire fight. Both men threw hard rights that landed on the necks of their counterparts. Then the fighters unleashed volleys of punches and counterpunches. Kilrain hit Sullivan with two shots below the belt, which raised cries of foul that went unheeded by the referee. John L. responded with terrible blows to Jake's ribs and body that sent him to the ground in agony. Mitchell and Donovan dragged their man back to his corner as chants of "Sullivan! Sullivan!" shook the Mississippi pines.

After the bombardment of the third round, Kilrain wanted no more of John L.'s big right. The challenger now implemented the same battle plan that had proven so effective for his field general, Mitchell. Particularly with the heat, Kilrain wanted to turn the fight into a footrace and wear down Sullivan. The challenger began to play a game of keep away—sidestepping, jabbing, and retreating from any toe-to-toe slugging.

The temperature would have reached one hundred degrees in the shade—had there been any shade. It grew so hot that fresh pine pitch bubbled up from the newly cut pieces of timber in the bleachers. According to some accounts, one southern belle tried to rise from her seat to discover her dress and underclothes stuck to the oozing grandstand. The scorching heat, however, couldn't break the fans of their formal Victorian-era dress code. Ties remained knotted. Long-sleeve shirts and dress coats stayed buttoned.

With temperatures already halfway to the boiling point, Mitchell knew it would take little for Sullivan's blood to bubble over, and he began to launch taunts in the champion's direction. John L. grew increasingly frustrated at Kilrain's evasion. "Why don't you stand and fight like a man?" he growled at his opponent after the fourth round.

Kilrain walked in circles in the fifth round, which drew boos and hisses from Sullivan's fans. In the sixth round, both men came to scratch breathing heavily. After a Kilrain hook to Sullivan's right ear, blood ran down the champion's sweaty body. The referee awarded the challenger first blood. Kilrain's backers cheered again as rolls of greenbacks changed hands. Their man had won the first two betting points, but Sullivan began to gain the upper hand in the larger battle. Wounded, he leveled Kilrain with the first knockdown punch of the bout—a sledgehammer right to end round six. Mitchell and Donovan carried their dazed fighter back to his corner. They tried to cool Kilrain with a palm-leaf fan as he sat with his head bowed. Masterson argued with the referee to squeeze any extra seconds he could for the challenger to recover.

When the champion returned to his corner, he refused to sit. "What the hell is the use? I just have to get back up again, don't I?" he told his seconds, who fanned him with towels that had soaked in ice water. The water grew more tepid by the minute as did the surly Sullivan. He repeatedly quarreled with Muldoon, which of course was nothing new between the two gladiators.

Sullivan continued to rush Kilrain as his opponent clinched and hugged to prevent the champion from firing off his shots. Still, John L. managed to land big blows that "sounded like a man hitting a bale of cotton with a stick." By the eighth round, Kilrain's face was swollen, and red splotches appeared on his chest. He continued to evade Sullivan, who cried out, "Stand up and fight! You're the champion, you know. Come, prove your title." Some of the spectators called Jake a cur and voiced their disapproval "over Kilrain's refusal to stand up and be thumped."

Suddenly, a commotion came from the crowd where a section of the temporary grandstand buckled and collapsed to the ground. The fighters were so engrossed that they barely noticed. The incident caused no serious injuries, just disappointment among the affected fans who no longer had a roost from which to watch the brawl. At least those spectators who lost seats could still keep tabs on the fight. The rest of the eager nation suffered the telegraph blackout. The inaugural edition of the *Wall Street Journal* published rumors of the fight's possible start on its front page amid the dividend reports and market updates, while the White House pestered the press room for any news from Richburg.

Sullivan continued to have the better of the fight, and in what would have been unthinkable just a couple months before, he proved to be the fitter man. The rounds shortened as Jake started to hit the ground to avoid his opponent. The challenger quivered. He was in great distress. The end appeared near. Yet Kilrain managed to stagger to the scratch each time.

Sullivan's fists began to swell like padded gloves from the punishment they delivered, and Kilrain hoped to just prolong the fight until John L. weakened. In the fifteenth round, the longest of the fight, he spent the better part of seven minutes racing away from Sullivan. With his feet constantly on the move, Kilrain accidentally spiked John L., gashing his left foot. Blood seeped through the top of Sullivan's boots. The champion's left eye also started to swell, and Kilrain managed to open up a cut with additional stingers. When Sullivan came back to his corner after the seventeenth round, Cleary sucked the blood out of his man's eye and sent him back out to scratch.

Kilrain now fell with just the slightest push or without even being touched, and John L. protested to the referee to no avail. The rounds piled up. Twenty. Twenty-one. Twenty-two. After Kilrain dropped to the ground to end the twenty-third round, a frustrated Sullivan jumped on his head with both knees. Fitzpatrick, however, dismissed the protests from Jake's corner.

Twenty-five. Twenty-eight. Thirty. Sullivan's left eye continued to swell. Blood flowed from Kilrain's ear. The challenger continued to dive to the turf as fans yelled, "Fight! Fight!" Muldoon asked Sullivan how long he could endure. "Until tomorrow morning, if it's necessary," he replied.

Thirty. Thirty-five. Forty. The fight now approached ninety minutes in length. Kilrain continued to play his waiting game, hoping that Sullivan's condition would change.

And then suddenly it happened.

Just after the call of time to start the forty-fourth round, Sullivan doubled over and vomited. The champion had been given cold tea laced with whiskey between rounds and apparently his system rebelled. John L. later claimed that there was too much whiskey in the concoction. "My stomach being in such a good condition, I threw it right off," he recounted in his autobiography. His friends knew better, however. They joked that Sullivan actually heaved the tea and kept down the booze.

Given the stomach ailments that had laid up Sullivan ten months prior, his backers feared the worst. Kilrain suddenly saw an escape from certain defeat. "Will you draw the fight?" he asked Sullivan. "No, you loafer," John L. snapped back. The champion punctuated his retort by knocking Kilrain down to end the forty-fourth. He sent Jake to the turf in the next round and then jumped in the air and landed on his opponent's head with both legs. Fitzpatrick did not call a foul.

Fifty. Fifty-five. Sixty. The fighters turned red from blood, lacerations, and the cauldron of the midday sun, which had broiled and blistered their exposed skin. Kilrain's seconds gave him whiskey shots between rounds to try to dull the pain. Sullivan continued to stalk his prey. He pounded away at a raw piece of skin over Kilrain's ribs that was "hanging like a big tumor." Through it all, the plucky Kilrain would not give up, but none of the gambling men in the crowd would risk even a nickel on him at this point in the fight.

Sixty-five. Seventy. Sullivan found little resistance to his repeated blows from his terribly weakened opponent. In the seventy-third and seventy-fourth rounds, Kilrain retreated all around the ring. In the seventy-fifth, Sullivan knocked the challenger around as he pleased. Kilrain returned to his corner extremely dazed. He could barely lift his arms. Donovan looked into Kilrain's glassy eyes and noticed that his neck could barely support the weight of his head.

In a reversal of Chantilly, this time it was Mitchell who came to Sullivan's corner to ask for $2,000 to get Kilrain to quit. Donovan, however, did not wait for Mitchell to complete his transaction. He had seen two exhausted fighters die in the ring before, and he vowed not to watch it happen again. Donovan tossed a sponge from his water pail into the middle of the ring. It was over.

Two hours and sixteen minutes after the men came to scratch, the referee announced Sullivan the victor. Although he had lost six and a half pounds during the battle, the champion had enough energy left to charge at Mitchell and challenge him then and there to fight. Muldoon and Cleary hustled John L. out of the ring as the crowd broke through the ropes. They harvested any souvenirs they could. Hats, water buckets, sponges, and towels all disappeared. The throng smashed the ring posts into splinters and even dug up the sacred turf.

The heat of that July afternoon in Richburg evaporated Fox's best, and ultimately last, shot in pursuit of his prey. Sullivan had whipped the man whom the *National Police Gazette* publisher touted for more than two years as the true heavyweight champion of the world. Fox lost much more than just face. He surrendered the $10,000 stake, $1,000 side bet, and thousands more bankrolling the expenses of Kilrain and Mitchell.

Even after abusing his body to the breaking point and displaying a waning interest in his vocation, Sullivan had proved that his superstardom burned as brightly as ever. The champion forever referred to the Richburg brawl as his greatest fight, and for the rest of his life, Kilrain insisted that the fight was swinging in his direction when Donovan, whom he accused of being "overexcitable" or on Sullivan's take, tossed the sponge. However, it was clear to all, even the *National Police Gazette,* that Sullivan was the heavyweight champion of the world. THE BIGGER BRUTE WON, sneered the *New York Times.*

Later that afternoon, Sullivan's sister, Annie Lennon, walked into the parlor of the family home on Parnell Street and handed her parents a telegram with the good news from Mississippi. That evening, Michael Sullivan sent his eldest boy the following dispatch: "Come home at once; mother is sick. M. Sullivan." The champion's parents may have assumed that their son could hurry home now that his marathon bout had ended, but Sullivan's fight in Mississippi had only just begun.

The legal drama that would unfold in the wake of the battle in Richburg would consume Sullivan for the better part of the next year and convince him to swear off bare knuckles forever. The champion's preference for gloves had driven the sport's transition from the London Prize Ring Rules to the Marquis of Queensberry Rules throughout the 1880s, a transformation that would eventually be completed with his decision to never again defend his title with naked fists. While often remembered as the last of the bare-knuckle heavyweight champions, Sullivan truly deserves instead to be remembered as the first of the gloved heavyweight titleholders.

The duel in the Mississippi sun turned out to be the final bare-knuckle championship fight in history. When Sullivan and Kilrain left the ring in Richburg, a 170-year era in boxing ended with it as the two fighters authored the closing chapter in a story first written by the naked fists of James Figg in 1719.

CHAPTER EIGHT

The Leading Man

BLOOD-STAINED SWEAT AND TEARS TRICKLED DOWN JAKE KILRAIN'S cheeks onto his bruised and blistered body. The fallen fighter groaned in agony as he was helped into a waiting buggy that brought him to the railroad tracks.

Around the bend from the depot, a special engine and car chartered by the Associated Press hid in wait to whisk its ten reporters back to New Orleans with the first news from Richburg. The sprinting fans leaving the ring dashed the newsmen's hopes for a quick getaway, however, once they spotted and boarded the secluded train. Even competing reporters climbed aboard the Associated Press special, and Kilrain's entourage coupled his railroad coach to the reporters' car to piggy-back a ride to New Orleans.

The pressmen furiously pulled on the bumper pin to unhitch Kilrain's car when they suddenly heard the click of a revolver. Looking up, they saw Bat Masterson with a six-shooter in his hand and "a merry twinkle in his eye." The gunslinger offered fifty dollars to any reporter who dared to pull the pin. Masterson found no takers, and the challenger's entourage joined the caravan back to the Crescent City.

The pitiable Kilrain, still wearing his fighting gear, slumped in his seat and sobbed. Swollen lips, puffy ears, a blackened left eye, and a raw field of crimson welts over his ribs testified to John L. Sullivan's terrible power, and a doctor injected Kilrain with morphine and brandy to quell the pain. John Fitzpatrick, the referee, walked the aisle of the train taking up a collection for the vanquished fighter, raising about $500. Fans tried to boost the spirits of the defeated man with three hurrahs, and reporters attempted to console Kilrain, but the boxer wouldn't listen. "No, I've lost my friends' money, and with their money goes their friendship," he said.

The lack of comfort being offered to Kilrain by his cornermen and backers in his lowest moment validated his statement. Like many gamblers, their interest in the fighter had never been personal. They were investors, not friends. Even Charley Mitchell, who had spent the better part of a year and a half with Kilrain, shunned the beaten brawler and called him a coward to all within earshot in the rear car. "I made the mistake of overrating Kilrain in his fight with Jem Smith," is all he could say to a reporter after the bout.

If Kilrain didn't have enough on his mind, Governor Lowry's directive to arrest the prizefighters who dared to brawl in Mississippi still loomed. The militia, determined to fulfill their orders this time, remained stationed at the state line. A squadron of troops stood on the tracks and waved for the train to stop as they spotted it chugging toward the Louisiana border. A friend of Kilrain assigned to ensure the engineer went straight through to New Orleans told him, "Pull your throttle wide open and let her go." With every pound of steam it could muster, the train roared by at thirty-five miles per hour as soldiers dodged for cover. The powerless officer in charge could only shake his fist at the mighty machine.

As he disembarked in New Orleans, Kilrain kept his head bowed and tried to hustle through the railroad station. One passerby, however, caught a glimpse of the fighter's cut-up face and yelled, "That's the bloke John L. Sullivan licked!" Kilrain swung at the lout, but much like many of his blows in Richburg, his right failed to connect. Once back in his quarters, the dutiful prizefighter telegraphed a brief message to his wife: "Nature gave out. Not hurt. Your husband, Jake."

An hour after Kilrain fled from Richburg, Sullivan, with little time to bathe in the afterglow of his epic victory, boarded the next train for New Orleans. As the engine idled near the scene of the crime, another train suddenly approached. Cries of "Police!" rattled around the Mississippi pines. "To the woods, John!" exhorted one of Sullivan's friends as passengers darted in every direction. "To the woods! The coppers are after us!"

The spooked Sullivan, dressed in his fighting togs underneath a big coat, demonstrated remarkable agility and dove headfirst through a window. He bolted into a nearby swamp for cover. Within minutes, word came that the alarm had been a false one. Grabbing his pants and coat from his friends, John L. emerged from the thickets to board the train, which sped away.

That evening, safely back in Louisiana, the champion returned to Mrs. Green's boardinghouse. He recuperated in a hot mustard bath and indulged in champagne and chicken. Tossing coins to the kids trailing behind his open carriage, Sullivan then paraded through the streets of New Orleans. For all the pounding he had taken, John L. emerged with just a scratch under his right eye and a small sore on his lip.

He also received $3,600 for his share of the excursion and gate receipts, in addition to the $1,000 side bet. Of course, Sullivan tried his best to divest of it throughout New Orleans the day after the fight. When he arrived back at her boardinghouse, Mrs. Green had an urgent message. "Mr. Sullivan, there is an officer here looking for you. He has a warrant from the authorities in Mississippi. He will be back pretty soon." The entourage scrambled. Sullivan slipped out of the house, while his backer Charley Johnston arranged for a special engine and coach to spirit them out of New Orleans as soon as possible.

Instead of leaving the Crescent City as the conquering hero, John L. absconded like a common criminal. The train ripped across the bayous and deposited Sullivan, Johnston, William Muldoon, Mike Cleary, Jack Barnett, and the rest of the fighter's party in Grand Bay, Alabama, just over the Mississippi state line. From there, they boarded a Louisville & Nashville sleeper heading north. The men smoked cigars and commented at how fortunate they were to escape Mississippi. With the danger of arrest apparently over, Sullivan could finally relax, and he settled in to sleep as the train blew through the night.

———

A big hand grasped Sullivan and stirred him from his sleep.

"What is your name?"

Through his dozy haze, John L. could make out a wall of uniformed men with nightsticks packed into his stateroom. His mind finally processed the policeman's question.

"My name is Jack Thompson. Let me sleep."

The most famous athlete in America had little chance of pulling off such a ruse, particularly with his face still bearing the relics of "the biggest sporting event of the century." The officer gave John L. another chance, but the champion again insisted his name was Thompson and refused to leave the train.

With that, the gang of eight Nashville police officers drew their revolvers. They handcuffed the champion and dragged him and Johnston through Union Station.

The incensed Governor Lowry had vowed to pursue the boxers and their backers beyond his borders for flagrantly violating Mississippi's antiprizefighting statute. Lowry, who huddled in his office for days with legal advisers amid piles of law books, wired the authorities in neighboring states requesting the capture and return of all involved in the fight.

Hours after their capture, Sullivan and Johnston appeared before a judge, who ruled that Tennessee had no right to arrest the men based upon a gubernatorial telegram rather than a warrant. The magistrate released the two men on a writ of habeas corpus, but not before Sullivan had spent $3,600, including $2,500 in legal fees, to secure his release. The expenses elicited howls that the champion had bought off justice—and the judge—but by nightfall, Sullivan and Johnston were once again riding the rails to Chicago.

The cautious Kilrain, meanwhile, had not even risked crossing into Mississippi on his flight on the rails north from New Orleans. And when news of Sullivan's arrest reached him at the depot in Seymour, Indiana, Kilrain panicked and fled the train with Mitchell and friend Johnny Murphy. They hired teams to drive them to nearby Shelbyville, but after hearing rumors that fourteen deputies were closing in, they bolted on foot into the tall pine woods. The battered fighter, who wanted more than anything to be back with his family in Baltimore, wandered aimlessly for a full day and night.

As a hurt and hungry Kilrain rambled the Indiana backwoods in fear of the authorities, an unconcerned John L. partied through the saloons of Chicago. Released from the rigors of training, Sullivan demonstrated little rustiness in returning to drinking form. He cloistered himself in

Tom Curley's saloon in "the lowest and most disreputable part of the city" where the liquor poured as heavily as the Windy City rain that pelted a mud-caked Kilrain when he finally arrived in Chicago.

As John L. continued to down drinks, his normally blunt words became sharpened to a knifepoint. When fellow fighter "Sailor" Charles Brown walked into Curley's bar a few nights after losing to the up-and-coming black heavyweight sensation Peter Jackson, Sullivan made his views on interracial fights clear. "So you're the fellow who fights n-----s, are you?" he slurred to Brown. The two exchanged blows before Sullivan's friends whisked him to safety in the saloon's backroom.

Undeterred by the setback in Nashville, Lowry continued his zealous pursuit from the Mississippi governor's mansion. He arrested Charles Rich, forced Fitzpatrick to surrender, signed formal extradition papers for the fighters on the charge of prizefighting, and dispatched one of his sheriffs to bring John L. back to Mississippi in handcuffs. If the "Big Fellow" worried about being arrested, he didn't show it. The champion's behavior, particularly in light of the news he had received after the fight about the poor health of his mother, appalled his friends and frayed his already-tenuous relationship with the strait-laced Muldoon. In a newspaper interview dated July 16, the disgusted trainer lit into John L. "All these stories about his great love for his parents and his generosity are the veriest bosh," Muldoon reportedly said. "A more unappreciative fellow I never saw, and it appears to be useless to induce him to behave himself." The next day, Muldoon denied making the statements—although he admitted that "a few unpleasant things occurred during our training." The reporter, meanwhile, stood by the veracity of the quotations.

After receiving a telegraph from his mother begging him again to come home immediately, Sullivan left Chicago on July 17. Fans in Boston kept a vigil outside of the family's Parnell Street home, but the champion never showed. Instead, Sullivan traveled to New York where he and his brother kept the champagne corks popping inside the city's sporting resorts.

On July 23, John L. finally received his payoff from the championship fight inside a small storefront on West Twenty-Eighth Street. Surrounded by backers Johnston, Jimmy Wakely, and Arthur Lumley, stakeholder Al

Cridge counted out forty-five hundred-dollar bills and placed them in the champion's hand. Sullivan kept half, and the other half went to his backers. After the handover of money, Cridge presented Sullivan with the *Police Gazette* belt. "Take the dog collar away," John L. barked. "Take it away! I wouldn't be found dead with it." He instead gave the belt to Johnston, who kept it on display inside his Brooklyn saloon.

Muldoon expected a sizable chunk of the $20,000 purse for his efforts in training Sullivan, but he was greatly disappointed when he received only $1,200 from Johnston and a paltry $200 payout from John L. The meager compensation further hardened him toward John L., who was developing bitter feelings of his own. The trainer was taking credit for molding a champion out of what he described as a "drunken, bloated, helpless mass of flesh and bone." Despite Sullivan's objections, the narrative of Muldoon as savior began to take hold. One book published soon after the bout even declared that "it was really Muldoon who won the fight."

If Muldoon had won the fight, then John L. could have been forgiven for wondering why he was the one being pursued by authorities. The Mississippi sheriff dispatched to handcuff John L. finally arrived in New York, where the governor agreed to honor Lowry's writ of extradition. On July 31, New York City police Chief Inspector Thomas Byrnes, who had been present at so many of Sullivan's fights inside Madison Square Garden, knocked on the door of the champion's room at the Vanderbilt Hotel and took him into custody. Sullivan declared his innocence—claiming he was compelled to appear at Kilrain's chosen location in Mississippi "or else be called by the world at large a coward"—and brazenly played the sick mother card to push for a postponement of the case. In spite of his protests, John L. again boarded a train to the South, this time to battle in court.

———

At every station along the way, ladies awaited on platforms with bouquets of flowers and cheering crowds hailed the arrested prizefighter like a hero. One thousand fans, including Charles Rich and Bud Renaud, welcomed Sullivan to the Mississippi capital of Jackson on August 4. They trailed his carriage to the Edwards House hotel and raised huzzahs that carried to the governor's mansion just three blocks away.

One of Sullivan's backers, Col. Jones Hamilton, arranged a reception at the hotel in which the ladies of Jackson lined up to shake hands with him "in a most cordial manner." When word of the lavish affair being given in the prisoner's honor filtered down the street, an enraged Governor Lowry ordered authorities to throw the fighter in jail until his court appearance the following morning. After a personal appeal from Hamilton, however, the governor relented and released John L. from lock-up.

Lawmen brought Sullivan to the Marion County seat of Purvis, where a grand jury convened on August 12 and two days later indicted Sullivan and Kilrain for prizefighting and assault and battery. The grand jury also indicted Muldoon, Cleary, and Mike Donovan for aiding and abetting the prizefighters. The decision outraged Donovan, who believed he should instead have been lauded for possibly saving Kilrain's life by throwing the sponge to end the fight.

Jury selection for Sullivan's trial started right away, and transcripts reveal the difficulty in seating an impartial panel given that most prospective jurors had actually been present at the bout or heard witnesses describe the scene. Most testimony focused on the pre-fight side bet between John L. and Kilrain, a wager that would have made the bout technically a prizefight. Sullivan's attorneys questioned witnesses on such minute points as whether they could tell if the bills were real or counterfeit, whether they could recall the ring specifically being called a prizefighting ring, and whether they could swear that Sullivan even fought Jake Kilrain since his real name was John Killion. In spite of the attempted obfuscation, it only took the jury a half-hour on August 16 to find Sullivan guilty of prizefighting. The following day, the judge levied no fine against John L. but imposed the maximum sentence: twelve months in jail.

A slice of America applauded the verdict. "Pugilism has received a severe blow, a black eye, a knock-down, and Mississippi has done it. The state deserves the greatest credit, and will have it from all right-minded men," declared one newspaper. A Christian newspaper editorialized "that the time has almost come when such public exhibitions of brutality as prizefights shall be extinct as bear-baiting and dueling." Sullivan's lawyers immediately appealed the ruling, and the court released the fighter on bond. John L. left Mississippi as fast as he could.

Kilrain, arrested in Baltimore in mid-August, arrived in Mississippi for his trial in the weeks before Christmas. Unlike Sullivan's jury, the panel weighing Kilrain's guilt acquitted him of prizefighting, yet convicted him of assault and battery, ironic considering how badly he was assaulted and battered in Richburg. The court sentenced him to two months' imprisonment and fined him $200. Fortunately for the challenger, he never did any hard time. Under a unique Mississippi law that turned prisoners over to the care of respectable private citizens to perform manual labor, the state released Kilrain into the friendly hands of Rich, who treated him as a houseguest for his two-month sentence.

Once again, though, poor Jake received it worse compared to John L. The Mississippi State Supreme Court in March 1890 reversed the judgment against Sullivan on a technicality and kicked the case back to the county court. John L. returned to Purvis where a grand jury again indicted him for prizefighting. This time, however, Sullivan pleaded guilty, paid a $500 fine, and walked out of the courthouse on June 24, 1890, a free man. The next day, Muldoon, Cleary, and Donovan entered guilty pleas as well. The court fined Muldoon $250 and Cleary and Donovan $100 each. Kilrain paid half of Donovan's fine. Sullivan defrayed none of the expenses incurred by Muldoon or Cleary for acting as his seconds. By this point, the relationship between John L. and Muldoon had truly unraveled, and the fighter accused his former trainer of seeking to turn state's evidence against him in return for immunity.

After vigorously pursuing justice for nearly a full year after the prizefight, Governor Lowry ultimately saw not one participant spend a day behind bars. Not that he didn't make Sullivan suffer through an ordeal. The champion estimated that between fines, legal bills, and associated expenses, it had cost him more than $18,000 to settle the charges, which was more than he earned in winning the fight. "I may say that I built a courthouse and school at Purvis," he quipped.

Not only did the legal wrangling deplete his earnings from the Richburg fight, it exhausted any desire of his to once again enter the ring with naked fists. "The country seems to be opposed to it, and there is no money in it," he told reporters on his way home. "I propose to respect the law hereafter. Announcing that you are going to fight a prizefight is like saying you are going to break into a house where there is an armed force waiting for you. It is suicide."

—◦—

After Sullivan left Mississippi following the appeal of his initial conviction, he returned to New York on the morning of August 19, 1889, and continued to face questions about his filial devotion to his invalid mother. John L. still showed little urgency in returning to Boston until Barnett and Annie Livingston finally convinced him to leave at once that afternoon.

The next day, the "Boston Strong Boy" came home. When his carriage pulled over, Sullivan bounded up the steps of the familiar wooden house at 8 Parnell Street and entered the parlor where his rheumatic mother reclined on a lounge. Joy burst across her face, which was as worn as the sitting room's faded carpet. "I feared you'd not come, John, till too late," she sobbed as the big fellow tenderly enveloped her in his mighty arms.

In spite of the emotional reunion, John L. did not stay long at his fifty-six-year-old mother's bedside. He woke up some time after noon the next day and left to visit his old haunts, Mike Clarke's saloon and Billy Hogarty's barbershop. Then he left with Barnett and friend Sylvie Gookin to Crescent Beach, where he had been laid up with such sickness less than a year before.

John L. was with his brother at the seaside location on the evening of August 30 when they received an urgent message to return home immediately. A priest had already arrived to administer last rites to Catherine Sullivan, who was surrounded by her husband, two sisters, daughter Annie, and Annie's husband, James Lennon. The brothers boarded the next train to Boston. They rushed inside the family home to see the grief-stricken faces. They were too late.

The *Boston Globe* reported that Catherine's funeral was the largest ever seen in the Roxbury Highlands. It took two vehicles just to hold the bountiful floral tributes sent from sporting men across the country. Four dark horses draped in black robes hauled the hearse through the streets of Boston. John L. and Michael trailed their mother's cedar casket into Roxbury's St. Patrick's Church for the funeral, and they rode in a one-hundred-carriage procession to her burial at Mount Calvary Cemetery.

On September 7, Sullivan, accompanied by his father and brother, made his first public appearance since losing his mother, a benefit in his honor at the New York Academy of Music. Hundreds of fans showered him with a crown of roses and well wishes before he donned the gloves for a tame three-round exhibition with Cleary.

The crowd buzzed that the champion's spar could be his last. Earlier that day in a stunning letter to the *New York Sun,* Sullivan, who had tossed his cap over the ropes before many a bout, announced that he was throwing his hat into the political ring. He declared that he would accept the Democratic nomination for Congress—should it be offered to him. A Gotham newspaper served as an odd mouthpiece for launching a political campaign in Boston, but the strange venue suggests that *Sun* reporter Arthur Brisbane scripted Sullivan's lengthy missive.

Sullivan vouched for his qualifications for public office—his honesty, his ability to keep a promise, his public-speaking abilities, and his work in upholding the "reputation of America among other nations." Like any aspiring politician, he tugged on patriotic heartstrings. "There isn't a self-respecting American, no matter what tomfool ideas he may have about boxing in general," the letter read, "who does not feel patriotic pride at the thought that a native born American, a countryman of his, can lick any man on the face of the earth. It is human nature." He also assured that "a man who can quiet a crowd in Madison Square Garden, as I have done, can make his presence felt in Congress." He signed the letter with his usual rhetorical flourish: "Yours truly, John L. Sullivan, Champion of the World."

Although viewed more as lawbreakers than lawmakers, boxers had been voted into public office in the past. New York City voters elected John Morrissey—with the backing of Tammany Hall—more than a decade after he defeated "Yankee" Sullivan, to the US House of Representatives in 1866. The Democratic machine bosses in Boston understood that Sullivan, like the two-term Morrissey before him, had tremendous popularity among Irish Americans, who now held the electoral balance of power in the city.

The news sent political tongues atwitter. "Is Sullivan really going to run for Congress? I think it is the most exquisite bit of humor if he does," New York politician Theodore Roosevelt wrote to his friend—and sitting Massachusetts congressman—Henry Cabot Lodge.

Sullivan said that his mother's death spurred him to pursue the drastic career switch, and he again vowed to make some serious lifestyle changes. "I've had my last drink for one year," he told the public. "In that year I propose to make some money, pay my debts, and settle down. I'm tired of being a sporting-man now. I'm going to be a gentleman." His pledge of sobriety lasted barely a fortnight.

While Sullivan blustered about higher office, Barnett organized a sparring tour of cities and towns around New York that included Sullivan, Cleary, Jimmy Carroll, Ike Weir, Liney Tracey, and Joe Lannan. On the combination's opening night in Brooklyn, however, John L. failed to appear. The champion was reportedly drunk in Boston. Fearing a similar occurrence three nights later, the promoter of his next scheduled appearance personally accompanied Sullivan from Boston and closely monitored him at his hotel. The intense supervision worked, and a sober John L. sparred with Cleary and Tracey.

Sullivan never fully committed to Barnett's company. After a string of canceled appearances, he dashed back to Boston claiming he needed to collect $6,500 from Livingston to whom he had given his earnings from Richburg. John L. never returned, and the show folded.

By the middle of October, newspapers reported the champion was "dead broke" and had already run through all of the earnings from the Kilrain fight. Then came a truly close shave at Hogarty's barbershop on October 26 when words flew between Sullivan and Thomas F. Keefe, alias Tommy Shea, who had recently served a three-year sentence for highway robbery. The pair, along with Sullivan's friend and former lightweight boxer Tommy Kelly, had spent the day crawling the bars of Boston before stopping by the barbershop. Shea was in an ugly mood and repeatedly blistered John L. with insults. Sullivan demonstrated remarkable restraint, but one comment finally set off Kelly, who seized a razor from one of the barber's hands, lunged at Shea, and slashed him under the left side of the jaw. Blood splattered the barbershop, and Hogarty jumped on Kelly's back and rushed him into the street. Sullivan grabbed a towel and administered first aid before Shea could get to the hospital, where he spent six weeks in recovery. A doctor said Sullivan's actions helped to save the man's life.

The constant news reports about the champion's debts and drinking, not to mention the ongoing legal problems in Mississippi, were too unseemly even by the lowered behavioral standards for American politicians. Sullivan's quest to serve in Congress, if it had ever been a serious proposition in the first place, fizzled. In later years, John L. put his distinctive spin on his brief political foray: "They wanted to send me to Congress, but I was too busy having a good time."

While his political career petered out, another profession outside of the ring soon called Sullivan. This vocation was perfect for a celebrity already experienced at being one of America's leading men.

In the year during which the outcome of the Mississippi court case remained in limbo, so did Sullivan's fighting career. Talk swirled of a rematch with Kilrain or a bout with Smith or Jackson, but John L. only appeared between the ropes for sporadic exhibitions. He certainly did not want to engage in any more prizefights, and he had little desire to resume the self-denial that serious training required.

In May 1890, a unique offer from the popular actor Duncan B. Harrison shook Sullivan out of his ambivalence. Harrison, who managed a traveling troupe appearing with him in a melodrama called *The Paymaster*, engaged the champion to spar four rounds with Lannan at the conclusion of each performance for the remaining six weeks of the theatrical season. For his efforts, Sullivan received $1,000 a week, while Lannan earned $300 weekly.

The double-bill may have seemed an odd pairing, but there had long been a traditional connection between the stage and the ring. Theaters served as common venues for fights, exhibitions, and benefits, and stage performers often joined the entertainment bill at exhibitions. As Sullivan expanded the popularity of the sport beyond the lower classes, boxing and theater began to appeal to similar audiences.

Sullivan was a hit when he debuted with *The Paymaster* in Proctor's Theatre in New York. "Well-dressed folks and women in equal numbers with the men" packed the house, and theaters turned away hundreds every night. The brief engagement proved a success and whet Sullivan's interest in the stage. John L. especially enjoyed the easy money, and Harrison realized Sullivan's tremendous power as a drawing card.

Once the theatrical season ended in June, Harrison feverishly scripted a melodrama that would thrust Sullivan into a starring role. Although John L. had experience performing as a living statue, a circus ringmaster, and a boxer, Harrison was still taking quite a risk. Relying on John L. to spar four rounds on stage was one thing; asking him to go toe-to-toe with a script for four acts was quite another.

Boxers had occasionally acted on stage in the past. In the 1870s, Jem Mace played Charles the Wrestler in William Shakespeare's *As You Like It*, and Muldoon appeared in the same role alongside Maurice Barrymore and Helena Modjeska. Sullivan, however, broke new ground as an athlete by taking on a starring role, rather than a bit part.

The champ's adoring—and curious—public packed Proctor's Opera House in Bridgeport, Connecticut, on August 28 to watch him take his star turn alongside Harrison in the melodrama *Honest Hearts and Willing Hands*. The play, set in Ireland, was billed as "a sensational comedy drama in five acts." John L. starred as the hero, the muscular village blacksmith James Daly. Harrison played his brother, John. The action followed the stock melodramatic formula: virtuous hero whips dastardly villain and gets the girl in the end.

The "wealth and fashion of Bridgeport" that filled the theater for opening night demonstrated Sullivan's crossover appeal. When the champion walked on stage for the first time, the audience cheered so wildly that Sullivan stood and bowed for several minutes until the play could proceed.

John L. sat out the second act but reappeared in the third at his blacksmith's forge. Nearly bursting through his dress pants and clad in a leather apron, he rolled up his sleeves to reveal his biceps, which fired like pistons as he pounded his anvil with loud blows that caused the balcony audience to cover their ears. At the close of the third act and before Sullivan was able to begin preparing for the fourth act, the audience's applause elicited a speech from Sullivan. He thanked the patrons for their reception. "This is my first appearance as an actor. I am not an Edwin Booth or a John McCullough, but having quit my other profession, I hope some day to be a star in this," he told the audience.

Harrison knew that Sullivan's fists were his greatest asset, so he penned a fifth and final act in which John L. and Lannan, who played the "hired thug" Tug O'Brien, sparred with gloves in a mock prizefight for a cup and a one-hundred-pound purse. When the boxers appeared for the climactic fight scene with Barnett acting as master of ceremonies, one critic noted "there was a flutter of curiosity among the feminine hearts present to whom prize fighting was a new thing." The audience tossed their hats into the air and cried out "Sock 'em Sully!" and "Give him an uppercut, Jawn!" They cheered as the fighting grew fiercer with each round, and they roared when John L. laid Lannan flat on the stage.

Sullivan delivered his lines with the same subtlety as his blows, but his deep, booming voice benefited him as an actor. And of course, he was at ease starring as the hero and lead of the show. After all, he had played the part of an American idol for nearly a decade.

In the end, any review of Sullivan's acting chops missed the point. Audiences didn't pack theaters expecting to be entertained by a renowned thespian any more than fans who paid to watch John L. umpire baseball games expected to see the sport's best arbiter. They just wanted to bask in the glow of a superstar.

Sullivan enjoyed his turn in the theater, which he said was much easier than boxing. "You've only got to walk around, get off your lines, mind your cues, and there you are," he told one reporter. Plus, it paid handsomely without any of the bothersome physical punishment, arrests, or training. Harrison tried in vain to get John L. to practice and polish his raw talent, but Sullivan relished rehearsals as much as training. The champion earned $100,000 during the two-year run of *Honest Hearts and Willing Hands*, and he quickly viewed himself as a member of the actors' guild rather than a part of the fighting fraternity.

When *Honest Hearts and Willing Hands* opened at Niblo's Garden in New York, it played to sold-out audiences every night. Although the manager paid at least one New York critic $400 to write a positive review and say that Sullivan had promise as an actor, the critiques of the boxer's performance generally benefited from critics' quite-low expectations. "I was surprised when I saw Sullivan act," confessed Nym Crinkle of the *New York World*. "There were none of the frills nor airs assumed by the usual aspirant for stellar honors. . . . Were any other actor in New York to essay the part as Sullivan plays it he would be credited with a fine bit of character acting."

Less than a week into his run at Niblo's Garden, Sullivan received a dispatch to return to Boston as quickly as possible. His father had taken ill. As with his mother, Sullivan showed up too late to say goodbye. Just hours before his son could arrive by train in the early morning hours of September 7, 1890, Michael Sullivan passed away from typhoid pneumonia at age sixty.

The end had come in just a matter of days. Only a week before, Michael had moved around the corner from the old family home into 26 Sawyer Street, the brick house that John L. had purchased for his parents in 1885 but which had been primarily used for rental income. Annie Lennon, ever the dutiful daughter, nursed her father when he took sick, and when Michael learned the severity of his illness, he asked for John L. to be summoned "that he might see him and grasp his big, muscular hand once more." When Sullivan arrived to find his father gone, he teared up and bent over Michael Sullivan's body to plant a kiss on his cold cheek.

Barely a year after laying his mother to rest, John L. had to make the same doleful trip to Mount Calvary Cemetery to bury his father as one newspaper headline declared: JOHN L. NOW AN ORPHAN.

After interring his father, Sullivan quickly returned to the stage in New York City before the troupe started its travels across the United States. It was a rudderless period for John L. He had lost both parents, and his tumultuous relationship with Livingston appeared to have finally ended. Once again, he was on the road. Once again, he was drinking.

For the most part, John L. managed to finely tune his imbibing so that he was just drunk enough to be a menace, yet never so inebriated that he couldn't run through his lines. In November 1890, he sent Harrison to the hospital with a kick in the back and nearly broke his own neck falling through a hotel window in Taunton, Massachusetts. In a Milwaukee hotel in January 1891, he reportedly punched a theater critic who had called on him, and he struck a bellboy repeatedly with his brush. In February, he howled through the saloons of Augusta, Georgia, while waiting for a train connection and grew so verbally abusive that a train hand took a swipe and knocked him out. The head of the Elks fraternal order even stripped Sullivan of his antlers for being a person "who is unworthy to associate with gentlemen and whose conduct has brought shame and discredit upon the order."

Sullivan's drinking helped at the box office, however. Whenever rumors swirled through a town that John L. was off on another bender during the day, curious fans snapped up tickets to watch the high-wire act as Sullivan attempted to stumble and slur through an evening performance.

As Sullivan traveled America from coast to coast during the 1890–1891 theatrical season, boxing fans and the press wondered in increasingly louder tones when the champion would offer a challenger a shot at his crown. One of those leading contenders, James J. Corbett, knew the only way he could get a glimpse of the champion was at the theater, so he dropped in at a January 1891 performance of *Honest Hearts and Willing Hands* in Chicago. Jim Corbett had made a name for himself after defeating Joe Choynski in a vicious twenty-seven-round fight aboard a barge in San Francisco Bay in June 1889, and he signaled his rise by downing Kilrain in New Orleans in February 1890 and knocking out Dominick McCaffrey two months later. The rangy San Francisco heavyweight, who sported a luxurious black pompadour haircut, had idolized Sullivan. The teenaged Corbett had been the first person to enter the gates of Mechanics' Pavilion when John L. defeated George Robinson in 1884, and he watched from the audience as Sullivan whipped Paddy Ryan for a third time in 1886.

But by the time Corbett arrived at Chicago's West Side Theatre, Sullivan was no longer his hero. He was an obstacle to the heavyweight crown. Corbett sent a messenger backstage with fifteen dollars and a request for a box seat. Back came the money with a message: "The big fellow would like to see you, Jim." In the champion's dressing room, Corbett shook the hand of Sullivan for the first time. After the show, John L. took the young fighter through a half-dozen Chicago saloons, where he set up the house on each occasion. As the bar tabs swelled, Corbett "became more and more amazed at the drinking ability of the champion."

Through his alcoholic haze, Sullivan still knew enough gamesmanship to beat his chest in the presence of a leading contender. He entered every watering hole with a fist pound on the bar and the declaration: "I can lick any son-of-a-bitch in the world." As the drinks piled up, Sullivan's statement started to come with a contemptuous glare at the young fighter. Corbett chafed and finally had enough. At the next saloon, the man known as "Gentleman Jim" informed John L. that the boast was "hardly courteous." He looked directly into Sullivan's eyes and for the first time saw the piercing stare that caused so many fighters to cower. Corbett never blinked, and John L. threw his arm around his guest and ordered another round.

Talk between the two fighters turned to Corbett's next opponent, the black heavyweight Peter Jackson. "Well, young fellow, I don't like the idea of you fighting a negro. I have drawn the color line." An insistence on adhering to the color line forever stained John L., both as a fighter and simply as a human being.

———

The measure of any fighter is as black-and-white as the printed pages in the boxing record books: the wins, the losses, the knockouts, the opponents. Scan the bout-by-bout listings for the "Boston Strong Boy," and one takeaway is crystal clear. John L. Sullivan never fought a black man.

The civil rights advances that had occurred in the United States in the decade following the Civil War and the abolition of slavery quickly eroded after the official end of Reconstruction in 1877. During the years of Sullivan's championship reign, Jim Crow laws legalized segregation, white supremacists latched onto social Darwinism as proof of their superiority, and race relations spiraled into violence. Lynchings of blacks more than tripled from 49 in 1882 to 161 in 1892. Even the US Supreme Court upheld the separation of races in 1883 by declaring the Civil Rights Act of 1875 unconstitutional.

The increasing institutional racism of the Gilded Age bled into the world of American sports. By the end of the 1880s, professional baseball barred African Americans from the diamond, a hardball segregation not to be broken until the Brooklyn Dodgers called up Jackie Robinson in 1947. Black jockeys had dominated horse racing in the decades following the Civil War—thirteen of the fifteen riders in the inaugural Kentucky Derby in 1875 were African American—but they began to be driven out of the sport in the 1890s.

Boxing, while not even close to being color-blind, was perhaps the most integrated sport—if not one of the most integrated segments of American society—in the late nineteenth century. Black and white fighters commonly met in the ring, although the crowds outside the ropes were almost purely white. The heavyweight championship, however, that symbol of physical prowess and dominance, was kept strictly in the grasp of white hands. The *National Police Gazette* offered a separate colored crown for black heavyweights. When Sullivan captured the heavyweight title, he felt a particular obligation to ensure that he would never yield it to an African American.

That pressure came in part from the Irish-American community that nurtured and supported him. Although many Irish immigrants personally experienced the sting of racism, they were among the most virulently racist groups toward African Americans after the Civil War. Following the abolition of slavery, Irish Americans found themselves battling against a new black labor pool for the manual jobs they had previously dominated. The competition bred antagonism.

John L. embodied the bigotry that flowed through Irish America. While he befriended black fighters such as featherweight George "Little Chocolate" Dixon, he didn't want to associate with them in the workplace. "It wasn't that I had any small grouch against the colored fighters, personally, because I like them," Sullivan wrote in 1907, "but it was the race idea." To John L., the color line wasn't anything personal; it was strictly business.

Sullivan was not immune to the poisonous racism that infected most of nineteenth-century America, but as a hero who carried the banner of a city with a proud abolitionist past, he failed terribly in the chance to use his powerful platform to take a courageous stand. And he had plenty of opportunities. In 1883, a group of Albany sporting men tried to match Sullivan with the black heavyweight C. A. C. Smith, who had just knocked out the Canadian champion Jack Stewart, but John L. reportedly refused because of Smith's skin color. The rationale left the *National Police Gazette* puzzled: "We do not see why Sullivan should refuse to arrange a match with Smith merely because he is a colored man."

Sullivan claimed that early in his career he had twice set a match with the Boston-bred black fighter George Godfrey, only to have police interfere and prevent the fight. When Godfrey was called forth from the audience at the Sullivan testimonial in May 1888, Sullivan blustered about fighting the black man but did nothing to press the matter. (Sullivan did agree to referee two matches involving Godfrey, however.)

The real clamor for John L. to fight a black man came with the rise of the Australian Jackson. The "Black Prince" was considered by most to be the greatest black heavyweight of his era and perhaps superior to Jack Johnson, who became the first black man to capture the world heavyweight championship in 1908. Jackson, who was born on St. Croix and emigrated to Australia as a boy, was a national sculling champion and a gifted swimmer who introduced the "Australian crawl" freestyle stroke to the United States. After finding work at sea as a teenager, Jackson discovered his fistic aptitude in a brawl with an officer aboard one of his ships.

When he had gained the Australian championship, Jackson came to the United States in 1888 with hopes of returning home with the world heavyweight crown. He dazzled with a clever, scientific style punctuated with quick footwork and an agile, yet powerful jab. He defeated Godfrey in eighteen rounds for the colored heavyweight title and also conquered notable white fighters such as Patsy Cardiff and San Francisco's Joe McAuliffe. Although the foreigner had defeated a hometown boy, Jackson's victory over McAuliffe set off the biggest celebration by San Francisco's African Americans since the signing of the Emancipation Proclamation. Unable to get a match with Sullivan in the months after the Richburg fight, Jackson sailed to the British Isles and defeated notables such as Jem Smith and Peter Maher.

In an interview given more than two decades after he left the ring, Sullivan claimed that he offered Jackson a title shot but that the challenger tried to dictate the terms and merely sought publicity rather than a fight. Indeed, John L. did make public challenges to the Australian in the newspapers, but when it came time to sign for the match, he always found a complicating factor: the legal case in Mississippi, the theatrical tour, the clampdown on prizefighting by the authorities. Unable to hammer out a fight with Sullivan, Jackson arranged a match with Jim Corbett for May 1891.

While Sullivan hid behind excuses when drawing the color line during his fighting days, his racist proclamations in the years after his retirement followed the mood of the country and grew increasingly stark. "A man who fights a negro should be whipped," he told one reporter in 1893. "If God had intended the black man as the equal of the white, he would have made him of the same complexion," he spouted to another a few months later. Newspaper columns printed under his bylines in the early 1900s were even more strident, stating that "the negro is inferior" and "a white man shouldn't fight a negro because it pulls the white man down to the negro's level without getting the negro up to the white man's class." Sullivan had been known to give editors the right to sign his name to any story he considered "right and proper," but if he had any reservations about the racist views that appeared with his name and photograph, he never voiced them.

Until 1908, heavyweight champions followed Sullivan's lead and honored the color line. Even some black fighters began to refuse to fight against their own race. The lightweight champion Joe Gans, who declared in 1906 that he would not fight another black man, said, "You don't get any credit if you lick 'em, and they are too tough to lick." It echoed a line that Sullivan himself had written just months before: "A white man has nothing to gain by swapping punches with a negro."

While the color line was a convenient excuse behind which white boxers could hide from black fighters, cowardice was a foreign emotion to John L. The roots of his decision to draw the color line were far more complex than simple primal fear, although he wrote in his post-retirement years without irony: "I had never shirked a fight, though I refused to fight a negro."

As the final curtain prepared to close on the 1891 theatrical season, fans clamored for John L. to return to the ring, possibly against Kilrain, Corbett, Jackson, or another Australian fighter, Frank Slavin. Even old foe Paddy Ryan asked the champion for a match. But Sullivan lacked the motivation to put on the gloves. "I am making more money than if I were fighting," he said, "and I hate like the devil to go into training anymore. Now I can enjoy myself. When I train, I have to half-starve."

Instead of booking an opponent, John L. booked passage down under. Sullivan and Duncan Harrison signed with Australian theatrical managers Charles and James McMahon to perform *Honest Hearts and Willing Hands* in their country during July, August, and September. The McMahon brothers expected to replicate the play's American box-office success by importing boxing's greatest star to a fight-loving nation.

Before sailing for Australia, Sullivan appeared on stage in San Francisco for the last American stop of *Honest Hearts and Willing Hands.* On opening night, John L. ran through his lines when a loud cheer suddenly interrupted him. He peered through the lights and made out a familiar pompadour. It was Corbett, who had arrived late to the performance. As Sullivan stewed, the audience turned its attention away from the world champion to salute boxing's rising star, who weeks before had fought Jackson to a sixty-one-round stalemate.

Following the first act, Corbett arrived backstage with a business proposition. He asked Sullivan to spar with him at a testimonial that had been scheduled in Corbett's honor for an even split of the gate. John L. agreed, but with one unusual stipulation—that they fight in full evening dress. "Gentleman Jim" needed the money and had no choice but to consent.

On June 24, three thousand fans crowded the Grand Opera House on Mission Street expecting a titanic slug. Instead, they watched a royal farce. The men came on stage in their dress suits and delivered their speeches. Corbett took a bow after someone in the crowd gleefully shouted, "You whipped the coon!"

Then each man shed his topcoat and entered the ring in shirt sleeves and six-ounce gloves. The fight started with the usual Sullivan rush, and John L. had Corbett on the defensive for the entire opening round before it was ended after about a minute to allow the puffing champion to regain his breath. In the second, Corbett "displayed great science" in dodging Sullivan's blows and delivering some of his own to the champion's nose. The Sullivan rushes and Corbett dodges continued in round three, but John L. could no longer deliver any of his signature rights. One reporter noted that Sullivan had the better of the first half of the fight and Corbett the latter half. The bout proved as tame as the fight scene in *Honest Hearts and Willing Hands,* which is exactly what Sullivan wanted.

John L. insisted he chose the formal fighting costumes simply to bring "professional etiquette" to the stage, but if he truly hoped the patronizing outfits would negate the strategic value of the bout to a potential challenger, it didn't work. The crafty Corbett dissected the champion's style throughout the fight. He tested his feints. He saw how Sullivan telegraphed his huge right by unconsciously dropping his head. "I can whip this fellow!" he confided to his cornerman Billy Delaney after the second round. "Just as sure as I get Sullivan in the ring with me, I will knock him out," he declared in a letter to Mike Donovan.

Two days after the preposterous set-to, Sullivan boarded the steamship *Mariposa* for the nearly month-long voyage to Australia. Corbett sent an emissary with a box of cigars as a going-away present. When Sullivan heard the smokes were "with Jim Corbett's compliments," he heaved them into San Francisco Bay. The surprise appearance of Jackson at the dock did little to improve his mood. Legendary West Coast boxing journalist W. W. Naughton introduced the champion to the black fighter, and Sullivan said he enjoyed his time with Jackson before adding, "but he is a n-----, and that settles it with me."

John L. set sail with Barnett, old colleague Frank Moran, and Jack Ashton, his sparring partner from the European trip who filled Lannan's role. The ship registry also recorded a "Mrs. J.L. Sullivan," although this mystery woman was neither one of the Annies—Sullivan or Livingston.

After six days at sea, the champion arrived in the kingdom of Hawaii. Due to the admonitions of the Christian missionaries, his Honolulu exhibition with Ashton drew a sparse crowd, but Sullivan did receive a royal audience with the sister of the recently deceased King Kalakaua. John L. described her as "a most entertaining and interesting person" who "seemed to greatly admire our Republic."

Following his departure from Hawaii, Sullivan apparently worked up quite a thirst in the middle of the Pacific Ocean. Reports arrived back in America of a particular binge in which John L. downed thirty-eight glasses of porter, attempted to slug the captain, and found himself locked up in his stateroom to dry out.

After stops in Samoa and New Zealand, Sullivan sailed into the marvelous natural harbor of Sydney, Australia, on July 20. Many of his Irish brethren had made their own voyages into the British colony under far more harrowing conditions during the previous century. After the Irish Rebellion of 1798, the British banished many Irish men fighting for their freedom to the faraway penal colony. Decades later, a Celtic tide washed upon Sydney's shores in the wake of the Great Hunger.

A tug carrying Harrison and a group of Australian sporting men greeted the *Mariposa*, but Sullivan stayed on board with Moran, who had taken sick a few days out from San Francisco. The people of Sydney hosted a banquet in honor of their guests the night after their arrival. Still, the frenzy that had greeted Sullivan in Great Britain did not translate to its southern colony.

The famed actress Sarah Bernhardt lodged in the room above the champion in the elegant Australian Hotel, but her constant nocturnal rehearsing disturbed Sullivan's sleep. After several restless nights, the champion passed his fellow thespian on the stairs and unleashed his famous glare. Bernhardt remained quiet for the remainder of her stay.

Honest Hearts and Willing Hands opened on July 30 at one of Australia's premier theatrical venues, Her Majesty's Opera House. Unlike their American counterparts, the Australian theater critics filleted the show. The *Sydney Times* grilled Sullivan for hurling "ungrammatical impromptu speeches at the heads of his audience who do not happen to have been educated down to his standard of histrionic importance." Following in the shadows of Bernhardt did nothing to help the reviews, and attendance flopped. A fed-up Harrison complained to audiences that the Australian press "were dead against everything American; particularly if it had an Irish name."

The American success of the melodrama could not be replicated in Australia simply because Sullivan was not a superstar down under.

Australian audiences actually cared about the quality of the acting and the content of the play. They were not going to pay just for the privilege of star-gazing.

The role in which Australians wanted to watch Sullivan was that of world champion prizefighter. Australians would have preferred one of his famous "knocking out" tours rather than seeing him knock about the stage. They desperately desired to see "the hurricane comet of the fistic firmament," as one sporting paper described him, put up his dukes against one of their native sons, be it Jackson, Slavin, or Joe Goddard. Some Australian voices taunted John L. and questioned his manhood for not facing their brawlers.

The show left Sydney to open a three-week engagement in Melbourne on August 15. The reception was no better. The irreverent "gallery gods had a high time" at Sullivan's expense. A frustrated John L. even stopped his performance at one point, advanced to the footlights, and threatened the audience. "I'll put a head on you fellows, see?" he fumed.

After the disappointments in the big cities, the troupe barnstormed through Victoria and South Australia. At the conclusion of the seven-week theatrical tour, Sullivan finally entered the ropes, but only to second Ashton in an eight-round loss to Goddard in Melbourne on October 2.

To little fanfare, he departed Australia three days later on the steamship *Alameda*. On October 29, Sullivan sailed through the Golden Gate into San Francisco Bay. The devout patriot felt as happy as ever to be back on American soil after his unexpectedly difficult foreign venture. Reporters found John L. sporting muttonchops and spewing profanity against the "set of bums" he encountered in Australia. "I never saw such a mean lot of people in my life," he muttered.

In December, Sullivan returned to the stage in *Honest Hearts and Willing Hands* along with another production penned by Harrison called *Broderick Agra*, a four-act romantic Irish comedy. John L. starred as the title character, a "typical young Irishman ready for fun, frolic, or fight at a moment's notice." Sullivan played a county boxing champion from Tralee, which happened to be the county town in which his father was born and bred. The play had all the stock components of an Irish melodrama: the damsel facing the loss of her ancestral home, the tyrannical landlord, the scheming butler, and even a duel. In the third act, John L. put on the gloves against Ashton, who played the champion of Dublin, to win the Irish championship and the prize money to save the heroine's mortgaged homestead. (Choynski filled in for Ashton at one San Francisco performance and drew a packed house.)

Sullivan's company performed both plays across the United States and Canada in December 1891 and the first half of 1892. John L. wrapped up his tour in Boston in June 1892, the "Boston Strong Boy" returning home after a year and a half that saw him travel to the ends of the earth and back. He had spent so much time before the footlights that a portion of America—and perhaps John L. himself—might have forgotten that he still ruled the heavyweight class. Outside of traveling with a small pair of dumbbells and Indian clubs, Sullivan had done little to keep in shape on his theatrical tours. Nevertheless, nearly three years after he last entered the ring, John L. finally felt the time had arrived to defend his title.

CHAPTER NINE

The Final Round

THE SECOND DECADE OF JOHN L. SULLIVAN'S HEAVYWEIGHT REIGN
dawned on February 7, 1892. Ten years had passed since he skipped out of
a ring in Mississippi City and streaked into superstardom. In an era when
the lifespan of a typical athletic career could be measured in months, the
champion's lengthy tenure at the zenith of his sport was phenomenal.

On the tenth anniversary of his victory over Paddy Ryan, John L.
chugged into the railroad town of La Junta, Colorado, with his theatrical
company. Complacent in virtual retirement from the ring, the old shipwreck of a fighter had just torn through Denver on a bender and remained
so drunk that he couldn't even stumble off the train for breakfast.

The champion had not defended his crown in the thirty-one months
since leaving a bloodied Jake Kilrain sobbing in his corner in Richburg.
Newspapers now coined Sullivan an "actor-pugilist," and he considered
himself more the former than the latter. These days, John L. only raised
his fists in character before the footlights.

The press and the sporting fancy, however, were growing increasingly impatient with the champion. Even from the remote edges of the
Great Plains, John L. could hear their calls to either fight or retire. And
as comfortable as Sullivan found the thespian's life, his alcohol habit and
open wallet to friends and strangers alike meant he needed another big
payday, a monetary infusion that could only come from a championship
prizefight.

John L. decided to answer the critics. On March 5, he fired a missive
to the press in which he challenged "all of the bluffers who have been trying to make capital at my expense." Sullivan called out three challengers

by name. The Australian Frank Slavin topped his list of preferred opponents "as he and his backers have done the greatest amount of blowing." He next ranked the English "bombastic sprinter" Charley Mitchell, whom he "would rather whip than any man in the world," followed by Jim Corbett, "who has achieved his share of bombast." The patriotic champion said he based his rankings on a desire to knock out a foreigner rather than another American.

Notably absent from the troika was the black fighter Peter Jackson. In his challenge, John L. drew the color line in the starkest terms yet. "I will not fight a negro. I never have; I never will," he wrote. Sullivan, finally done with bare knuckles, also insisted that the fight be a gloved one governed by the Marquis of Queensberry Rules. "I want fighting, not foot racing," he asserted.

"First come, first served," Sullivan declared, and Corbett proved his agility was not limited to the ring. Within days, he and his manager, William A. Brady, had recruited enough sporting men to cover the sizable side bet. On March 15, Corbett and Jimmy Wakely, who with Charley Johnston again served as Sullivan's principal backers, met in New York to sign the articles of agreement. Both sides consented to a fight to the finish on Wednesday, September 7 at the Olympic Athletic Club in New Orleans, where prizefighting had been legalized in 1891. They agreed to an astronomical $25,000 purse, which at Sullivan's insistence would be winner-takes-all. Both fighters made an additional wager of $10,000 a side. The total take for one night's work would be just $5,000 shy of the annual salary earned by President Benjamin Harrison.

Corbett hoped for a power shift at the top of the heavyweight division, much like the one taking place in boxing's power structure. Richard K. Fox no longer ruled the sport—or even the sports pages. Charles A. Dana, William Randolph Hearst, Joseph Pulitzer, and other print barons had cribbed Fox's successful formula of sensationalism and sports, and by the 1890s, the pink pages of the *National Police Gazette* had given birth to yellow journalism. As daily newspapers such as Pulitzer's *New York World* hired sporting editors and developed sports sections that extensively covered boxing, the masses no longer needed to wait a week for the arrival of Fox's tabloid to satisfy their pugilistic fix.

Boxing had become such a big business that when it came time for Wakely and Corbett to sign the articles of agreement, they bypassed Fox's lair for the planet's tallest skyscraper—the *New York World* Building. Pulitzer's new journalistic palace, which opened in 1890, had been the first structure in Manhattan to surpass the spire of Trinity Church, a signal that the mass media now lorded over Gotham. From atop the dome crowning his twenty-story building, Pulitzer looked down upon the rest of New York—and his journalistic rivals, including Fox.

As Sullivan's theatrical tour wound down in May, Sullivan expressed little venom toward his challenger. "I have no word of disparagement for him, or for any of the professional boxers," John L. told a reporter before punctuating his thought with a natural addendum—"except Mr. Mitchell." Such kind words for his forthcoming opponent wouldn't last.

The broad brush strokes of Corbett's youth looked familiar to Sullivan. The challenger was born in San Francisco in 1866 to Irish-Catholic immigrants who came to America in the wake of the Great Hunger. Corbett's parents dreamed that their son would join the priesthood like his uncle back in Ireland. When Patrick Corbett learned of his boy's true calling as a prizefighter, he flew into a rage.

Like Sullivan, Corbett showed promise as a baseball player. (His younger brother Joe pitched professionally for the Washington Senators, Baltimore Orioles, and St. Louis Cardinals.) He developed into an all-around athlete, excelling at sports from handball to swimming. Unlike John L., Corbett received a formal ring education from instructors at San Francisco's Olympic Club. By the age of eighteen, he captured the club's heavyweight championship, and soon he had the field to himself because no other fighters wanted to subject themselves to a surefire whipping.

In spite of his nickname, "Gentleman Jim" could be every bit as rough-and-tumble as his contemporaries. He was expelled from parochial school for striking one of the brothers and sparred with the toughs who caroused through the Barbary Coast poolrooms along the waterfront. He proved his courage and stamina in his bloody brawl with Joe Choynski and the marathon stalemate with Peter Jackson.

Unlike the millions of his Celtic brethren who toiled in manual jobs, Corbett first found employment as a clerk for the Nevada Bank. He preferred highbrow hotels to Sullivan's choice of lowly saloons. While John L. immersed himself in the Irish drinking culture, Corbett found "it was the most boring thing in the world to be mauled around by a lot of drunks." Corbett had the good looks and elegance of a matinee idol. Dressed in his neatly tailored suits, brown derby, and cane, "Gentleman Jim" looked "more like a divinity student than a prize fighter." His face carried no scars. Not a tooth was missing, not a hair out of place.

Corbett's sophisticated and polished manner made it more difficult for Irish Americans to connect with him on the same visceral level with which they bonded with John L. The "fancy dude" from California and the ruffian from Boston represented a clash of cultures. "Lace-curtain" Irish versus "shanty" Irish. White collar versus blue. Book smarts versus street smarts. Milk versus whiskey. Pompadour versus mustache.

Their differing personalities also manifested themselves in contrasting ring styles. The slugging Sullivan constantly charged with a frantic energy. The more measured Corbett employed calculating strategy and a scientific approach. He delivered precision punches and demonstrated clever feinting. He had fast feet and even faster hands. Corbett possessed many of the same skills as Mitchell, a fighter who had given Sullivan so much trouble, but with the formidable addition of size and power.

The contrasts between Sullivan and Corbett augured well for a delicious battle in the ring, a matchup the press hyped as a "set-to between animal force and a thinking brain." To further feed the publicity machine, Brady tore a page from Sullivan's promotional playbook and sent his fighter on an exhibition tour of the country in which he sparred with partner Jim Daly and offered one hundred dollars to anyone who could last four rounds with boxing's rising star. (Unlike Sullivan, though, Corbett did have to pay out one night in Milwaukee.)

While the challenger toured the country staying in fighting trim, John L. finished up his theatrical season topping the scales at more than 250 pounds. The champion needed another crash training program. Johnston and Wakely tried to convince Muldoon to reprise his role as trainer, but the falling-out between him and John L. had been too bitter. Instead,

Sullivan's backers gave the thankless task of trying to replicate Muldoon's success to world champion handball player Phil Casey, a husky forty-eight-year-old Irish immigrant from Brooklyn with no experience training a championship fighter.

Although Casey inked the deal to train Sullivan on May 20, the champion spent much of May and June lounging in Boston and New York. Less than four months remained until the fight, but Sullivan felt little urgency to shed his pounds or rust. "Why, all the training I need for that fellow is a haircut and a shave," he boasted.

In mid-June, Corbett settled into his training ground at a modest house near Asbury Park, New Jersey, not far from Brady's summer home. Although he had not fought an important match since defeating Jackson in May 1891, the challenger required little work to round into peak shape. Overtraining was his primary worry, as Corbett poured himself into his workouts like Sullivan poured himself into his drinking. The challenger kept busy rowing, swimming, punching the bag, running, sparring with Daly, and playing handball as many as three hours a day. He trained along to phonograph music to perfect the timing of his punches and incorporate rhythm and grace into his hooks, crosses, and leads.

Corbett relaxed by betting on the horses at the local racetrack and walking the seaside boardwalk with his pet dog, Ned. After a particularly grueling day of training, the challenger indulged himself—at a local ice cream parlor. He could have used a few extra scoops in the eyes of some of his backers, who grew concerned that Corbett had shed too much weight. Although trainer Billy Delaney tried to get Corbett to ease up on his workouts—a problem that never confronted Sullivan's trainers—the challenger could not be stopped. To assuage his backers, Corbett agreed to a public weigh-in. His weight of 197 pounds eased their concerns, but unbeknownst to them, Corbett had concealed nearly twenty pounds of weights in his trouser pockets.

Losing too much weight was not a concern for Sullivan, who did not begin his training until the final days of June when he joined Casey in Brooklyn. Their initial workouts primarily consisted of handball games on Casey's court. In mid-July, the two men, along with Sullivan's regular sparring partner Jack Ashton, left the city for quieter—and cooler—training quarters at the Canoe Place Inn on eastern Long Island. The historic inn, which predated the American Revolution, served as a popular summer retreat for New York's Tammany Hall bosses. Straddled by Peconic Bay to the north and Shinnecock Bay to the south, the picturesque resort stood on a breezy strip of land once used as a Native American canoe portage.

A colossal bust of Hercules, which had served as a figurehead on the USS *Ohio*, guarded the inn's entrance. Daily throughout the summer, hundreds of fans walked past that old warship relic to watch the old warhorse—the American Hercules—at work. Inside the inn's wooden barn, which had been transformed into a makeshift gymnasium, Sullivan skipped rope, punched a bag suspended from the rafters, and sparred with Ashton. He played handball with Casey against a wooden fence and took twelve-mile walks in a heavy sweater. Sullivan labored through rheumatism in his knees and feet, but the arrival of his brother-in-law, James, and his namesake nephew, John L. Lennon, lifted his spirits.

The press reported that the "Big Fellow" was restricting his drinking to just Vichy water and soda, but Sullivan swam in more than just the Peconic Bay during his training. Bass Ale flowed freely. Casey could hardly match Muldoon's ability to get John L. to buckle down. The weeks to New Orleans dwindled. The champion was still fat and was spreading himself too thin.

While Sullivan struggled with the discipline required to tone his body, he also lacked the singular focus that the task required. He spent hours honing his lines for his latest theatrical production, *The Man from Boston*, which would begin less than two weeks after the title bout. On top of balancing training and rehearsals, John L. also spent time on Long Island putting the finishing touches on his autobiography.

When it was announced earlier in the year that Sullivan had signed a contract with a Boston publishing firm, the news hardly stirred the ghosts of Thoreau, Emerson, Alcott, Longfellow, or any of the literary gods who sprouted from Boston's soil. But much as John L. broke new ground for an athlete by taking to the stage, he did the same by taking up the pen, not that he likely did any heavy lifting of a writing instrument. A ghostwriter's hand scripted at least a portion of Sullivan's memoir, which—with the three-hundred-page book due to be released just days before the encounter in New Orleans—required the champion's input to stay on schedule.

The book's title—*Life and Reminiscences of a Nineteenth Century Gladiator*—did not roll off the tongue, and the memoir hardly told all. "Who has had more living than me? Nobody!" the champion boasted, but this recounting of his adventurous life left out many of the saucy chapters. The autobiography failed to delve into his drinking. It doesn't mention his son, John Jr., nor the women—marital or extramarital—in his life. The book focused mainly on his ring exploits and reads at times like a scrapbook of newspaper clippings.

The most fascinating feature of the autobiography is actually the appendix, a physical examination of Sullivan by Dr. Dudley A. Sargent, America's first professor of physical education and director of Harvard University's campus gymnasium. Sargent and his colleagues examined Sullivan in Boston on June 2 and visited Sullivan at his training ground on August 13. They measured nearly every part of the champion's body from the length of his forearms to the girth of his ankles.

In his report, Sargent presented a scientific analysis to explain why Sullivan excelled as a fighter. He compared the champion's vitals against a data set he had compiled from the examination of several thousand Harvard students and athletes. Sargent announced that Sullivan's height surpassed nearly 90 percent of the sample. His seventy-four-inch armspan charted in the top 6 percent. His lung capacity measured in the top 5 percent. Not surprisingly, Sullivan's prodigious neck was the largest Sargent had ever measured.

The doctor reported that Sullivan excelled far above the normal man in all physical respects but one: thigh length. Even then, Sargent conceded that Sullivan's short thighs could be advantageous in boxing by affording the necessary quickness for starting and rapidly changing positions. The doctor warned, however, that Sullivan's breathing appeared hurried and labored, and he expressed concern "that Sullivan's respiratory apparatus is his weak point vitally."

Although John L. had said his autobiography could "be placed on the family table beside the Bible without fear," the two full-length nude photographs of Sullivan taken from behind that were published with Sargent's examination surely caused many Victorian cheeks to blush. In spite of its literary shortcomings, the tome proved popular with Sullivan's legion of fans, including a pregnant Irish-American woman in Manassa, Colorado, who read it over and over to her unborn son. "I decided that if you turned out to be a boy, you could be just like him," she told her boy, the future heavyweight champion "Jack" Dempsey.

—✦—

As *Life and Reminiscences of a Nineteenth Century Gladiator* rolled off the printing presses, its author, reportedly down to 206 pounds, broke his training camp on August 29. That evening, four thousand fans filled Brooklyn's Clermont Avenue Rink to judge Sullivan's form for themselves. Stripped to his waist, John L. sparred three rounds with Ashton, and "the fistic cognoscenti scanned him as thoroughly as though he were some rare plant." The champion's backers expressed their pleasure at his shape and his show of speed and power.

John L. demonstrated that his braggadocio was in peak form. "I will win quickly if Corbett will fight," Sullivan predicted. "I am told he has been devoting much of his time to practicing getting away." The cocky champion continued, "I think this job's the easiest one I ever had. I do, really. I do not think it will be a long fight. Maybe it won't last two rounds."

Four miles away from the champion, the challenger also spent the day preening before the boxing fancy. Brady had scored a coup by booking for his fighter the city's most coveted venue, the second incarnation of Madison Square Garden. The new athletic palace, which opened in 1890, featured an arena, a concert hall, a theater, a roof garden, and a soaring Moorish tower topped by a gilt copper nude statue of the Roman goddess Diana sculpted by Augustus Saint-Gaudens.

Under the cover of Diana's outstretched hunting bow, six thousand fans filed into the Garden for what amounted to a public workout session. The audience watched the challenger skip rope, toss the medicine ball, play handball, punch the bag, and even eat a meal before he finally sparred three rounds with Daly.

Three days later, Sullivan boarded a six-car special train in Weehawken, New Jersey, along with Casey, Ashton, Wakely, Johnston, and old acquaintance Frank Moran. For the third time in his life, he headed south to New Orleans for a title fight.

What an incredible change had occurred since his first venture to the Crescent City a decade ago. The then-chiseled, little-known challenger was now a doughy champion and a household name. Gray frosted his temples. His neck and waistline had thickened. Like notches on a gunslinger's belt, the lines on his face recorded the thousands of drinks he had downed. His tremendous power endured, but the agility of a decade ago had decayed.

Boxing had been transformed in the previous decade as well, in large part due to Sullivan himself. By the force of his personality and his ring dominance, he delivered the sport from the backwoods to the front pages. By championing the Marquis of Queensberry Rules, he pulled boxing from the antediluvian, bare-knuckle age to the modern gloved era. In 1882, Sullivan travelled south fully prepared to break the law and raise his bare knuckles at an unknown location in the hinterlands. Ten years later, he readied himself to legally don gloves inside an electrically lit, tenthousand-seat arena in the middle of New Orleans. In 1882, prizefighting was an outlawed endeavor; now, it was a regulated commercial enterprise.

On this trip to New Orleans, there would be no militiamen, no gubernatorial proclamations, and no veil of secrecy. Instead, there would be all the trappings of the first modern heavyweight championship. Leading newspapers from around the country dispatched reporters to cover the every move of the two men around New Orleans. Western Union employed fifty operators to handle the special dispatches from ringside that would provide round-by-round results to millions around the country. Special telegraph lines were installed in hotels, saloons, and athletic clubs—and even in the home of Corbett's parents—to deliver instantaneous news from New Orleans. Theaters in New York planned to announce regular updates to curious audiences during performances. Pulitzer even planned to turn his *New York World* Building into a virtual scoreboard by lighting a red beacon from the skyscraper's dome when Sullivan was in the ascendancy and a white beacon when Corbett had the advantage.

The Olympic Club planned for the Sullivan-Corbett fight to culminate a three-day "fistic carnival" that featured the lightweight championship between Jack McAuliffe and Billy Myer on September 5 and the featherweight championship between George Dixon and Jack Skelly on September 6. The unprecedented pugilistic spectacle marked the coming-out party of the gloved age that John L. pioneered.

The hype machine, fueled in part by the enormous sums of money wagered on the fight, churned for months. In drawing rooms and corner stores, America talked of nothing else but the clash of heavyweights. By the beginning of September, the fight sucked all the oxygen out of other stories in the news, including the upcoming presidential election between the current and previous occupants of the White House—Benjamin Harrison and Grover Cleveland—the continuing saga of Lizzie Borden, and fears that the raging worldwide cholera pandemic would reach American shores any day.

While the contagion remained at bay, boxing fever infected the country. The national frenzy greeted Sullivan at every station on his way to New Orleans. Seven thousand fans welcomed him to Dayton. Ten thousand jammed the train station in Cincinnati. Mayors led welcoming delegations. Village bands serenaded the champion. Men "leaped up and down like marionettes" just to steal a glimpse of Sullivan inside his car.

The trip to New Orleans was not without its challenges. The baggage car specially equipped with exercise equipment for Sullivan's use en route was left in Buffalo, and the railroad company also failed to attach a dining car to the train, which forced Casey to fight through the crowds at station after station to bring Sullivan his meals. "That's just like these railroad companies," groused Moran. "They get your money and then don't care a damn."

John L. also caught word that a hostile reception awaited him in Tennessee, thanks to the never-ending legal saga in the aftermath of the Kilrain fight in Richburg. The legal team that assisted Sullivan and Johnston after their arrest in Nashville claimed the men had failed to fully pay their bills, and authorities waited in Chattanooga to arrest the two men. When the train pulled into Chattanooga, police boarded and searched every car in vain for the wanted men. In a bit of trickery, Sullivan's car had been decoupled on the outskirts of the city and pulled through a belt line by a special engine to meet back up with the rest of the cars on the other side of Chattanooga.

Corbett, fearful of being infected by malaria in New Orleans and seeking to remain in familiar environs as long as possible, trailed two days behind Sullivan. The challenger brought his own water and even his own bed aboard the train, and like the champion, he had a baggage car fitted with weights and a punching bag. The makeshift training quarters caused Corbett his own brush with southern justice in North Carolina. On a stopover in Charlotte on Sunday, September 4, Corbett squeezed in some brief road work, worked out in his private car, and wrestled and boxed with Daly for an hour. The challenger intended to leave Charlotte early the next morning, but he was roused by Delaney in the middle of the night. The trainer told his fighter that police sought his arrest for desecrating the Sabbath with his workout. Corbett scrambled and stowed away in a sleeping car, which was towed by a special engine safely over the state line.

Earlier on that Sunday morning, Sullivan arrived in New Orleans. As he had three years earlier, before the Kilrain fight, John L. checked into Mrs. Green's Rampart Street boardinghouse. Wakely and Johnston soon decided, however, that the lodgings had too many distractions, particularly "the presence in the house of some pretty quadroon girls in whom it was feared Sullivan might become too much interested." Sullivan's backers checked him into the St. Charles Hotel the next day.

When John L. stepped onto the scales for the first time at the Young Men's Gymnastic Club, where he also had made last-minute preparations for the Kilrain fight, the news was not good. He had gained nine pounds since leaving Long Island, and the hours were growing short.

Corbett arrived in New Orleans the morning before the battle, by which time the city blazed with excitement. Specially chartered rail cars arrived and poured out sporting men from around the country into the epicenter of boxing. The saloons and gambling houses crackled with energy. Hacks, hoteliers, and whores all did brisk business. Men and boys wore buttons proclaiming their allegiance. Peddlers circulated through the French Quarter selling replicas of each man's colors. Visitors paused in front of store windows festooned with photographs of Sullivan and Corbett. Large crowds watched John L. try to shed excess flesh at the Young Men's Gymnastic Club, and a slightly smaller contingent watched the challenger's final workouts at the Southern Athletic Club.

In New Orleans alone, estimates of the money wagered on the fight approached half a million dollars. With three fights on which to wager, gambling men reveled in all the betting options, the parlays and trifectas. The lobby of the St. Charles Hotel resembled a trading room floor with prices constantly fluctuating. The long, lithe "Gentleman Jim" possessed the edge in youth, speed, and science. Sullivan had not fought for three years. Still, Sullivan was a 4–1 favorite on the streets of New Orleans. The American public still had tremendous faith—and love—for its champion.

The betting line puzzled the confident Corbett. "They ought to be ten to one on me—at least ten to one," he told a reporter. "That fellow couldn't hit me in a year. I'll take my time, but I don't think he'll win a round." "Gentleman Jim" told his manager to put everything he had on him to win. "I know I can lick him without mussing my hair."

The start of the fistic carnival was finally at hand on September 5. The event had been months, and really years, in the making. Athletic clubs grew in popularity in New Orleans during the 1880s as the city's commercial elite amassed greater wealth and more leisure time. Crescent City businessmen who earned their fortunes in lumber, coal, cotton, and real estate joined with doctors, lawyers, and public servants to found the Olympic Club in 1883. They constructed a four-story masculine playground on Royal Street between Montegut and Clouet Streets that featured smoking and reading rooms covered with fine art, a bar, a dining room, a billiards parlor, a bowling alley, a rifle range, a swimming pool, and a gymnasium.

Even with all it offered, the manly lair lacked one thing its members greatly desired: boxing. The patrons put their money and political connections to work, and in 1890, New Orleans and Louisiana legalized gloved contests—with stipulations. Bouts could only take place in athletic clubs and under the watchful eyes of the police. Alcohol sales and Sunday bouts were prohibited, and fifty dollars from each match had to be given to charity.

With the measure, New Orleans supplanted New York as the American mecca of boxing, and the Olympic Club positioned itself as the country's premier fight venue after staging the January 1891 middleweight title bout in which Bob Fitzsimmons defeated "Nonpareil" Jack Dempsey. Later that year in court, the club successfully tested the portion of the Louisiana law that still prohibited prizefights, which cleared the way for the Olympic Club to post the $25,000 purse to land the Sullivan-Corbett heavyweight title fight and eventually arrange for the three-night boxing extravaganza.

To stage the "Triple Event," the Olympic Club constructed a wondrous, electrically illuminated arena on an adjacent cotton press yard just a block from the Mississippi River. The fans who came inside to watch the opening night saw the undefeated lightweight champion McAuliffe, who was born in Ireland's County Cork but came to America as a boy, knock out Myer, the "Streator Cyclone," in the fifteenth round to maintain his unblemished record.

The following evening, Sullivan's fellow Bostonian, the diminutive featherweight champion Dixon, entered the ropes to defend his crown against Skelly. The presence of the African-American champion, nicknamed "Little Chocolate," stirred controversy in the heart of the Jim Crow South. Black men were normally prohibited from the Olympic Club, but in this case, the patrons made an exception, although African-American fans entered through a separate entrance and were segregated from the white spectators in seven hundred seats in the upper gallery. Skelly, whose nose was broken in training two days before the fight, offered little resistance, and Dixon knocked him out in the eighth round. Even white hands clapped for Dixon's demonstration of skill and fitness.

Dixon's victory set off loud celebrations among the African Americans of New Orleans. "The colored people on the levees are so triumphant over the victory of the negro last night that they are loudly proclaiming the superiority of their race, to the great scandal of the whites, who declare that they should not be encouraged to entertain even feelings of equality, much less of superiority," reported the *New York Herald*. Due to the backlash, Dixon would be the first and only African-American fighter to appear at the Olympic Club, and years passed before another integrated audience witnessed a boxing match in New Orleans.

As darkness descended upon the fight-crazy metropolis on the evening of September 7, boxing's biggest star streaked into the New Orleans night. Cleanly shaven, freshly shorn, and refreshed after a short nap, Sullivan stepped out of the St. Charles Hotel with Casey, Johnston, Wakely, and the rest of his entourage, which now included McAuliffe. As he chewed on a quilled toothpick, John L. tipped his brown derby hat and bowed to the crowd "as an emperor might in acknowledgment of the cheers of his loyal people." About ninety minutes before the 9 p.m. fight time, America's fistic king stepped into an open-air carriage and rode in royal style to the grand glove contest.

Sullivan asked his driver to find a quiet street where he wouldn't be recognized, but that was an impossible request. John L. was swept away in a current of ten thousand fans who flowed down Royal Street like the Mississippi River coursing its way to the delta. A symphony of clomping horses and clanging streetcar bells drifted through the downtown streets. Men shouted themselves hoarse trying to find a hack, any hack to take them on the two-mile journey to the Olympic Club.

Sullivan and McAuliffe sang old Irish ballads as the coach rattled over the cobblestone streets. As they drew closer to the arena, their progress slowed. The streets around the Olympic Club had been jammed since 5 p.m. Locals crowded their stoops and waved fans to cool themselves as they watched the passing parade. The temporary barrooms and lunch counters that had sprouted on the side streets around the arena found a bountiful supply of thirsty and hungry fight fans.

A roar trailed the champion through the streets of New Orleans, and the growing crescendo heralded his arrival as his open carriage approached the Olympic Club. "I never felt better in my life," Sullivan boasted to a

New York Sun reporter as he disembarked the carriage and bounded up the steps. "The fight will be all over in ten rounds, providing that Corbett doesn't jump the rope before that time." One reporter who got a glimpse of Sullivan's eyes afire prayed that he would not kill Corbett.

The challenger had arrived at the Olympic Club early and rested on a cot in his dressing room as his seconds fanned him. Hours earlier, Corbett had eaten his pre-fight meal with Myer, who had lost to McAuliffe two nights before. Through a black eye and cracked lip, the vanquished fighter had warned Corbett, "You may look worse than I do when Sullivan gets through with you tonight."

"No, Billy," the challenger replied, "Sullivan won't have to hit me as many times as McAuliffe did you, to lick me. If it's done, it will be done with one punch!"

To the disgust of his trainer Delaney, Corbett had dressed in his finest duds: a light summer suit, a straw hat, and a little bamboo cane. He had left his quarters and boarded a carriage with the men who would be his seconds—Brady, Delaney, and the veteran fighter "Professor" John Donaldson. Another carriage transporting Mike Donovan, who had served as a valued instructor, and the rest of Corbett's entourage trailed behind. As the challenger rode to the Olympic Club, the constant chanting of his opponent's name percussed in his ears.

Ticket holders with reserved seats filed in the arena from Royal Street. Fans with fifteen-dollar general admission tickets rushed the Chartres Street entrance to grab seats as close to the action as they could. Speculators sold ringside seats for an unfathomable one hundred dollars. If fans needed a reminder that the biggest purse in boxing history awaited the winner, they could glance at the money bags and piles of coins emblazoned on the tickets they clutched in their hands.

The atmosphere inside the arena was truly electric. Sixty bright bulbs bathed the ring with golden light. Fans were charged up, too, burning nervous energy by chewing gum, chattering, and smoking cigars, the glowing embers of which danced like fireflies in the arena's murky outer reaches.

In the dressing rooms, a priest gave Corbett a blessing, while a relaxed Sullivan cracked jokes with McAuliffe. The champion heard the constant rumble of the crowd that crested in periodic waves whenever a prominent person arrived. Fans applauded the entrance of fighters such as Fitzsimmons and Joe Choynski and even the famous Mississippi duelist J. J. Kennedy, "the deadliest shot in the South." Loud cheers erupted when the previous night's victor, Dixon, arrived with J. Madison Vance, a prominent African-American politician. The Olympic Club had already made an exception to its whites-only policy that evening for Dixon, but Vance's presence was too much. They asked the politician to leave, then relented after Dixon threatened to storm out as well. Throughout the night, Vance and Dixon would be the only black men in an ocean of white faces.

In the soaking humidity, sweat beaded on the foreheads of the fans and on the ginger ale, sarsaparilla, and soda water sold by the vendors. Although state law prevented the Olympic Club from selling alcohol, nearly everyone toted bottles of whiskey in their hind pockets for quick nips. The night was so sticky that the tarpaulins that covered the arena, with the exception of one directly above the ring, had been rolled back for ventilation—and perhaps to allow the heavens to peer in. About a half-hour before the fight, an unexpected rainstorm blew through New Orleans. Rain streamed down upon the spectators. Umbrellas shot up, and fans raised chairs over their heads as workers scrambled to engage the makeshift roof.

Safe and dry from the quick cloudburst that delivered welcome relief from the heat, Brady entered Sullivan's dressing room for the toss for corners. Corbett's representative won the flip and selected the same corner that had been used by the victorious McAuliffe and Dixon the two previous nights. In a city where voodoo superstition hovered as thickly as the soupy summertime air, this was not a good sign for the champion, who emerged from his dressing room shortly before 9 p.m. in green tights and black shoes. Johnston, McAuliffe, Casey, and Joe Lannan, a last-minute replacement for Wakely, who had injured his ankle walking, accompanied the champion as his seconds.

As soon as the ten thousand fans saw Sullivan, a hurricane of voices shook the arena. He took his seat, and then Corbett—clad in greenish-brown tights, green socks, and black boots—followed to a more modest reception with his seconds. Bat Masterson served as the timekeeper for Sullivan's challenger, as he had in Richburg for Kilrain. Moran kept time for John L.

Corbett looked like a panther, muscular but sleek. He appeared his usual cool self. He politely bowed to the crowd and smiled. By practicing his charges and sidesteps, he tested the traction of the ring surface, which was covered with solidly packed reddish-brown earth taken from the bottom of the Mississippi River.

The respected "Professor" John Duffy, owner of a St. Charles Street saloon and Olympic Club boxing instructor, refereed the fight, as he had the previous two nights. Duffy, who had a solid reputation for honesty and impartiality, had been in close proximity to Sullivan in New Orleans once before. When John L. appeared at the St. Charles Theatre on his "knocking out" tour in 1884, Duffy boxed Peter Burns in a preliminary match. Now, he was part of the main event as he announced the champion at 212 pounds and the challenger at 178 pounds.

In addition to more than thirty pounds, the nearly thirty-four-year-old champion also had eight years on Corbett. He was also three inches shorter than the challenger. Still, Sullivan knew one punch was all he would need, and he still possessed his big right, not to mention his ferocious glare.

Corbett knew that Sullivan half-whipped his opponents with his fearsome scowl before a punch had ever been thrown, so he treated the eyes of the world's biggest superstar as he did the brightly burning sun. He refused to look directly at them. When Sullivan, with his fists clenched, shot his wicked eye at his opponent in the opposite corner, Corbett laughed and pretended to wave to friends. Even when Duffy called the fighters to center to go over the instructions, the challenger refused to let the champion look him dead in the eye. When told to shake hands, Corbett looked down with a dismissive smile and then disdainfully threw his hand aside after a quick, hard grip. Corbett returned to his corner to don his five-ounce gloves, pointed at Sullivan, and cracked jokes that caused Brady and Delaney to "explode with laughter."

Sullivan nearly came to a froth as the bell clanged.

At the signal, Sullivan charged like an animal at his insolent opponent. Determined to get Corbett "right at the jump," John L. barreled at his opponent with his signature aggression.

While Sullivan sought to end the fight then and there, the clever Corbett was choreographing the bout dozens of rounds into the future. The challenger, whose mind was as powerful a weapon as his fists, opened the fight by dissecting the champion's style. Corbett believed the greatest danger facing him was to be cornered by Sullivan when he was tired or dazed, so he deliberately let the champion corner him while he was still fresh, so he could learn what his opponent intended to do with him when he had him trapped. It was a risky strategy, one that could only be employed by a fighter confident in his abilities.

As John L. rushed, Corbett backpedaled and nestled in the corner. He saw Sullivan give a quick slap to his thigh with his left hand, the telltale sign of an impending right that Donovan had warned about. Corbett sidestepped, pulled back his head, and felt the breeze from Sullivan's huge right, which missed connecting by an eighth of an inch. At ringside, instinct overtook Fitzsimmons, who snapped back his own head and hit that of a fan in the row behind.

The crafty Corbett slid back to the middle of the ring and used his superior speed to dance and dodge around the champion for the rest of the round. With every Sullivan charge, Corbett allowed John L. to draw nearer so that he could judge just how close he could get to deliver one of his own blows and still be out of Sullivan's reach. This intellectual approach to the ring was foreign to Sullivan. To Corbett, a prizefight was like a chess match, and he envisioned the board many moves ahead. Sullivan, however, tried trampling all the pieces on the board.

Corbett lured Sullivan into thinking he was controlling the action, when the exact opposite was true. The challenger continued to allow John L. to back him into each corner of the ring until he had gathered all the necessary data and mastered the calculations. He understood just where to position his head to dodge a blow in case Sullivan should corner him later in the bout.

In the second round, the nimble challenger "flew about the arena like a hunted deer" and used his sidesteps and feints to escape the charging brawler. Sullivan could not catch up to his opponent to land a big blow, and he grew infuriated at Corbett's prancing. The crowd grew impatient as well. They hissed at Corbett and jeered "Sprinter!" The challenger turned away from the champion, waved both hands to the crowd, and yelled to the hecklers, "Wait a while! You'll see a fight."

The fans feared that Corbett would turn the fight into a footrace like Mitchell and Kilrain before him, but the challenger had more power than Sullivan's former foes and the Marquis of Queensberry Rules meant he could not play a similar game of keep-away or drop to the ground at a whim to escape an onrushing Sullivan. Although Corbett had yet to land a solid punch, he would have to engage John L.

He chose to do so in round three. Corbett wanted his first punch to be a particularly powerful blow so that the champion would respect his hitting ability. As the round opened, he floated lightly backward on his toes like a "ballet master" and allowed Sullivan to corner him. The champion expected Corbett to slither away as he had in the previous two rounds. Corbett darted his eyes left, then right, as if he was searching for an escape. Sullivan's head moved in tandem with his opponent's eyes to block his outlet. As John L. set to launch his big right hand, Corbett drove "his long, lean left arm straight up in a piston-like blow" that connected with full power to the champion's face. Sullivan's head snapped back. Corbett charged with more punches. He backed Sullivan into his corner. The crowd yelled. Men jumped on top of their chairs and swung their coats in the air.

As Corbett returned to his corner at the end of the round, he believed that the rally proved he was the better man. Sensing that he could deliver a quick knockout, he told his seconds he wanted to continue to take the fight to Sullivan, but his corner convinced him to stick with his more patient strategy to wear down the champion.

Across the ring, John L. seethed. So far, he did not appear to be the champion of old, but simply an old champion. Still, he felt confident because he always possessed a knockout wallop.

He knew that one big punch, one big punch was all he needed.

Pouncing out of his corner, the angry Sullivan started the fourth round. The men exchanged blows, but the champion still could not land a big punch. The agile Corbett continued to glide across the ring like an ice skater, while the lumbering Sullivan "moved with all the slowness and majesty of an iceberg." Frustrated at Corbett's waiting game, John L. barked, "Come on and fight like a man!" Corbett only laughed.

The challenger launched a savage attack in the fifth round. He popped Sullivan in the nose. The champion looked down and saw red rivulets trickling down his chest. After Sullivan clutched his opponent, the champion's blood slathered both fighters. The challenger jabbed Sullivan's nose several more times. He hit Sullivan and then danced away. John L. felt himself fading. Between rounds, he "lay like a huge porpoise, puffing and blowing to regain his lost breath." Sullivan knew his endurance was limited. He felt even more urgency to land that knockout punch.

As the rounds piled up, the challenger continued to play a waiting game. He delivered a pugilistic potpourri of blows and escaped punishment with ever-increasing ease. Corbett felt confident in victory and decided to play it safe even if it prolonged the bout. "Gentleman Jim" wanted to wear the champion out and neutralize any potential danger.

He knew that one big punch, one big punch was all John L. needed.

As his fans grew dispirited, John L. gasped for air, struggling to land any kind of solid blow on his challenger. His lungs burned. His legs weakened. He began to ache from the increasingly harder shots Corbett delivered against his weakened defenses. By the sixteenth round, the champion could barely see out of his swollen left eye. He could taste the blood from his split lips. He could feel himself tiring, but he knew he would never quit. He continued to answer the bell round after round.

Sullivan just could not get close enough to Corbett to connect with his best weapon, the right to the jaw. In the nineteenth round, Corbett connected with four straight jabs to the face as the crowd roared. The champion's friend Yank Sullivan walked out of the arena rather than witness what he thought was the inevitable end. An exhausted Sullivan tried to hold on as the storm of blows washed over him.

He knew that one big punch, one big punch was all he needed.

In the twentieth, Sullivan missed wildly and Corbett hammered a hard right to his stomach. "That was a good one," complimented the champ. He returned to the corner groggy, a spent shell of a fighter.

When the twenty-first round started, Corbett finally felt he had disarmed the wearied champion. John L. could barely raise his guard. Corbett rushed and delivered three quick punches to the stomach. The ferocious glare could not be found behind Sullivan's glassy eyes. The champion's arms dangled limply at his side. Corbett knew the time had come. He delivered a staccato of left and right hooks and sent John L. to the ropes. The crimson rivulets on Sullivan's chest now rushed like the swollen Mississippi in a deluge. Corbett launched a right. The fist crashed against Sullivan's jaw. The mighty champion buckled. He dropped in a heap.

Felled by his own signature punch, Sullivan laid on his stomach on the gritty ring floor. He struggled to stand up. He heard Duffy begin the count. He gazed up and saw the knees of Corbett, who hovered over the champion with another fusillade ready to discharge. His fans clasped their hands in a collective vigil as they prayed for their idol to rise.

For the first time in his storied ring career, the champion felt a strange sensation. He felt as if he were standing on a bridge surrounded by water. He tried to rise with his hands and knees to a sitting posture. His legs refused. They buckled. He could feel himself plummeting into the water. He couldn't break his fall and slammed the surface with his face as he heard a torrent of water filling his ears.

An "uproar like Niagara tumbling over the cliffs" shook the arena as Duffy stood over the prostrate fighter and cried, "Ten!"

For the first time ever, John L. took the count.

Corbett's knockout right sent shockwaves pulsating around the world. The result still ranks as one of the greatest upsets in boxing history. From the distance of a half-century, legendary sportswriter Grantland Rice called it "the most sensational single episode in the history of American sport."

To millions, the news from New Orleans was a national calamity. Blinded by Sullivan's fame, America refused to see—or couldn't see—that the champion was aging and out of shape. Distraught youngsters could not understand what happened to their idol. Through their tears, they ground their heels into photographs of the new champion and vowed to beat up Corbett to avenge their hero. When the news of the knockout arrived at the Chicago Armory, one incredulous Irish American named Thomas Jefferson Dolan asked, "On whose authority?" When told the authorities were Western Union and the telegraph operator, the doubting Thomas blurted, "They're both damned liars."

The result was also a financial calamity for Sullivan's backers, and some of his faithful friends and fans went bust as a result. Cleveland sporting man Tom Costello, who had served as Sullivan's timekeeper in Richburg, lost $30,000 on John L. Steve Brodie, the famed daredevil who boasted of surviving a jump off the Brooklyn Bridge in 1886, lost all his money on the champion. He pawned his jewelry and borrowed train fare just to return to New York.

In Boston, Billy Hogarty had borrowed cash and hocked his barbershop to put as much money as he could on his good friend. With his South End tonsorial parlor gone, Hogarty eventually started a new career as a bartender at the downtown Quincy House hotel. McAuliffe had given a friend every penny of his winnings from the lightweight title fight two nights earlier to lay on Sullivan, but luckily—and wisely—his friend did not make the wager.

Back in Corbett's hometown of San Francisco, his brother Harry had tens of thousands of extra reasons to rejoice when the news crossed the telegraph wires. He had mortgaged his billiard hall to wager $10,000 on his brother. He won considerably more. Corbett's father reiterated his disappointment at his son's career choice but acknowledged he was happy that, if his son must be a fighter, at least he was the champion.

In Chicago, the future gambling kingpin of the Stockyards, Big Jim O'Leary, bet everything he had on the 4–1 underdog. It was his first big hit, a good break for the young man who was two years old when the blame for the Great Chicago Fire was placed on the cow owned by his mother, Mrs. O'Leary.

The atmosphere was quite different in Sullivan's hometown. September 7, 1892, had already been a dark day in Boston with the passing of one of the region's literary giants, the legendary poet and abolitionist John Greenleaf Whittier. That evening, thousands thronged Newspaper Row to await the latest boxing bulletins. The crowd swirled with anticipation under the flickering gaslights, but they grew more somber as the bad news chattered across the telegraph. They expected a victory party, but the black Boston night grew even darker when the final news flashed from New Orleans. They scattered home with shattered hopes and bank accounts.

The following morning, the front page of the *Boston Globe* featured a banner headline, six columns of text, drawings of both fighters, and even illustrations of their closed fists, while news of Whittier's death was buried on the fourth page. The respective coverage of the stories struck a segment of America as a head-shaking commentary on the country's cultural priorities, the power of celebrity, and the relative value of brains and brawn.

In New York, the skyline broadcast the result to the entire metropolis. The redder Sullivan's face grew with blood, the whiter the light glowed from the *New York World* Building to signal that Corbett was the better man. The scene was somber inside Johnston's Brooklyn saloon and Brodie's watering hole on the Bowery, which had a huge oil painting of Sullivan hanging outside. Newspapers estimated that three-quarters of the twenty thousand people who stood for hours inside Printing House Square to follow the round-by-round results left disappointed.

Similar scenes played out in city after city. Twenty thousand people gathered in Pittsburgh and in Chicago. Streetcars in St. Louis could not pass through the thick throngs that clogged the streets. When news of Corbett's victory arrived, saloons around the country spit out fans who howled through the streets. As midnight arrived in America, the dark skies resounded with the cries of newsboys hawking extra editions, still hot from the printing presses, in their ink-stained hands.

—◦—

As soon as Duffy counted out Sullivan, Brady and Donovan rushed the ring and flung their arms around the new champion. True to his word, barely a black hair in Corbett's pompadour had been mussed during his one hour and twenty minutes in the ring.

Sullivan's seconds helped him to his corner and propped him up in his chair. They poured water on their man, lifted ammonia underneath his nose, and fanned him with a towel. John L. turned to McAuliffe and asked, "Say, am I licked? Did that young fellow do it?" McAuliffe broke the truth.

Corbett walked to Sullivan's corner to shake hands with the vanquished boxer. The sudden dynastic succession and the shifting allegiance of the fans from Sullivan to Corbett jarred the new monarch. "I was actually disgusted with the crowd, and it left a lasting impression on me," Corbett wrote in his autobiography. "It struck me as sad to see all those thousands who had given him such a wonderful ovation when he entered the ring turning it to me now that he was down and out."

Bruised, bleeding, and beaten, the deposed fistic king insisted on addressing his subjects. He staggered to his feet and teetered until he fell against the ropes on the opposite side of the ring. He slid his hand along the top rope until he felt one of the posts for support. Raising the imperial right arm that had silenced so many opponents, Sullivan quieted ten thousand people. His deep bass voice rumbled from his bloody lips.

"Gentlemen, all I've got to say is, I stayed once too long. I met a young man. I'm glad the championship remains in America, with one of her own people." The ever-patriotic fighter signed his eulogy with his typical rhetorical flourish, "Very truly yours, John L. Sullivan." The "Boston Strong Boy" melted into the arms of his seconds, but the country never forgot the graceful punctuation mark Sullivan placed on the story of his heavyweight reign.

In sports, youth ultimately wins out. Sullivan had traveled the inescapable arc of a professional athlete's career, but he had arrived in New Orleans overweight and overconfident, undertrained and underprepared. He had been thoroughly licked. Corbett didn't level him with a lucky shot, but overwhelmed him with a cacophony of unanswered blows.

After leaving the Olympic Club, Corbett rode to the Southern Athletic Club where sixteen hundred people feted the new champion. While his friends toasted Corbett's victory with wine, the new champion poured himself a glass of milk. He left a short time later for his quarters, turned off the light, and fell asleep in the familiar bed he had brought with him from Asbury Park.

For the rest of his life—no matter his other achievements in the ring—Corbett found himself defined in relation to Sullivan. He was more apt to be described as "the only man to defeat John L. Sullivan" than "heavyweight champion of the world." When Corbett died in 1933, the banner headline in the *Boston Herald* read: JOHN L. SULLIVAN'S CONQUEROR SUCCUMBS TO HEART DISEASE AT NEW YORK. And although Corbett was every bit as Irish as John L., he never felt the love from his Celtic brethren as Sullivan did. The new champion wasn't vilified by any means, but a segment of Irish America couldn't forgive him for dethroning their hero.

While Corbett slept soundly after sipping his glass of milk, Sullivan attempted to drown his sorrows. They proved too buoyant, however, and surfaced every so often in uncontrollable sobs. Sullivan had ushered in the modern age of sports on the same night he was ushered out of the championship he had held for more than a decade. As he mourned his loss in the hours after his defeat, John L. could only mutter, "What has happened? What'll become of me?"

CHAPTER TEN

"I'm Still John L. Sullivan—
Ain't That Right?"

AMERICA AWOKE ON SEPTEMBER 8, 1892, WITH A HANGOVER.
Waves of titanic change had battered the country's moorings during the previous decade. Edison had electrified the nation. Civil rights
for African Americans had been strangled in Jim Crow's noose. Corporate titans had built magnificent palaces as immigrants sank deeper
into slums. Labor unrest had rocked American cities. Through it all,
though, the country could always rely on a declarative sentence amid a
sea of questions: John L. Sullivan is heavyweight champion. Now with its
touchstone pulverized, America lost its bearings.

Sullivan arose the morning after losing to Jim Corbett with an unfamiliar moniker: *former* champion. John L. certainly hadn't prepared for
the inevitable. He never entered the ring without expecting to win. He
couldn't process the concept of defeat, let alone think about what he
would do if he lost. And none of the fallen fighters who came before
him could guide him through this chapter of his life. No boxer had ever
achieved the heights that Sullivan had, which meant no fighter had ever
fallen so far. No script existed for what a sports deity should do when he
plunged from the heavens.

Once again, John L. found himself a pioneer. He was the first athlete
forced to answer this question: What happens when the world's most
famous sports superstar loses the grip on what made him exalted in the
first place?

A man so drawn to fame couldn't stop living a public life any more
than he could stop living, but he had no idea if the crowds had idolized

him because he was Sullivan or because he was the reigning heavyweight champion. A comeback would require severe discipline and a radical life-style change for a thirty-three-year-old alcoholic on the steep downside of a ring career, not attractive options for John L., but he had also seen what could happen to fighters when they decided to leave the ring. Even boxers who hadn't lived in the glare of the limelight struggled in retire-ment. Ex-pugs tended to burn hot before being snuffed out, drunk, and broke. As Sullivan boarded the train out of New Orleans, he faced the possibility of becoming what every fighter fears: a has-been.

—

Corbett and Sullivan rode separate excursion trains bound for New York. Cheers greeted "Gentleman Jim" along his triumphant journey, but the crowds were drawn not by affection for the new champion, but by curios-ity to see what kind of man could possibly have knocked out the mighty Sullivan.

America still struggled to explain the inexplicable. Some saw a sym-bolic triumph of science over primitive force that befit the new age of Edison. Army surgeon A. A. Woodhull pointed to the fight as proof that speed and agility were traits for the military to develop through physical training. Conspiracy theorists had a simpler explanation. They surmised that Sullivan must have been the victim of foul play. Rumors circulated that gamblers with money on Corbett drugged John L. before the fight. One of Sullivan's backers, Lee Townsend, said that as soon as his man set foot in the Olympic Club ring, the doctor who had declared him physi-cally sound earlier that day turned to him and exclaimed, "There's some-thing wrong here! That's not the same man I examined this afternoon." Townsend suspected Sullivan's final meal before the fight, which was not inspected by Phil Casey as usual, had been tampered with. But the betting line didn't support the gossip; money did not rush to Corbett as the fight approached. "Don't say anything about that drugging business," Sullivan told reporters. "It is a pure baby act, and there is nothing in it. I was beaten by a good man."

Casey served as a convenient scapegoat among the gamblers who lost big on Sullivan, and William Muldoon joined in the chorus criticiz-ing Sullivan's trainer. He blasted Casey for indulging his fighter's "every extravagant whim" and added that "it would have been a thousand times better for Sullivan if he had been taken half-drunk from a New Orleans bar-room and put in the ring" than engaged in such mismanaged training. The disgusted "Iron Duke" announced he would back John L. for $5,000 and train him to fight any comers to prove Casey was the problem.

Sullivan, however, carried no thoughts of entering the ring again when he arrived in New York's Grand Central Depot on September 11 along with Charley Johnston and Jimmy Wakely. John L. still bore the scars—puffy lips, swollen eyes, and a stitched-up nose—from the southern battlefield. The trio, returning with thin wallets, "looked like mourners at a funeral." The fallen king, unsure of what kind of reception he would receive from his subjects, walked in a numbed haze with his head bowed until he reached the platform gate where hundreds greeted him with handshakes, encouraging words, and three cheers for "the greatest champion yet known." The reception elicited a smile that had been absent for days.

The day after the fight, Corbett graciously offered to appear at a benefit for Sullivan, who, due to his insistence for a winner-takes-all bout, had left New Orleans with nothing. Initially, Sullivan's pride prevented him from accepting the overture. Gods don't take charity. "Corbett is a good young fellow, and he beat me fair," Sullivan told reporters, "but I don't want his services or his money. Ain't I John L. Sullivan yet?"

Within twenty-four hours, Sullivan had changed his mind. At an exhibition featuring Corbett the following night at Madison Square Garden, William Brady announced to the three thousand fans in attendance that John L. had agreed to the benefit. The mere mention of Sullivan's name elicited cheers that rained down from the galleries. A New York newspaper noted the contrast between the sea of empty boxes and seats that confronted Corbett in the Garden and the packed houses that had consistently greeted Sullivan.

The day before the Sullivan benefit, Corbett courageously ventured to Boston, the den of the vanquished. Bostonians had lost their money, their idol, and their "Strong Boy." They took the loss personally, and the new champion, who had been booked for a show at the Grand Opera House, wondered if he might be received about as warmly in Boston as the Redcoats had been a century prior. As his train pulled into the Park Square depot, Corbett scanned the waiting faces trying to gauge the popular mood. Thousands of eyes smiled back and shouts of approval sent startled pigeons darting. The relieved champion flashed a boyish grin as a police escort valiantly cleared a pathway through the well-wishers to his waiting carriage.

Back in New York, crowds trailed Sullivan, too, as he rehearsed *The Man from Boston*, Edmund E. Price's "romantic four-act drama." With only a week to go before the curtain raised on the show, Sullivan had little time to be introspective about the overthrow of his reign. As he went through final rehearsals, so many fans gathered outside the Windsor Theatre that police swept in to keep traffic moving on the Bowery. Fans waited for hours just to catch a glimpse of Sullivan, in part to see how badly Corbett had punished him. The fans erupted when John L. finally appeared, and small boys chased behind his carriage shouting, "Three cheers for Sullivan!" The old warhorse was no longer their champion, but he was still their hero.

—◦—

If Sullivan's boxing career was indeed dead, the September 17 benefit at Madison Square Garden served as an old-fashioned Irish wake, filled with laughter, tears, and plenty of memories. In contrast to the half-empty arena that had greeted Corbett a few nights prior, a full house paid their respects to Sullivan. For four blocks surrounding the Garden, the streets were "a solid mass of pushing, jostling humanity" as speculators, commanding as much as six dollars for a reserved seat, prowled for prey. Even after the benefit started, two thousand fans without tickets lingered outside just to be near history.

They all came. Rich and poor. Businessmen and sporting men. Cops and criminals. Boozers and teetotalers. New money and old. Fighters and preachers. Men, women, and kids. Corrupt politicians and the merely crooked lawmakers. This was an American melting pot that only the former champ could stir together.

After the warm-up bouts, the defeated gladiator emerged from his dressing room. Waves of applause thundered off the arena's steel roof. The new incarnation of Madison Square Garden shook as it never had before. Men in the galleries waved their hats. Women in the boxes twirled their handkerchiefs. Ten thousand voices cried Sullivan's name. Even without a crown on his head, John L. was still their king.

Many of the notable figures from Sullivan's career—from Al Smith to Billy Madden to Mike Donovan—saluted the former champion. The clean-shaven brawler, wearing a green shirt and black trunks, walked to the center of the ring and waited for the adoration to ebb. The cheers crescendoed again when Corbett appeared. The dethroned shook hands with his successor. For most of the night, the presence of the reigning champion was a mere afterthought—he "might as well have been the croquet champion of the world" for all the attention he received noted one reporter—but "Gentleman Jim" carried himself with a dignity befitting his nickname.

Sullivan finally silenced his subjects with an outstretched arm and boomed his thanks. "I have nothing to say but bestow good honors on the present champion," he said. "I was defeated and have no excuses to make. When a defeated man begins to make excuses, he makes the mistake of his life." Sullivan placed his meaty hand on his shirt and took a deep bow. Corbett, shirtless and in white trunks, then said a few words, but the timbre of his voice couldn't resonate through the cavernous athletic palace like Sullivan's mighty bass. "Louder!" shouted the crowd.

With the orations complete, the two men toed the scratch, shook hands, and sparred three rounds with "gloves as big as feather pillows." While some speculated that Sullivan might try to land an unexpected shot on Corbett to prove his bite remained, such an underhanded move wasn't in the character of the man who boasted of always being "on the level." The men "tried to see just how easy they could hit each other," but it was conceded that Corbett "clearly demonstrated his superiority as a boxer."

In spite of all John L. had done to elevate Madison Square Garden, arena management insisted on taking half of the benefit's box office. Still, Sullivan walked away with more than $6,000 and perhaps the even deeper adulation of his public. He may not have been the heavyweight champion anymore, but he remained the people's champion.

Jake Kilrain, touted by Richard K. Fox as "champion of the world," fought seventy-five rounds against Sullivan in 1889 in the last bare-knuckle title bout. *THE PORTRAIT GAL-LERY OF PUGILISTS OF AMERICA AND THEIR CONTEMPORARIES* (1894)

William Muldoon, who trained Sullivan for his 1889 epic brawl with Jake Kilrain, toured the country with John L. posing as "living statuary" in 1885. LIBRARY OF CONGRESS

Workers clear the pine trees and build the makeshift grandstands for the Sullivan-Kilrain 1889 title fight. LIBRARY OF CONGRESS

Sullivan and Jake Kilrain shake hands before their marathon seventy-five-round bare-knuckle title fight on July 8, 1889. LIBRARY OF CONGRESS

Sullivan and Jake Kilrain circle each other during their epic seventy-five-round bare-knuckle title fight on July 8, 1889. LIBRARY OF CONGRESS

Sullivan and Jake Kilrain pound each other with bare fists for seventy-five rounds in triple-digit heat on July 8, 1889. LIBRARY OF CONGRESS

An 1890 handbill advertises Sullivan's starring role in a Philadelphia performance of *Honest Hearts and Willing Hands.* LIBRARY OF CONGRESS

James J. "Gentleman Jim" Corbett met Sullivan for the heavyweight championship of the world on September 7, 1892. LIBRARY OF CONGRESS

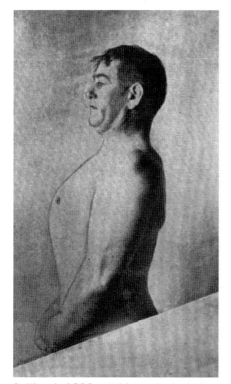

Sullivan's 1892 autobiography includes photographs, such as this side view, taken during a physical examination prior to his title fight with Jim Corbett. *LIFE AND REMINISCENCES OF A NINETEENTH-CENTURY GLADIATOR* (1892)

James J. "Gentleman Jim" Corbett feuded with Sullivan for years after their 1892 heavyweight title fight. *THE PORTRAIT GALLERY OF PUGILISTS OF AMERICA AND THEIR CONTEMPORARIES* (1894)

A flabbier Sullivan strikes a fighting pose later in his championship reign. LIBRARY OF CONGRESS

A three-story-tall electric sign outside Dante's Inferno Cafe, Sullivan's Manhattan saloon, lit up Broadway in 1899. MILSTEIN DIVISION OF UNITED STATES HISTORY, LOCAL HISTORY & GENEALOGY, THE NEW YORK PUBLIC LIBRARY, ASTOR, LENOX AND TILDEN FOUNDATIONS

After leaving the ring, Sullivan continued to draw crowds as a tuxedo-clad monologist. AUTHOR'S COLLECTION

Two of America's foremost celebrities—Sullivan and William F. Cody, "Buffalo Bill"—shake hands in 1908. YALE COLLECTION OF WESTERN AMERICANA, BEINECKE RARE BOOK AND MANUSCRIPT LIBRARY

Sullivan poses with former heavyweight champions Tommy Burns, Jim Corbett, and Jim Jeffries prior to the 1910 "Fight of the Century" between Jeffries and Jack Johnson. DON SCOTT, *BOXING COLLECTORS' NEWS*

Prior to Jack Johnson's 1910 fight against Jim Jeffries, Sullivan shook hands with the reigning heavyweight champion. DON SCOTT, *BOXING COLLECTORS' NEWS*

Australian Peter Jackson was one of the great heavyweight fighters of the Gilded Age, but Sullivan denied him a championship shot because of the color of his skin. *THE PORTRAIT GALLERY OF PUGILISTS OF AMERICA AND THEIR CONTEMPORARIES* (1894)

A smiling Sullivan poses for photographs on board the *Ivernia* in 1910 before departing on his honeymoon with his second wife, Kate. YALE COLLECTION OF WESTERN AMERICANA, BEINECKE RARE BOOK AND MANUSCRIPT LIBRARY

Months after their 1910 nuptials, Sullivan and his second wife, Kate, pose in front of Hollow Tree in Stanley Park on a stopover in Vancouver, Canada. YALE COLLECTION OF WESTERN AMERICANA, BEINECKE RARE BOOK AND MANUSCRIPT LIBRARY

Sullivan and his second wife, Kate, share a light moment in this undated photograph. YALE COLLECTION OF WESTERN AMERICANA, BEINECKE RARE BOOK AND MANUSCRIPT LIBRARY

Sullivan raises his dukes playing around with "Young John L.," a son of a friend whom the champion and his wife reared on their farm in Abington, Massachusetts.

The 1916 lithograph *Introducing John L. Sullivan* by George Bellows captures the champion in the moments before the Jess Willard–Frank Moran title bout.

Sullivan in his later years feeding chickens on his farm in Abington, Massachusetts.

Pallbearers flank the hearse carrying the "Boston Strong Boy" through the city streets on the frigid morning of February 6, 1918.

Two days after the benefit, *The Man from Boston* opened in Providence, Rhode Island. Sullivan didn't know whether the public would buy tickets to see a *former* champion on the stage, but a full house packed the Providence Opera House. A "deafening cheer" greeted John L. when he stepped out to his mark for the first act, and the crowd insisted he come to the footlights and make a speech before uttering any of the lines he had duly rehearsed. Tears trickled from his eyes as a large floral harp was pushed on stage after the first act. After the final curtain, John L. received a large floral horseshoe and three encores.

Sullivan's character in *The Man from Boston* wasn't much of a stretch. He basically played himself. John L. starred as a pugilist with a poor reputation who assumes the identity of the nattily attired Captain Harcourt of the yacht *Wonder* as he embarks on a series of scattershot adventures. John L. maintained a constant stage presence through the entire four acts. He rescued a man from drowning; thwarted villains trying to obtain money by forgery; and even lined up on a mock gridiron for a football game, which he won for Yale by crashing over the line for a last-second touchdown. After Captain Harcourt was revealed in the final act to be Sullivan, "the man from Boston," the former champion sparred three gloved rounds with Jack Ashton and punctuated the play with a knockout. Night after night, Sullivan's loyal right-hand man made sure that his opponent's big right hand sent him to the ground for the amusement of thousands.

One reviewer saw a marked improvement in Sullivan's acting from *Honest Hearts and Willing Hands* and noted that John L. prompted his "inferior" support when they forgot their lines. Reviewers were not as kind to the play itself. "Possibly worse plays have been seen on the stage," damned one reviewer with faint praise. "For dullness and lack of originality however, it is certainly a remarkable success."

From Providence, the "Boston Strong Boy" came home. Given the amount of money the city lost on the fight, Sullivan, like Corbett, may have questioned what type of reception awaited, but he received a welcome more suited for victor than vanquished. More than three thousand well-wishers who waited at the Park Square depot gave a wild cheer the moment his train was first spied chugging under the Berkeley Street

Bridge. As he drove off to his sister's house, several hundred jovial men and boys chased behind for almost a mile.

A dozen years after he first took to the Howard Athenaeum's stage to fight Donovan, Sullivan returned to the floorboards of the hometown venue. The audience greeted him with "violent, uncontrollable joy." Applause thundered with each Sullivan entrance, and he could barely get through his lines without being interrupted by cheers. The crowd yelled for "Our John" even when he was off stage. Every show sold out, and ushers tried in vain to keep the standing-room audience from seeping into the aisles.

The Madison Square Garden benefit and the successful launch of *The Man from Boston* eased any concerns Sullivan may have had about whether he could still command public attention as a former champion. The set in Boston was a financial success as well, with Sullivan's share estimated to be more than $2,000. John L. supposedly used some of the money to make amends with at least one of his fans. In Providence, he overheard a story about a local who had mortgaged his wages, furniture, and even his wife's wedding ring betting on him against Corbett. The former champion reportedly bought back the keepsakes at the pawnshop and returned them to the man's wife. When the woman asked Sullivan if he was a city missionary, he simply pointed to the large poster on a nearby fence with a picture of himself dressed as Captain Harcourt.

The box-office receipts, unfortunately, also became seed money for a return of Sullivan's benders. With the burst of hometown love behind him and his whirlwind schedule finally calming, the reality of the loss to Corbett began to confront him.

Sullivan raged as *The Man from Boston* criss-crossed the East. In October, John L. showed up intoxicated at a New York performance, and his sparring "was so ludicrous that the audience hissed." The following month he tore through York, Pennsylvania, and forcibly removed a passenger, who happened to be a police detective, from a cab. The detective obtained an arrest warrant for assault and battery, but Sullivan's manager threw money at the problem and settled the case before John L. could be handcuffed.

When Sullivan was seen stumbling drunk around a train platform, his accompanying enablers simply attributed his unsteady gait to "bad corns."

While Sullivan toured American stages, Corbett traveled the theater circuit as well. Although Brady had entered the fight game when he took on the management of his childhood friend Corbett, he was a show-business entrepreneur at heart. He even called the fight in New Orleans "just a publicity stunt" to promote a new production not-so-loosely based on (and not-so-loosely named for) his charge: *Gentleman Jack*. In the play written by Charles T. Vincent at Brady's behest, Corbett starred as a bank clerk in love with the same girl as the villain, who frames Jack for a bank robbery that gets him fired. The villain imports an English boxer named Charlie Twitchell (think "Charley Mitchell") to fight Jack, but in the end, the hero triumphs over the fighter in a twenty-four-foot ring complete with referee, timekeepers, seconds, and hundreds of extras posing as spectators.

Gentleman Jack did brisk business. In reviewers' eyes, Corbett outclassed Sullivan on the stage, just as he did in the ring. "Corbett played his role with considerable more subtlety and conviction than did John L. Sullivan in *Honest Hearts and Willing Hands*," wrote one. Sneered another critic, "Corbett may have talent, and certainly has education and appearance, but John L. has none of the three."

Sullivan likely felt irked that Corbett followed him so closely down the trail of American sports celebrity he had blazed. In the days following his defeat in New Orleans, John L. told reporters that Corbett deserved credit for the result. "I was whipped, and that's all there's to it," he told one reporter. "I've got no excuses to make." Yet, in short order, the excuses flowed.

He began to attribute his defeat to the "rapid life" he had led rather than to Corbett's talents and strategy. "He did not knock me out at New Orleans," he told reporters six months after the fight. "I simply fell from exhaustion in the twenty-first round. True, he hit me almost at will, but of all the blows he delivered not one was sufficiently hard to knock out an ordinary man." The following year, he told another reporter, "Anybody could have beaten me the night I fought." For years, Sullivan grumbled about Corbett's tactics in their encounter, which he was just as apt to call a "footrace" as a "fight."

The famed novelist Theodore Dreiser encountered Sullivan shortly after the Corbett fight at a moment when the former champion seemed at peace with his new status. Dreiser, then a young reporter for a St. Louis newspaper, found himself quickly smitten by the "prizefighting J.P. Morgan" who was holding court in a room scattered with cigar boxes, champagne buckets, and beer bottles. "I'm ex-champion of the world, defeated by that little dude from California," he howled, "but I'm still John L. Sullivan—ain't that right? Haw! Haw! They can't take that away from me, can they?"

— ◡ —

They couldn't take Sullivan away from his drinking either. Alcohol continued to land him in scrapes, barroom and otherwise. In January 1894, he needed the assistance of a porter to stagger back to his room at Buffalo's Tifft House in the early morning hours. Minutes later, a hysterical woman rushed into the lobby, screaming, "Send for a doctor, quick. Mr. Sullivan is dying." The unidentified woman had pounded the former champion on the head with a three-pound Indian club and knocked him unconscious. It took doctors an hour to revive him. Some newspapers reported that Sullivan had struck "his wife" several times before she retaliated. That June, a barroom argument in a Boston hotel, which reportedly broke out over Paddy Ryan's "scrapping" abilities, landed Sullivan in an emergency room with stitches for a gash delivered by a bottle on his right cheek.

The worst headlines that Sullivan received occurred in May 1893 for an incident inside a Pullman car as he railroaded through Maine with *The Man from Boston* company. Once again, John L. had been drinking when local lawyer Max L. Lizotte reached in front of the former champion to shake hands with another member of his party. After an exchange of words, Sullivan reportedly kicked Lizotte in the groin and traded blows. Maine authorities arrested John L. for assault and battery, which was bad press enough, but the public relations disaster became complete when it was revealed that Lizotte only had one arm.

Despite his handicap, the single-winged lawyer didn't shirk from fighting a man who in theory could have whipped him with one arm tied behind *his* back. Lizotte clinched John L. and turned him over a car seat before they were separated. Another member of Sullivan's entourage punched the lawyer in the face, cutting his lip and bloodying his nose, and Sullivan went back in to choke the man. After learning of the man's handicap, however, John L. reportedly sent word that "he would not have attacked him if he had known that he had only one hand." Even drunk heavyweights had a code of honor.

Sullivan proclaimed his innocence but spent a night in jail. He said that Lizotte tried to throw the first punch and his errant blow struck his manager, John J. Howard, who then fought back. Several impartial eye-witnesses, including newspaper correspondents and a Boston justice of the peace, corroborated the story, but Sullivan settled the civil suit with Lizotte for $500, paid hundreds more in legal fees, and caught a train to Portland where he appeared on stage that night. The brief flicker of fame touched Lizotte. One Boston newspaper cheekily printed a riff on the popular saying of the day: "Down in Maine they are yearning to grasp the hand that grasped Sullivan's windpipe."

A few months later in August, another drunken argument resulted in a narrow escape in the barroom of Manhattan's Vanderbilt Hotel. Sullivan had been drinking hard and "was in an ugly mood" when he lurched into the room and ordered wine for everyone in the place. As he approached one man at the end of the bar who refused the drink, Sullivan recognized him as an old Boston enemy named McClusky. They traded words, then fists. After one blow knocked McClusky to the floor, John L. saw his foe reach for his hip pocket. Sullivan bolted for the door as an errant bullet sped by him. Sullivan's friends wrestled the weapon away from the shooter before he could get off another round, and hotel officials hustled the fighter out into the summer air where he sped away in a carriage.

Fire was another constant danger of the day, and in February 1895, Sullivan fled an inferno that burned the Denison Hotel in Indianapolis along with a trunk of his prized photos and scrapbooks. Two months later, he tried to play a hero during a stay at a Boston boardinghouse when cook Margaret Donnelly overturned a kettle of boiling fat that splattered all over her and set her clothes ablaze. Hearing screams, Sullivan rushed downstairs and tried to extinguish the flames with a mat and his hands, burning himself in the process. Although initial reports stated that John L.

was a lifesaver, the woman unfortunately passed away hours later at City Hospital. Sullivan asked police not to mention his role in the incident, but news leaked out and one newspaper commented about his big hands: "At last they have done something of which their owner may be proud."

The press not only delivered plenty of backhanded praise but had written Sullivan off for dead multiple times. In 1894, newspapers reported that Sullivan had committed suicide. Shortly after the news flash, John L. was spotted in a railway station in Zanesville, Ohio. In Sullivan's case, news of a dead man walking wasn't as amazing as the fact that he was sober. "John L. Sullivan is not dead as reported," stated the clarification. "The press dispatches say he is not even drunk."

Although fewer than eighteen months had passed since his loss in New Orleans, Sullivan seemingly passed directly into old age. His hair and mustache were nearly all gray. Thoughts of mortality hovered as members of his fighting circle started to pass away. Ashton, just thirty years old, died days after appearing on stage with Sullivan in January 1893 from a lethal skin infection that developed from a small scratch. In September, Mike Cleary died of consumption in Belfast, New York, the hamlet he fell in love with while training Sullivan for the Jake Kilrain title bout. Weeks later, Pete McCoy fell off a boat and drowned in Long Island Sound.

While the newspapers continued to call Sullivan "the picture of health," the "Big Fellow" was living up to his name. Now that he had no pretense for training or staying in shape, John L. let go. Pudge turned into paunch, and Sullivan again tipped the scales at well over 250 pounds. His legs, always a little short for his body, made him appear even more top-heavy.

John L.'s burgeoning appetites shrank his bank account, and once again—although *The Man from Boston* proved successful enough to earn a second run in the theatrical season of 1893–1894—he relied on the kindness of his fans and fellow fighters to replenish his wallet. In May 1894, twenty-five hundred fans in Boston attended a grand testimonial in his honor that climaxed with a three-round spar between Sullivan and Ryan. (To his credit, John L. donated a quarter of the net proceeds to victims of the Great Roxbury Fire, which days before wiped out whole blocks of the neighborhood he once roamed as a child.) The two fighters who ruled the sport just a decade earlier were so out of shape that they could only last a minute per round before returning to their corners puffing away.

Though Sullivan was buried under rolls of flesh, the once elite prizefighter remained the sport's greatest drawing card as a brand-new entertainment industry emerged: motion pictures. Boxers were among the first subjects filmed by Thomas Edison, an enthusiastic fight fan who foresaw the market potential in screening fights in his kinetoscope parlors, where patrons dropped coins into slots and peered through peephole viewers to watch films. A pair of unknowns—Mike Leonard and Jack Cushing—boxed a six-round exhibition on film in June 1894, but Edison needed a true star for his movies. He wanted Sullivan.

John L., however, wanted an astronomical $25,000 for his services. The film company balked and found Corbett willing to do it for just $5,000. In September 1894, "Gentleman Jim" donned four-ounce gloves—and shorts more suited to a sumo wrestler—for a six-round fight with Pete Courtney, champion of New Jersey, inside Edison's famous "Black Maria" production studio at his West Orange, New Jersey, laboratory. The first fight ever shown commercially was a box-office success, and Corbett, who became the first motion picture actor to ever perform under contract, grossed thousands in royalty checks. Once again, Corbett had gotten the better of Sullivan.

Corbett may have been boxing's first movie star, but John L. remained a matinee idol as he returned to the stage for the 1894–1895 theatrical season, which he vowed would be his last before retiring to the eighteen-acre farm he had purchased near Greenfield, Massachusetts. Sullivan grew corn and tobacco there and hoped to expand into breeding cows and sheep. Although planning to leave acting behind, he was excited about his new role as John Desmond, "a gentlemanly land overseer," in the comedy farce *A True American,* which like *The Man from Boston* sprang from the pen of Edmund E. Price. As with the previous Sullivan plays, *A True American* concluded with Sullivan in the ring, appearing in full costume to fight with Dan Dwyer, who had replaced Ashton as his regular sparring partner.

From the start, the production struggled with money issues and Sullivan's debauched drinking sprees. He stumbled drunk around the stage, and his cursing caused cast members to quit the production. In February 1895, Sullivan's drinking finally brought down the curtains on *A True American*. As he arrived in Jacksonville, Florida, he denied reports he had beat up a passenger on the train and insisted he was "attending strictly to business." Drinking, however, was the only business he strictly attended to after playing to a packed house at the Park Opera House. He tore through the Jacksonville saloons reportedly with the aid of the receipts from that night's performance. When he spent all his money, he reportedly started to pawn the diamonds from his championship belt.

His cast mates, who claimed they hadn't been paid in weeks and stayed in poor boardinghouses while Sullivan lodged in fine hotels, quit en masse. One of them, Viola Armstrong, told the sheriff that Sullivan owed her $200. The lawman took the clothes off Sullivan's back by seizing his two large wardrobe trunks. The *National Police Gazette* reveled in the news, reporting of Sullivan that "it looks now as if his public career had come to an inglorious close indeed."

While his clothes remained in Florida, where they were eventually auctioned off for one hundred dollars, Sullivan returned to Boston with his drinking habit firmly in tow. In March, John L. staggered into the Suffolk Athletic Club to watch a fight between his old foe Jake Kilrain and Steve O'Donnell. The crowd, which normally would have given him a rousing ovation, whispered about his pathetic, alcohol-sodden condition. Sullivan made himself "very much in evidence during the evening." He forced himself into Kilrain's dressing room, sat behind his corner during the fight, and profanely offered unsolicited advice on technique. At the end of the eight rounds, he climbed onto the stage to berate referee Patsey Sheppard and had to be restrained from charging O'Donnell's corner after one of the fighter's entourage called Sullivan a "mutton head."

A sober Sullivan appeared at Madison Square Garden for a June benefit for former middleweight champion "Nonpareil" Jack Dempsey, who was struggling with consumption. He sparred a three-round exhibition with Dempsey, but Corbett was the man Sullivan really wanted to face.

"Gentleman Jim" charitably offered to appear at a separate benefit for Sullivan, and on June 27, a crowd of seven thousand filed into the Garden. After a feast of twenty preliminary bouts that included stars such as Jack Skelly, George Dixon, Joe Choynski, Peter Maher, and Jack McAuliffe, a roar went up as Corbett and Sullivan, both stripped to the waist, squeezed through the delirious crowd flanking the narrow aisle leading down to the arena floor. Everyone wanted to shake the hand of the former champion or simply pat him on the shoulders. Sullivan, wearing black tights, entered the ring first. Corbett trailed behind "like a dutiful son." Unhappy with the position of the stools in the ring, John L. moved his seat to another corner and "imperiously waved his hand as a signal for Corbett to do likewise." Corbett obeyed.

The difference in the paths taken by the two men since their meeting in New Orleans was readily evident in Sullivan's corpulence. It became more striking when the sparring began. Corbett "simply played with the 'old fellow,'" getting in soft blows and, for sympathy's sake, allowing John L. to land a punch every now and then. (In spite of Corbett's chivalry toward him, Sullivan still couldn't even feign courtesy toward the reigning champion afterward, telling an audience in October, "I want it distinctly understood that he is no friend of mine and I am no friend of his.")

Sullivan's financial drama continued at the arena's box office as the fists flew inside. While the benefit was in progress, the police arrived to attach the receipts to a judgment obtained against Sullivan for $2,345 in unpaid printing bills for *The Man from Boston*. The benefit promoters had caught wind that an attempt might be made and craftily drew up a bill of sale by which Sullivan sold all interests to Chicago sporting man Charles "Parson" Davies and Max Hirsch for $5,300. As a result, the deputy sheriff could not serve papers.

These periodic benefits for Sullivan, which continued for years to come, boosted his ego, but they also reminded the public about his profligate spending and raised questions—although the public largely knew the answer—about where the money was going. Still, the public continued to show up at the altar of the boxing god with offerings in hand.

That summer in Boston, John L. became a regular fixture inside the saloons of the South End. Sullivan also passed the days keeping a three-week vigil at the bedside of his only brother, Michael, who was laid up inside the Brook Avenue home of his sister. On August 9, 1895, Michael died of complications of Bright's disease and heart trouble at the age of twenty-eight. Annie Lennon was now John L.'s only surviving blood relative.

His brother's death further fueled Sullivan's alcoholic binges around Boston until Davies brokered a deal to have Sullivan and Paddy Ryan join the touring company of *The Wicklow Postman*, a comedy-drama set in Ireland that starred popular comedian Eugene O'Rourke, and spar in a three-round exhibition after the performance. In December, Sullivan left to meet the production in Chicago, and the two old warriors proved more popular than the play itself, although they did little more than tap each other. Sullivan, who looked to be on the "brink of premature decay," had grown so obese that Davies had to cut short the rounds for the benefit of his badly winded fighter. The old foes spent months traveling a giant loop of the West by train, a mode of transportation that soon proved perilous for John L.

In January 1896, Sullivan stepped off a Rock Island and Peoria express, which wouldn't have been noteworthy except that the train was speeding along at forty miles per hour at the time.

Not surprisingly, alcohol played a role in the incident. John L. had been on a tear after a show in Davenport, Iowa, and caused a ruckus at depots throughout Illinois on his way to Springfield. After insulting several passengers as the train rumbled between Galva and LaFayette, Sullivan stumbled through the rear of the rail car to find the bathroom. He mistakenly threw open the back door, continued walking, and plummeted. Passengers frantically pulled the bell, and the engineer stopped the iron horse. Afraid Sullivan could be dead, the passengers experienced several anxious minutes until the train backed up and they discovered the ex-champ lying facedown in a muddy ditch, just as surly as ever. He brushed himself off, staggered aboard, and ordered the conductor to get moving or "he would clean out the train."

With his head wounded, face battered, and eyes blackened, Sullivan arrived in Springfield looking like he had taken a licking worse than any he had absorbed in the ring. Incredibly, though, he didn't break any bones and John L. insisted on taking the stage that night. Sullivan spent a week recuperating in the Palace Hotel, where he was nursed by a woman the newspapers referred to as "his wife." The report drew a stinging rebuke and a request for a correction from the pen of his true spouse, Annie Sullivan, who said the woman was "a notorious character from Boston by the name of Maggie Lee."

Sullivan soon rejoined *The Wicklow Postman* traveling company. The accident didn't dampen his drinking—one newspaper reported he was under the influence during five performances a week—and he became more indifferent to the impact it was having on his health and wallet. "A short life and a merry one is my motto," he told Davies when he raised concern about the former champion's drinking. "There's a good deal of rot in all this talk about saving up for a rainy day," he told a reporter on a swing through St. Paul. "What's the use of saving up your money till you're so old you can't have any fun spending it? What's the matter with enjoying it when you're young and can get some good out of it?" The only rainy days John L. wanted to save for were ones showered with liquor.

When the show completed its run, Sullivan returned to Boston. He summered in Nantasket Beach, where his old sparring partner Joe Lannan ran the Fairhaven Hotel. Sullivan followed suit in the hospitality business and signed a lease to manage the Clarendon Hotel on Tremont Street, a popular hangout for the theatrical and sporting crowd just blocks from his South End birthplace.

In 1896, a theatrical season started without Sullivan for the first time since his loss to Corbett. In August, however, he entered the Madison Square Garden ring to exchange blows in a four-round exhibition with "Sailor" Tom Sharkey, who had recently fought Corbett to a four-round draw. The age difference between the twenty-two-year-old Sharkey and the thirty-seven-year-old "grand old man" wasn't as shocking as John L.'s appearance to the fight fans who had seen him in his prime. Noting his portliness, Sullivan told the forty-five hundred fans, "I hope you won't say any harsh things." The crowd may not have, but the press did. One newspaper reported he was "hog fat" with "the skin of his abdomen hanging in a fold over the waistband of his trunks." Sharkey danced all around the ring; Sullivan could barely move. The matchup was so lopsided that Sharkey could get in little useful work.

The Sharkey exhibition came just days after news arrived of the death of Harry Hill, and the following week in New York, Annie Livingston died suddenly at Bellevue Hospital from acute gastritis. The former champion did not attend the funeral of the woman whom many newspapers still referred to as "the common-law wife of John L. Sullivan." He sent a pillow of roses with the word "friend" attached and telegraphed word through Billy Hogarty that he would defray the funeral costs, but the Actors' Fund had enough money to cover the expenses.

It turned out that John L. had been racking up big bills sending floral arrangements for the passing of friends and acquaintances. In October 1896, the same month doctors removed a melanoma from Sullivan's right hand, a judgment was obtained against him for a $318 unpaid bill with a Boston florist. The police officers who went to his address at 23 Folsom Street, however, could not find any property of Sullivan's to satisfy it. In December, Bostonians packed into debtors court to watch Sullivan testify as lawyers grilled him about the whereabouts of the fortune he had earned in the ring. He eventually settled with the creditors the following month.

Sullivan briefly returned to the stage in February 1897, opening in Gloucester, Massachusetts, with a thirty-person company that performed minstrelsy, comedy, burlesque, and vaudeville. In addition to appearing as the interlocutor for the minstrel show, Sullivan returned to appearing as living statuary, the act that had caused a sensation when he was champion. More than a decade later, however, Sullivan did not carry quite the same chiseled figure as he had in 1885. This time, Hercules packed more of a paunch.

In March 1897, Sullivan traveled west to Carson City, Nevada, to cover the heavyweight championship between Corbett and challenger Bob Fitzsimmons for the *New York World* and syndicated newspapers—and incredibly to issue a public challenge to the winner. The train conductor slowed at every station along the way so that Sullivan could wave his shiny top hat from his Pullman car and bow to the faithful who still thronged to see him. Although the actual writing was done by a young reporter named William Inglis, the news business stoked Sullivan's competitive juices again. "[My] report of the fight will not take a back wash from any of the other newspapers that will be represented there," he vowed.

Sullivan was ringside in the outdoor arena on St. Patrick's Day when the British-born Fitzsimmons shocked Corbett by knocking him out with a solar plexus punch in the fourteenth round. The man who had defeated John L. had now been vanquished. If Sullivan felt pleased with the outcome, he masked it from his readers, telling them he was upset that his pre-fight pick had failed to uphold the honor of America. "It is pretty hard to understand how a foreigner can beat an American," Sullivan wrote while getting in a dig at Corbett, "and when it does happen, you can be pretty sure that the foreigner has not met the best American, or that the American has not been taking care of himself."

Days after Fitzsimmons decked Corbett, Sullivan's new manager, showman and theater owner Frank Dunn, posted $1,000 with a stakeholder to bind a gloved match with the new champion within nine months. "Barring his obesity," Dunn said without a touch of irony, "Sullivan is as strong and good as ever he was, and can surely get to 190 hard pounds of fighting flesh." John L. claimed he weighed 250 pounds, which surely undershot his true heft. Much like his persistent pledges to give up alcohol, he constantly blustered about how easy it would be for him to shed weight.

Few took Sullivan seriously, believing the challenge to be a publicity stunt concocted by him and Dunn, but John L. pointed out that at thirty-eight years old, he was a year younger than Joe Goss had been when he defeated Tom Allen for the heavyweight championship. Of course, thanks to Sullivan, the boxing world had changed in the past two decades, with a greater quantity and higher quality of fighters. Still, his championship reign had crashed so suddenly in New Orleans that fight fans questioned whether he might not be able to reclaim his title. Did Corbett defeat him or just the bottle? "There yet remains a knockout blow in John L.'s mighty right hand," reported one Boston paper.

Fitzsimmons brushed off Sullivan, suggesting he defeat Corbett first before bothering him. "Let him go and get a new reputation," said the champion, echoing the words that Ryan had uttered to Sullivan when John L. was a rising star. Back on stage touring with a vaudeville company, Sullivan incorporated a demonstration of the solar plexus punch that crippled Corbett into his stage performances along with a showing of a motion picture reenactment of the fight, complete with stand-ins for Corbett and Fitzsimmons.

After the theatrical paths of Sullivan and Fitzsimmons crossed in Buffalo in early June, the new champion agreed to meet for an exhibition match at Ambrose Park in Brooklyn on July 5, 1897, with the understanding that a prizefight between them would be negotiated if Sullivan proved a credible challenger.

John L. immediately went into training, and in an attempt to dial back the clock and reduce his waistline, he turned to the best trainer he ever had: Muldoon. But eight years and many more pounds after they had last worked together, Muldoon thought the venture foolhardy. Sullivan did not get Muldoon's personal touch, simply joining the standard conditioning program with Muldoon's wealthy clients at his White Plains, New York, health farm.

Fight day in Brooklyn arrived, but so did the police, who warned the men if they even put up one duke, they would be arrested for "a gross violation of the Horton law," which only permitted bouts inside athletic clubs. Although the men assured the police that it would be only a friendly spar, the authorities didn't budge. Sullivan announced to the crowd that there would be no fight. Dunn said John L. hadn't given up trying to fight Fitzsimmons, but a meeting never materialized.

In the summer of 1897, Boston buzzed about the hand that *didn't* shake the hand of John L. Sullivan. At an August reception for rower Edward Hanlan Ten Eyck, the first American to win the Diamond Sculls championship at England's Henley Royal Regatta, Sullivan extended his hand to Boston mayor Josiah Quincy, who did not reciprocate. Whether intentional or not, Sullivan made this perceived snub a cause célèbre. Once again, John L. saw the old Brahmin guard thumbing its nose at a lowly Irish pugilist. Not only did John L. rescind his endorsement of Quincy for re-election, he growled about running against Quincy for mayor on a platform "of honest assessing, low taxes, and impartial handshaking by the Chief Executive." Amid the corrupt mire of Boston municipal politics, he vowed his ballot designation would be "independent and honest." BIG 'UN WILL RUN declared one Boston newspaper.

As with the Fitzsimmons fight, select newspapers speculated that this was just a publicity stunt with the theatrical season in the fall of 1897 approaching and the champion launching a new stage venture—the "John L. Sullivan Comedy and Big Vaudeville Company." Boston newspapers called it "a pretty cheap joke" and asserted that the mayoralty was being used "as a theatrical billboard." Still, representatives of Quincy's political machine tried to dissuade Sullivan from running and even intimated that he might find a profitable city job if he chose to stay out of the race.

As he continued to mull public office, Sullivan left for Maine in September 1897 to headline his large variety troupe and star as the ship captain clad in a "natty outing costume" in a one-act musical farce, *A Trip Across the Ocean,* that opened the show. The production again kept Sullivan within his comfort zone, including a closing gymnasium scene that promised to show him "in strict training" in which he punched the bag, jumped rope, and sparred three rounds with his trainer, Ed B. White, who also demonstrated a scientific-boxing and bag-punching act with his wife, Rolla. Newspapers noted that the playlet put Sullivan in a new role "of a light comedian," although it could be argued that depicting John L. "in strict training" was just as much of a stretch for the old gladiator.

Sullivan kept his name in the news during his trip to Maine, but for all the wrong reasons. In Bangor, he verbally assaulted the proprietor of the Bangor House hotel after Dunn protested their room charge. Three days later in Lewiston, a hackman called on Sullivan for an unpaid fare. John L. threatened to lick the driver before enlisting his assistant William Cowan as a proxy. The obedient "Billy" attempted to hit the hackman with a chair before the melee was broken up. Police arrested Sullivan and Cowan prior to that evening's performance in Biddeford in a $1,000 civil suit brought by the driver.

As with most of John L.'s managerial relationships, the one between Sullivan and Dunn quickly frayed. The two men argued over money at the close of a performance in New York in October, leading Sullivan to "administer physical chastisement." Once again the brawny fighter sent the 120-pound Cowan into battle in his stead. This time, Sullivan raised Cowan high in the air and hurled him at Dunn. After being struck by the human projectile, Dunn took a swing at the valet, and Sullivan barked at Cowan: "Now you lick him, or I'll lick you." Given the choice, Cowan made the easy decision and lit into Dunn. Two weeks later, police arrested Sullivan in Providence for $5,000 in damages for alleged assault and debts owed to his now-former manager. (After the jury decided in his favor the following June, Sullivan thanked them and told them "there was a box for them all at his show.")

Following all the bad press, the news eventually came in December that "The Big 'Un" was not running for mayor. Although he likely never intended to run, Sullivan, like a true politician, cloaked his decision in the noblest of terms, supposedly sacrificing personal ambitions for the sake of the people. He said he received countless letters from friends who were city employees begging him not to run because they feared the Quincy machine would toss them out of their jobs or, with Sullivan splintering the vote, that a Republican administration would come in and turn over the workforce. John L. reiterated that he would not vote for a man who "refuses to shake hands with a citizen of the Hub whose claims to greatness are not based on fights that took place in 1812."

Even if he eschewed public office, John L. served his country in other ways, particularly after "Remember the *Maine!*" became the national rallying cry following the explosion of the United States warship in Havana, Cuba, in February 1898. As newspaper publishers William Randolph Hearst and Joseph Pulitzer pounded the drums of the Spanish-American War, vociferous patriots joined in the crescendo, and few Americans waved the flag as hard as Sullivan.

In March 1898, Sullivan headlined a huge benefit event at Madison Square Garden sponsored by Hearst's *New York Journal* to raise money for a monument in memory of the sailors killed aboard the USS *Maine*. The program featured cycling races, lacrosse and football games, "Buffalo Bill's Wild West" show, and patriotic tunes. Reigning heavyweight champion Fitzsimmons received a warm welcome when he came out to punch the bag, but it paled in comparison to the hearty cheers that greeted Sullivan. Women waved their handkerchiefs, and men yelled, "Speech!" John L. obliged. "Ladies and gentlemen, before Spain talks about fighting us she should go out and get a reputation," he bellowed. "Spain wants war, but I don't think she could lick a postage stamp."

By the end of the summer, the guns had fallen silent and Sullivan returned to his vaudeville company and *A Trip Across the Ocean* for a second straight theatrical season. There was one new addition, however; Sullivan's bare-knuckle foe Jake Kilrain joined as his sparring partner in the climactic three-round exhibition. The pair famous for their naked fists donned gloves this time as they headlined variety bills from coast to coast.

And debts continued to hound Sullivan. By January 1898, Sullivan even owed his manager, William H. Sherwood. A regular parade of creditors took John L. to court for unpaid wages from various theatrical performances. He couldn't even fully pay Frank McElroy, the lawyer who had assisted him with creditors since he left the ring. "You know that things in some people's life do not come smashing at all times," he wrote to McElroy. Sullivan asked for a little more time to pay his bills and in the interim invited McElroy to stop in his bar "and have a small bottle and good cigar with me."

Then a few days before Christmas 1899, Sullivan declared under oath in a Manhattan courtroom that he was "broke." He had earned approximately one million dollars by some accounts in the 1800s, and not a cent made the journey with him into the twentieth century.

CHAPTER ELEVEN

Undiluted Sullivan

AT THE DAWN OF A NEW CENTURY, MORAL CRUSADERS MADE INROADS against two pillars of Sullivan's life: the boxing ring and the booze bottle. The Anti-Saloon League in 1900 launched a campaign against bars that sold during prohibited hours, including on Sundays. In addition, a series of fixed fights, crooked decisions, and violent deaths in the ring resulted in the repeal of the Horton Law, which had legalized certain boxing matches in New York State in 1896. Sullivan predicted that what happened in New York would be "copied all over the country," and that's precisely what happened as anti-boxing legislation passed in states and municipalities in the ensuing years. Sullivan insisted the sport was less brutal than football and far less hazardous than simply walking across the street where a person could "be killed by electricity from a stray broken wire." As far as the rash of fixed fights, the dives taken by some fighters outraged John L., but they also boosted the public affection for the retired boxer who prided himself on always being "on the level."

Two days before the official repeal of the Horton Law, Sullivan returned to Madison Square Garden for a benefit in his name. The sale of tickets and subscriptions to the August 29, 1900, event raised a very healthy $15,000 to be held in a trust that would invest the money and pay the interest to John L. Before the main feature—a four-round exhibition between Sullivan and reigning heavyweight champion James Jeffries, who had defeated Bob Fitzsimmons in 1899—Tom Sharkey, Fitzsimmons, and Peter Maher all sparred.

The following night at the Garden, John L. watched as Kid McCoy appeared to take a dive against Jim Corbett in what he described "as barefaced a robbery as was ever perpetrated."

"I did much to make these men, and make it possible for them to earn big money," fumed Sullivan. "I took boxing out of the filth of disrepute and made something of the game." Now it was returning to the mire, and when the repeal of the Horton Law took effect the following night, Madison Square Garden went dark as the mecca of boxing until the Roaring Twenties.

Sullivan suspected Corbett was in on the fix, which only stoked his animosity toward "Gentleman Jim." The two ring rivals were now also foes in the saloon business. In the spring of 1899, sixteen years after he had opened his first saloon on Washington Street in Boston, Sullivan came to New York to sling liquor once again. His new bar opened near Herald Square on the east side of Sixth Avenue between Thirty-Fifth and Thirty-Sixth Streets. Sullivan's Gotham taproom, which he opened with a partner, rivaled his old Boston saloon. Incandescent lights brilliantly illuminated the lavishly decorated bar with walls bearing oil paintings, mirrors, and frescoes. Behind the mahogany bar was an oval mirror twenty-five feet long and five feet high, and the rear of the cafe featured a small garden with a portable canopy.

Corbett, who owned a cafe a couple blocks south on Sixth Avenue, reportedly attended the opening of Sullivan's bar. Being in such close proximity to the man who knocked him out of the ring wasn't the best salve for John L.'s enduring wounds. On one of his sprees around New York, Sullivan barreled into Corbett's saloon and called out, "Do you know what brought me here? It was to lick the man that owns this place, and I can do it, too. Show out, Corbett! I want him, and I want him quick. I can make him look like five cents' worth of lard in a paper sack." The two old gladiators didn't brawl. Sullivan could settle for the satisfaction, however, that his bartender had whipped Corbett's brother Tom in a street fight a few weeks before.

Sullivan ran through New York saloon partners as quickly as he did managers. In November 1899, he bought into a new venture: Dante's Inferno Cafe at 1177 Broadway near Twenty-Seventh Street. A three-story-tall electric sign spelling out Sullivan's name lit up the Great White Way, and a cutout of "Buffalo Bill" on horseback waving his cowboy hat stood over the entrance. Paintings inside depicted scenes from its namesake's epic, and the fighter's prized championship belt stood on display over the bar. Sullivan served as the manager, and Thomas Allen the chief owner. The partnership lasted only eight months. Three weeks after Sullivan spent a night in Greenwich Village's Jefferson Market Courthouse jail for assault, he was back in its courtrooms in a dispute with Allen over the belt. When John L. severed his interest in the bar, Allen refused to give him the belt, and the matter was tied up in litigation for months.

Within weeks, Sullivan joined up with "Brooklyn Jimmy" Carroll to partner in yet another cafe, this time on Forty-Second Street near Sixth Avenue. In October 1900, Sullivan's new business partner rushed him to Polyclinic Hospital after he complained of a severe pain in his abdomen. John L. had blamed the discomfort on eating seven chickens inside of four hours, but doctors operated on him, without ether or chloroform, for a strangulated hernia, which had been exacerbated by his drinking. It took 120 stitches, consisting of the tail skin of a kangaroo and fiddle string, to close up the huge incision. Sullivan was flat on his back for five weeks and shed thirty pounds to return to "his normal weight of 280 pounds." Once again, he took the pledge. "No more bug juice for me! I ain't had a drop in months, and I don't want any more ever again."

To no one's surprise, it took just a couple weeks for John L. to fall "off the water wagon with a splash," and soon America's foremost boozehound attracted the attention of the country's preeminent temperance advocate when Carrie Nation came to New York on August 28, 1901. The anti-alcohol crusader from Kansas had, like John L., achieved fame with a smashing right. Hers wielded a hatchet that left a trail of shattered bar glass, splintered bar tops, and broken alcohol bottles throughout the Midwest. The pug-faced Nation, who described herself as "a bulldog running along at the feet of Jesus, barking at what he doesn't like," was not some little old lady. She was an imposing figure, nearly six feet tall, usually dressed in black, and certainly not intimidated by the former champion who reportedly threatened to "throw her down the sewer" if "that old woman ever comes around to my place."

After she was physically ejected from Police Headquarters for making life uncomfortable for the city's top cops, Nation told her driver to head north to Sullivan's Forty-Second Street bar, although it had recently closed. Reporters tailing the saloon-smasher salivated at a possible showdown between two of America's biggest celebrities. When her carriage pulled up at the curb, she gave her card to a messenger and stayed in her vehicle. After a few minutes, the messenger returned to say John L. was sleeping and could not be disturbed.

Underneath her poke bonnet, Nation's brow furrowed. "I don't allow any man to stick me into a sewer hole—not while I have my hatchet with me. Now you go back messenger, and tell Mr. Sullivan that Mrs. Nation is here and insists on seeing him."

The messenger refused and warned her that "Mr. Sullivan is a very dangerous man when he's 'roused, ma'am."

"Tell Mr. Sullivan, then, that when I next come to town I will visit him and see if he'll stick me in any sewer hole. I'll see him and there'll come a reckoning. Get up, driver."

The battle-axe's carriage rattled away, and reporters saw the shutter in John L.'s upstairs room slowly open.

Sullivan floundered from one commercial venture to another in 1901. He tried a brief stint as a whiskey wholesaler, but with his direct personality, he couldn't master the soft sell. He performed even worse as a bookmaker at Brooklyn's Sheepshead Bay Race Track. He quickly lost patience with the flocks of gamblers who swarmed him and nearly knocked him off the high stool on which he roosted. In addition to threatening his jostling customers with violence, Sullivan lacked the requisite math skills for a bookie, and he lost his shirt—and his job—when a 100–1 shot named Little Gem won by a nose. He then tried to join up with a minstrel show and put on exhibitions in upstate New York with George Bush, a New Hampshire fighter who had served as his sparring partner in the past, but the local sheriff threatened him with arrest if he attempted to throw a single punch.

John L. finally found steady work playing one of the most notorious characters of the American stage, Simon Legree, the cruel slaveowner in *Uncle Tom's Cabin*. Sullivan relished his turn as a villain, although his fellow actors complained that Sullivan was too vigorous with his whip. Newspapers had fun joking that Eliza would not be able to make her escape across the river after Sullivan grabbed all the ice to make highballs, and his drunken sprees with the traveling company generated regular headlines. In January 1902, John L. howled through Norwalk, Connecticut. On a previous stopover in the town, he had hijacked an organ grinder and monkey, piled them into a carriage, and driven like a madman while making the terrorized musician play for hours. On his alcohol-fueled return trip, he threw fistfuls of coins into the crowds and pushed a dawdling bartender out of the way to mix his own gin fizzes and Manhattans.

Five days later, Sullivan and his troupe found themselves at Jersey City's Pennsylvania Station at 7 a.m. with three hours to kill. To John L., it was never too early for a tipple. His early-morning grouchiness quickly morphed into joviality after a visit to the bar. He wandered into the train shed and performed some impromptu carpentry before treating all the workers to a drink. He also played fashion police. "Your hat is out of style," he barked at a young man wearing a derby he didn't approve of before crushing the offending headgear with his mighty right hand and tossing a five-dollar bill at him with instructions to buy a new one.

The traveling production of *Uncle Tom's Cabin* fizzled to a close in early 1902, and the company disbanded. Sullivan didn't exit the stage, however. He shifted full-time from melodrama to monologue in the fall of 1902. He hitched his star to the vaudeville circuit where he appeared under the floodlights with a cavalcade of acts. At one performance at Boston's Howard Athenaeum, he performed alongside a ventriloquist, acrobatic bull terriers, sketch teams, comedians, dancers, jugglers, and two other acts reflective of Jim Crow America: black-face comedian Lew Hawkins and Clara Adams, who sang a repertoire of "coon songs."

The idea of John L. delivering soliloquies elicited snickers from theater critics and intellectuals at first. Then again, so did the thought of Sullivan as thespian. The monologue act attracted a curious segment that wanted to see whether John L. or the English language got the better of the tussle, but the reviews were decent and surprisingly it was "one of the theatrical sensations of the season." When Sullivan appeared at the Grand Theatre in Boston for a dozen performances in November 1902, he reportedly earned the largest salary ever paid in the United States for a single monologue act. The role of monologist suited a man who was a natural storyteller, flashed a sense of humor, prized a good memory, and had no qualms talking about himself. With the mighty lungs encased in his barrel chest, the ability to project was never a concern.

Sullivan appeared on stage for his act adorned in a formal frock coat with a shiny white paper dickey blanketing his massive chest. He bristled his mustache, puffed his chest out like a robin, tugged on the sides of his jacket, anchored himself to a spot on the stage, and never let go as, in rapid-fire sentences, he recounted memories from his prizefighting career, shared tales from his travels, and told disjointed Irish stories. The thirty-minute performance of "undiluted Sullivan" climaxed with John L., accompanied by slow music and moving his powerful right arm in graceful motions, reciting a melodramatic four-stanza ode, "A Toast to Woman."

In spite of the stage success of the monologue, Sullivan's finances still suffered. On November 28, 1902, Sullivan, who gave his residence as the Vanderbilt Hotel in Manhattan, was "duly adjudicated bankrupt" by the United States District Court in New York in order to prevent his arrest by a creditor in Boston. His debts totaled $2,658, mostly liabilities from his days in the saloon business including $1,600 for beer from the Anheuser-Busch Company. His assets consisted of only sixty dollars in apparel. Sullivan was eventually discharged from bankruptcy in February, but in the interim, he was sued for an alleged breach of contract by play-wright Charles Horwitz, who claimed he had not been paid a promised $250 for penning Sullivan's monologue.

John L.'s boxing hardware fell victim to his shattered fortunes. In July 1903, he pawned the old "dog collar," the *Police Gazette* belt he had won after defeating Kilrain, for $1,600. For John L., it was no big loss. "With a white flannel suit and a pair of tan shoes it would look out of sight on a hot day at Coney Island," he told a reporter. Four months later, the diamond-studded championship belt presented to him by the citizens of Boston, which he was forced to pledge to a pawnbroker in 1900, was sold to a second-hand jewelry dealer in the Bowery.*

---

* The belt ended up in the hands of Baltimore man James King, languished in a safety deposit box, and was reportedly melted for gold by the United States Mint in Philadelphia in 1926. An imitation belt crafted for the 1901 World's Fair was later donated to the Smithsonian Institution.

Sullivan's regular alcoholic binges contributed to his decrepit finances. On December 16, 1902, Sullivan weaved to his mark on the stage of The Avenue in Detroit. Instead of delivering his standard opening line— "Ladies and gentleman, you all know me. I'm yours truly, John L. Sullivan"—he sputtered, "Ladies and gentlemen, you all know me. I'm . . . I'm . . . I'm . . . drunker than a fiddler's bitch." With that opening salvo, the curtain plummeted. The audience saw a rush of bodies bulging from behind the drapery and heard scuffling and cursing. A second attempt, with Sullivan barely able to stand, ended with the curtain brought down again as the audience hissed. Management cancelled his afternoon performance and tried in vain to sober him up at a Turkish bath for the evening engagement, but he was thoroughly inebriated.

After "one of the most lamentable happenings in local vaudeville history," the theater manager cancelled Sullivan's contract for the rest of the week as well as his appearance the following week in Toledo. That just freed up John L. to rampage through Detroit on a two-day bender. He tore through saloon after saloon in downtown Detroit before hitting the barroom of the elegant Russell House. His salty language drove out the female patrons and brought in a patrolman who asked John L. to leave with him. "Go get a bigger patrolman," Sullivan shot back, and that's what the cop did. In came James "Big Jim" Sprott, a six-foot, five-inch former London bobby, who picked up John L. and carried him out. Local folklore grew that Sprott had whipped Sullivan into submission, but John L. may have been passed out by the time Sprott arrived. Either way, the physical feat of single-handedly removing the mountainous Sullivan would have been impressive, and Sprott ended up with a raise and promotion.

Sullivan sobered up in a jail cell with a platter of tenderloin and brown rice along with a kettle of coffee. The manager convinced the police to drop the charges, and after getting John L. to pledge that he'd drunk his last swig of booze, he allowed him to continue his engagement, no doubt aware that the news stirred by the spree guaranteed sold-out audiences. Sure enough, a rousing ovation greeted Sullivan's return to the stage two nights later when he admitted to making a mistake, "as all good fellows do," and asked for forgiveness.

Although supposedly in the prime of his life, John L. looked like a physical wreck. And he felt as bad as he looked. In early 1904, after four months on the road, his stomach made it impossible to eat, and his eyes started to quit. The doctors didn't know the precise cause, but they told John L. "some sort of germs poisoned the optic nerves." Friends feared he would become totally blind.

Broke and nearly sightless, Sullivan convalesced at his sister's home in Roxbury where a parade of ring greats that even included old foe Charley Mitchell pilgrimaged to his bedside in Annie Lennon's darkened parlor. When Fitzsimmons visited, the press couldn't help but note the physical difference between the robust forty-year-old light-heavyweight champion and the forty-five-year-old dissipated relic. Five decades, rather than five years, seemed to separate the gladiators, and the deep blue goggles Sullivan wore to protect his eyes made him appear even more elderly. Sullivan drank only milk and water along with a dash of salt as he recovered; tobacco became his nourishment. "Damned if the pipe ain't as good as eating and drinking to me," he told "Ruby Robert" in his deep, guttural tone. "I tell you, Bob," he muttered, "a fellow can't play with the kind of water I've been up against, and still hope to be there."

As John L. recovered, his defiance returned. "Tell them that I'm not dead yet," he wrote Fitzsimmons. "When I go, it will be quick and sudden. They won't ever hear that I'm sick, and all of a sudden they'll see it in the papers some morning—'old John L. is counted out for good.'"

The realm of fistiana came together once again to aid its former king. After visiting Sullivan's bedside, Fitzsimmons, a former blacksmith and champion horseshoer of Australia, returned to the forge at a Boston blacksmith shop, rolled up his shirt sleeves, and hammered out a horseshoe to be auctioned for a benefit fund for Sullivan. Stars such as Fitzsimmons, Sharkey, Mitchell, and Jack McAuliffe gathered in Boston Theatre on April 28, 1904, to raise money for John L. When the fists fell silent after sixteen exhibition bouts, Sullivan was led onto the same floorboards where Boston had presented him with his diamond belt in 1887. He still wore the dark goggles to protect his eyes from the floodlights. After several minutes of applause and three lusty cheers, Sullivan thanked the three thousand in attendance, delivered a brief monologue, and walked off the stage with tears trickling from beneath his goggles.

He also walked away from the box office with $2,500, and the following week, the world champion Boston Americans, who had won the inaugural 1903 World Series with Sullivan in attendance, and Connie Mack's Philadelphia Athletics donated 20 percent of the gate from their baseball game at the Huntington Avenue Grounds to Sullivan's benefit fund. John L. threw out the first pitch and showed a good arm based on the smack heard when the ball landed in the umpire's bare hands.

Soon enough, Sullivan felt well enough to drink again. In August, he was arrested in Roxbury for drunkenness after struggling to keep his balance and launching a profane tirade at a policeman at the Dudley Street elevated railway terminal. Just as he did at the Boston Theatre in April, Sullivan drew an overflow crowd when he arrived for his court appearance. He was found guilty and fined five dollars for drunkenness and ten dollars for profanity. Between the illness and the arrest, the "Boston Strong Boy" felt he needed a break from his hometown. Luckily, an invitation arrived from more than a thousand miles away.

In 1904, St. Louis hosted both the Summer Olympics and a World's Fair. The world had descended upon the Gateway to the West, but it kept walking right on by the saloon at 604 Market Street. Hurting for business, its owner John Gillespie contacted Sullivan with an enticing proposition for a man down on his luck: If John L. lent his name to the bar and shook the hand of any patron who bought a drink, he would receive a half interest in the profits with no money to invest.

In September, John L. headed west to become a professional greeter. Even though his new job entailed sitting in a bar all day, Sullivan pledged he was through with liquor, "as far as drinking it is concerned, at any rate." Upon setting foot in the long, narrow watering hole, he immediately redecorated. He tore down the life-size picture of Corbett hanging on the wall. "I can't do any business with that fellow around," he grumbled. Then he went to work sitting in a big chair at the end of the bar to be gawked at and pawed. Business boomed so much on his first day that a rope was strung around John L. to prevent him from being crushed by his admirers.

Within weeks, however, the novelty dissipated. The saloon returned to its former non-glory, populated by outcasts, grifters, and criminals. The depressing surroundings, contemptuous patrons, and menial work dragged Sullivan down. The ex-champion sat around at the end of the bar with a perpetual scowl—that is when he didn't fall asleep in his chair—verbally swatting at the stray barflies who buzzed too long in his airspace. A surly greeting of "What in the hell do you want?" awaited slack-jawed gawkers. The advertising cards that boasted Sullivan "will meet all comers in any number of rounds at his buffet" further chafed the dignity of former ring royalty.

Predictably, the boozing returned. He brawled with the bartender, who jumped through a plate-glass window to avoid Sullivan's hooks. When old Boston friends visited, he howled through the city on the eve of delivering a scheduled temperance lecture in East St. Louis. A grand jury issued a subpoena for Sullivan due to abnormally heavy voter registration conducted from the saloon, but he couldn't be found for days.

In early 1905, Sullivan traveled to Jefferson City, Missouri, to deliver a lecture. Two people showed. At two dollars a ticket, Sullivan hauled in four dollars. Humiliated, Sullivan refused to speak and then borrowed money to pay for the railroad ticket back to St. Louis. Back along the banks of the Mississippi, he contracted pneumonia after another drunken spree and had to cancel two weeks of lectures. "It's the worst knockdown I ever got," he whispered hoarsely. Once again, newspapers printed headlines that Sullivan was dying.

The next news flash about Sullivan from St. Louis just days later was stunning, but it had nothing to do with his death. From his sickbed, he publicly challenged Corbett to a rematch, a dozen years after the whipping in New Orleans. John L. said that he had ordered his new manager, Chicago theater promoter Frank Hall, to post a $1,000 forfeit. All he needed were eight months of training to be ready to "wallop that dude," he said. Newspapers attempted to explain Sullivan's deluded grasp for faded glory, speculating that he "evidently feels the need of notoriety in his old age, or else he was drunk." Likely, the answer was both. Corbett brushed off John L. in a telegram from Cincinnati: "I wish he had the health and youth to be able to fight me or anybody else. That's all the bad luck I wish the poor old fellow." Sullivan had become so pathetic that he could only elicit pity, rather than animus, from his greatest enemy.

John L. insisted the challenge was "on the level." Few in the sporting world doubted it, which made it just that more laughable.

The "Big Fellow" claimed his neck, legs, and arms were all the same size as during his fighting days. The same surely could not have been said of his waistline. He had assumed the build of a geriatric alderman, not a prizefighter. Every indulgence could be read on his face. The trademark mustache still flowed proudly, but when framed with sagging jowls, a puffy face, and a bulbous nose, it gave him the appearance of a walrus. The hand that shook the world was a massive mitt of meat and bone. His snow white hair made his coal black eyebrows stand out even more when he unfurled his legendary scowl. Huge black marks around his eyes made him look like a victim of an assault. In fact, he had been beaten up, by liquor. Side-by-side photographs of Sullivan in 1894 and a decade later that ran in a St. Louis newspaper highlighted Sullivan's ghastly transformation.

Sullivan's entire stay in St. Louis had been a disaster. The ring idol to millions was a sick and humiliated drunk. He was a forty-six-year-old leviathan who could pass for a man of seventy.

CHAPTER TWELVE

The Fight of His Life

Alone in St. Louis at the beginning of 1905, John L. Sullivan was stuck in one of the lowest troughs of his life. The inevitable ebbs that come in the course of a lifetime can plunge awfully deep for a former champion athlete, let alone an alcoholic one like John L. But as any fighter knows, sometimes all it takes is one punch, one instant to reverse a man's fortune.

Although rebuffed by Jim Corbett and recovering from pneumonia, the old warhorse pushed ahead with his plan to return to the ring. He scheduled a four-round bout with Canadian heavyweight John W. Phillips as part of a weeklong engagement at Smith's Opera House in Grand Rapids, Michigan. When Phillips backed out, Sullivan scrambled for a replacement. He sent for Jim McCormick, a veteran heavyweight from Galveston, Texas, with an impressive record of twenty-two victories to one defeat.

McCormick, who had been training in Arkansas for a fight with Kid McCoy, barely made his rail connection in Chicago and showed up in Grand Rapids just hours before the fight on the evening of March 1, 1905. Side by side in the ring, the 273-pound Sullivan and the 196-pound McCormick, a man half his age, looked like a mismatch.

An older boxer, especially a forty-six-year-old brawler, never has stamina in his corner, so John L. took the fight to his challenger as soon as the first round started. Sullivan popped McCormick in the face and rushed the younger man around the ring. His opponent returned fire with a right and a left to Sullivan's face, but John L. had the better of it at round's end. McCormick retreated to his corner bruised and concerned.

Sullivan, his chest heaving and falling like a storm-tossed sea, continued the onrush in the second round with a left and a right to the body. McCormick countered with a left to the face and a right to the ribs.

More heavy blows from Sullivan forced his opponent into a neutral corner. McCormick tried to fight his way out. And then it happened.

The long-dormant "Strong Boy" returned to the ring.

Sullivan unleashed a straight right to the jaw that dropped McCormick cold to the floor. The referee counted to ten, but the Texan never heard him. Unconscious for ten minutes, McCormick also missed the deafening roar from the sold-out audience and the chaos when frenzied fans broke chairs and furniture in the orchestra pit in their excitement to reach the stage and congratulate the old champion.

The punch that had made Sullivan world-famous had added one more notch to his belt. Sullivan immediately issued a public challenge to fight Corbett, Bob Fitzsimmons, Jim Jeffries, or any of the "top-notchers" for eight or ten rounds.

The fight warranted a three-paragraph item in the sports pages of the *Grand Rapids Herald,* but as news of Sullivan's unexpected fistic thunderbolt crossed the country, the shock waves grew in size the farther they moved away from the epicenter. The *National Police Gazette* featured a big spread on the bout, and back home in Boston, the knockout made front-page news.

Sullivan pointed to his victory as proof of his continuing relevance. "I'm only forty-six, and that is not too old," he insisted as he cited Fitzsimmons and Joe Goss as fighters who still brawled in their forties.

Two days after Sullivan's defeat of McCormick, the *Boston Journal* printed a cartoon depicting John L. asleep in his fighting trunks and dreaming of knocking out Corbett, Fitzsimmons, and Jeffries. Drawn next to the snoozing ex-champ was an anthropomorphized bottle laying the licking on him. The caption read "the real fight."

For thirty years, John L. Sullivan marinated himself in alcohol. He was a superstar imbiber who backed his boast that he could drink any man in the country under the table with the same ferocious certitude he used to prove that he could lick any son-of-a-bitch in America. One newspaper surmised that John L. "bought more drinks for people he knew and didn't know than any other American," and Sullivan's bills for broken glassware and busted bar mirrors were mere incidentals to his astronomical bar tab.

The bottle had been his only habitual companion for three decades, but according to Sullivan, he quit drinking with the same suddenness that he floored McCormick. John L. said he had an epiphany, and the road to Damascus ran straight through Terre Haute.

The Indiana city was Sullivan's next stop after packing up from Grand Rapids. While the specific details of the moment when John L. said he decided to quit drinking invariably changed with each telling, a few facts remained constant: that it happened in Terre Haute; that it happened on March 5, 1905; and that he quit booze cold.

Most of Sullivan's accounts placed him at a hotel bar, sometimes with his manager Frank Hall and sometimes with another friend, where he ordered either a glass of ale or a bottle of champagne. Sullivan, perhaps having a letdown following the high in Grand Rapids and hearing the silence that greeted his ring challenge, felt depressed. As he held the glass of spirits in his hand, he estimated that he had pushed half of the money he had ever earned, at least half a million dollars, across the polished bartops of saloons around the world.

"I thought of the contracts I had lost because of my battle with the black bottle, of the newspaper stories that had been printed about my drinking," he said. "I tumbled to it quick that I had been making a fool of myself." He took his glass, poured its contents into a cuspidor, and pledged aloud to never take another drink. Laughter greeted the proclamation. His friends had heard Sullivan make similar declarations with regularity and expected the predictable cycle: Binge. Repent. Repeat.

Sullivan claimed that he never had a "liquor habit" or a craving he needed to satisfy. "I drank like most people do—for conviviality's sake, to be a good fellow," he said. The signs all point to his being an alcoholic, though, and how he apparently willed himself to stay on the wagon forever this time amazed and puzzled even his closest friends.

The initial weeks of sobriety challenged Sullivan. "I had a feeling something like an appetite which I had been in the habit of satisfying with liquor," he said. "Whenever this feeling came over me, I ate something—I found just a bit would satisfy. After two or three weeks, I never experienced the feeling again."

With his newfound sobriety and his headline-grabbing knockout, Sullivan continued to verbally challenge his old foes as he toured the country performing in sparring exhibitions and delivering his monologue. He even made the preposterous claim to still be the reigning undefeated world heavyweight champion since no one had ever taken the title away from him under the bare-knuckle London Prize Ring Rules.

Sullivan finally found a taker when he signed articles of agreement to face longtime nemesis Charley Mitchell in a fifteen-round fight in Tacoma, Washington, in September 1905. John L. insisted his show business itinerary wouldn't impede his training because he'd simply take ten-mile sprints between midnight and sunrise. The claim did little to dissuade the segment of the American public who thought the fight was just a ploy to sell theater tickets. Indeed, the bout with Mitchell never came off, and Sullivan's shocking knockout in Grand Rapids proved to be his valedictory. However, John L. returned to breaking playhouse attendance and receipt records and proving he "still retained the hero worship that the multitude has always given him since his ring career began."

Every Sunday, his worshippers read the gospel according to Sullivan in "Jolts from John L.," a weekly column that ran from 1905 to 1909 in newspapers around the country. In his typically blunt style, Sullivan shared memories from his ring days, championed the color line, groused about the state of the heavyweight division, and offered his opinion on everything from tariff bills to the legalization of Sunday baseball games. He shared his distinctive views on war ("If the nations would agree to pick a dozen of their boxers to settle arguments with their fists you'd get just as much satisfaction and there wouldn't be half the damage done.") and even women's hats ("These styles are made up in Paris by women who would get pinched as street walkers if they hung out over here."). He rarely missed a chance to disparage Corbett—"a ladylike fighter"—or mention his friendship with the former Prince of Wales or exalt his new political hero, President Theodore Roosevelt.

Although the Knickerbocker aristocrat and the Irish ruffian sprouted from different backgrounds, excelled in vastly disparate arenas, and even belonged to opposing political parties, they were kindred spirits. Roosevelt and Sullivan—born just fifteen days apart—attacked life, took pride in always being "on the level," and had little use for "mollycoddles."

From his days as a sickly youth, Roosevelt boxed to stay in shape. While Sullivan ascended through the ranks of Boston fighters in 1879, across the Charles River in Cambridge, the 135-pound future president boxed for Harvard University's intramural lightweight championship. Harvard's Dr. Dudley Sargent, the physician who so thoroughly evaluated Sullivan before the Corbett fight, examined Roosevelt three months before his graduation and warned the young man of fatal consequences if he did not give up the "strenuous life" and find a sedentary occupation. "Doctor, I'm going to do all the things you tell me not to do," Roosevelt said. "If I've got to live the sort of life you have described, I don't care how short it is."

Roosevelt continued to box and credited the sport with steeling him with the temper and courage he displayed on San Juan Hill during the Spanish-American War. In the White House, he regularly sparred with Mike Donovan and others until a punch from a young artillery officer smashed a blood vessel and left him nearly blind in his left eye. Much to the First Lady's disdain, boxing was a frequent dinnertime topic with guests, and Roosevelt had particular esteem for Sullivan, whom he considered "as game and straight and honest a fighter as ever stepped in the ring," and their mutual admiration morphed into friendship.

When John L. visited the White House on May 9, 1907, however, he came to discuss family business rather than fisticuffs. His nephew and namesake, US Marine Corps private John Lawrence Lennon, had been convicted by court-martial for desertion in Cuba the previous December. Private Lennon received a dishonorable discharge and a one-year sentence that he was serving at Fort Jay in New York Harbor.

Sullivan took his appeal directly to the commander-in-chief. Although it was an afternoon meeting, he donned his finest evening wear—a tuxedo coat, a low-cut white waistcoat, and a large diamond. As he sat in the White House waiting to be announced, Secretary of War William Howard Taft waddled by, and the two portly men compared their vitals. Sullivan said he hit the scales at 335 pounds, while the future president claimed he was down to a slim 283. "Guess I got you skinned a block," John L. quipped.

Once ushered in to see Roosevelt, John L. sat down and offered the chief executive an expensive cigar. The president said he didn't smoke, but that didn't deter Sullivan. "Put it in your pocket," he insisted. "Take another; put both in your pocket." After dispensing with his offerings, John L. explained that his nephew hadn't intended to desert but merely overstayed his leave of absence by three days. "That boy I just cannot understand," John L. told the president as a poignant look came across his eyes. "I did my best to bring him up the way he ought to go. But there was just nothing to be done with him. His tastes were naturally low. He took to music!"

Roosevelt choked the chortle that overtook him and agreed to take the matter under advisement. The president interceded with the Navy to pardon Lennon and allow him to re-enlist to serve out his full term of four years. Roosevelt caught political blowback for his decision because, while he clearly had the power of pardon, the legal officers of the War Department and most military officials believed an act of Congress was the only way to restore a dishonorably discharged serviceman to active duty.

Sullivan made one final trip to visit Roosevelt at the White House in early 1909 and presented the president with a gold-mounted rabbit's foot that he ended up carrying with him on safari to Africa after he left the presidency. The two men remained in regular touch, exchanging birthday telegrams and meeting in person on occasion. TR even defended Sullivan after a Kentucky senator called him the most vile of names for a boxer or a celebrity: a "has-been." "I set him right with a jump," Roosevelt assured John L.

⸺

Much as in Roosevelt's business, boxing made for strange bedfellows. Fighters could find themselves battering each other in the ring one day and then working the same corner the next. After the encounter in Grand Rapids, McCormick joined Sullivan's tour as a sparring partner, and John L. briefly served as the Texan's trainer, working McCormick's corner in August 1905 when he fought Gus Ruhlin. In 1907, John L. and former foe Jake Kilrain—now a park policeman in Somerville,

Massachusetts—agreed to revive the sparring act that they had briefly performed in 1898 as part of *A Trip Across the Ocean.*

Their act began with a brief introduction from Frank Hall followed by Sullivan's monologue, which had evolved to include opinions on the boxing news of the day and a warning of the evils of alcohol. After taking his bows, John L. changed into a gym shirt, flannel trousers, and boxing shoes and donned the gloves with Kilrain in a three-round exhibition. (Occasionally, Kid Cutler joined the circuit as a sparring partner.) As an added lure for boxing fans, the act sometimes featured original fight films, such as ones from the Corbett-Fitzsimmons and Joe Gans–Kid Herman bouts.

The cauldron of Richburg, Mississippi, had forged Sullivan and Kilrain together in the American memory, and nostalgia for the bare-knuckle era tugged old-timers into the theaters, even if this time the fighters were trading blows with gloves. Although silver now frosted the hair and mustaches of the gladiators, both forty-eight years old and a generation removed from their famous fight, they proved to be one of the vaudeville circuit's biggest drawing cards. When they arrived in the Pacific Northwest, a local newspaper reported the act "has created more interest than anything in the theatrical line that has been seen in Seattle for years." Even when they appeared in the same city numerous times in a single year, Sullivan and Kilrain filled theaters from pit to dome.

The schedule of week after week on the road could be grueling and the temptation to drink constant, but Sullivan never wavered from his pledge to theater owners to attend "strictly to business." A May 1908 newspaper item noted that John L. had not missed one performance in 163 consecutive weeks. Sobriety treated Sullivan well. The newspapers referred to him as a virtual renaissance man: "pugilist, actor, philosopher, lecturer, and temperance talker." His cheeks grew ruddier, his eyes brightened, and his gait quickened.

The health of his bankroll improved as well. John L. earned several hundred dollars a week and regularly sent money to his sister to place in a trust. By 1907, according to one report, the account had grown to $40,000.

John L. could now be found on the road spending evenings in the company of priests, something unimaginable during his bar-prowling days, but a development that would have pleased his mother. He also made company with fellow teetotalers. When he met up with William Cody at a Wild West show stop outside Boston in 1908, Sullivan and "Buffalo Bill" revisited old times for two hours over tall drinks of ginger ale as costumed cowboys and Indians hovered to listen to their anecdotes.

Although nearly two decades and dozens of pounds separated Sullivan from his championship reign, he remained the face of boxing, the epitome of American masculinity, and one of America's foremost celebrities. "It is a dollar to a nickel that he is known to more people in this country than George Washington," stated the *National Police Gazette* in 1905. Letters from fans merely addressed to "John L. Sullivan, Boston, Mass." still found their way into the champion's hands. Ernest Thompson Seton, who fostered the Boy Scout movement in the United States, declared in 1910, "I do not know that I ever met a boy that would not rather be John L. Sullivan than Darwin or Tolstoi."

None of the heavyweight champions who succeeded Sullivan—men such as Corbett, Fitzsimmons, and Jeffries—had anywhere near the same hold on the American public. When Seattle vaudeville impresario John Cort built an arena on the Pay Streak adjacent to the Alaska-Yukon-Pacific Exposition in 1909, he bypassed any of the subsequent heavyweight title holders and constructed a twenty-five-foot-tall alabaster statue of a mustachioed Sullivan in a fighting post to guard the main entrance.

Sullivan turned fifty in October 1908, and the traveling started to exhaust him. He announced that he was taking a break from the theater and went to Hot Springs, Arkansas, for a respite. "A man past fifty shouldn't do much toward reducing his weight. The effort will do more harm than good," Sullivan told a reporter, and he did his best to fulfill that assessment. Sullivan weighed well over three hundred pounds. His sleeveless gym shirt revealed his beefy arms, and his body resembled a hot-air balloon in his enormous trousers. He spent his days smoking his pipe, writing letters, and playing solitaire but doing little exercise outside of five minutes work with light dumbbells and brushing his hair one hundred times a day to stimulate blood flow to his scalp.

By this time, John L. had decided to legally end his shattered marriage to Annie Sullivan. He filed preliminary papers for divorce in

Brooklyn in July 1908 and claimed that his wife had violated her marriage vows several times in the prior five years. The news surprised many Americans because they simply forgot that Sullivan had ever been married in the first place. After all, it had been more than two decades since John L. and Annie Sullivan lived in the same house. Many of those who thought they remembered Sullivan's wife mistakenly recalled Annie Livingston instead.

Back in Centerville, Rhode Island, the news stunned Annie Sullivan as well. She still felt the sting of the contested divorce proceeding she had brought twenty-three years before. "We have been through all this divorce business once before," she told the press who descended upon her home, the same family cottage she had shared with her sister when she fell in love with John L. The former champion dispatched a lawyer to Rhode Island to pay off Annie in return for an uncontested divorce this time around, but she vowed to pay him back for fighting her divorce suit by doing the same to him. She even managed to deliver her own low blow in the press: "I have not seen John in a long time, although I hear every now and then that he looks more and more like Bismarck."

After returning from Hot Springs, Sullivan formally filed for divorce in December 1908 in superior court in Cook County, Illinois. The fighter so associated with Boston blamed his vagabond lifestyle for the strange legal venue. Sullivan told the court that he had no permanent home but had lived at Hall's residence, listed as 3327 Michigan Avenue, for the previous two and a half years.

Sullivan named the late Salvation Army captain Henry Howland of Centerville as a co-respondent, and Hall testified that "Mrs. Sullivan several years ago confessed to having transferred her affections to the clergyman." John L. told the court that during their years together Annie "craved a life of gayety, and shunned domestic responsibilities." Sullivan also claimed he sought the divorce because of greater concerns about his afterlife rather than his days on earth. "I don't want that woman to have my bones," he said of his Protestant wife. "She may outlive me, but if I die first I want to feel that I'll have a decent Catholic burial by my blood relatives. I've always fought shy of the divorce courts on account of my religion, but there is a time to draw the line."

The judge granted the divorce on grounds of desertion. Annie fumed. She had only learned about the divorce proceedings through the press. The court served her no notice. She had no chance to testify. "How any one can go and get a divorce in that fashion is more than I can conceive," she said. "It's all a rank outrage."

⎯⎯

February 7, 1910, was a grand day for the Boston Irish. Their excitement over the inauguration of John F. Fitzgerald as mayor for a second time forced the swearing-in ceremony to be shifted from City Hall to the much larger Faneuil Hall, but even that historic venue could not contain the throng that clamored to watch "Honey Fitz" take his oath. Men scaled awnings and climbed through open windows. Women fainted in the crush, and police pressed through the mob to escort Fitzgerald into the hall. Inside, the crowd's enthusiasm overflowed when they spotted the hulking figure of their hero, the "Boston Strong Boy," taking a seat among the political dignitaries.

As soon as the inauguration finished, Sullivan leapt to his feet, slapped his prodigious palm on the mayor's back in congratulations, and gripped his legendary right around that of Fitzgerald, whose daughter Rose would give birth to the thirty-fifth president of the United States in 1917. Thus, whenever John F. Kennedy exchanged handshakes with his grandfather, the most famous Irish American of the twentieth century shook the hand that shook the hand of the most famous Irish American of the nineteenth century.

Hours after Fitzgerald's oath, John L. took one himself. Sullivan's vows, however, shocked even his best friends and landed a photograph of him, not Fitzgerald, on the front page of the *Boston Globe*. After leaving the inauguration, John L. journeyed the few blocks to the Parker House hotel where, inside a room rented by Hall, he stood before justice of the peace Fred Ingalls and wed Catherine Harkins.

Rumors of impending nuptials had trailed Sullivan for years, even before the courts granted him the divorce with Annie Sullivan in 1908. Newspapers reported that he planned to wed a wealthy woman who was the widow of Charley Johnston. Despite his public denials, John L. *was* in love. It just wasn't with the woman identified by the press.

Kate Harkins, five years Sullivan's junior, was born in East Boston to parents who had emigrated from County Donegal in the north of Ireland. The press had already written the script of John L. wooing a moneyed widow and tended to typecast Kate in that role, but she wasn't wealthy and had never been married. She lived at 285 Roxbury Street, near the neighborhood where she and John L. grew up. Newspapers reported the pair were "childhood sweethearts," although the age difference and reports that their previous relationship ended when "differences arose because of his methods of life" suggest that any prior romance didn't occur during Sullivan's schooldays and would have ended shortly before he met Annie Bates Bailey. The long arcs of their lives intersected decades later, particularly after he was laid up with temporary blindness at his sister's house in 1904. Kate, a quiet, prim woman he called "mother," helped to nurse him back to health, and Sullivan's journey to sobriety also blazed his way back to her.

Kate attended mass regularly, but given Sullivan's divorce, there could be no Catholic wedding. The civil ceremony was quiet and simple, in contrast to the chaotic scene John L. had experienced at Faneuil Hall earlier in the day. Sullivan wore a new suit, his bride a plain traveling gown. A tall woman scraping the six-foot mark, Kate matched the groom in stature and in the gray shade of her hair. Sullivan beamed as the justice of the peace pronounced them man and wife shortly after four in the afternoon. Hall served as the best man. Nellie Kelly was the lone bridesmaid. The only others in attendance were Hall's wife and son, three relatives of the bride, Sullivan's nephew Arthur Lennon, and two of his friends and advisors.

Sullivan had so vigorously denied intentions to remarry that few, even his closest acquaintances, knew of his plans. "I did not want my friends to trouble themselves by sending me any presents," he explained. To keep the secret, Kate, rather than John L., went to the city register that afternoon to apply for the marriage license. She listed his residence as 3327 Michigan Avenue, Chicago, the same address he had provided for the divorce proceedings in Cook County. Sullivan's occupation was listed as "lecturer," which raised grumbles among some sporting men who wondered if John L. had disowned anything to do with the ring and turned "mollycoddle."

After dinner with their guests, the newly betrothed boarded the steamer *Ivernia*, scheduled to set sail in the morning for Ireland. The trip mixed business and honeymoon as John L. had scheduled a ten-week theatrical tour with Kilrain across the British Isles. The Halls and Kilrains stayed in rooms adjoining the Sullivans' stateroom. Once the newspapers learned of the nuptials, reporters swarmed the *Ivernia*. Sullivan greeted them with smiles, pleased almost as much with giving them the slip as with the wedding itself. "I'm just about the happiest man on this big earth tonight," he told them with an affectionate glance at his new bride.

Sullivan was eager to return to Ireland and Great Britain and renew acquaintances with the man he considered his old friend, King Edward VII, the former Prince of Wales who had succeeded Queen Victoria in 1901. Sullivan waved a large silk American flag as the *Ivernia* sailed out of Boston Harbor. Friends and well-wishers cheered back, giving the newlyweds their own royal send-off.

———

Sullivan's voyage was considerably calmer than his last transatlantic crossing, the tempestuous transit with Annie Livingston in 1888. The newlyweds arrived in Queenstown, Ireland, on February 16, 1910, and toured the rugged beauty of the south and west of the Emerald Isle for a week before Sullivan's first scheduled appearance in Dublin.

Unlike his first trip to Ireland, Sullivan spent time exploring the Celtic roots of his family tree. On the morning of February 21, the couple arrived by train in Tralee to visit Michael Sullivan's family farm. John L. had few specifics about the whereabouts of his late father's birthplace. "I do not know whether his place was in Tralee or Abbeydorney," he confessed. As word spread through Tralee of the world-famous man in their midst, crowds inundated the Central Hotel where he was enjoying a brief respite. Sullivan congratulated the men of County Kerry for the name they had made for themselves in the civilized world, and then the couple drove off in a sidecar with a local to the Sullivans' Laccabeg homestead where they were welcomed by his first cousin, Eugene.

Two days later, John L. received a great public welcome in his late mother's hometown of Athlone. A throng of townspeople and the

Athlone National Brass Band gathered outside Sullivan's quarters at the Prince of Wales Hotel (the name of which surely pleased Sullivan). The former champion addressed the crowd from his hotel window and drew cheers by expressing to "his fellow townsmen" his pride in his Irish origin and local connection. Later that day, half of Athlone poured into Denis O'Connell's public house to shake Sullivan's hand. The next morning, John L. and Kate visited the Kellys of Curramore before leaving for Dublin, where he opened a two-week engagement at the Theatre Royal.

Twice nightly as part of a vaudeville act, Sullivan took to the stage in top hat and white gloves as the band played "Come Back to Erin." He delivered his monologue and then donned gloves to spar three rounds with Kilrain. He made good money—$750 a week—but Irish newspapers couldn't help but notice the precipitous difference in his appearance since his previous visit more than twenty years earlier. "Years and years ago, John L.'s brawny chest was the admiration of the world. There's a change in front since then," noted the *Irish Independent*.

After closing in Dublin, Sullivan and Kilrain brought their act to Scotland and England. Much as they had nearly a quarter-century before, the British came out in force, standing five deep along the city streets just to glimpse a passing John L. in Glasgow. Then Sullivan performed before approximately forty thousand people per week in various theaters around London.

The three-month foreign tour was a financial success, but Sullivan regretted not being able to meet up with Roosevelt, who was traveling through England at the same time, or the king, who had taken ill not long after the Sullivans set sail from Boston. The British monarch died on May 6, 1910, while Sullivan was performing in Manchester.

Everywhere that Sullivan traveled through the British Isles, reporters asked him about the big boxing news that had inflamed the passions of America: thirty-five-year-old former champ Jeffries had agreed to come back after a five-year retirement in a quest to recapture the heavyweight championship from Jack Johnson, who had become the first black man to hold the title after he knocked out Tommy Burns the day after Christmas in 1908. The victory by the son of former slaves threw segments of white America into a panic and upended theories of racial superiority and social

Darwinism. "Is the Caucasian played out?" fretted the *Detroit Free Press*. "Are the races that we have been calling inferior about to demand to us that we must draw the color line in everything if we are to avoid being whipped individually and collectively?"

Whites such as author Jack London believed only Jeffries, who had retired undefeated, could be their savior. "Jeffries must emerge from his alfalfa farm and remove the golden smile from Jack Johnson's face," London wrote. "Jeff, it's up to you. The white man must be rescued." John L. joined in lobbying "the great white hope." On behalf of a group of money men, he offered a purse of $75,000 to make the match. Jeffries had followed Sullivan's lead in drawing his own color line, but as Johnson continued to dispatch white challengers with ease, "The Boilermaker" felt obligated to subvert the principle ultimately to "demonstrate that a white man is king of them all."

The Irish newspapers quoted Sullivan as saying, based on his personal experience squaring off against Corbett after a three-year absence from the ring, that it would be extremely difficult for Jeffries, who had exploded to more than three hundred pounds, to get into fighting form. One newspaper reported that although John L. expressed his natural desire to see the white challenger win, he said, "I cannot see that he can with such a man as Johnson before him." According to the *Irish Independent*, he even went so far as to suggest that a victory by Jeffries would mean the fix was in because the film rights to the bout had sold for $200,000 and "the cinematograph pictures would be worthless if Johnson won, for nobody would go to see a n----- beat a white man."

In April, Sullivan signed with the *New York Times* and syndicated newspapers to cover the Jeffries-Johnson bout, scheduled for July 4 near San Francisco, and the last two weeks of the fighters' training. Now being paid for his opinion, Sullivan retreated from the comments that had appeared in Ireland. "Lots of stuff has been written as coming from me about the fight, but it's all bosh. I am saying nothing about who will win," he told *Times* readers. By the time he landed back in America at the end of May, he was telling the papers that if Jeffries was in condition that he'd "whip" Johnson and "take that coon and bite his ears off."

After a one-week engagement at New York's Plaza Theater, John L. boarded the rails for San Francisco with Kate and a *New York Times* sporting editor charged with polishing the former champ's raw thoughts into readable prose.

Sullivan almost missed the Chicago Limited, however, because like a giddy schoolboy, he glued his eyes to the skies instead of his watch, searching for any glimpse of aviation pioneer Charles M. Hamilton, who was attempting to be the first man to make a round-trip flight between New York and Philadelphia. John L. had never before seen an airplane aloft, and the disappointed fighter would have to wait for another day to see the new marvel of transportation.*

Sullivan chose a leisurely route to the Golden Gate by way of Chicago and Seattle because he insisted that Kate, who had never been out of New England before their marriage, see the majesty of the Canadian Rockies. Sporting men and old friends of the fighter joined them along the way, and by the time they reached St. Paul, they had an entire luxury rail car to themselves. Cigar smoke and memories of the old days wafted through the air as they crossed to the Pacific. With the train's westward movement, the newspaper bylines "with the John L. Sullivan party on the way to the fight" marked their progress: "Enderlin, North Dakota," "Swift Current, Saskatchewan," "Ashland, Oregon."

John L. couldn't help but notice the striking difference between the luxurious style in which he was traveling to the championship fight compared to years ago when he had sneaked into Mississippi City and Richburg like an outlaw. Political opposition to the fight game still existed, however, and under pressure from religious groups, California governor James Gillett banned the title bout from his state. It was a decision ironically lauded by Sullivan's employer, the *New York Times*, which led one puzzled reader to ask "by what reasoning or morality you justify the engagement of an ex-prizefighter to report in your columns the details of a criminal proceeding which you officially condemn." The paper responded

---

* Although Sullivan expressed his admiration for Hamilton to reporters, he insisted it was strictly "terra firma for yours truly, John L."

with the tired, lame excuse that its coverage should not be construed as an endorsement of prizefighting and that it was actually performing a public service by exposing the brutality of prizefighting.

After arriving in San Francisco, Sullivan visited Johnson's training camp at the Seal Rock House where he posed for photographs and checked in with the champ. John L. came away from his meeting impressed at the "husky piece of humanity." Indeed, if Sullivan had been able to see past the color of Johnson's skin, he would have been quite familiar with what he saw. The flamboyant, boisterous "Galveston Giant" dominated his sport and had continual run-ins with the law. He inflamed the establishment by refusing to subjugate himself. He was an ethnic hero, but just as Sullivan offended the "lace curtain" Irish, Johnson's behavior earned him the rebuke of some African Americans. "His actions do not meet my personal approval, and I am sure they do not meet with the approval of the colored race," wrote Booker T. Washington.

Johnson's ascent renewed talk of the color line, which John L. continued to advocate staunchly in his pre-fight reports. "I do believe that the negroes should fight in a class by themselves," he told his readers. "Many times during my career I was urged by outsiders to throw reason to the winds and fight a black man. But I always refused."

Sullivan left San Francisco for Reno, Nevada, where promoter Tex Rickard found a new home for the fight. Within hours, John L. was not only reporting the news, he was making it. Jeffries had hired Corbett to help him train, and "Gentleman Jim" had read Sullivan's spoutings from Ireland that Jeffries would only win if the fight was fixed and that "old, decrepit" boxers like Corbett couldn't possibly give the challenger the workouts he required.

While Sullivan had made peace with old enemies such as Kilrain and Mitchell, the rivalry with Corbett endured. The bad blood soon spilled onto the front pages of newspapers around the country.

Although Sullivan caught wind that he might receive a hostile welcome, he made the challenger's training quarters his first stop in Reno. "Gentleman Jim" promised to make John L. "as welcome as a rat at a suffragette meeting," and he watched as Sullivan, in a gray suit and straw hat, shuffled from the trolley stop and approached the front gate of the Jeffries camp. Other brawny members of the challenger's entourage, such as Joe Choynski, guarded the gate with Corbett. Jeffries remained inside the cottage, but his wife emerged to watch the coming storm. Reporters positioned themselves to get the best vantage of the first punch.

As Sullivan reached for the gate, Corbett clasped it shut and barked, "Say, you. I've got something to say to you."

"What have you got to say to me?" growled Sullivan.

"Mr. Jeffries left word that if you called here he did not want to see you or have you around."

"What does he mean by that?"

"Well, he means that you have been knocking this fight and trying to put him in bad," Corbett said.

"I have never done him any wrong."

"Yes, you have," Corbett shot back. "You have been quoted in newspapers all over this country and in England as saying this fight was to be a fake, and that Johnson was to lay down, and that Jeffries couldn't win it on the level."

"I never said the thing the paper claimed I did," Sullivan exclaimed. "I'll say now that I want Jeffries to win this fight, and that he will if he's as good as he was five years ago."

"What do you say about the cracks you made in the Howard Theatre in Boston when the match was made? Did you give it out there that the fight was to be a fake and Johnson was to quit?"

Although the *Boston Globe* quoted him otherwise, John L. denied it. "You didn't hear me say it, did you?"

"No, I didn't hear you say it, not personally, because I wasn't in the Howard that week, but every newspaper in Boston quoted you as making the crack, and there was no contradiction of it."

"I can't help what the papers say," replied the man in the employ of a newspaper syndicate. "There are twenty papers in Boston that are always panning me, and I can't stop it."

Then Corbett ripped open the old wound at the root of their animosity. "You have no use for him, and have never had any use for me since I licked you. You have always been knocking me, even when I appeared at both your benefits; but I don't hold that against you. I have got it against you, though, because you have acted so meanly about this match."

"I ain't knocking the fight business," Sullivan said. "I have done more for it than any man living."

"Is that so?"

"By boosting for big purses, sticking out for something worth while," John L. said.

"You and I fought for twenty-five thousand dollars, and I guess I had something to do with making that big purse."

Sullivan felt compelled to correct Corbett and reminded him that it was actually $45,000 since there was an additional $20,000 side bet. They glared at each other like savages until John L. declared that he had enough. In his younger days, Sullivan might have attempted a swing, but instead he tottered away. "This is all bunk and don't get anybody anything," Sullivan muttered. Corbett went inside to fill Jeffries in, saying, "He has been a butter-in and a knocker all his life, and it's about time somebody called him on it."

The re-ignition of the Sullivan-Corbett battle became the unwelcome big story from Reno. TONGUE LASHING FOR OLD JOHN L. blared the front page of the *Boston Globe,* which said Corbett "publicly humiliated" him for the second time in his life. The peacemakers went to work immediately. Rickard tried to defuse the story, and William Muldoon, the friend of both men who had just arrived in Reno, convinced Corbett to accept, at least in public, Sullivan's claim of being misquoted. It would be for the good of the sport, already suffering from an image problem after being booted from California.

The next day, Corbett sent for Sullivan. This time when John L. arrived with Muldoon, he received a more gentlemanly greeting.

"Well, John, old boy," Corbett said with a hearty handshake, "I am glad to see you again."

"Jim, old boy, I am glad to see you, too."

"John, the big fellow would like to meet you," Corbett said as he ushered him over to meet Jeffries.

The three former heavyweight champions shook hands and posed for the photographers and film crews. Grainy film captured Corbett and Sullivan playfully putting up their dukes and John L. giving a quick feint and demonstrating a little millwork. The film crew also shot John L. throwing rights and lefts at a speedbag bouncing around like a balloon. The silent movie provides a rare glimpse of what Sullivan must have looked like in the ring. Somewhere beneath the wrinkles, the fat, and the decades of rust, the raw talent still shined through.

By fight day, the focus had returned to "The Fight of the Century." As the United States celebrated its birthday and the adoption of the document that declared "all men are created equal," most of the country lusted for the white man to pound the black man back into subjugation. In the early morning, special trains from across the West deposited "heavy loads of perspiring humanity." African-American porters and cooks placed their wages on Johnson and returned to the train station. The spectators, nearly all white, stood in a half-mile line to enter the enormous specially constructed outdoor arena. Sullivan settled in ringside and took his seat in front of the motion-picture cameras and opposite the timekeeper. Although he announced that he had made his final pick for the fight, John L. kept his readers guessing "because I have not any logical reason for my decision. It is just like one of those woman things—I just feel it, and that's all." (He revealed the following day that Johnson was his choice.)

Before the main event, twenty thousand fight fans cheered as Sullivan stepped inside the ring and joined a lineup of fistic gods that included Muldoon, Fitzsimmons, Tom Sharkey, Stanley Ketchel, Battling Nelson, Jack McAuliffe, and Sam Langford. Then entered Johnson and Jeffries, the betting favorite. By this point, the fighters had ceased to be men. They had become vessels carrying the hopes and fears of millions around the world. From the start, Johnson had the better of it. Between the fifth and sixth round, he leaned over the ropes to Sullivan and said, "John, I thought this fellow could hit."

"I never said so," John L. replied, "but I believe he could have six years ago."

"Five or six years ago ain't now, though," Johnson said.

Jeffries couldn't wipe the golden smile off the champion's face, and it ended in the fifteenth round with one last knockdown. Rickard lifted the arm of the black man as the challenger's trainers sprayed Jeffries with water to revive him.

Never had the culmination of a sporting event sparked so much silence. In the stadium, there were no boos, just a few random cheers emanating from the twenty thousand. The reaction was the same among the thirty thousand in Times Square when the bulletin flashed: "Johnson Wins." As the crowd departed in disbelief, one fan mumbled, "Old John L. was right when he said they never come back." Not all remained quiet that Fourth of July night in America. From sea to shining sea, race riots and assaults crackled. The violence claimed eleven lives and injured hundreds, most of them African-American. Fearing even more disorder, censors across the country banned the screening of the movie of the bout, and Congress followed suit by outlawing the interstate transportation of fight films. A generation passed before the public could freely watch Johnson whip Jeffries again.

The opening line of Sullivan's column the next morning, in which he felt compelled to restate his "well-known antipathy" to Johnson's race, succinctly captured the news: "The fight of the century is over and a black man is the undisputed champion of the world."

CHAPTER THIRTEEN

From Glory to Gutter to God

AFTER A WHIRLWIND FIVE MONTHS, JOHN L. AND KATE RETURNED TO Massachusetts and finally exhaled. A few weeks before their marriage, the couple had bought a farm in Abington, a rural community of fifty-five hundred people twenty miles south of Boston. A stable, poultry house, piggery, and comfortable eleven-room farmhouse at 704 Hancock Street dotted seventy pastoral acres of woods and meadows in a section of town known as the "Thicket." Fields of blueberry bushes stretched back to Beaver Brook, which bubbled into a large pond with two private islands. For the first time in a quarter-century, since he left Annie Sullivan in 1885, John L. had a true "home" of his own.

Using the nest-egg that his sister had held for him, he poured the money that he hadn't squandered on booze into upgrading the old farm. He hired workmen to build a stone bungalow just south of the bright red farmhouse and fitted a small gym in the barn. Like the "Big Fellow" himself, the farmhouse was strong, solid, and of fine vintage, dating back to the War of 1812.

Friends doubted that John L. could make it as a "gentleman farmer." They remembered how he hated the seclusion of Muldoon's farm and predicted the boy born in the South End tenements would be back in Boston in a matter of weeks. After all, the only thing he had experience raising was hell.

But Sullivan loved the simple life on the farm with Kate. He allowed the frantic engine that had driven his life at full speed to idle. Clean living and clean air suited him well now. He enjoyed waking up with the roosters rather than in some strange hotel with a hangover. He lolled away in a hammock while Kate tended to flower beds. Well-wishers, temperance leaders, and reporters who made unannounced pilgrimages to the farm often found Sullivan puffing away on his pipe and holding court from his rocking chair on the portico or underneath one of the large trees shading the farmhouse. He was "the most contented man to be found in all New England."

Sullivan's beloved horse-drawn Irish jaunting car was a familiar fixture on the country roads of Plymouth County. With a cigar in his mouth, Sullivan drove to town every morning to pick up farm supplies and visit the post office. Little boys who ran after the car shouting Sullivan's name always received a friendly wave in return. Still not overly religious, Sullivan did accompany Kate to church and began to carry a little leather prayer book in his vest pocket. "I am going to stay here until I die," he pledged. These were the happiest years of John's life.

The couple christened their humble estate Donelee-Ross Farm as a reminder of their shared Irish ancestry. The name was a mash-up of Donegal, the home county of Kate's parents; Tralee, the ancestral county town of Sullivan's father; and Roscommon, the county where his mother was born. And in some respects, Donelee-Ross completed the circle on a Celtic journey that had begun when Michael Sullivan and Catherine Kelly fled Ireland after the Great Hunger. Like his Irish forebears, John L. planted his roots in the soil. Ironically, the crop that Donelee-Ross excelled at producing was the same one whose failure drove his parents to America: the potato. The farm grew almost enough potatoes to supply Abington for an entire winter. "My boy," he bragged one day to a reporter as he patted a newly dug spud, "there is a Murphy that would make the heart of an Irishman glad."

John L. became beloved in his adopted town. He was a ring god to the adults, but the neighborhood boys and girls also idolized the "Big Fellow," not because of his boxing exploits but because of the personality of their new playmate. Even shy girls intimidated at first by his big voice and bigger frame soon grew attached to him. Sullivan let the children pick his ripened berries and apples, and the little ones ate up the fruit along with his gripping tales of adventure. Kids always seemed to be at his heels, scrambling for the coins he scattered on his trips into town or shaking the hand that touched those of kings and presidents. Kate stayed active volunteering as a visiting nurse, and the couple were admired for their charity.

In short order, the old fighter became Abington's most treasured asset, but John L. was also the biggest man in town in more ways than one. Kate's home-cooked meals contributed to his ever-expanding corpulence. Reporters who visited the farm often saw Sullivan's gargantuan bib overalls flapping in the breeze like a battle flag. His jowls drooped. When he ate, the fat below his chin shook like a pelican devouring a fish. He grew so fleshy that he earned formal membership in the Boston chapter of the United States Fat Men's Club.

"Farmer John" surrounded himself with a veritable menagerie: pigs, goats, rabbits, geese, pheasants, chickens, horses, turkeys, and milk cows. He also loved dogs. During his years in Abington, he owned bulldogs, Scotch collies, Irish setters, and bull terriers. Soon after he and Kate moved to Abington, the couple also took an eight-year-old orphan, William Kelly, into their home. The boy Sullivan nicknamed "Kell" had been living with an adopted family in a nearby town, but after the father of the family suddenly passed away, the mother of eight was unable to care for William any longer. When Kate heard the priest tell the terrible story at mass, she suggested to her husband that they bring him to their new home. "Sure, my dear, fetch him along," the former champion said. Sullivan had been a disinterested father at best to John Jr. three decades earlier, but perhaps he felt he had been given a chance for redemption. Kelly was often referred to in the press as Sullivan's "adopted son," but whether the designation ever became legal is unknown. A reporter who visited Donelee-Ross in 1915 also found a six-year-old boy, the son of a close friend struggling with health issues, nicknamed "Young John L." living there. "What's a home without kids?" John L. asked a reporter.

Despite his pledge to swear off long-distance theatrical tours of the country, he continued to spend a few weeks every year headlining vaudeville acts and delivering his monologue to "pick up a little sugar."

The blissful life on the farm was shattered around 1913, however, when doctors diagnosed Kate with breast cancer. She struggled for years and was operated on three times. "Well, old pal, Kate has been a very sick woman for the last three years," he wrote to a friend in February 1916. "Had part of her breast cut out . . . I am all broke up—don't know what I am doing half of my time . . . my courage has forsook me." A distraught John L. began to lose hope that his wife could survive.

A decade after his sobering epiphany in Terre Haute, Sullivan announced in 1915 the launch of yet another phase of his career. "I am quitting the farm and 'coming back' to have a go with a bigger champion than I ever was—the champion of champions—John Barleycorn," he told a magazine reporter.

As an anti-drinking crusader, John L. completed the transformation from boozed fighter to booze fighter, although he rejected the "temperance" label. During his drinking days, he had too many run-ins with temperance advocates, such as Carrie Nation, who he felt were consumed by self-aggrandizement. Sullivan preached abstinence from alcohol without being preachy. He didn't couch the issue in moral terms or cloak himself in religion. He simply pointed to himself as a cautionary tale to the power of demon rum.

Sullivan supported anti-saloon legislation but insisted he was not a "prohibition crank." "If we can teach our drinkers to stop drinking," he said, "and teach our boys never to start drinking, we won't need any prohibition laws." Sullivan also foresaw the failure in national prohibition legislation. "I realize that people who want liquor will get it. If they can't buy it openly or surreptitiously, they will manufacture it," he said.

There was an inherent class component in the temperance movement as upper-crust Yankees moralized against working-class drinkers, many of them Irish Americans. Sullivan experienced the searing disdain of elite society himself after being personally recruited to address the Anti-Saloon League's national convention in Atlantic City in July 1915. Boston-bred General Nelson A. Miles, a distinguished Civil War and Spanish-American War veteran who presided over the convention, threatened to boycott the event if a man with a prizefighting past was given a spot on the program. When Sullivan heard the report, he telegrammed a response, crafted by his new business manager, D'Arcy O'Connor: "I have no desire to address a convention where bigotry and narrow-mindedness hold sway with a pretense of doing good and which is presided over by an arrogant, self-centered, strutting old peacock now in his dotage. I have never been jealous of any fighter; why should Miles be jealous of me? Yours for temperance, John L. Sullivan." The general spoke as planned, but Sullivan declined to speak as scheduled two nights later. "I refuse to appear on any platform where General Nelson A. Miles has strutted. The referee's decision is with me. Let us call it quits."

Undeterred by the controversy, Sullivan launched his own anti-alcohol lecture tour a few weeks later in Asbury Park, New Jersey. His speech—which was written by O'Connor—reflected the arc of his life. It was entitled, "From Glory to Gutter to God."

The newspapers called again when Jess Willard, who had defeated Johnson for the heavyweight crown in 1915, announced his defense against challenger Frank Moran. A syndicate hired Sullivan to cover the scheduled ten-round bout, and he sat ringside for the March 25, 1916, battle inside Madison Square Garden.

Before the start of the fight, Sullivan was beckoned into the ring for an introduction along with the other former heavyweight greats in attendance. He clung to the ropes like a lifeline to lift his bulk on top of the temporary press desks, which somehow didn't collapse. With some difficulty, he ducked through the ropes and waddled into the ring. Ring announcer Joe Humphreys introduced Jim Corbett, Bob Fitzsimmons, Kid McCoy, and then finally Sullivan, who was showered with an ear-splitting applause that drowned the lingering reception for the previous fighters. Sullivan removed his hat and bowed to the four corners of the Garden. Then a surprise. Moments earlier, Humphreys had been given the colors that Sullivan wore in his 1888 draw against Charley Mitchell in France. He passed the colors to Corbett to present them to Sullivan. John L. kissed the silk flag and tucked it in his vest pocket over his heart. The two former foes shook hands firmly and cordially in a rare thaw during their cold war.

The moment brought tears to Sullivan's eyes. "Sullivan had sworn in a ring, glared in a ring, and run amuck in a ring. That, I think, was the first time he ever sobbed in a ring," Humphreys said. John L. said it was the happiest moment of his life.

American artist George Bellows, who lived a few blocks from Madison Square Garden and worked in a studio opposite Tom Sharkey's famed saloon and boxing club at Broadway and Sixty-Sixth Street, immortalized the moment in his lithograph *Introducing John L. Sullivan*. While many of the artist's drawings depict the drama, athleticism, and brutality of the ring, this still life captures the grizzled fifty-seven-year-old former champion clad in a dark suit and wing collar with his mighty chest inflated, his famous right hand clutching a gray fedora at his side. Stark black eyebrows dominate his slivered eyes. Sullivan is built like a bullet compared to the spindly figure of Humphreys with his mouth agape. Willard sits on his stool as trainers tend to him in his corner, while the mountain of a man in the middle soaks up the attention. Sullivan appears to be rooted in the ring, a mighty stump that couldn't be budged. Outside of a few fans at ringside, everything outside the ropes is darkened, the light forcing the eye to Sullivan.

Back in Abington, Kate continued to deteriorate. The old gladiator remained at her bedside day and night until she passed away at age fifty-two from the breast cancer on May 25, 1916. Three days later, John buried her in the family plot at Mount Calvary Cemetery.

Kate had been his foundation in the decade after he gave up drinking. For the first time, he had discovered a relationship that had stabilized his life.

It was a hard blow.

Sullivan made sure his mailman, George Manley, drove him to Kate's grave every other week, and he played her favorite song on the phonograph at the same time every night. Although he tried to keep it a secret, John L.'s health had been sliding as well. He suffered occasional bouts of rheumatism. One day Kate had discovered him passed out after complaining of chest pains, but he managed to convince her and his sister it was merely indigestion from overeating. Perhaps scared by the episode, he cut back to two meals a day and began an electric massage over his heart. Fearful of being on his own after Kate's death, particularly if another attack occurred, Sullivan asked his old sparring partner George Bush to move in with him and William Kelly.

As Sullivan broke down, so did the farm. It withered from neglect. The hay and grain stocks became depleted. Friends lent him stock for the barns. Money problems returned, too. Although the press referred to him as a "wealthy squire," Sullivan was far from it. He lost thousands after purchasing an interest in a Brockton, Massachusetts, theater in 1913, and he tossed away thousands more in a railroad investment gone bust. Given Sullivan's turn as a temperance speaker, stage dates became more difficult to book because theaters were afraid of losing patrons if they became identified with prohibition.

Blackballed by theaters, John L. tried his hand at movies. On St. Patrick's Day in 1917, his lawyer, Clarence W. Rowley, also counsel for "Buffalo Bill," incorporated the John L. Sullivan Motion Picture Company. Sullivan proposed to produce physical education films, starring himself, to illustrate "methods of making young men clean, able-bodied citizens." The movies would not be shown as stand-alone features but as accompaniments to a lecture delivered by Sullivan. They would depict John L. training and at work on his farm demonstrating everything from "practical gardening" to "poultry raising." The former champion made several trips to New York City to raise the $25,000 in working capital he sought, but he found little interest in the venture.

John L. drifted after the loss of his wife, but he never returned to the bottle. Love of country renewed him with a sense of purpose. When the United States entered World War I in April 1917, the patriot mobilized and even expressed his willingness to go "over there."

Sullivan's boosterism for the Allied cause was not necessarily a popular sentiment among sons and daughters of Ireland, who were conflicted about fighting in support of Great Britain particularly as their homeland continued to struggle for independence in the wake of the 1916 Easter Rising. But although John L. was an Irish American, he viewed himself first, foremost, and always as an American. He espoused the same view as Theodore Roosevelt that "a hyphenated American is not an American at all."

Much as Sullivan blustered for years about getting back in the ring, Roosevelt lobbied President Woodrow Wilson to let him back on the battlefield and lead a volunteer army to France. John L., also seeking to restoke that hot fire of youth, pledged to follow wherever the hero of San Juan Hill led him.

Asserting that "Colonel Roosevelt is the only man in America the Kaiser is afraid of," Sullivan took it upon himself to muster the troops in Boston to press the cause for his fellow old warrior. He headlined a rally for Roosevelt and the war effort in Faneuil Hall. Following in the footsteps of Bostonians such as Sam Adams, William Lloyd Garrison, and Daniel Webster who delivered fiery orations for the cause of freedom inside the "Cradle of Liberty," John L. thundered the Hub's great civic meeting space. "If the time prevails and the opportunity avails, your uncle, John L. will be there. I've got to die sooner or later, but I have no fear of death in this fight of democracy," he told the crowd.

The meeting overwhelmingly adopted a resolution to urge President Wilson to send to France an expeditionary force of two hundred thousand men under Roosevelt's direction. Roosevelt and Sullivan never received the call to the front, however. Even the most gallant of old warriors never get sent back into the ring. In spite of the disappointment, Sullivan continued to channel Uncle Sam. He never turned down an invitation to speak at a flag raising or a recruiting rally, and to aid in conservation efforts, he planted a large crop of potatoes at Donelee-Ross Farm.

His military ambitions spurned by his country, the patriotic Sullivan found solace in the national pastime. A month after umpiring an amateur baseball game at Fenway Park, he returned to Boston's new ball yard in September 1917 as an honorary first-base coach at an all-star benefit game for the family of recently deceased *Boston Globe* baseball scribe Tim Murnane. Will Rogers entertained the seventeen thousand fans by galloping around Fenway demonstrating rope tricks before the Boston Red Sox took the field against a team of all-stars that included "Shoeless" Joe Jackson, Ty Cobb, Walter Johnson, and Tris Speaker. As Sullivan took to the coaching box for the all-stars, he stood on the same field as another noted athlete, Red Sox phenom Babe Ruth, who toed the rubber as the starting pitcher after easily winning the pre-game hitting competition by launching a ball 402 feet. Sullivan had little work to do as Ruth scattered just three hits in five scoreless innings against a pantheon of baseball legends. On Fenway's emerald turf, the lives of the greatest American sports superstars of the nineteenth and twentieth centuries briefly intertwined. The men shared big egos, big mouths, and bigger appetites. But while Sullivan may be referred to in some quarters as the "Babe Ruth of boxing," the Bambino's prodigious eating, headline-grabbing benders, womanizing, and sporting achievements all echoed those of Sullivan forty years earlier. In truth, Ruth was the "John L. Sullivan of baseball."

Sullivan also stayed active in the other game of hardball popular in Boston—politics. Irish Catholics may have felt politically powerless when they arrived in Boston, but by the early twentieth century, they controlled the ballot box. "The day of the Puritan has passed; the Anglo-Saxon is a joke; a new and better America is here," declared Boston mayor James Michael Curley in 1914. For some of the Boston Irish, the political machine offered a better chance at upward mobility than the ring, although a strong fist was a prerequisite for both. In Boston, "they open campaigns with baseball bats and close them with ambulances," Sullivan once wrote. Campaigns were often bare-knuckle affairs among Irish ward bosses—latter-day civic chieftains—and no one knew that better than Curley, who was raised on the same neighborhood streets as Sullivan.

As Mayor Curley campaigned for re-election in 1917, he knew his friend Sullivan was "weary and depressed" following Kate's death. He invited his pal to join him on the campaign trail and promised to give him a job as collector if the voters returned him to City Hall. Curley also knew that a surrogate who was more adept at literal blows than verbal ones could be valuable under the London Prize Ring Rules of Boston politics. At one rally, Sullivan accompanied the mayor onto the South Boston turf of a rival candidate. Even the presence of John L. didn't dissuade the rival "goon squads" from taunting Curley and barricading the exit to the hall. Curley relied on his own "strong boys" to execute a flying wedge to clear the path for him and Sullivan. Once they had safely escaped, John L. turned to the mayor and asked whether they had just been at a rally or a massacre.

On election night, Sullivan sat in Curley's office as the disappointing results trickled in. "I'm taking the count," the mayor told him. "I know what it is to take the count," the former champion sympathized. Curley believed that Sullivan took the loss harder than he did, and a few weeks after Election Day, in December 1917, the mayor spoke at a banquet in Sullivan's honor at the United States Hotel. "No man in the history of Boston has done more to perpetuate the fame of this city in a manly way than has John L. Sullivan," Curley said.

In a reflective mood, the old warrior told the audience, "If the good Lord should call me right now, I may say I have seen it all. I know the game of life from A to Z, from soda to hock."

New England shivered through the winter of 1918. The season's icy grip clutched the region and choked its harbors with a tenacity few Yankees had ever seen. The thermometers of Boston cracked the freezing mark only eight times in December and January, and wartime coal embargoes only sharpened the bite.

A couple of weeks after New Year's, a fluttering heart drove Sullivan to Abington physician J. Frank Curtin. The doctor began treatment, but John L. did not let the chill or ailing health slow him down. He continued to venture into Boston. He easily scaled six flights of the downtown Old South building and playfully demonstrated his limberness to his friends by touching his toes without bending his knees.

In spite of his health issues, the "Boston Strong Boy" still felt invincible. His lawyer Rowley urged John L. to compose a will, but he refused to do so, he said, for at least twenty more years. "When you make a will, it looks as if you were getting ready to die," Sullivan growled. "I'm going to live to be one hundred, so I have plenty of time before bothering about a will." How could Rowley doubt him? When the former champion set his mind to do something, he usually did it. After all, he was still John L. Sullivan, wasn't he?

The temperature had nearly sunk to zero when the sun rose on Saturday, February 2, 1918. In spite of the freeze, Sullivan decided to keep his plans to meet friends in Boston. He had news to share. He was returning to the ring—albeit a circus one. The night before, O'Connor visited Donelee-Ross to get Sullivan's signature on a contract to tour that upcoming summer with Ringling Brothers Circus. Under the deal, Sullivan was to receive $1,000 a week to ride in an Irish jaunting car with an Irish bagpiper and deliver a ten-minute address in the center ring.

As Sullivan prepared to depart, Bush heard groaning emanating from the bedroom. He rushed in and found that John L. had fainted on the bed. Unable to reach Dr. Curtin, Bush contacted another Abington doctor, R. B. Rand, who revived the former champion and gave him a heart stimulant. "I'm all right now," Sullivan reassured Bush as he sat on his bed. "Telephone the people in Boston that I'll be along and that I'm sorry I'm late." Shortly after Dr. Rand left, Bush again heard Sullivan groaning and complaining about the sharp pain in his chest. Sullivan began to slip away after this second attack. By the time Dr. Curtin finally arrived, it was too late. At 11:45 a.m., John L. Sullivan passed away with Bush, Kelly, Curtin, and neighbor George Harris at his bedside.

Although he had been having heart trouble for the previous three weeks, the death of the old gladiator "came as a bolt from a clear sky." That death had visited Sullivan so quickly, and at the age of fifty-nine, may have been stunning, but the cause of his demise—"fatty degeneration of heart" was listed on the death certificate—would not have surprised John L. in the least. Although death had brushed him several times, from barroom bullets to a drunken stumble off a rushing passenger train, Sullivan always knew his heart would do him in. He had predicted it a quarter-century earlier. "I have always had it in my head that it is heart disease that is to be my ending," he told a reporter in 1893. "My mother died of heart disease, and I take after her physically. It has to come some time, and I am not looking for it in a hurry, but when it does come I had rather be snuffed out quickly by something like heart disease than to suffer with a lingering illness."

The news quickly spread across Abington before it radiated out to the front pages of evening newspapers around America. Hundreds of Sullivan's neighbors made the pilgrimage that afternoon to the forlorn farm. Inside, fourteen-year-old Kelly, an orphan once again, sobbed for his best friend and the man he knew as a father for half his life. John L.'s favorite pet collie, Queenie, wandered from room to room whining for the "Big Fellow." Within the next week, perhaps in a quest to follow their master, a cow, a bulldog, two collies, and Sullivan's favorite horse, "Colonel Corn," all dropped dead on the farm.

The "Strong Boy" returned to Boston in the company of his lifelong friend, undertaker Timothy J. Mahoney. The mortician could find no coffin in metropolitan Boston to hold this mountain of a man, so a specially ordered mahogany casket was shipped from New York. The day after his death, Sullivan's body was brought to his sister's Roxbury house, the closest thing John L. had to home for so many years before he remarried. The house on Brook Avenue may have been just over a mile from where he was born on East Concord Street, but the road he had traversed between those two bookends of his life had been a truly long one. As he was carried inside the house, tears welled in the eyes of the neighborhood kids who knew John L. not as the first American sports superstar, but as their "pal."

For the ensuing three days, a slow march of mourners trudged through Annie Lennon's darkened parlor. In spite of war and subzero temperatures, fighters, sporting men, patrolmen, soldiers, sailors, laborers, doctors, clergymen, politicians, reporters, old-timers who remembered him as a boy from the South End, new neighbors from Abington, temperance advocates, sons and daughters of Erin, curiosity seekers, souvenir hunters, neighborhood kids he entertained with tales of princes and presidents, and hundreds of fellow citizens of Boston knelt before the bier from early morning until well after midnight. Their constant presence testified that Sullivan's mighty fists still retained a firm grasp on the American public.

The coffin was as big as a bed, lined with white satin, and affixed with a simple silver nameplate with his name engraved. Given that the end had come suddenly, Sullivan looked "natural in death." With an open collar and black bow tie, he appeared ready to deliver one of his theatrical monologues. His favorite Prince Albert coat, with a white flower in the lapel, cloaked his colossal frame. His iconic white mustache flowed gallantly, with fine curls on each end. The lifeless right hand that had once delivered such violent punishment clenched a black rosary. A large photograph of the former champion in full evening dress surveyed the room from the wall above his head, while a portrait of his father hung on the wall at the foot of the casket.

Through the entire wake, Annie, who had now lost both her parents and both her siblings, rarely abandoned her post at the head of John's casket. Even as neighbors huddled around the old-fashioned stove belching out heat in the kitchen while swapping stories, Annie kept a constant vigil at her brother's side amid a garden of lilies, roses, and floral horseshoes. "Her big Sullivan eyes rested continually on the great warrior's silent face," reported one observer.

Seventy-five-year-old Dan Dwyer, one of Sullivan's first foes and a longtime sparring partner, made the ninety-mile journey and shed tears as he gazed upon the champ. Kilrain was there, too, recounting his friendship and their epic battle under the Mississippi sun.

Hundreds of telegrams piled up at the Western Union office from well-wishers who couldn't make it to Boston. Theodore Roosevelt sent his regrets from Sagamore Hill: "He was an old and valued friend, and I mourn his death." A pallbearer spot had been reserved for Roosevelt, but Sullivan's idol was preparing for an operation to remove a thigh abscess resulting from an infection he had contracted years before on an expedition through Brazil. The slow train travel due to the weather prevented Muldoon from arriving from upstate New York. Corbett telegraphed that, although Sullivan's passing was a "great blow," he couldn't make it due to a theatrical engagement in New York that he couldn't break. Both men sent floral horseshoes in their steads.

With no will, Sullivan's estate passed to his only surviving relative, Annie. His possessions were meager when compared to the estimated one million dollars he had earned in the ring and on the stage. The only item found in his coat pocket was a slip from a Brockton bakery. Sullivan had already given most of his ring relics to his personal friends years ago, although Annie still had a trunk with mementoes such as the watch he was given by the Prince of Wales and the cleats from the Mitchell draw, still caked with French mud and dead grass caught in the spikes. His debts were valued at $2,514, and his final estate—consisting of a small savings account, a Liberty bond, and the farm, which sold for $3,500—totaled $3,624.71. It may not have been much, but unlike many pugs before and after him, John L. did not die penniless.

It was four degrees outside as day broke on February 6, but that was a veritable thaw in such a hard winter. The previous day had been one of the most bitter in living memory. Temperatures had dipped to ten degrees below zero, and Boston moved in slow motion. Ice floes had trapped steamers and tugs in their berths. Trains and trolleys could only creep along the rails. City hospitals had reported a record number of frostbite cases. With the limited wartime coal shipments unable to enter the frozen harbor, dozens of schools closed, and the city announced embargoes on coal deliveries to stores, office buildings, and factories.

Through it all, Bostonians kept coming to pay respects to the old gladiator. The bereaved were still filing through the Lennon house when the time came to leave for the 10 a.m. funeral mass around the corner at St. Paul's Catholic Church. A monochrome world of gray light, pale snowbanks, and darkly dressed mourners greeted the Lennon family as they left the house. The hearse squeezed through the narrow streets of the Roxbury Highlands on the short procession. Neighbors craned their necks from their doorsteps as friends and family walked slowly on the icy streets behind the hearse. They trampled the sand and cinders that had been scattered for traction much like the loose change Sullivan used to sprinkle for packs of children.

When the procession arrived at St. Paul's, the family found that once again John L. had commanded a standing-room audience. Mourners stood in the packed aisles, vestibules, and the choir gallery. Scores who were not among the two thousand inside the church huddled amid the mounds of snow on Woodward Park Street. And as had happened so many times during Sullivan's life, the police needed to clear a path for John L. through an adoring crowd, this time from the hearse to the front door. The men in the crowd removed their hats as the ten pallbearers—including Curley, Rowley, and Billy Hogarty—carried Sullivan up the steps of St. Paul's. (Kilrain, too crippled by rheumatism to carry the casket, was among the ushers.)

They gathered in the little wooden church dedicated to another man famed for a mid-life conversion. They came not to say "good-bye"—John L. hated that word and the finality that came with it—but simply to wish him "good luck." The hardened, calloused hands of laborers and the soft palms of brokers and lawyers clasped in prayer as Father Frederick Allchin, assisted by Father John Lyons of Abington's St. Bridget's Church, celebrated mass. Although Sullivan would have been disappointed that Roosevelt couldn't make it, he would have been pleased that his funeral commanded a future White House resident—Massachusetts lieutenant governor Calvin Coolidge, who officially represented the citizens of the commonwealth.

Following the mass, the pallbearers, clad in Prince Albert coats and top hats, flanked the hearse, and the mourners trudged behind. The snow crunched underneath the wheels of the hearse as it wound through Roxbury, Dorchester, and Roslindale. As station bells rang, firefighters stood at attention in front of their red trucks draped in black crepe, an honor usually reserved for department members. Flags on public buildings saluted at half-mast as Bostonians stood in deep snowbanks to say farewell to "Our John." Hundreds who couldn't make it inside the church tried to walk behind the procession to the burial, but the cold and ice proved too much for most.

The procession creaked to a stop at the Sullivan family plot on the east side of Mount Calvary Cemetery. One hundred and fifty heads bowed as the devout congregated on the gentle slope where John L. had buried his mother, his father, his brother, and his dear Kate. As flurries danced in the air, the wind bit the bare heads of the men clasping their hats between their frozen fingers. Father Lyons blessed the grave of his parishioner and reminded all that his greatest triumph had come out of the ring, his victory over the bottle.

Frigid gales whipped Father Allchin's robe as he prayed while cemetery employees struggled to extricate from the hearse the hefty mahogany casket, bearing Sullivan with his world-famous right hand resting on top of his heart. As the chapel bell tolled, they lowered the coffin into the rock-hard ground, soil so solid following the unprecedented streak of below-zero temperatures that prior to the burial cemetery employees were forced to abandon their spades and instead carve his resting place with dynamite.

As they blasted the frozen ground of Boston, the city quaked for its "Strong Boy."

For one final time, John L. Sullivan shook the world.

ACKNOWLEDGMENTS

"The art of writing is a fight," penned John L. Sullivan, and there's little doubt that the written word can be just as humbling—and bruising—a foe as a heavyweight champion. While few pursuits may appear to be more solitary than boxing or writing, the truth is that both fighters and authors require strong support teams working their corners.

I'm deeply indebted to many people without whom this book could not have been possible. Thanks first to Nicole Vecchiotti for suggesting that John L. would make a fascinating subject for a biography. As always, it was advice well taken.

My sincere thanks go to the descendants of relatives of John L. on both sides of the Atlantic who were very gracious with their time. I am grateful to Maureen Sullivan, Brian Westwater, and Larry Westwater—all descendants of Sullivan's sister, Annie Lennon—for providing me with detailed information on the Sullivan family tree and showing me treasured family heirlooms. Thanks to Kathleen Barrett, who offered valuable information on the roots of the Sullivan family tree back in Ireland, and to Bridget O'Sullivan, who also provided me with information on the Sullivan ancestral farm in Laccabeg. I'm also grateful to Joe Hunter for sharing his genealogical research into the Sullivan family. Thanks to Bob Gardiner for sharing information about distant relation Sylvie Gookin and to Daniel Robinson, Jerry Burnham, and Steve Vance for doing the same about Richard K. Fox.

Great assistance was given to me by the members of the International Boxing Research Organization who always prove to be an incredible font of knowledge about the sport of boxing. Thanks to Dan Cuoco, Harry D. Boonin, Joe Page, and Enrique Encinosa. I'm particularly indebted to Don Scott of *Boxing Collectors' News* and Tracy Callis for taking the time and trouble to provide me with photographs and illustrations. Clay Moyle provided tremendous assistance with not only photographs, but selections from his vast collection of boxing literature.

Joe Lannan was extremely gracious with his time. He shared memories of his namesake as well as several extremely fruitful research sources. Richard Johnson of The Sports Museum in Boston is a walking encyclopedia of Boston sports knowledge. I am so grateful for his assistance and his opening of the museum archives to me. Christine Lewis was a tremendous help in sparking new ideas about John L. and guiding me to other boxing historians and experts. I raise my glass to toast Jerry Burke of Doyles Café. If there is a bigger Sullivan fan in Boston, I don't know who he is. Slainte!

Bill Heaney assisted me with the history of Belfast, New York. Thanks also to Scott Burt of the Bare Knuckle Boxing Hall of Fame, Dave Edwards, Eric Jay Dolin, Mike Quinlin, Sujit Chawla, Peter Nash, Douglas Cavanaugh, Jim Houlihan, Joe Donovan, Stephanie Schorow, and Mike Walters.

No research project would be possible without the collective memory stored inside our treasured libraries and archives. Special thanks to the librarians and archivists at Memorial Hall Library in my hometown of Andover, Massachusetts; the Boston Athenaeum; the Boston Public Library; the Bostonian Society; the Beinecke Rare Book and Manuscript Library at Yale University; the New York Public Library; the Library of Congress; the Museum of History and Industry in Seattle; the Tisch Library at Tufts University; the John J. Burns Library at Boston College; the Kerry Archaeological Historical Society; and the Dyer Memorial Library in Abington, Massachusetts. Thanks in particular to Robert Johnson-Lally of the Archdiocese of Boston, Elizabeth Bouvier of the Massachusetts Supreme Judicial Court Archives, Marta Crilly of the City of Boston Archives, and Cindy Lawler at the McCain Library and Archives at the University of Southern Mississippi. In Ireland, I'm grateful for the help of Gearoid O'Brien of the Westmeath County Library Service, Michael Lynch of the Kerry Library, and Frank O'Donovan of the Abbeydorney Development Committee.

My deepest gratitude to my agents John Taylor "Ike" Williams and Katherine Flynn of Kneerim, Williams & Bloom. Katherine in particular has been a source of invaluable advice and a reassuring voice shepherding me through the long journey from book proposal to completed manuscript.

I am deeply indebted to my editor at the Lyons Press, Keith Wall-man, who has shared my enthusiasm for telling the story of John L. I am so grateful for the confidence he has shown in me and in the story, and I am thankful for both his patience and his deft pen in sharpening the prose of this book. Thanks as well to the rest of the Lyons Press team that contributed to the production of the book.

Finally, this book would not have been possible without the love, patience, and unwavering support of my family. My parents, Tom and Mary Ann, instilled in me a love of history and—in a house filled with newspapers and books—nurtured a passion for the written word. My wife, Erin, and my children, Drew and Sydney, have been my biggest boosters. They have been sources of boundless encouragement and inspiration. Quite simply, I couldn't do what I do without them, and for that I am eternally grateful.

Sources

Prologue: Rumble on the River

ix. . . . a nefarious moonlight excursion.: *New York Clipper,* May 21, 1881

ix. . . . island of "unadulterated deviltry": *National Police Gazette,* January 10, 1880

ix. . . . like "Hell's Half Acre" and "Satan's Circus.": *National Police Gazette,* January 3, 1880

ix. . . . the fifteen thousand prostitutes: James William Buel, *Mysteries and Miseries of America's Great Cities* (St. Louis: Historical Publishing Co., 1883), 61

ix. . . . in the shadows of police stations polluted with corruption.: Timothy J. Gilfoyle, *City of Eros: New York City, Prostitution, and the Commercialization of Sex, 1790–1920* (New York: W.W. Norton & Co., 1992), 255

x. . . . turpentine on his hands to blind his opponent.: Rex Lardner and Alan Bodian, *The Legendary Champions* (New York: American Heritage Press, 1972), 36

x. . . . pitched the twenty-four-foot ring on the barge deck.: William Inglis, *Champions Off Guard* (New York: The Vanguard Press, 1932), 44

x. . . . West Forty-Third Street a little after 9 p.m.: *Baltimore Sun,* April 15, 1904

x. . . . to locate the "suspicious barge.": *New York Tribune,* May 17, 1881

x. . . . the murky midstream bed of the Hudson.: *Denver Post,* January 20, 1910

xi. . . . felt the river roll softly beneath his feet.: *Denver Post,* January 20, 1910

xi. . . . of whiskey and cigars hovering over the barge.: Lardner and Bodian, *The Legendary Champions,* 36

xi. . . . few friends in the heart of Gotham.: *National Police Gazette,* June 4, 1881

xi. . . . 3–1 odds.: Inglis, *Champions Off Guard,* 43

xi. . . . Flood's backers had second thoughts.: John L. Sullivan and Dudley A. Sargent, *Life and Reminiscences of a Nineteenth-Century Gladiator* (Boston: Jas. A. Hearn & Co., 1892), 46

xi. . . . destruction" manifest in flesh and blood.: *Harper's Weekly,* December 3, 1910

xi. . . . and ability to rapidly change positions.: *New York Herald,* May 17, 1881

xii. . . . Paddy Ryan, who was aboard the barge.: *New York Herald,* May 17, 1881

xii. . . . tirelessly working with Madden.: *Boston Globe,* December 5, 1887

xii. . . . Flood carried a nearly identical build: *National Police Gazette,* June 4, 1881

xii. . . . toughest neighborhood in America's toughest city.: *New York Clipper,* May 21, 1881

xii. . . . a bath rather than taking one themselves.: *Denver Post,* January 20, 1910

xii. . . . gouge his eyes with a cane.: *Boston Globe,* July 14, 1907

xii. . . . perfectly square fight under his watch.: *National Police Gazette,* June 4, 1881

xii. . . . protect their hands than cushion their blows.: *Denver Post,* January 20, 1910

xiii. . . . run up the rise to start each round.: *Baltimore Sun,* April 15, 1904

xiii. . . . Smith called time at 10:40 p.m.: *National Police Gazette,* June 4, 1881

xiii. . . . He met Flood at the peak,: *Baltimore Sun,* April 15, 1904

xiii. . . . rattled away at close quarters.: *New York Herald,* May 17, 1881

xiii. . . . face and stomach with rights and lefts.: *Denver Post,* January 20, 1910

xiii. . . . drove Flood against the ropes: *National Police Gazette,* June 4, 1881

xiii. . . . punctuated his two-minute fistic storm: *New York Sun,* May 18, 1881

xiii. . . . on the bent knee of his second, Dooney Harris.: Inglis, *Champions Off Guard,* 44

xiii. . . . traded ninety seconds of fireworks: *New York Sun,* May 18, 1881

xiii. . . . in a "most unscientific manner": *New York Herald,* May 17, 1881

xiii. . . . John L. throwing Flood to the deck.: *National Police Gazette,* June 4, 1881

xiii. . . . The fighters froze in fear.: *Boston Herald,* May 18, 1881

xiii. . . . police may have finally discovered them.: *Denver Post,* January 20, 1910

xiii. . . . barely see through his swollen eyes.: *Boston Herald,* May 18, 1881

xiii. . . . offered little resistance in the seventh,: *Baltimore Sun,* April 15, 1904

xiii. . . . I'll give the fight to this Boston man.": *Baltimore Sun,* April 15, 1904

xiv. . . . had the ropes of the ring not been there.: *Pelham Sun,* February 6, 1931

xiv. . . . and carried him to the corner.: *Baltimore Sun,* April 15, 1904

xiv. . . . declared the unblemished Sullivan the victor.: *Boston Herald,* May 18, 1881

xiv. . . . Flood sprawled on the deck of the barge.: *National Police Gazette,* June 4, 1881

xiv. . . . and we part as friends.": *New York Clipper,* May 21, 1881

xiv. . . . collect ninety-eight dollars for the loser.: *National Police Gazette,* June 4, 1881

xiv. . . . to Ryan, "I'll get you next!": *Denver Post,* January 20, 1910

CHAPTER ONE: THE STRONG BOY FROM BOSTON

1. . . . consumed seven million tons of potatoes a year,: John Burrowes, *Irish: The Remarkable Saga of a Nation and a City* (Edinburgh, Mainstream Publishing, 2003), 39

1. . . . dead infants in their arms as they begged for food.: John Kelly, *The Graves Are Walking: The Great Famine and the Saga of the Irish People* (New York, Henry Holt and Co., 2012), 1

1. . . . dogs fed on human corpses.: Kelly, *The Graves Are Walking,* 1

1. . . . sprinkled their crops with holy water.: John Crowley, William J. Smyth, Michael Murphy, and Charlie Roche, *Atlas of the Great Irish Famine* (New York: New York University Press, 2012), 30

2. . . . to remind me of my former condition.": *Liberator,* March 27, 1846

2. . . . and own land, horses, guns, and swords.: Edward Laxton, *The Famine Ships: The Irish Exodus to America* (New York: Henry Holt, 1997), 20–21

2. . . . "that calamity must not be too much mitigated.": Tim Pat Coogan, *The Famine Plot: England's Role in Ireland's Greatest Tragedy* (New York: Palgrave Macmillan, 2012), 63–64

2. . . . lived in adjacent cottages: Kathleen Barrett e-mail, January 2, 2013

2. . . . William Crosbie, was larger than most.: Griffith's Valuation

2. . . . shed 40 percent of its population between 1841 and 1851.: *A Comparative View of the Census of Ireland in 1841–1851* (London: House of Commons, 1852), 40

3. . . . minimally converted cargo ships: Laxton, *The Famine Ships,* 7–8

3. . . . three-thousand-mile journey that lasted at least four weeks,: Laxton, *The Famine Ships,* 18

3. . . . eighteen inches of bed space—children half that.: Stephen Puleo, *A City So Grand: The Rise of an American Metropolis, Boston 1850–1900* (Boston: Beacon Press, 2010), 65

3. . . . on the bed of the cobalt Atlantic.: Arthur Gribben, ed., *The Great Famine and the Irish Diaspora in America* (Amherst: University of Massachusetts Press, 1999), 137

3. . . . more than a quarter of Boston's population.: Crowley et al., *Atlas of the Great Irish Famine,* 226

4. . . . and tossed it in the Potomac River.: Julia Schaffer, *The Washington Monument* (New York: Chelsea Clubhouse, 2010), 33

4. . . . than those of feasting on humans.: Gail Collins, *Scorpion Tongues: Gossip, Celebrity, and American Politics* (New York: William Morrow, 1998), 20

4. . . . all but four seats in the House chamber.: Thomas H. O'Connor, *The Boston Irish: A Political History* (Boston: Northeastern University Press, 1995), 76

4. . . . the "mother country" to be close family.: Oscar Handlin, *Boston's Immigrants, 1790–1880: A Study in Acculturation* (Cambridge, MA: Belknap Press of Harvard University Press, 1959), 124

4. . . . death if they happened to be caught escaping.: O'Connor, *The Boston Irish*, 14

4. . . . by torching a papal effigy.: O'Connor, *The Boston Irish*, 15

4. . . . doctrines were "subversive of society.": Thomas H. O'Connor, *Boston Catholics: A History of the Church and Its People* (Boston: Northeastern University Press, 1998), 10

5. . . . Catholic patients in the city hospital until 1859,: Puleo, *A City So Grand*, 71–72

5. . . . Protestant version of the Lord's Prayer.: Jim Vrabel, *When in Boston: A Time Line and Almanac* (Boston: Northeastern University Press, 2004), 172

5. . . . "the most class-bound city in America,": James Michael Curley, *I'd Do It Again: A Record of All My Uproarious Years* (Englewood Cliffs, NJ: Prentice-Hall, 1957), 2

5. . . . and homogeneity of their blood.": O'Connor, *The Boston Irish*, 1

5. . . . lump in the community, undigested, undigestible.": Handlin, *Boston's Immigrants*, 55

5. . . . "No Irish person need apply.": *Boston Traveler*, August 19, 1853

5. . . . Back Bay neighborhood to escape them.: Handlin, *Boston's Immigrants*, 63

5. . . . 1850, half of Boston's laborers were Irish,: Crowley et al., *Atlas of the Great Irish Famine*, 226

6. . . . November 6, 1856, inside St. Patrick's Church,: Archdiocese of Boston Records

6. . . . built to house only eight hundred paupers.: Gearoid O'Brien, Westmeath County Library Service e-mail, February 25, 2013

6. . . . Kiltoom shed 25 percent of its population,: *A Comparative View of the Census of Ireland in 1841–1851*, 4

6. . . . birth certificate lists the date as October 12, 1858,: City of Boston Records

6. . . . baptism the following day at St. Joseph's Church.: Archdiocese of Boston Records

6. . . . tenements owned by the heirs of Samuel Salisbury: City of Boston Records

7. . . . with the affairs of other people.": *Boston Evening Transcript*, October 12, 1858

7. . . . "the 'Dublin' of America,": *Christian Examiner*, July 1858

7. . . . eleven thousand souls in unmarked graves.: *Boston Herald*, August 11, 1912

8. . . . at battlefields such as Antietam and Gettysburg.: O'Connor, *The Boston Irish*, 77

8 (fn). . . . one thousand who took up arms for the Confederacy.: Ancestry.com

8. . . . "was as strong as a bear.": *Morning Herald*, July 15, 1889

8. . . . "a model of womanly vigor": *Boston Globe*, December 5, 1887

8. . . . around 180 pounds.: Sullivan and Sargent, *Life and Reminiscences*, 21

8. . . . and never topped 130 pounds.: *Charlotte Observer*, May 14, 1905

8. . . . temper came courtesy of his father,: Inglis, *Champions Off Guard*, 22

8. . . . the fifteen dollars a week he earned as a mason and day laborer.: *State*, January 14, 1906

8. . . . where they lived next to extended family.: City of Boston Records

9. . . . took his beating without a whimper: *Kalamazoo Gazette*, January 30, 1895

9. . . . became a hero to the other boys.: Sullivan and Sargent, *Life and Reminiscences*, 24

9. . . . done with his formal schooling.: *Boston Journal*, September 27, 1903

9. . . . shot marbles and spun tops.: Sullivan and Sargent, *Life and Reminiscences*, 24

9. . . . sail in and out of Boston Harbor.: *Boston Globe*, July 7, 1907

9. . . . Sullivan was not a neighborhood bully,: *Morning Herald*, July 15, 1889

9. . . . in response to any perceived injustice.: *Boston Globe*, September 6, 1892

9. . . . enjoyed nothing more than baseball.: *Morning Herald*, July 15, 1889

9. . . . dissect each player's strengths and flaws.: *Boston Globe*, October 5, 1896

9. . . . beyond the center field of the South End Grounds.: *Baseball Magazine*, May 1901

9. . . . violation of the city's puritanical laws.: *Boston Globe,* June 7, 1908

9. . . . local nines that barnstormed New England.: *Kalamazoo Gazette,* January 30, 1895

9. . . . during the 1879 and 1880 seasons,: *State,* May 21, 1905

9. . . . president could not recall such an offer.: *Sporting Life,* October 23, 1909

9. . . . enrolled at Boston College for a time: *Kalamazoo Gazette,* January 30, 1895

9. . . . has no records of his matriculation.: Kathleen Williams e-mail, January 11, 2013

10. . . . scrap with a more experienced journeyman.: Sullivan and Sargent, *Life and Reminiscences,* 25

10. . . . disagreement with one of his co-workers.: *Kalamazoo Gazette,* January 30, 1895

10. . . . taking off to play baseball ended in blows.: *Boston Globe,* December 5, 1887

10. . . . not provide living wages for even the leading brawlers.: Melvin L. Adelman, *A Sporting Time: New York City and the Rise of Modern Athletics* (Urbana: University of Illinois Press, 1986), 236

10. . . . "drifted into the occupation of a boxer,": Sullivan and Sargent, *Life and Reminiscences,* 28

10. . . . weighing nearly two hundred pounds,: *State,* November 12, 1905

10. . . . Jack Scannell or Mike Scannell or even as Mike Scanlon: *State,* March 11, 1906

11. . . . and sent him into the orchestra.: *Boston Globe,* January 12, 1910

11. . . . and three shattered fiddles.: *State,* November 12, 1905

11. . . . simplest of nicknames—"Strong Boy.": *Boston Globe,* March 15, 1879

11. . . . against veteran John "Cockey" Woods.: *Boston Globe,* March 15, 1879

11. . . . Sullivan is the coming man,": *Boston Globe,* March 15, 1879

12. . . . in the main event with the feted fighter.: *Springfield Republican,* January 25, 1925

12. . . . can't be made out of a stiff.": Sullivan and Sargent, *Life and Reminiscences,* 66

12. . . . by watching other fighters in action: *Kalamazoo Gazette,* January 30, 1895

12. . . . flying into the stage wings.: *Duluth News-Tribune,* May 27, 1906

12. . . . without a moment of retreat.: *Literary Digest,* February 23, 1918

12. . . . as a bull dog is from a spaniel.": John Boyle O'Reilly, *Ethics of Boxing and Manly Sport* (Boston: Ticknor and Co., 1888), 79

13. . . . right to the neck or jaw of his disarmed foe.: Inglis, *Champions Off Guard,* 35

13. . . . to the other fellow's heart.": *Boston Globe,* March 22, 1908

13. . . . as hard as you can and hit him first.": Jerome W. Power, *The Boston Strong Boy.* US Work Projects Administration, Federal Writers' Project (Folklore Project, Life Histories, 1936–39); Manuscript Division, Library of Congress, 1937

13. . . . will not effectually weaken him otherwise.": *Denver Post,* February 2, 1910

13. . . . as Prime Minister Sir Robert Walpole watched from the crowd.: Patrick Robertson, *Robertson's Book of Firsts: Who Did What for the First Time* (New York: Bloomsbury, 2011), 87

14. . . . McCloskey" in a three-hour brawl in 1841: Adelman, *A Sporting Time,* 230–31

14. . . . brought their fistic tradition with them to worksites: James R. Barrett, *The Irish Way: Becoming American in the Multiethnic City* (New York: Penguin Press, 2012), 26–27

15. . . . a golden era of boxing in the United States.: Elliott J. Gorn, *The Manly Art: Bare-Knuckle Prize Fighting in America* (Ithaca, NY: Cornell University Press, 1986), 69

15. . . . at ringside during the thirty-seventh round.: Richard Briggs Stott, *Jolly Fellows: Male Milieus in Nineteenth-Century America* (Baltimore: Johns Hopkins University Press, 2009), 234–35

15. . . . until he lost consciousness.: Gorn, *The Manly Art,* 113

15. . . . friends returned and shot Poole dead.: *New York Times,* February 26, 1855

15. . . . fifty thousand New Yorkers greeted him on his return to America.: Adelman, *A Sporting Time,* 234–35

15. . . . in the awful slaughter of the Civil War.": *The Life of John L. Sullivan* (New York: Richard K. Fox Publishing Co., 1892), 5

15. . . . one of the sport's strongest advocates, in 1870.: Stott, *Jolly Fellows*, 225

16. . . . and "tend to breaches of the peace.": Jeffrey T. Sammons, *Beyond the Ring: The Role of Boxing in American Society* (Urbana: University of Illinois Press, 1988), 6

16. . . . named for John Sholto Douglas, the ninth: Linda Stratmann, *The Marquess of Queensberry: Wilde's Nemesis* (New Haven, CT: Yale University Press, 2013), xi–xii

16. . . . Chambers, an accomplished oarsman and champion race walker.: Stratmann, *The Marquess of Queensberry*, 69

17. . . . drummer boy on General William T. Sherman's March to the Sea.: *New York Times*, March 24, 1918

17. . . . struck by the youngster's physique.: Mike Donovan, *The Roosevelt That I Know: Ten Years of Boxing with the President—and Other Memories of Famous Fighting Men* (New York: B.W. Dodge & Co., 1909), 37–44

17. . . . well-proportioned "mass of sinew.": *Daily Inter Ocean*, February 8, 1882

17. . . . his shirts had to be made to order.: Power, *The Boston Strong Boy*

17. . . . hands on you," Donovan informed his opponent.: *Outing*, December 1903

17. . . . the fall broke his nose.: *Pearson's Magazine*, September 1912

17. . . . feared that he had killed him.: *Boston Globe*, March 22, 1908

18. . . . breaking his right wrist in the third round.: Donovan, *The Roosevelt That I Know*, 37–44

18. . . . fought the coming champion of the prize-ring.": Donovan, *The Roosevelt That I Know*, 37–45

18. . . . pounding a piece of iron into shape.": Donovan, *The Roosevelt That I Know*, 44

18. . . . The Coming Champion of America!": *The Modern Gladiator: Being an Account of the Exploits and Experience of the World's Greatest Fighter, John Lawrence Sullivan* (St. Louis: Athletic Publishing Co., 1889), 16

18. . . . "in honor of the Highland boy.": *Boston Globe*, April 7, 1880

18. . . . easy on his opponent in the final round.: *State*, May 28, 1905

18. . . . as his first bout of any account.: *State*, May 14, 1905

19. . . . renowned fighter from near Albany, New York.: Sullivan and Sargent, *Life and Reminiscences*, 38

19. . . . Goss in eighty-six rounds in Colliers Station, West Virginia.: *Boston Globe*, May 18, 1880

19. . . . carried to his dressing room.: *Boston Globe*, June 29, 1880

19. . . . "extreme heat" for his unsteady gait and performance.: *National Police Gazette*, June 26, 1880

20. . . . They referred to him as "John Sullivan,": *National Police Gazette*, April 9, 1881

20. . . . "Jack L. Sullivan": *National Police Gazette*, April 30, 1881

20. . . . "John E. Sullivan.": *Cincinnati Daily Gazette*, December 11, 1880

20. . . . knocked out his opponent in less than three minutes.: *National Police Gazette*, April 16, 1881

20. . . . and the scientific sparring of Donaldson.: *Cincinnati Daily Gazette*, December 13, 1880

21. . . . "I refuse to fight him.": *Boston Globe*, January 14, 1910

21. . . . wishing he hadn't listened to the audience's pleas.: *Charlotte Observer*, June 11, 1905

21. . . . Sullivan accepted and remained in Cincinnati: *Boston Globe*, January 14, 1910

21. . . . to fight right in the middle of Cincinnati.: *Cincinnati Commercial Tribune*, December 26, 1880

21. . . . owned by an Indiana brewing company.: *Cincinnati Commercial Tribune*, December 1, 1880

21. . . . and all entered unobserved by the police.: *Cincinnati Commercial Tribune*, December 26, 1880

22.... in the Vine Street side of the storefront.: *Cincinnati Commercial Tribune*, December 25, 1880

22.... from the barrel organ and bass drum: *Cincinnati Commercial Tribune*, December 25, 1880

22.... drown out all noise from the prizefight.: *Cincinnati Daily Gazette*, December 25, 1880

22.... sitting on the edge of an old trunk: *Boston Globe*, July 14, 1907

22.... and laced up his gloves.: *Cincinnati Commercial Tribune*, December 25, 1880

22.... side bet of $500.: *Boston Globe*, January 14, 1910

22.... and Abe Smith seconded Donaldson.: *Cincinnati Commercial Tribune*, December 25, 1880

22.... no rules about the fight at all.": *Cincinnati Daily Gazette*, December 25, 1880

22.... defeat never entered Sullivan's mind.: *Literary Digest*, February 23, 1918

22.... seconds told him to keep fighting.: *New York Herald*, December 28, 1880

23.... corn could the scythe," reported one newspaper.: *New York Herald*, December 28, 1880

23.... including the twenty he had deposited.: *Boston Globe*, January 14, 1910

23.... could carry a ten-year prison sentence.: *Cincinnati Commercial Tribune*, December 26, 1880

23.... a running match and not a fight.: *Cincinnati Commercial Tribune*, December 30, 1880

23.... of the two men he had assisted in the ring.: *Cincinnati Daily Gazette*, December 30, 1880

23.... with the prosecutor, witnesses, and fighters.: *Cincinnati Commercial Tribune*, December 30, 1880

24.... the trial proved there was a corner at Sixth and Vine.: *Cincinnati Daily Gazette*, December 30, 1880

24.... by news of Sullivan's legal battle in Cincinnati.: *Boston Globe*, January 4, 1881

24.... kick where it would be the most assistance.": *Duluth-News Tribune*, July 26, 1908

24.... "as a cat does with a mouse.": *Boston Globe*, January 4, 1881

24.... "altogether uninteresting" spar with Goss,: *Boston Herald*, January 4, 1881

24.... while tending bar at Keenan's sporting house.: Billy Edwards, *Gladiators of the Prize Ring* (Chicago: The Athletic Publishing Co., 1895), 39

25.... and perfected his straight hitting.: *Cincinnati Commercial Tribune*, November 28, 1881

25.... lay low a full-grown Texan steer.": *Boston Globe*, March 22, 1881

25.... showered Donovan with crude remarks.: Donovan, *The Roosevelt That I Know*, 46

25.... police broke it up in the third round.: *Boston Globe*, March 22, 1881

25.... for at least $1,000 a side.: *National Police Gazette*, February 26, 1881

25.... "You go get a reputation first.": Donovan, *The Roosevelt That I Know*, 37–41

25.... power brokers to facilitate a trip to New York.: Edward Van Every, *Muldoon, The Solid Man of Sport* (New York: Frederick A. Stokes Co., 1929), 71–74

CHAPTER TWO: AMERICAN HERCULES

26.... Get out of my way.: Luc Sante, *Low Life: Lures and Snares of Old New York* (New York: Farrar Straus Giroux, 1991), 62–63

26.... as "black-eye fixers.": Sante, *Low Life*, 65

26.... and fighting dogs than anywhere else in the world,": Inglis, *Champions Off Guard*, 42

26.... the heads off mice for a dime and off rats for a quarter.: Adelman, *A Sporting Time*, 241

26. . . . well-known in New York City as Broadway,": *Records and Proceedings of the Senate Committee Appointed to Investigate the Police Department of the City of New York* (Albany: State of New York, 1895), 1927

27. . . . as Central Park and the Metropolitan Museum of Art.: Parker Morell, *Diamond Jim: The Life and Times of James Buchanan Brady* (New York: Simon and Schuster, 1934), 33

27. . . . prohibition of foul language and misconduct.: Timothy J. Gilfoyle, "Barnum's Brothel: P.T.'s 'Last Great Humbug,'" *Journal of the History of Sexuality*, September 2009, 502

27. . . . went elsewhere to finalize their transactions.: Stott, *Jolly Fellows*, 238, 240

27. . . . "grand sacred concerts" on Sunday.: *National Police Gazette*, February 26, 1881

27. . . . his first big break at Harry Hill's: Thomas A. Green, ed., *Martial Arts of the World: An Encyclopedia, Volume Two, R–Z* (Santa Barbara, CA: ABC-CLIO, 2001), 677

27. . . . any fighter who wanted to stage a benefit.: *Records and Proceedings of the Senate Committee*, 1939–1940

27. . . . booked John L. on boxing's biggest stage,: Van Every, *Muldoon, The Solid Man of Sport*, 71–74

28. . . . to Wall Street bankers in top hats: Lloyd R. Morris, *Incredible New York: High Life and Low Life of the Last Hundred Years* (New York: Random House, 1951), 50

28. . . . a long counter for ordering drinks: Morris, *Incredible New York*, 51

28. . . . without Uncle Tom," said one newspaper.: Gilfoyle, *City of Eros*, 227

28. . . . well beyond its appointed closing time.: *New York Times*, August 28, 1896

28. . . . that will stand before him for four rounds.": *Boston Globe*, January 15, 1910

28. . . . trained Paddy Ryan for his title fight against Joe Goss.: Edwards, *Gladiators of the Prize Ring*, 41

29. . . . threw up his handkerchief to surrender.: *Boston Herald*, April 1, 1881

29. . . . he can do the walking.": *Sports Illustrated*, February 18, 1963

30. . . . fighter was properly attired to enter Fox's lair.: Van Every, *Muldoon, The Solid Man of Sport*, 72–73

30. . . . gnawed his tobacco like a cow masticating its cud.: *National Police Gazette*, May 30, 1925

30. . . . he would back Sullivan against Ryan.: *National Police Gazette*, April 9, 1881

30. . . . and declined his backing.: *The Life of John L. Sullivan*, 10

30. . . . spending a decade at the *Belfast News-Letter*.: Guy Reel, *The National Police Gazette and the Making of the Modern American Man, 1879–1906* (New York: Palgrave Macmillan, 2006), 14

30. . . . became business manager for the *National Police Gazette*.: Reel, *Making of the Modern American Man*, 42–43

30. . . . in 1876 for nothing more than assuming its debts.: Reel, *Making of the Modern American Man*, 42–43

30. . . . hawked pornographic cabinet photographs,: *National Police Gazette*, July 2, 1887

30. . . . and "premature debility.": *National Police Gazette*, May 7, 1881

31. . . . had no interest in seeing it exterminated.: *National Police Gazette*, January 3, 1880

31. . . . by the constant bustle of modern life.: David B. Sachsman, S. Kittrell Rushing, and Roy Morris, eds., *Seeking a Voice: Images of Race and Gender in the 19th Century Press* (West Lafayette, IN: Purdue University Press, 2009), 291

32. . . . baseball began to emerge as the "national pastime.": Robert Weir, "Take Me Out to the Brawl Game," *Historical Journal of Massachusetts*, Spring 2009, 35

32. . . . could be seen "at all hours of the day.": *Boston Globe*, March 15, 1879

32. . . . walk distances of nearly five hundred miles.: Adelman, *A Sporting Time*, 218

32. . . . Trickett of Australia to capture the world championship.: *National Police Gazette*, November 22, 1881

33. . . . such as grand pigeon shooting matches, dog fights,: *National Police Gazette,* April 23, 1881

33. . . . bleeding and "raw as beefsteak.": *National Police Gazette,* February 3, 1883

33. . . . no sport could sell newspapers like boxing.: *Sports Illustrated,* February 18, 1963

33. . . . facilitate matches even after several arrests.: George Washington Walling, *Recollections of a New York Chief of Police* (New York: Caxton Book Concern, 1887), 373

34. . . . "the most promising Knight of the Fives in America,": *New York Clipper,* May 21, 1881

34. . . . bare knuckles. The fighter refused.: *National Police Gazette,* July 2, 1881

34. . . . to the law," Sullivan later wrote in his autobiography.: Sullivan and Sargent, *Life and Reminiscences,* 242–43

34. . . . with bare knuckles," the *National Police Gazette* proclaimed.: *National Police Gazette,* June 25, 1881

35. . . . take the chances of getting arrested,": *National Police Gazette,* June 25, 1881

35. . . . to face some true competition.: *National Police Gazette,* July 30, 1881

35. . . . Following an exhibition with Madden in Trenton,: *Trenton State Gazette,* July 13, 1881

35. . . . none could have beaten that young fellow, Sullivan,": *Chicago Tribune,* August 6, 1881

35. . . . Dalton, a tugboat captain on the Great Lakes.: *Daily Inter Ocean,* August 13, 1881

35. . . . nearly forty pounds lighter than Sullivan,: *Boston Globe,* September 8, 1907

35. . . . knocked out the plucky challenger in the third.: Sullivan and Sargent, *Life and Reminiscences,* 50

35. . . . fifty dollars in appreciation of his effort.: *Daily Inter Ocean,* August 15, 1881

35. . . . local sporting man Charles "Parson" Davies.: *Daily Inter Ocean,* August 8, 1881

35. . . . a rematch, this time in a friendly spar,: *Daily Inter Ocean,* August 27, 1881

36. . . . who stood six feet, three inches tall.: *Daily Inter Ocean,* September 2, 1881

36. . . . into the second row of the orchestra seats.: Sullivan and Sargent, *Life and Reminiscences,* 51

36. . . . four rounds with the "Boston Strong Boy" evaporated.: *National Police Gazette,* October 1, 1881

36. . . . Gallagher did not show after saying he would accept the offer.: *Daily Inter Ocean,* September 14, 1881

36. . . . none of the angry fans stepped forth to the stage.: *National Police Gazette,* October 29, 1881

37. . . . blind eye to its anti-prizefighting ordinances.: *National Police Gazette,* October 22, 1881

37. . . . he opened a saloon in Albany.: *Lockport Union-Sun & Journal,* February 27, 2010

37. . . . first, and only, voyage into the prize ring.: *National Police Gazette,* January 14, 1882

37. . . . Madden, middleweight Pete McCoy, and lightweight Bob Farrell: *Cincinnati Commercial Tribune,* November 28, 1881

38. . . . last appeared for the Donaldson fight.: *Cincinnati Commercial Tribune,* November 28, 1881

38. . . . seemed to be that he was not his equal.": *Daily Picayune,* January 8, 1882

39. . . . the other side in the matter.": *New York Clipper,* January 28, 1882

39. . . . Too convenient for Sullivan.: *Daily Picayune,* January 24, 1882

39. . . . giggled as they touched the boxers' fists.: Jose Marti, *The America of Jose Marti: Selected Writings* (New York: Noonday Press, 1954), 118

39. . . . finely tuned anatomical specimens in person.: *National Police Gazette,* February 18, 1882

39. . . . a sand bag, that Sullivan had fired Madden,: *National Police Gazette,* February 18, 1882

39. . . . Sullivan had been arrested.: *Boston Globe,* February 6, 1882

39. . . . considered so evenly matched,: *Boston Globe,* February 2, 1882

40. . . . eyes on one of his impromptu visitors.: *National Police Gazette,* February 18, 1882

40. . . . a human ring around the combatants.: *National Police Gazette,* February 18, 1882

40. . . . wagered on the fight in New York City alone.: *New York Times,* February 8, 1882

40. . . . it is classic," he gushed to a reporter.: *National Police Gazette,* February 11, 1882

40. . . . been this enthralled by a title fight.: *National Police Gazette,* March 11, 1882

40. . . . Sullivan drew eight hundred fans,: *New York Clipper,* February 11, 1882

40. . . . his lackluster sparring performance against Goss,: *Boston Globe,* February 5, 1882

41. . . . that ever put on a glove.": *National Police Gazette,* February 11, 1882

41. . . . nature's weapons unadorned are two different things.": *National Police Gazette,* January 7, 1882

41. . . . in New Orleans the night before the battle.: *Boston Globe,* February 7, 1882

41. . . . free of "magisterial interference.": *Daily Picayune,* September 29, 1881

41–42. . . . to stop the fight from soiling his state's turf,: *New York Sun,* February 8, 1882

42. . . . destination unknown to all but a select few.: *New York Sun,* February 8, 1882

43. . . . and offering no regrets as he clung to Dixie's glory.: *New York Times,* February 6, 1882

43. . . . and jail on the way to the hotel.: *Daily Picayune,* February 8, 1882

43. . . . for Biloxi to officiate an estate sale.: *New York Sun,* February 8, 1882

43. . . . home to the University of Mississippi.: David G. Sansing, *The University of Mississippi: A Sesquicentennial History* (Jackson: University Press of Mississippi, 1999), 22

43. . . . a promise to dredge it a proper harbor.: *The Picayune's Guide to New Orleans* (New Orleans: the *Picayune,* 1903), 187

43. . . . lazed away summer days on the verandah.: *Daily Picayune,* August 30, 1898

43. . . . danced on the hotel's lush emerald lawn,: *New Orleans Times,* September 1, 1874

44. . . . highly coveted vantage on the hotel's verandah.: *Boston Herald,* February 8, 1882

44. . . . fishermen rowing out to the catch.: *Boston Herald,* February 8, 1882

45. . . . about the location or results of the fight.: *Boston Globe,* February 8, 1882

45. . . . bound to win."—buoyed his spirits.: *Boston Globe,* February 7, 1882

46. . . . with the spittle from their angry lips.: *Daily Picayune,* February 7, 1882

46. . . . outnumbered those of Sullivan by three to one,: *New York Clipper,* February 18, 1882

46. . . . impatient Goss bellowed to Ryan's camp.: *Daily Picayune,* February 8, 1882

46. . . . his white flannel breeches, stockings, and undershirt.: *The Life of John L. Sullivan,* 23

46. . . . John L. saw the worry in Ryan's eyes.: *New York Clipper,* February 18, 1882

47. . . . as compact as a rampart," a reporter marveled.: *Boston Globe,* February 5, 1882

47. . . . the English heavyweight championship in 1795.: Arne K. Lang, *Prizefighting: An American History* (Jefferson, NC: McFarland & Co., 2008), 10

47. . . . became the 100–80 favorite.: *New York Clipper,* February 11, 1882

48. . . . shoved against me endways," he said after the fight.: Sullivan and Sargent, *Life and Reminiscences,* 82

48. . . . He was the superior man.: Sullivan and Sargent, *Life and Reminiscences,* 91

48. . . . spectators outside than the fighters inside.: *The Life of John L. Sullivan,* 22

49. . . . arms of a windmill with the kick of a mule.": *Kansas City Star,* February 7, 1922

49. . . . Ryan "done and might kill him.": *New York Clipper,* February 25, 1882

49. . . . a disdainful smile after every round.: *National Police Gazette,* March 11, 1882

49. . . . in a heap, bloodied and broken.: *The Life of John L. Sullivan,* 31

49. . . . "It's no use, Johnny. I am too weak.": *St. Paul Globe,* February 12, 1882

50. . . . liable to kill a man with a blow.": *The Life of John L. Sullivan,* 31

50. . . . blackening over his left eye from a Ryan head-butt.: *Daily Inter Ocean,* February 8, 1882

50. . . . while Sullivan was stealing his crown.: *National Police Gazette,* February 25, 1882
50. . . . Sullivan can hit he can whip.": *National Police Gazette,* February 25, 1882
51. . . . "thump us little fellows at school.": *Boston Globe,* February 8, 1882
51. . . . Fox had lost thousands,: *New York Times,* February 8, 1882
51. . . . three hundred thousand copies, twice its normal run.: Reel, *Making of the Modern American Man,* 125

CHAPTER THREE: THE CHAMPION OF CHAMPIONS
52. . . . "the most talked-of man in the world.": *Boston Globe,* May 20, 1906
52. . . . newest head that wore the crown.: *New York Clipper,* February 18, 1882
52. . . . before it puffed out of the station.: Sullivan and Sargent, *Life and Reminiscences,* 94
53. . . . and watched the ruse in peace.: *Chicago Tribune,* February 12, 1882
53. . . . receive his stakes on March 2.: Sullivan and Sargent, *Life and Reminiscences,* 95
53. . . . handed over $4,000.: *New York Herald,* March 3, 1882
53. . . . by a horseshoe of wax flowers.: *Boston Herald,* March 10, 1882
53. . . . "ready to fight any man in the world,": *National Police Gazette,* March 11, 1882
53. . . . as if the feeling was mutual.: *Boston Globe,* August 22, 1882
53. . . . a position amenable to the law.": Sullivan and Sargent, *Life and Reminiscences,* 95
53. . . . will have to do it my fashion.": *National Police Gazette,* March 11, 1882
53. . . . defend his title with bare knuckles.: *National Police Gazette,* March 11, 1882
54. . . . and "lank, green amateur": *New York Times,* March 28, 1882
54. . . . before being finished by the champion.: Sullivan and Sargent, *Life and Reminiscences,* 96–97
54. . . . to more than 1,200.: O'Connor, *The Boston Irish,* 65
54. . . . one illegal grog shop for every ninety-seven people.: Stephanie Schorow, *Drinking Boston: A History of the City and Its Spirits* (Wellesley, MA: Union Park Press, 2012), 50–51
54. . . . Boston repealed prohibition in 1875: *Plain Dealer,* October 6, 1912
54. . . . from eight gallons in 1878 to seventeen gallons in 1898.: Schorow, *Drinking Boston,* 48
54. . . . male bachelor subculture that nurtured John L.: Steven A. Riess, *City Games: The Evolution of American Urban Society and the Rise of Sports* (Urbana: University of Illinois Press, 1989), 16
54. . . . never gone to excess in drinking.": *Chicago Tribune,* February 12, 1882
55. . . . pressed upon me by good fellows," Sullivan said.: *Boston Globe,* May 20, 1906
55. . . . terrorize policemen, hackmen, and bartenders: *New York Times,* February 3, 1918
55. . . . a $500 bond, appealed the sentence,: *New York Times,* April 27, 1882
55. . . . pleaded guilty and paid an eleven-dollar fine,: *Boston Globe,* July 30, 1882
55. . . . at the "prizefighting bully.": *Cincinnati Commercial Tribune,* April 27, 1882
55. . . . lost her husband when she was sixteen.: *New York Times,* May 29, 1885
55. . . . or pianist on the stages of Boston.: *Providence Journal,* January 4, 1981
55. . . . brunette of "majestic proportions.": *Boston Globe,* May 28, 1885
56. . . . three hours as man and wife.": *Cleveland Leader,* May 29, 1885
56. . . . while women entered for free: *New York Times,* July 5, 1882
56. . . . "the lovers of the manly art of self-defense.": *Boston Globe,* June 26, 1880
57. . . . began just before fight time.: *New York Tribune,* July 5, 1882
57. . . . Fenian invasion of Canada in the 1860s,: Undated newspaper article, Lannan scrapbook
57. . . . a bout he lost in twelve rounds.: Undated newspaper article, Lannan scrapbook
57. . . . and roofs of the neighboring houses.: *New York Herald,* July 5, 1882
58. . . . to the delight of the crowd.: *New York Times,* July 5, 1882

58. . . . bloody layer of skin from his back.: *New York Herald*, July 5, 1882

58. . . . crimson stream onto the platform.: *New York Herald*, July 5, 1882

58. . . . and slipped him fifty dollars.: *New York Herald*, July 5, 1882

58. . . . December 22 rematch with the champion,: *National Police Gazette*, January 13, 1883

58. . . . after claiming he acted in self-defense.: *New York Times*, January 4, 1894

59. . . . opponent broke his own arm and had to stop.: *National Police Gazette*, July 8, 1882

59. . . . if he could stand up for four rounds: *The Life of John L. Sullivan*, 42

59. . . . Sullivan had said following the Ryan fight.: Lloyd Lewis and Henry Justin Smith, *Oscar Wilde Discovers America: 1882* (New York: Harcourt, Brace and Co., 1936), 180

59. . . . champion at 215 pounds.: *New York Herald*, July 19, 1882

59. . . . "I can do him with a punch.": *New York Herald*, July 19, 1882

59. . . . but only for a few weeks a year.: Joseph Durso, *Madison Square Garden: 100 Years of History* (New York: Simon and Schuster, 1979), 19

59. . . . weren't huge money-makers.: George Clinton Densmore Odell, *Annals of the New York Stage, Volumes 12–13* (New York: Columbia University Press, 1940), 540–41

60. . . . or stop him in four three minute rounds.": *New York Herald*, July 16, 1882

60. . . . through the gates of the arena.: *New York Times*, July 18, 1882

60. . . . fans pleaded to be allowed inside.: *Chicago Tribune*, July 18, 1882

60. . . . "Hundreds of respectable citizens": *New York Times*, July 18, 1882

60. . . . its representative," reported one local newspaper.: *New York Times*, July 18, 1882

60. . . . and blue stockings, gazed across at Wilson.: *New York Times*, July 18, 1882

61. . . . like an infant" compared to the champion.: *The Life of John L. Sullivan*, 42

61. . . . hissed the "artful dodger,": *Boston Globe*, January 26, 1910

61. . . . to the count of nine each time.: *The Life of John L. Sullivan*, 42–46

61. . . . before he regained his feet.: *New York Times*, July 18, 1882

61. . . . fumes that swam through the soupy air.: Mark Caldwell, *New York Night: The Mystique and Its History* (New York: Scribner, 2005), 190

61. . . . fell twenty-eight times during the bout,: *Boston Globe*, February 16, 1908

61. . . . back to England with his thousands.: *Boston Globe*, January 26, 1910

61. . . . fight topped $16,000.: *New York Herald*, July 19, 1882

62. . . . as well as tolerated in these days.": *Boston Globe*, July 19, 1882

62. . . . for shooting the outlaw in the back.: Odell, *Annals of the New York Stage*, 140

62. . . . a stake of $500.: Sullivan and Sargent, *Life and Reminiscences*, 103

62. . . . defeated young challenger Henry Higgins.: Sullivan and Sargent, *Life and Reminiscences*, 108–9

62. . . . until the police stopped the fight.: *Critic-Record*, November 18, 1882

62. . . . blacksmith S. P. Stockton out cold.: *Cleveland Leader*, October 17, 1882

62. . . . "wanted to know if he fell off a barn.": *Boston Globe*, January 27, 1910

63. . . . a "wind-bag and a fraud,": *Boston Globe*, October 30, 1882

63. . . . took over the company's management.: *Cincinnati Daily Gazette*, October 25, 1882

63. . . . relationship between John L. and Madden severed,: *Cincinnati Daily Gazette*, October 24, 1882

63. . . . "thinks that he is a Vanderbilt.": *Boston Globe*, October 30, 1882

63. . . . to pit against his former favorite.": *National Police Gazette*, November 18, 1882

63. . . . to be matched against Sullivan.: *Cleveland Leader*, December 20, 1882

63. . . . moved in together at 4 Lovering Place: *Boston Journal*, December 20, 1882

63. . . . Given that a psychic medium: *Facts*, March 1883, 109

64. . . . Thousands more were turned away.: *Boston Globe*, March 20, 1883

64. . . . sporting men," reported a local newspaper.: *Boston Herald*, March 20, 1883

64. . . . local boxer named Jake Kilrain.: *New York Times*, March 20, 1883

64. . . . Sullivan watched from the audience.: *New York Herald*, April 10, 1883

64. . . . "exhibition" at Madison Square Garden.: *Boston Globe,* January 29, 1910

65. . . . so much blood that he fainted.: *Plain Dealer,* April 25, 1883

65. . . . instructed the champion to get married.: *Cleveland Leader,* May 29, 1885

65. . . . parents were married twenty-seven years before.: Archdiocese of Boston Records

65. . . . due to "rum and hard knocks.": *Muskegon Chronicle,* April 27, 1883

65. . . . blamed the episode on a cold: *Truth,* April 25, 1883

65. . . . sequestered himself just outside of Boston: *Rocky Mountain News,* May 7, 1883

65. . . . Abbey sporting house on Harrison Avenue.: *Boston Globe,* December 27, 1912

65. . . . prizefighter to the banker and broker.": *New York Times,* May 15, 1883

65. . . . for use as makeshift seats.: *New York Times,* May 15, 1883

66. . . . it gave rise to his nickname.: Herbert Asbury, *The Gangs of New York: An Informal
    History of the Underworld* (New York, London: Thunder's Mouth Press, 2000), 217

66. . . . of the Supreme Court," Williams allegedly boasted.: Mike Dash, *Satan's Circus:
    Murder, Vice, Police Corruption, and New York's Trial of the Century* (New York: Crown
    Publishers, 2007), 50

66. . . . "poster boy for graft and excessive force": Richard Zacks, *Island of Vice: Theodore Roos-
    evelt's Quest to Clean Up Sin-Loving New York* (New York: Anchor Books, 2012), 169

66. . . . will have some tenderloin now.": *Records and Proceedings of the Senate Committee,* 5569

66. . . . of "an ox and a lamb.": *New York Times,* May 15, 1883

66. . . . annihilate Madden's chosen man.: *The Life of John L. Sullivan,* 48

66. . . . cleanest knock-down ever seen,": *The Life of John L. Sullivan,* 48

66. . . . child might have pushed me over,": *State,* April 8, 1906

67. . . . "like a bull at a red flag": *Boston Globe,* January 29, 1910

67. . . . headfirst into the crowd below.: *The Life of John L. Sullivan,* 49

67. . . . on the stage and stopped the battle.: *The Life of John L. Sullivan,* 49

67. . . . kill him?" the captain responded.: *Boston Globe,* January 29, 1910

67. . . . topped $15,000.: *New York Times,* May 15, 1883

67. . . . player in the field," noted a reporter.: *New York Times,* May 29, 1883

68. . . . pitcher lobbing the ball to him.: *Boston Globe,* May 29, 1883

68. . . . around $1,200.: *New York Times,* May 29, 1883

68. . . . runs in a 15–2 rout.: *Philadelphia Inquirer,* June 2, 1883

68. . . . back into the local economy.: *Boston Globe,* April 5, 1908

68. . . . bounce off his prodigious chest.: *Sporting Life,* October 23, 1909

68. . . . a board underneath his vest.: *Boston Globe,* June 7, 1908

68. . . . took on Bunyanesque proportions.: *New York Times,* February 3, 1918

69. . . . placed it back on the rails: Sullivan and Sargent, *Life and Reminiscences,* 28

69. . . . after six men failed in the task.: Sullivan and Sargent, *Life and Reminiscences,* 28

69. . . . "Blood, my son. Nothing but blood.": *Boston Globe,* February 3, 1910

69. . . . uninspired performance with Steve Taylor.: *Boston Globe,* June 22, 1883

69. . . . struck his wife in a fit of anger.: *New York Times,* June 12, 1883

69. . . . falsehoods should be made public.": *Truth,* June 15, 1883

69. . . . a little morose and surly.": *National Police Gazette,* June 30, 1883

70. . . . newspaper establishment in New York.": *National Police Gazette,* March 10, 1883

70. . . . head of a fox lorded over the entrance,: *Sports Illustrated,* February 18, 1963

70. . . . whiskey in the religious editor's office,: *National Police Gazette,* June 16, 1883

70. . . . modeled after pieces in the Louvre.: David McCullough, *The Great Bridge: The Epic
    Story of the Building of the Brooklyn Bridge* (New York: Simon and Schuster, 1972), 526

71. . . . an Irish whaler and a Maori mother.: *New York Times,* January 27, 1883

71. . . . for the championship of the world.: *National Police Gazette,* January 13, 1883

71. . . . "half-breed" as if he were some dog.: *New York Times,* December 27, 1882

71. . . . beast back from a savage land.: *New York Times,* January 27, 1883

71. . . . overlooking picturesque Scituate Harbor.: *Boston Globe,* August 5, 1883
71. . . . just north of two hundred pounds.: Sullivan and Sargent, *Life and Reminiscences,* 121
71. . . . He "sparred like an automaton.": Inglis, *Champions Off Guard,* 62
72. . . . and headfirst into the crowd.: *Charlotte Observer,* July 9, 1905
72. . . . butcher's axe," reported the *National Police Gazette.: National Police Gazette,* August 18, 1883
72. . . . much of a fight to stop.: *Charlotte Observer,* July 9, 1905
72. . . . as high as $15,000.: *The Life of John L. Sullivan,* 52–54
73. . . . broke away and fell to the floor.: *Boston Globe,* August 8, 1883
73. . . . etched with the champion's initials.: *New York Times,* August 9, 1883
73. . . . on the opening night alone,: *New York Times,* September 19, 1883
73. . . . to a customer who lacked money.: *Boston Globe,* May 20, 1906
73. . . . a third whiskey, and a fourth brandy,": *New York Times,* September 19, 1883

CHAPTER FOUR: AMERICA TAKES ITS BEST SHOT

74. . . . Boston and Providence Railroad depot.: *Boston Herald,* September 27, 1883
75. . . . lick any son-of-a-bitch alive!": Barrett, *The Irish Way,* 27
75. . . . imposing figure at six feet, two inches tall.: Donovan, *The Roosevelt That I Know,* 90
75. . . . experience for a future title bout.: *State,* November 26, 1905
75–76. . . . Munzinger was hired as the treasurer.: *National Police Gazette,* April 15, 1905
76. . . . would join the traveling party—Annie.: *Boston Globe,* September 19, 1883
76. . . . drink and stand up in the ring.": *Boston Globe,* September 19, 1883
76. . . . from their Madison Square Garden encounter,: *Baltimore Sun,* September 29, 1883
77. . . . to personally deliver the whippings.: *Boston Globe,* April 26, 1908
77. . . . "temperance and good shows.": *New York Herald,* September 28, 1883
77. . . . "disreputable resort in Railroad Street.": *New York Times,* October 13, 1883
77. . . . escaped and left for Wilkes-Barre.: *New Haven Register,* October 13, 1883
77. . . . galloping to their downtown hotel.: *Cincinnati Post,* October 15, 1883
77. . . . tossed them around like footballs: *New York Times,* October 14, 1883
77. . . . tried to break up the crowd.: *Boston Herald,* October 14, 1883
78. . . . the mob dispersed after midnight.: *New York Times,* October 14, 1883
78. . . . fought with the champion of the world.": Sullivan and Sargent, *Life and Reminiscences,* 138–40
78. . . . the fight at the one-minute mark.: *New York Herald,* November 4, 1883
79. . . . with Slade sprinting alongside.: *Cleveland Leader,* November 5, 1883
79. . . . of abandoning tour dates to return.: *National Police Gazette,* December 1, 1883
79. . . . "just face Sullivan one second.": Sullivan and Sargent, *Life and Reminiscences,* 146
79. . . . the "strongest man in Iowa,": Sullivan and Sargent, *Life and Reminiscences,* 146–47
80. . . . sent Sheehan away with one hundred dollars: *San Antonio Express,* October 8, 1905
80. . . . to over eighty-seven thousand.: *Report on Transportation Business in the United States at the Eleventh Census 1890* (Washington, DC: Government Printing Office, 1895), 4
80. . . . stoked the United States in the 1880s.: Andrew Carnegie, *Triumphant Democracy or Fifty Years' March of the Republic* (New York: Charles Scribner's Sons, 1886), 1
80. . . . "living locomotive going at full speed.": *New York Times,* July 5, 1882
81. . . . ", and I don't like funerals.": *Seattle Daily Times,* June 21, 1925
81. . . . to the enemy and fight all the time.": *Boston Globe,* July 5, 1908
82. . . . and other "gilded haunts.": J. J. Lee and Marion R. Casey, eds., *Making the Irish American: History and Heritage of the Irish in the United States* (New York: New York University Press, 2006), 451
82. . . . and pugnacious Irish buffoon.": Lee and Casey, *Making the Irish American,* 451

82. . . . the Sunday mining camp circuit.: Sammons, *Beyond the Ring,* 22

82. . . . Business came to a stop in the town.: *State,* May 6, 1906

83. . . . would have been a dead man.: Sullivan and Sargent, *Life and Reminiscences,* 148

83. . . . and second-generation Irish Americans.: James Patrick Walsh, *Michael Mooney and the Leadville Irish: Respectability and Resistance at 10,200 Feet, 1875–1900* (University of Colorado Dissertation, 2010), iii

83. . . . McCoy dodged the projectile,: *New York Times,* December 30, 1883

83. . . . Sullivan was taken to his hotel.: *New York Times,* December 31, 1883

83. . . . Leadville people," the local newspaper reported.: *Walsh, Michael Mooney and the Leadville Irish,* 71–72

84. . . . he had Robinson knocked out.: *National Police Gazette,* April 15, 1905

84. . . . boxing than in anything I know of.": *Boston Globe,* January 7, 1907

84. . . . knocked him cold for fifteen minutes.: Sullivan and Sargent, *Life and Reminiscences,* 149–50

85. . . . exhibition starring the Canadian idol.: *Daily British Colonist,* February 8, 1884

85. . . . "a state of beastly intoxication.": *Daily British Colonist,* March 1, 1884

85. . . . gracious majesty?" asked the dignitary.: *Boston Herald,* April 23, 1905

85. . . . Come on, Gillespie,": *National Police Gazette,* April 15, 1905

85. . . . "withdrew in high dudgeon.": *Daily British Colonist,* February 9, 1884

85. . . . drinking to the health of English monarchs.": *Boston Herald,* April 23, 1905

85. . . . out of the supper room in one round.: *Daily British Colonist,* February 15, 1884

85. . . . reputation behind him wherever he goes,": *Daily British Colonist,* February 12, 1884

85. . . . erratic footsteps" toward their city.: *Daily British Colonist,* February 12, 1884

85. . . . he will not leave the coast alive.": *Daily British Colonist,* February 21, 1884

86. . . . head-butt that bloodied his nose.: *San Francisco Bulletin,* February 25, 1884

86. . . . will reach home again,": *San Francisco Chronicle,* February 25, 1884

86. . . . in for having a good time.": *San Francisco Chronicle,* January 22, 1884

86. . . . for the audience to connect the dots.: *Daily British Colonist,* February 27, 1884

86. . . . quivering mass of insensible humanity.": *Daily British Colonist,* March 1, 1884

87. . . . might be killed or maimed for life.: *New York Times,* December 29, 1883

87. . . . Irish-born or the children of Irish immigrants.: Patrick Myler, *Gentleman Jim Corbett: The Truth Behind a Boxing Legend* (London: Robson Books, 1998), 9

87. . . . thirty-five pounds heavier than his opponent.: *The Life of John L. Sullivan,* 53

87. . . . wear eight-ounce versions instead.: *The Life of John L. Sullivan,* 53

88. . . . used "every trick and device": *The Life of John L. Sullivan,* 54

88. . . . voted unanimously to expel Robinson.: *The Life of John L. Sullivan,* 55

88. . . . to the dressing room to go to sleep.: *Boxing Illustrated,* August 1964

88. . . . it would be different with Marx.: *National Police Gazette,* June 6, 1925

89. . . . unconscious for ten minutes before he came to,: *National Police Gazette,* June 6, 1925

89. . . . to pay for the destroyed drum.: *Boston Globe,* July 14, 1907

89. . . . with the combination on a nightly basis.: *Daily Picayune,* April 15, 1884

89. . . . out of the building to his home.: *Macon Telegraph,* May 4, 1884

89. . . . "Did I lick him?": *Boston Globe,* January 12, 1908

90. . . . against Duncan McDonald in Butte,: *Boston Globe,* May 27, 1884

90. . . . to ovations all along the route.: Donovan, *The Roosevelt That I Know,* 69–70

90. . . . to board the next train out of the city.: *Plain Dealer,* May 26, 1884

90. . . . four rounds with the champion.: *National Police Gazette,* April 15, 1905

91. . . . some credible local toughs.: *National Police Gazette,* June 6, 1925

91. . . . $42,000 in expenses.: Sullivan and Sargent, *Life and Reminiscences,* 156

91. . . . $110,000 outside of expenses.: *National Police Gazette,* April 15, 1905

91. . . . $5,000 home to his mother: *National Police Gazette,* April 26, 1884

91.... brawn evidently holds first place over brain,": *San Francisco Chronicle*, January 22, 1884

91.... after his fighting days were done.: *Boston Globe*, January 31, 1910

92.... to say of me what it pleases.": *Once a Week*, May 10, 1892

92.... kept it and had it engraved.: *New York Times*, July 21, 1913

92.... the teacher of John L. Sullivan.": *Boston Herald*, June 28, 1901

92.... and challenged all comers.: *New York Times*, April 9, 1922

92.... the dream of one day meeting Sullivan.: Gerald Martin Bordman, *The American Musical Theatre: A Chronicle* (New York: Oxford University Press, 1978), 84

93.... the clerk couldn't achieve his dream,: John Charles Franceschina, *Harry B. Smith: Dean of American Librettists* (New York: Routledge, 2003), 83

93.... that grasped the hand of Sullivan.": *Brooklyn Daily Eagle*, September 20, 1886

93.... through the city streets to Sullivan's saloon.: *Boston Globe*, May 27, 1884

CHAPTER FIVE: BATTLES WITH BRAWLERS AND BOTTLES

94.... John Lawrence Sullivan, Jr.: *Providence Journal*, April 26, 1956

94.... appropriately hefty eleven pounds.: *Daily Register,* April 14, 1884

94.... Aunt Annie Lennon the godmother.: *Providence Journal*, April 26, 1956

94.... when he was just nine months old.: *Kansas City Times*, July 30, 1886

94.... state of Rhode Island," Sullivan groused.: *Denver Post*, April 30, 1907

95.... I get my jewelry at Tiffany's,": *New York Times*, September 13, 1885

95.... the children flock to the riches.: *State*, November 26, 1905

95.... how to enjoy life as it goes.": *State*, November 26, 1905

96.... leave New York with two-thirds of the gate.: *New York Tribune*, May 27, 1884

96.... for the rematch with Mitchell.: *New York Herald*, June 29, 1884

96.... training in Pleasure Bay, New Jersey.: Donovan, *The Roosevelt That I Know*, 92–93

96.... The fight was back on.: *New York Herald*, June 29, 1884

96.... McCoy also heaved out of the train.: *New York Tribune*, July 1, 1884

97.... on the elevated wooden platform.: *New York Times*, July 1, 1884

97.... Then the crowd waited.: *New York Times*, July 1, 1884

97.... a doctor here'll prove it.": *New York Tribune*, July 1, 1884

97.... is that I'm willing to spar.": *New York Tribune*, July 1, 1884

97.... management extinguished the gaslights.: *New York Tribune*, July 1, 1884

98.... would say it was gin," John L. complained.: *New York Tribune*, July 1, 1884

98.... who held legitimate tickets.: *State*, May 13, 1906

98.... the $8,000 gate,: *San Francisco Bulletin*, July 2, 1884

98.... give his share to charity.: *State*, May 13, 1906

98.... business relationship between the men.: *National Police Gazette*, March 31, 1888

98.... exhibitions of that nature in this city.": *New York Tribune*, July 1, 1884

98.... if only for half an hour.": *Irish-American Weekly*, July 19, 1884

99.... a wake a day or two prior.: *National Police Gazette*, August 30, 1884

99.... it grew even worse.: *National Police Gazette*, December 11, 1887

99.... carried upstairs by Annie's brothers.: *Boston Herald*, May 29, 1885

99.... and knocked her over a trunk.: *Boston Globe*, May 28, 1885

99.... uncanny resemblance to Thomas Edison,: *Irish-American Weekly*, February 6, 1892

100.... a sporting house in Chicago.: *New York Times*, December 13, 1909

100.... see him return from his walk.: Sullivan and Sargent, *Life and Reminiscences*, 161

100.... a polite, but firm refusal.: Sullivan and Sargent, *Life and Reminiscences*, 159–60

100.... was a few pounds heavier.: *The Life of John L. Sullivan*, 56

100.... five thousand fans that included Edison.: *Boston Journal*, November 11, 1884

101. . . . around his opponent in a bid to survive.: *The Life of John L. Sullivan,* 57–59

101. . . . with the $7,500: *The Life of John L. Sullivan,* 59

101. . . . a four-round gloved contest,: *The Life of John L. Sullivan,* 60–61

102. . . . to disrespect of law and order.": *National Police Gazette,* December 6, 1884

102. . . . a white flannel shirt with a blue ribbon: *New York Herald,* November 18, 1884

102. . . . "Lord bless you, no!".: *Boston Globe,* February 3, 1910

102. . . . not change based on the result.: *New York Times,* November 18, 1884

102. . . . sparring match until the following night.: *New York Times,* November 18, 1884

102–103. . . . around 160 pounds.: *The Life of John L. Sullivan,* 60–61

103. . . . at the end of the opening round.: *The Life of John L. Sullivan,* 61–62

103. . . . a big left. A right. A left.: *The Life of John L. Sullivan,* 62

103. . . . think I think?" he shot back.: *New York Herald,* November 19, 1884

104. . . . undercut their police chief.: Walling, *Recollections of a New York Chief of Police,* 374

104. . . . stare as he delivered the verdict.: Edward Van Every, *Sins of New York: As "Exposed" by the* Police Gazette (New York: Frederick A. Stokes Co., 1930), 271–74

104. . . . And then he won't have a chance.": Van Every, *Sins of New York,* 261, 269

104. . . . punched the other equine in the face.: *Boston Globe,* January 31, 1885

105. . . . "left the place on the best of terms.": *National Police Gazette,* January 17, 1885

105. . . . for the champion on opening night.: *New York Times,* January 1, 1885

105. . . . settled with the waitress out of court,: *Jackson Daily Citizen,* January 2, 1885

105. . . . cruelty in beating a horse.": *New York Times,* January 31, 1885

105. . . . and Commonwealth Avenue admirers.": *Boston Herald,* January 13, 1885

105. . . . at the slightest sign of violence.: Caldwell, *New York Night,* 191

105. . . . that resulted in their closure.: Gilfoyle, *City of Eros,* 193

105. . . . as their trainers rubbed them down.: *New York Times,* January 20, 1885

106. . . . of the gallery," reported the *New York Times.*: *New York Times,* January 20, 1885

106. . . . $11,000 for a brief night's work.: *New York Times,* January 20, 1885

106 (fn). . . . to the baseball diamond on a Sunday.: *Baltimore Sun,* September 15, 1885

106. . . . Sullivan would die with his boots on.: *Baltimore Sun,* March 26, 1885

107. . . . and threatened to kill her.: *New York Times,* May 28, 1885

107. . . . glances in his wife's direction.: *Cleveland Leader,* May 28, 1885

107. . . . beverages in her whole life.: *Boston Herald,* May 29, 1885

107. . . . thrown bottles and books at him.: *New York Times,* May 29, 1885

108. . . . for fifty-eight dollars to prove it.: *Boston Herald,* May 29, 1885

108. . . . drunkard" nor engaged in the cruel acts.: *New York Times,* May 30, 1885

108. . . . and its furniture over to Annie,: *Boston Globe,* July 12, 1908

108. . . . moved to 7 Carver Street,: *Daily Picayune,* August 4, 1885

108. . . . 26 Sawyer Street, a nine-room house: *Boston Herald,* October 6, 1885

108. . . . his parents' Parnell Street residence.: *Elkhart Daily Review,* October 12, 1885

108. . . . on the back of his neck.: Sullivan and Sargent, *Life and Reminiscences,* 168

108. . . . the fighters shook hands.: *Brooklyn Daily Eagle,* June 14, 1885

108. . . . in landing spots on fight cards.: Donovan, *The Roosevelt That I Know,* 102

108. . . . boils on Sullivan and broke them.: *Boston Globe,* July 28, 1907

109. . . . "done the better fighting.": *Brooklyn Daily Eagle,* June 14, 1885

109. . . . principals of a planned prizefight.: *Cincinnati Post,* October 7, 2006

109. . . . not a prizefight and could continue.: *Ring,* July 1994

109. . . . at Tom Denney's benefit in Boston,: *Boston Herald,* August 14, 1884

110. . . . SULLIVAN IS SOBER,: *New York Times,* August 28, 1885

110. . . . the encounter proved bizarre.: *Cincinnati Post,* October 7, 2006

110. . . . his biggest asset was speed.: *Ring,* July 1994

110. . . . chased the challenger around the ring.: *The Life of John L. Sullivan,* 65–66

110. . . . don't you force the fighting?": *Ring,* July 1994
110. . . . of range of taking a risky blow.: *The Life of John L. Sullivan,* 65–66
110. . . . announced the end of the round.: *Ring,* July 1994
111. . . . down heavily with Sullivan on top: *The Life of John L. Sullivan,* 65–66
111. . . . done enough fighting here today.": *Ring,* July 1994
111. . . . platform collapsed. Chaos reigned.: *Ring,* July 1994
111. . . . had the better of the match.": *Ring,* July 1994
112. . . . among the saloons of Cincinnati.: *Ring,* July 1994
112. . . . "the first heavyweight title fight of the modern era.": *Ring,* July 1994
112. . . . to open a corner saloon in Manhattan.: Sullivan and Sargent, *Life and Reminiscences,* 172
112. . . . poses of famous ancient and modern sculptures.: *Boston Globe,* September 13, 1908
112. . . . and *Dying Gladiator: New York Herald,* May 29, 1885
112. . . . statues which adorn the Louvre.": *Boston Globe,* May 29, 1885
112. . . . to 237 pounds.: *Ring,* July 1994
112. . . . "charming vocalist and actress.": *Boston Herald,* August 5, 1883
112. . . . a statuesque blonde beauty.: *Wheeling Register,* September 10, 1896
113. . . . to enter the theatrical world.: *Boston Journal,* September 7, 1896
113. . . . married, and had a daughter, Eva.: *National Police Gazette,* December 17, 1887
113. . . . living with her paternal grandparents.: *Boston Journal,* September 7, 1896
113. . . . again at the Howard Athenaeum: *Wheeling Register,* September 10, 1896
113. . . . buy a copy of the Sunday *Daily News.*: *Boston Globe,* January 6, 1886
113. . . . was so "sickly and inoffensive": *Albuquerque Morning Democrat,* January 5, 1886
113. . . . prevented the fight from taking place.: *Brooklyn Daily Eagle,* May 31, 1886
114. . . . and tailed him to the Steel City.: *State,* November 24, 1905
114. . . . in Allegheny City that night.: *Boston Globe,* September 13, 1907
114. . . . thirteen hundred fans entered the Coliseum Rink.: *Weekly Auburnian,* September 24, 1886
114. . . . and dance around the ring.: *Weekly Auburnian,* September 24, 1886
114. . . . after desperate infighting.: *The Life of John L. Sullivan,* 68
114. . . . Newell declared Sullivan the victor.: *The Life of John L. Sullivan,* 69
115. . . . to give speeches but not fight: *Daily British Colonist,* December 10, 1886
115. . . . "amicably settled their differences,": *Critic-Record,* October 27, 1886
115. . . . passed away on October 28, 1886.: *Boston Herald,* October 29, 1886
115. . . . for his own child's grave.": *National Police Gazette,* December 17, 1887
115. . . . the happiness of the absent father.": *Providence Journal,* April 4, 1981
115. . . . ever visited his son's grave: *Boston Globe,* July 12, 1908
115. . . . beside her boy in 1917.: *Providence Journal,* April 4, 1981
116. . . . savage blows with Ryan leading.: *The Life of John L. Sullivan,* 72
116. . . . the crowd made the rafters ring.": *The Life of John L. Sullivan,* 73
116. . . . JOHN L. SULLIVAN THE INVINCIBLE, read the headline.: *National Police Gazette,* November 27, 1886
116. . . . and then left the ballpark.: *San Francisco Examiner,* November 15, 1886, in Dean A. Sullivan, *Early Innings: A Documentary History of Baseball, 1825–1908* (Lincoln: University of Nebraska Press, 1995), 144–46
116. . . . before ten thousand spectators.: *The Life of John L. Sullivan,* 69
116. . . . 230-pound champion.: *The Life of John L. Sullivan,* 70
117. . . . tried his best to mask his suffering.: *Oregonian,* February 12, 1905
117. . . . by Sullivan the rest of the night.: *The Life of John L. Sullivan,* 71
117. . . . would not have emerged victorious.: *The Life of John L. Sullivan,* 72
117. . . . plaster cast for five weeks.: Sullivan and Sargent, *Life and Reminiscences,* 175

117. . . . in Hartford, Connecticut, on July 4.: *Boston Globe,* March 23, 1887
118. . . . JOHN L. SULLIVAN rather than vice versa.: *Cincinnati Post,* April 4, 1887
118. . . . that shook the hand of Sullivan.": Collins, *Scorpion Tongues,* 85
118. . . . and the name stuck.: *Boston Herald,* July 9, 1889
119. . . . wouldn't do it, then Kilrain would.: *National Police Gazette,* December 31, 1887
119. . . . representing the championship of America.: *Cincinnati Commercial Tribune,* June 5, 1887
119. . . . a mere "dog collar.": *National Police Gazette,* June 25, 1887
119. . . . is requested to let him alone.": *National Police Gazette,* June 25, 1887

CHAPTER SIX: THE KING AND THE PRINCE
120. . . . smaller plates of sixteen-karat gold: *Boston Globe,* March 23, 1887
120. . . . and the Stars and Stripes.: *Boston Globe,* May 7, 1925
120. . . . more than thirty times: Alexander Klein, "Personal Income of US States: Estimates for the Period 1880–1910," *Warwick Economic Research Papers,* no. 916, Department of Economics, University of Warwick, 2009
121. . . . as studded as the forty-four-inch championship belt.: *Boston Globe,* May 7, 1925
121. . . . That an "open law-breaker": *Zion's Herald,* August 17, 1887
121. . . . "culture, piety, and decency of the Hub.": *Christian Union,* August 18, 1887
121. . . . but among toughs we're kings.": *Boston Herald,* February 3, 1918
121. . . . strains of "Hail to the Chief,": *Christian Union,* August 18, 1887
122. . . . buckled the belt around his waist.: *Boston Globe,* April 4, 1926
122. . . . make a better speech yourself?": *Boston Globe,* April 20, 1913
122. . . . an exhibition with Mike Donovan.: *Boston Globe,* April 4, 1926
122. . . . was a tremendous success.: *Boston Globe,* March 23, 1887
122. . . . "two-weeks drunk at the Ocean House.": *National Police Gazette,* December 17, 1887
122. . . . torn through another manager.: *Denver Post,* May 2, 1904
123. . . . a hermit out of a prominent pugilist.": *Boston Herald,* September 2, 1887
123. . . . alcohol while under his care.: *Boston Globe,* October 6, 1887
123. . . . champion pedestrian in the 1870s.: *New York Herald,* October 29, 1887
123. . . . column until his recent firing,: *Plain Dealer,* April 28, 1888
123. . . . whip his old boss with a cowhide.: *New York Times,* October 25, 1887
123. . . . "who the real champion is,": *Boston Globe,* September 29, 1887
123. . . . matchup with either Smith or Kilrain.: *Boston Globe,* October 6, 1887
123. . . . $1,100 each.: *Boston Globe,* October 23, 1887
124. . . . and the ship cast off its lines.: *Boston Herald,* October 28, 1887
124. . . . press reported to be his "wife": *Boston Journal,* October 27, 1887
124. . . . passenger lists recorded as "Annie Sullivan.": Boston Passenger and Crew Lists, 1820–1943
124. . . . "Where is your other wife?": *National Police Gazette,* December 17, 1887
124. . . . the champion pugilist," was aboard.: *New York Herald,* October 28, 1887
124. . . . the pilothouse of one tug,: *Boston Herald,* October 28, 1887
124. . . . they flapped in the breeze.: *New York Herald,* October 28, 1887
124. . . . Sullivan's parents cried softly.: *New York Herald,* October 28, 1887
124. . . . "Auld Lang Syne" faded: *Boston Herald,* October 28, 1887
125. . . . exemplar," reported one British newspaper.: *Sheffield & Rotherham Independent,* November 10, 1887
125. . . . equivalent to $600).: Sullivan and Sargent, *Life and Reminiscences,* 177
125 (fn). . . . enter the country with the *Police Gazette* belt.: *Boston Globe,* October 23, 1887
125. . . . to await his sail home.: Sullivan and Sargent, *Life and Reminiscences,* 179

125. . . . quarters at the Grand Hotel.: Sullivan and Sargent, *Life and Reminiscences,* 182
125. . . . he boarded a train to London.: *Irish Times,* November 8, 1887
125. . . . scaled the roof of Sullivan's train: *Pall Mall Gazette,* November 8, 1887
125. . . . attempts to shake his hand.: *New York Herald,* November 8, 1887
125. . . . estimated as high as twelve thousand: *Pall Mall Gazette,* November 8, 1887
125. . . . walking sticks in the air.: *Pall Mall Gazette,* November 8, 1887
125. . . . that swallowed them whole.: *York Herald,* November 8, 1887
126. . . . and sent everyone to the cobblestones.: *York Herald,* November 8, 1887
126. . . . and delivered a brief thank-you.: *York Herald,* November 8, 1887
126. . . . poet, preacher, or artist": *Pall Mall Gazette,* November 8, 1887
126. . . . the flag of its former colony.: Don Russell, *The Lives and Legends of Buffalo Bill* (Norman: University of Oklahoma Press, 1960), 330
126. . . . double the regular prices: *Boston Globe,* December 6, 1887
127. . . . Queensberry himself watched from the audience.: *Penny Illustrated Paper and Illustrated Times,* November 19, 1887
127. . . . and disappointing" opening exhibition.: *Morning Post,* November 10, 1887
127. . . . "Slugger Sullivan" in each issue: *Boston Globe,* November 24, 1887
127. . . . four rounds with the champion.: *New York Herald,* October 28, 1887
127. . . . such as Leicester and Manchester.: Sullivan and Sargent, *Life and Reminiscences,* 178
127. . . . at Bingley Hall in Birmingham: *Boston Globe,* December 6, 1887
127. . . . La Belle Fatma Ben-Eny, the beauty of Tunis.: *Times of London,* November 28, 1887
127. . . . whenever he appeared on stage.: *Boston Herald,* December 11, 1887
128. . . . a suit for divorce was on.": *Evening News,* December 5, 1887
128. . . . traveled to England at his side.: *National Police Gazette,* December 17, 1887
128. . . . puritanical mother did nothing to stop him either.: *Daily Mail,* March 22, 2010
129. . . . too drunk for the assignment.: Oliver Carlson, *Brisbane: A Candid Biography* (New York: Stackpole Sons, 1937), 88–89
129. . . . tell the prince what you like.": *Evening News,* January 16, 1918
129. . . . only for the American press.: *Riverside Independent Enterprise,* March 10, 1901
129. . . . included Lord Randolph Churchill,: Sullivan and Sargent, *Life and Reminiscences,* 186
129. . . . first world heavyweight championship bout.: Sullivan and Sargent, *Life and Reminiscences,* 186
129. . . . reflected the rays of the gaslight,: *New York Sun,* December 10, 1887
130. . . . wanted to meet in coming to England.: Sullivan and Sargent, *Life and Reminiscences,* 187
130. . . . fought—yes, fought—in Detroit.: *Manchester Guardian,* December 28, 1887
130. . . . the twenty- by twenty-four-foot ring,: *Reynold's Newspaper,* December 11, 1887
130. . . . for the forty members of high society: *Boston Globe,* December 10, 1887
130. . . . attending seven funerals by proxy.: *Manchester Guardian,* December 28, 1887
130. . . . to the ancient Celtic king Brian Boru.: *Manchester Guardian,* December 28, 1887
130. . . . for the prince's enjoyment: *Manchester Guardian,* December 10, 1887
130. . . . on the floor, applauded, and smiled.: *New York Sun,* December 10, 1887
130. . . . "the strength of his eye.": *New York Sun,* December 10, 1887
130. . . . offered John L. his congratulations: *Manchester Guardian,* December 10, 1887
130. . . . knocks the men delivered to each other.: *Weekly Irish Times,* January 7, 1888
130. . . . a celebrated cordon bleu from Paris.: *Manchester Guardian,* December 28, 1887
131. . . . reportedly infuriated Queen Victoria.: *Huddersfield Daily Chronicle,* December 23, 1887
131. . . . shake hands with John L. Sullivan.": *Zion's Herald,* January 4, 1888
131. . . . never have entered the building.": *Weekly Irish Times,* January 7, 1888
131. . . . speech when addressing the Prince.": *Weekly Irish Times,* January 7, 1888

131. . . . I have often heard of you.": *Literary Digest*, February 23, 1918

131. . . . be sure and look me up.": *Literary Digest*, February 23, 1918

131. . . . hat off to speak to Sullivan.: *Manchester Guardian*, December 23, 1887

131. . . . with Britain's blue bloods,: *National Police Gazette*, March 10, 1888

131. . . . and introduce your family to.": *Manchester Guardian*, December 28, 1887

132. . . . his references to "King Ed,": *New York Times*, May 9, 1907

132. . . . shook his flipper and wished him well.": *Oregonian*, March 19, 1905

132. . . . was the Lord Mayor of Dublin.: *Manchester Guardian*, December 7, 1887

132–133. . . . to fight him, wouldn't you?": *Denver Post*, March 31, 1902

133. . . . the president's are tied by Congress.": *Denver Post*, March 31, 1902

133. . . . and "The Wearing of the Green.": Sullivan and Sargent, *Life and Reminiscences*, 193

133. . . . "he was proud to call his own.": *Freeman's Journal and Daily Commercial Advertiser*, December 12, 1887

133. . . . a lush ocean of meadow grass.: Jack Anderson, "A Champion in Ireland: The Visit of John L. Sullivan," *The CBZ Journal*, May 2002

134. . . . and congratulations for his bravery.: *Freeman's Journal and Daily Commercial Advertiser*, December 15, 1887

134. . . . "the local sporting event of the year.": *Belfast News-Letter*, December 19, 1887

134. . . . and one Irish tweed suit.: Sullivan and Sargent, *Life and Reminiscences*, 196

134. . . . prize ring" by the *National Police Gazette*.: *National Police Gazette*, December 31, 1887

134. . . . might be Sullivan's next opponent.: *National Police Gazette*, December 31, 1887

134. . . . he understood that to be Smith.: *Irish Times*, December 16, 1887

135. . . . sixteen-foot enclosure that John L. preferred.: Sullivan and Sargent, *Life and Reminiscences*, 197–98

135. . . . sporting men hurried Sullivan away.: Sullivan and Sargent, *Life and Reminiscences*, 198–99

135. . . . through Glasgow, Dundee, and Edinburgh.: Sullivan and Sargent, *Life and Reminiscences*, 182

135. . . . easily dispatching him in the third.: *New York Herald*, January 7, 1888

135. . . . an impressive five thousand pounds.: Sullivan and Sargent, *Life and Reminiscences*, 195–96

136. . . . through the streets of Windsor,: *National Police Gazette*, March 24, 1888

136. . . . suggest the royal viewing actually occurred.: Sullivan and Sargent, *Life and Reminiscences*, 196

136. . . . George McDonald remained with Sullivan: *Columbus Enquirer-Sun*, February 13, 1888

136. . . . left Boston weighing over 225 pounds,: Daniel M. Daniel, "Sullivan-Mitchell Aroused Rancors," unknown publication, 1944

136. . . . 196 in time for the fight.: *Boston Globe*, February 14, 1888

136. . . . has the gang to break [it] up,": Jake Kilrain letter to Johnny Murphy, January 23, 1888

136. . . . as it had been for Kilrain and Smith,: *Boston Globe*, March 9, 1888

137. . . . an eight-vehicle procession: *Boston Globe*, March 11, 1888

137. . . . of Baron Alphonse Rothschild near Chantilly.: *New York Herald*, March 11, 1888

137. . . . sheltered from view by trees.: *Boston Globe*, March 11, 1888

137. . . . the world's worst criminals.: Daniel, "Sullivan-Mitchell Aroused Rancors"

137. . . . elegant blue coat with velvet collar,: *Literary Digest*, February 23, 1918

137. . . . and bank burglars in America.": *Defenders and Offenders* (New York: D. Buchner & Co., 1888), 107

137. . . . over in Europe "on business.": *New York Sun*, June 23, 1888

137.... anyone interfering with the bout.: *Literary Digest,* February 23, 1918

137.... his hair cropped to stubble,: *Plain Dealer,* April 28, 1888

137.... five-hundred-pound note as a side bet,: *Observer,* March 11, 1888

137.... in the legendary fight with Sayers.: *Daily Inter Ocean,* March 12, 1888

137.... Smith's second ten weeks earlier.: *National Police Gazette,* January 14, 1888

138.... it was an "idiotic exhibition.": *New York Sun,* March 11, 1888

139.... to give his man a breather.: *New York Sun,* March 11, 1888

139.... you son of a bitch, if you can.": Anderson, *"A Champion in Ireland"*

139.... John L. couldn't comprehend why.: *Guardian,* March 8, 1999

140.... babies at home crying.": *Boston Globe,* March 18, 1897

140.... Mitchell's eye started to swell shut.: *Observer,* March 11, 1888

140.... thirty-four minute round came to a close.: Daniel, "Sullivan-Mitchell Aroused Rancors"

140.... bribe him into accepting the draw.: Daniel, "Sullivan-Mitchell Aroused Rancors"

141.... Kilrain laughed and taunted Sullivan.: *New York Sun,* March 11, 1888

141.... next most astonished man is Mitchell.": *New York Sun,* March 11, 1888

141.... pointed his gun at Baldock's head.: *New York Sun,* March 12, 1888

141.... to the gendarmerie in the town of Senlis.: *New York Herald,* March 11, 1888

141.... "to prevent their hanging themselves": *Richmond Times Dispatch,* September 21, 1927

141.... did nothing for Sullivan's chills.: *Irish Times,* March 13, 1888

141.... parleyvoos I couldn't understand.": *National Police Gazette,* July 29, 1905

141.... provide them both with some brandy.: *National Police Gazette,* July 29, 1905

141.... in court the following morning.: Sullivan and Sargent, *Life and Reminiscences,* 202

142.... and started back to London.: *Irish Times,* March 13, 1888

142.... and six days' imprisonment.: *Weekly Irish Times,* March 24, 1888

142.... never fight with his bare fists again.: *New York Herald,* March 12, 1888

142.... takers for Mitchell could be found.: *New York Sun,* March 11, 1888

142.... "This is a cold day for us.": *New York Herald,* March 11, 1888

142.... overconfident and did not half train.": *New York Herald,* March 11, 1888

142.... and he's broken the fiddle.": *National Police Gazette,* April 7 , 1888

143.... for the removal of his whiskers.: *Freeman's Journal and Daily Commercial Advertiser,* March 27, 1888

143.... selling its "Strong Boy" on the short.: *Christian Union,* March 22, 1888

143.... championship belt back in tow.: *New York Sun,* April 13, 1888

143.... terrorized the fourteen hundred passengers: *New York Herald,* May 7, 1888

143.... his head upon waking up.: *New York Herald,* May 7, 1888

143.... stewards hid under tables with the lights off.: *Plain Dealer,* April 28, 1888

143.... captain threatened to put him in irons.: *Duluth Daily News,* April 27, 1888

143.... kept the passengers awake: *Plain Dealer,* April 28, 1888

143.... her four children out of his way.: *Duluth Daily News,* April 27, 1888

143.... a championship sculler from South Boston: Bob Gardiner e-mail, January 7, 2013

144.... apologies to his fellow passengers.: *Milwaukee Journal,* April 28, 1888

144.... who are their shame and disgrace.": *Independent,* May 3, 1888

144.... from the injury to his reputation,": *New York Sun,* March 11, 1888

144.... declared his fighting days "finished.": *Boston Globe,* March 11, 1888

144.... to uphold the honor of the Stars and Stripes.: *National Police Gazette,* April 7, 1888

CHAPTER SEVEN: THE EPIC BRAWL

145.... rowed toward the mighty steamship,: *Boston Globe,* April 24, 1888

145.... when he left Boston six months ago.: *National Police Gazette,* May 5, 1888

145. ... for $10,000 a side.: *Boston Globe,* April 24, 1888
146. ... with flags and bunting, awaited.: *National Police Gazette,* May 5, 1888
146. ... joined in the festivities.: *Wheeling Register,* April 25, 1888
146. ... champ set foot on American soil.: James Bernard Cullen, *The Story of the Irish in Boston: Together with Biographical Sketches of Representative Men and Noted Women* (Boston: James B. Cullen & Co., 1889), 335
146. ... THE OTHER CAN FOLLOW AFTER.: *Wheeling Register,* April 25, 1888
146. ... to claim victory against Mitchell.: *Boston Globe,* April 26, 1888
146. ... won the fight forty times over,": *York Herald,* May 7, 1888
146. ... and proposed three cheers.: *Boston Globe,* April 26, 1888
147. ... claimed Phillips helped to bankroll.: *Boston Herald,* May 3, 1888
147. ... without the champion's knowledge.: *Daily Picayune,* April 11, 1897
147. ... "dirty backstabber" Holske, fumed.: *Boston Globe,* April 24, 1888
147. ... is not worth answering.": *National Police Gazette,* May 19, 1888
147. ... "accuse John L. of cowardice,": *National Police Gazette,* May 19, 1888
147. ... or back bone of a fighter": *National Police Gazette,* May 19, 1888
147. ... in front of the Prince of Wales.: *Boston Globe,* May 13, 1888
147. ... bribe Baldock according to some reports: *New York Telegraph,* February 10, 1918
148. ... sparring with Lannan and Ashton.: *Boston Globe,* May 16, 1888
148. ... "I don't get a cent of the receipts.": *Boston Globe,* May 16, 1888
148. ... GONE, declared the *New York World.*: *National Police Gazette,* June 23, 1888
148. ... Ashton sparred at each performance.: *Boston Herald,* July 12, 1888
148. ... tricks he had taught the horse.: *Boston Globe,* July 13, 1888
149. ... even buy bran for its steeds.: *Evening Star,* July 30, 1888
149. ... was "perfectly sober.": *Boston Globe,* July 17, 1888
149. ... hisses from his hometown fans.: *Aberdeen Daily News,* July 29, 1888
149. ... smashing into another coach.: *Springfield Republican,* August 12, 1888
149. ... paid a five dollar fine,: *Boston Journal,* August 15, 1888
149. ... in training with Ike Weir: *Daily Inter Ocean,* August 6, 1888
149. ... ballooned his weight to 230 pounds.: *Sacramento Daily Recorder,* August 11, 1888
149. ... TWO IDIOTS, screamed one newspaper headline,: *Sacramento Daily Recorder,* August 23, 1888
149. ... before attempting the same stunt.: *Haverhill Bulletin,* August 23, 1888
149. ... as "Mrs. John L. Sullivan.": *St. Louis Republic,* September 21, 1888
150. ... and liver complaint all combined.": Sullivan and Sargent, *Life and Reminiscences,* 204
150. ... from the Mitchell fight in March: *Saginaw News,* September 28, 1888
150. ... filthy conditions of the circus.: *Boston Globe,* February 11, 1910
150. ... SULLIVAN NOT DEAD.: *New York Times,* September 20, 1888
150. ... cancelled her theatrical plans.: *St. Louis Republic,* September 21, 1888
150. ... at the risk of eternal perdition.: *Open Court,* November 15, 1888
150. ... to go back on her now.": *Grand Forks Herald,* September 22, 1888
150. ... extract along with his medicine.: *St. Louis Republic,* September 21, 1888
151. ... on crutches another six.: Sullivan and Sargent, *Life and Reminiscences,* 205
151. ... same again after the ordeal,: *Saginaw News,* September 28, 1888
151. ... fun enough," he told a reporter.: *Boston Herald,* October 15, 1888
151. ... never to drink again," he pledged.: *Boston Globe,* October 29, 1888
151. ... "splendid physical condition,": *Brooklyn Daily Eagle,* September 1, 1888
151. ... "John L. to put up or shut up.": *National Police Gazette,* September 1, 1888
152. ... leave a Harrison Avenue saloon.: *New York World,* January 24, 1889
152. ... owned by Tom Hagerty and Mike Clarke.: *National Police Gazette,* February 23, 1889
152. ... rushed him out the doors: *New York Times,* March 10, 1889

152. ... "lively drunk" in Bridgeport and New Haven.: *Boston Herald,* March 12, 1889

152. ... proprietor Frederick Willetts: *The Modern Gladiator,* 108

153. ... linked the Allegheny River with the Erie Canal.: Interview with Bill Heaney, Belfast Town Historian

153. ... in 1878, its population shrank.: Arch Merrill, *A River Ramble: Saga of the Genesee Valley* (Rochester, NY: L. Heindl & Son, 1943), 45

153. ... with Muldoon on May 11, 1889.: *Boston Herald,* May 12, 1889

154. ... curtains that dimmed the sunlight.: *St. Paul Globe,* June 2, 1889

154. ... the whole country," Sullivan muttered.: *St. Paul Globe,* June 2, 1889

154. ... once been called Podunk,: Allegany County Historical Society website, www.allegany history.org

154. ... as the champion's sparring partner.: *National Police Gazette,* June 6, 1925

155. ... wrote in his autobiography.: Sullivan and Sargent, *Life and Reminiscences,* 206

155. ... assisted with the champion's management,: *New York Times,* June 9, 1938

155. ... animosity between Sullivan and Muldoon.: *National Police Gazette,* June 6, 1925

155. ... rest" upon his arrival in Belfast.: *Boston Herald,* May 12, 1889

155. ... Black Creek, Angelica, and Caneadea.: *St. Paul Globe,* June 2, 1889

155. ... expander was mounted on the wall.: *St. Paul Globe,* June 2, 1889

155. ... stuffed with twelve pounds of hair,: *The Modern Gladiator,* 223

155. ... milking cows, and plowing fields.: *Post-Standard,* June 9, 2012

156. ... legal in the fight with Kilrain.: *National Police Gazette,* June 6, 1925

156. ... searching for tumblers of gin.: *Collier's,* September 27, 1930

157. ... two thousand fans flooded the ring: *New York World,* May 31, 1889

157. ... "roughs, toughs, and plug uglies.": *New York Herald,* May 27, 1889

157. ... for boxing and wrestling bouts.: *New York Times,* July 10, 1914

157. ... a hotel nor a road house.: *St. Paul Globe,* June 2, 1889

157. ... to the baby-buying trade.: *Investor's Business Daily,* November 2, 2000

158. ... gave any reporter in my life.": *St. Paul Globe,* June 2, 1889

158. ... Fox for the better part of a decade,: *New York Times,* June 9, 1938

158. ... and an Irish golden harp.: *New York Illustrated News,* July 27, 1889

158. ... or killed during the fight.: *National Police Gazette,* February 23, 1889

158. ... benefit for the Johnstown Flood victims.: David McCullough, *The Johnstown Flood* (New York: Simon and Schuster, 1968), 224

159. ... him leaving his training quarters.: *Aberdeen Daily News,* June 15, 1889

159. ... drew a chorus of hisses,: *New York Herald,* June 14, 1889

159. ... helped himself to the liquor.: *Oregonian,* June 17, 1889

159. ... the state of his investment.: *Daily Inter Ocean,* July 2, 1889

159. ... as proof of his stamina.: "When John L. Hid in Southern Swamp to Avoid Militia," John Lawrence Sullivan Papers, John J. Burns Library, Boston, undated

160. ... a law banning prizefighting.: *Hattiesburg American,* July 8, 1970

160. ... for the apprehension of two pugilists.: *Clarion Ledger,* July 4, 1889

160. ... Alabama, and even Nebraska: *Boston Herald,* July 9, 1989

160. ... until Muldoon discovered the ruse.: *Wheeling Register,* July 21, 1889

161. ... postpone lovemaking until after the fight.": *Wheeling Register,* July 21, 1889

161. ... was a "short, chunky man,": Donovan, *The Roosevelt That I Know,* 113

161. ... "in his book of lives,": *Boston Herald,* July 9, 1889

161. ... stand tall against the champion.: Donovan, *The Roosevelt That I Know,* 110–14

161. ... moved in Sullivan's direction.: *Wheeling Register,* July 7, 1889

161. ... bearing the fighters and spectators.: *Boston Herald,* July 8, 1889

161. ... victory vanished from his mind.: Donovan, *The Roosevelt That I Know,* 115

162. ... baseball diamond on a small hilltop.: *Hattiesburg American,* July 8, 1938

162. . . . Rich's house in an orange glow.: Van Every, *Muldoon, The Solid Man of Sport*, 150–51

162. . . . forty dollars for the ducats.: *Plain Dealer,* July 9, 1989

163. . . . the entire flock of deadbeats.: "When John L. Hid in Southern Swamp to Avoid Militia"

163. . . . swallowed up the ticket taker,: *National Police Gazette,* July 27, 1889

163. . . . breached the exterior picket fence.: *Hattiesburg American,* July 8, 1938

164. . . . in a Turkish bath rug: *National Police Gazette,* July 20, 1889

164. . . . as the crowd parted.: "When John L. Hid in Southern Swamp to Avoid Militia"

164. . . . chanting, "Sullivan! Sullivan!": Transcript of testimony of T. R. White from prize-fighting trial of John L. Sullivan, Sullivan-Kilrain Fight Collection, McCain Library and Archives, Hattiesburg, MS, undated

164. . . . excited fans exchanging bets.: *Boston Globe,* February 12, 1910

164. . . . tumultuous approval of the fans.: *The Life of John L. Sullivan,* 81

164. . . . glare of disdain upon the challenger.: *Boston Herald,* July 9, 1889

164. . . . as he stepped into the ring: *Collier's,* September 27, 1930

164. . . . spirit of ensuring "fair play,": Robert K. DeArment, *Bat Masterson: The Man and the Legend* (Norman: University of Oklahoma Press, 1979), 339

164. . . . Mitchell toted two pistols.: DeArment, *Bat Masterson,* 340

164. . . . of the sovereign state of Mississipp164.: *National Police Gazette,* July 27, 1889

164. . . . slipped him $250.: "When John L. Hid in Southern Swamp to Avoid Militia"

164. . . . combat with the rest of the crowd.: *Collier's,* September 27, 1930

165. . . . old tin pails at five cents a dip.: *Ring,* 1932

165. . . . all vouched for his honesty.: *The Modern Gladiator,* 178

166. . . . for the championship of the world.: *National Police Gazette,* July 27, 1889

166. . . . bets taken on the first fall.: *National Police Gazette,* July 27, 1889

166. . . . give you enough of that.": "When John L. Hid in Southern Swamp to Avoid Militia"

166. . . . would have pleased Muldoon.: *National Police Gazette,* November 11, 1905

167. . . . unheeded by the referee.: *Daily Picayune,* July 9, 1889

167. . . . Sullivan!" shook the Mississippi pines.: *National Police Gazette,* November 11, 1905

167. . . . stuck to the oozing grandstand.: *Hattiesburg American,* July 8, 1970

167. . . . opponent after the fourth round.: *National Police Gazette,* July 27, 1889

167. . . . and hisses from Sullivan's fans.: *Daily Picayune,* July 9, 1889

167. . . . sledgehammer right to end round six.: *Daily Picayune,* July 9, 1889

168. . . . grew more tepid by the minute: *National Police Gazette,* July 27, 1889

168. . . . hitting a bale of cotton with a stick.": *National Police Gazette,* July 27, 1889

168. . . . spectators called Jake a cur: *Boston Herald,* July 9, 1889

168. . . . stand up and be thumped.": *The Life of John L. Sullivan,* 86

168. . . . from which to watch the brawl.: *Boston Herald,* July 9, 1889

168. . . . amid the dividend reports and market updates,: *Wall Street Journal,* July 8, 1889

168. . . . press room for any news from Richburg.: *Boston Herald,* July 9, 1889

168. . . . stagger to the scratch each time.: *Daily Picayune,* July 9, 1889

169. . . . John L., gashing his left foot.: *Daily Picayune,* July 9, 1889

169. . . . sent him back out to scratch.: *Times-Democrat,* July 9, 1889

169. . . . as fans yelled, "Fight! Fight!": *Times-Democrat,* July 9, 1889

169. . . . if it's necessary," he replied.: Sullivan and Sargent, *Life and Reminiscences,* 211

169. . . . I threw it right off,": Sullivan and Sargent, *Life and Reminiscences,* 209

169. . . . and kept down the booze.: *Fight Stories,* Fall 1947

169. . . . loafer," John L. snapped back.: *Boston Herald,* July 9, 1989

169. . . . Fitzpatrick did not call a foul.: *National Police Gazette,* July 27, 1889

170. . . . to try to dull the pain.: Donovan, *The Roosevelt That I Know,* 128

170. . . . "hanging like a big tumor.": "When John L. Hid in Southern Swamp to Avoid Militia"
170. . . . pounds during the battle,: *The Modern Gladiator,* 356
171. . . . "overexcitable" or on Sullivan's take,: *New York Times,* December 23, 1937
171. . . . mother is sick. M. Sullivan.": *Boston Globe,* July 9, 1889

CHAPTER EIGHT: THE LEADING MAN

172. . . . onto his bruised and blistered body.: *Morning Herald,* July 15, 1889
172. . . . hid in wait to whisk its ten reporters: *Hattiesburg American,* July 8, 1970
172. . . . with the first news from Richburg.: *Daily Picayune,* July 9, 1889
172. . . . bumper pin to unhitch Kilrain's car: *Hattiesburg American,* July 8, 1970
172. . . . who dared to pull the pin.: *National Police Gazette,* July 27, 1889
172. . . . morphine and brandy to quell the pain.: Sullivan and Sargent, *Life and Reminiscences,* 212
172. . . . raising about $500.: *Irish Times,* July 10, 1889
173. . . . within earshot in the rear car.: Alpheus Geer, *Mike Donovan: The Making of a Man* (New York: Moffat, Yard & Co., 1918), 135
173. . . . say to a reporter after the bout.: *Irish Times,* July 10, 1889
173. . . . shake his fist at the mighty machine.: *National Police Gazette,* July 27, 1889
173. . . . bloke John L. Sullivan licked!": *New York Times,* July 7, 1945
173. . . . his right failed to connect.: *Daily Picayune,* July 9, 1889
173. . . . Your husband, Jake.": *New York Tribune,* July 9, 1889
173. . . . The coppers are after us!": *National Police Gazette,* July 27, 1889
174. . . . the train, which sped away.: Sullivan and Sargent, *Life and Reminiscences,* 213
174. . . . through the streets of New Orleans.: *Collier's,* September 27, 1930
174. . . . and a small sore on his lip.: Sullivan and Sargent, *Life and Reminiscences,* 213
174. . . . share of the excursion and gate receipts,: *Evening Star,* July 23, 1889
174. . . . they were to escape Mississippi.: Sullivan and Sargent, *Life and Reminiscences,* 214
175. . . . "the biggest sporting event of the century.": *National Police Gazette,* July 27, 1889
175. . . . and Johnston through Union Station.: *New York Herald,* July 12, 1889
175. . . . Mississippi's anti-prizefighting statute.: Sullivan and Sargent, *Life and Reminiscences,* 217
175. . . . return of all involved in the fight.: *New York Times,* July 20, 1889
175. . . . again riding the rails to Chicago.: Sullivan and Sargent, *Life and Reminiscences,* 216
175. . . . drive them to nearby Shelbyville,: *Boston Globe,* September 29, 1907
176. . . . "the lowest and most disreputable part of the city": *New York Herald,* July 18, 1889
176. . . . when he finally arrived in Chicago.: *Clarion Ledger,* July 18, 1889
176. . . . safety in the saloon's backroom.: *Worcester Daily Spy,* July 16, 1889
176. . . . poor health of his mother, appalled his friends: *New York World,* July 15, 1889
176. . . . to induce him to behave himself.": *Saginaw News,* July 17, 1889
176. . . . "a few unpleasant things occurred during our training.": *St. Louis Republic,* July 18, 1889
176. . . . stood by the veracity of the quotations.: *New York Herald,* July 13, 1890
176. . . . Sullivan left Chicago on July 17.: *New York Herald,* July 18, 1889
176. . . . outside of the family's Parnell Street home,: *New York Herald,* July 14, 1889
176. . . . inside the city's sporting resorts.: *New York Herald,* July 21, 1889
177. . . . on display inside his Brooklyn saloon.: *Boston Globe,* July 21, 1907
177. . . . $200 payout from John L.: *New York Herald,* July 13, 1890
177. . . . helpless mass of flesh and bone.": *Salt Lake Herald,* July 12, 1890
177. . . . Muldoon who won the fight.": *The Modern Gladiator,* 230

177. . . . and took him into custody.: *New York Times,* August 1, 1889
177. . . . called by the world at large a coward": Sullivan and Sargent, *Life and Reminiscences,* 217
177. . . . for a postponement of the case.: Sullivan and Sargent, *Life and Reminiscences,* 218
178. . . . governor's mansion just three blocks away.: *The Modern Gladiator,* 210
178. . . . "in a most cordial manner.": Sullivan and Sargent, *Life and Reminiscences,* 218–19
178. . . . find Sullivan guilty of prizefighting.: *Philadelphia Inquirer,* August 17, 1889
178. . . . from all right-minded men": *Independent,* August 22, 1889
178. . . . extinct as bear-baiting and dueling.": *Christian Union,* August 22, 1889
179. . . . and fined him $200.: *Repository,* December 16, 1889
179. . . . into the friendly hands of Rich,: *Collier's,* September 27, 1930
179. . . . and Donovan $100 each.: *Springfield Republican,* June 27, 1890
179. . . . Cleary for acting as his seconds.: *Plain Dealer,* July 12, 1890
179. . . . against him in return for immunity.: *Rocky Mountain News,* July 3, 1890
179. . . . $18,000 to settle the charges,: Sullivan and Sargent, *Life and Reminiscences,* 221
180. . . . for you. It is suicide.": *Wheeling Register,* June 29, 1890
180. . . . devotion to his invalid mother.: *Baltimore Sun,* August 20, 1889
180. . . . to leave at once that afternoon.: *New York Herald,* August 21, 1889
180. . . . as the sitting room's faded carpet.: *Morning Herald,* July 15, 1889
180. . . . not come, John, till too late,": *Boston Herald,* August 21, 1889
180. . . . such sickness less than a year before.: *Boston Herald,* August 22, 1889
180. . . . boarded the next train to Boston.: *Boston Globe,* August 31, 1889
180. . . . They were too late.: *Boston Herald,* August 31, 1889
181. . . . St. Patrick's Church for the funeral,: *Boston Globe,* September 3, 1889
181. . . . her burial at Mount Calvary Cemetery.: *New York Evangelist,* September 19, 1889
181. . . . three-round exhibition with Cleary.: *Boston Herald,* September 8, 1889
181. . . . Congress—should it be offered to him.: *Boston Herald,* September 8, 1889
181. . . . John L. Sullivan, Champion of the World.": *Boston Herald,* September 8, 1889
182. . . . Massachusetts congressman—Henry Cabot Lodge.: Theodore Roosevelt letter to
        Henry Cabot Lodge, August 28, 1889
182. . . . I'm going to be a gentleman.": *New York Evangelist,* September 19, 1889
182. . . . combination's opening night in Brooklyn,: *Wheeling Register,* September 22, 1889
182. . . . sparred with Cleary and Tracey.: *Boston Herald,* September 27, 1889
182. . . . never returned, and the show folded.: *Daily Inter Ocean,* July 3, 1892
182. . . . the earnings from the Kilrain fight.: *Boston Herald,* October 14, 1889
182. . . . under the left side of the jaw.: *National Police Gazette,* November 9, 1889
183. . . . actions helped to save the man's life.: *San Antonio Express,* October 15, 1905
183. . . . I was too busy having a good time.": *Denver Post,* March 31, 1902
183. . . . at the conclusion of each performance: *Wheeling Register,* May 11, 1890
183. . . . earned $300 weekly.: Sullivan and Sargent, *Life and Reminiscences,* 220
184. . . . turned away hundreds every night.: *Philadelphia Inquirer,* May 25, 1890
184. . . . in William Shakespeare's *As You Like It,*: Myler, *Gentleman Jim,* 72
184. . . . balcony audience to cover its ears.: *Boston Globe,* December 18, 1966
185. . . . "Give him an uppercut, Jawn!": *Boston Globe,* February 21, 1932
185. . . . laid Lannan flat on the stage.: *Trenton Evening Times,* August 28, 1890
185. . . . cues, and there you are,": *Weekly Irish Times,* September 9, 1890
185. . . . relished rehearsals as much as training.: *Boston Globe,* August 18, 1907
185. . . . two-year run of *Honest Hearts and Willing Hands,*: *Boston Globe,* December 18, 1966
186. . . . Sullivan had promise as an actor,: T. T. Williams, "Temptations of a Young Journalist,"
        Cosmopolitan, April 1906
186. . . . a fine bit of character acting.": *Philadelphia Inquirer,* September 14, 1890

186. . . . plant a kiss on his cold cheek.: *Boston Globe,* September 8, 1890
186. . . . JOHN L. NOW AN ORPHAN.: *Boston Globe,* September 8, 1890
186. . . . returned to the stage in New York City: *Philadelphia Inquirer,* September 14, 1890
186. . . . appeared to have finally ended.: *Plain Dealer,* November 12, 1890
187. . . . hotel window in Taunton, Massachusetts.: *San Francisco Call,* November 23, 1890
187. . . . bellboy repeatedly with his brush.: *Evansville Courier and Press,* January 10, 1891
187. . . . swipe and knocked him out.: *Evansville Courier and Press,* February 27, 1891
187. . . . and discredit upon the order.": *Cleveland Leader,* January 25, 1891
187. . . . and slur through an evening performance.: *San Francisco Chronicle,* June 1, 1891
187. . . . defeated George Robinson in 1884,: *Boston Globe,* February 17, 1910
188. . . . at the drinking ability of the champion.": *Montgomery Advertiser,* March 13, 1918
188. . . . his guest and ordered another round.: James J. Corbett, *The Roar of the Crowd: The True Tale of the Rise and Fall of a Champion* (New York: G.P. Putnam's Sons, 1925), 117–21
188. . . . I have drawn the color line.": *Montgomery Advertiser,* March 13, 1918
188. . . . from 49 in 1882 to 161 in 1892.: University of Missouri–Kansas City Law School, Lynchings: By Year and Race, http://law2.umkc.edu/faculty/projects/ftrials/shipp/lynchingyear.html
189. . . . featherweight George "Little Chocolate" Dixon,: *Boston Herald,* July 31, 1911
190. . . . because he is a colored man.": *National Police Gazette,* August 4, 1883
190. . . . freestyle stroke to the United States.: *Los Angeles Sentinel,* January 29, 1992
190. . . . with an officer aboard one of his ships.: *Los Angeles Sentinel,* June 9, 1999
190. . . . since the signing of the Emancipation Proclamation.: *San Francisco Examiner,* December 30, 1888
191. . . . should be whipped," he told one reporter in 1893.: *Boston Globe,* February 18, 1893
191. . . . he spouted to another a few months later.: *Boston Globe,* September 25, 1894
191. . . . stating that "the negro is inferior": *Boston Herald,* June 18, 1905
191. . . . negro up to the white man's class.": *Boston Globe,* December 22, 1907
191. . . . and photograph, he never voiced them.: *National Police Gazette,* June 20, 1925
191. . . . and they are too tough to lick.": William Gildea, *The Longest Fight: In the Ring with Joe Gans, Boxing's First African-American Champion* (New York: Farrar, Straus and Giroux, 2012), 60
191. . . . by swapping punches with a negro.": *Charlotte Observer,* May 14, 1905
191. . . . though I refused to fight a negro.": *Boston Globe,* February 17, 1910
192. . . . Ryan asked the champion for a match.: *Daily Picayune,* June 29, 1891
192. . . . When I train, I have to half-starve.": *Boston Globe,* February 12, 1891
192. . . . shouted, "You whipped the coon!": *Daily Picayune,* June 29, 1891
193. . . . the fight and Corbett the latter half.: *Daily Picayune,* June 29, 1891
193. . . . bring "professional etiquette" to the stage,: *San Francisco Chronicle,* June 27, 1891
193. . . . by unconsciously dropping his head.: Inglis, *Champions Off Guard,* 85–86
193. . . . "I can whip this fellow!": Corbett, *The Roar of the Crowd,* 147–50
193. . . . declared in a letter to Mike Donovan.: Inglis, *Champions Off Guard,* 86
193. . . . heaved them into San Francisco Bay.: Corbett, *The Roar of the Crowd,* 150
193. . . . and that settles it with me.": *San Francisco Chronicle,* June 27, 1891
193. . . . exhibition with Ashton drew a sparse crowd,: *New Orleans Item,* July 29, 1891
193. . . . "seemed to greatly admire our Republic.": Sullivan and Sargent, *Life and Reminiscences,* 229–30
194. . . . locked up in his stateroom to dry out.: *Cleveland Leader,* August 7, 1891
194. . . . sick a few days out from San Francisco.: Sullivan and Sargent, *Life and Reminiscences,* 230

194.... did not translate to its southern colony.: Sullivan and Sargent, *Life and Reminiscences*, 230

194.... quiet for the remainder of her stay.: *New York Times*, July 24, 1910

194.... venues, Her Majesty's Opera House.: Sullivan and Sargent, *Life and Reminiscences*, 231

194.... to his standard of histrionic importance.": *Weekly Journal Miner*, October 14, 1891

194.... particularly if it had an Irish name.": *New Orleans Item*, October 27, 1891

195.... Jackson, Slavin, or Joe Goddard.: Sullivan and Sargent, *Life and Reminiscences*, 232

195.... a high time" at Sullivan's expense.: *South Australian Register*, August 17, 1891

195.... "I'll put a head on you fellows, see?": *St. Albans Daily Messenger*, October 16, 1891

195.... barnstormed through Victoria and South Australia.: Sullivan and Sargent, *Life and Reminiscences*, 231

195.... eight-round loss to Goddard in Melbourne on October 2.: *Argus*, October 3, 1891

195.... three days later on the steamship *Alameda*.: *Australian Town and Country Journal*, October 10, 1891

195.... bums" he encountered in Australia.: *Chicago Herald*, November 13, 1891

195.... people in my life," he muttered.: *San Francisco Bulletin*, November 17, 1891

195.... or fight at a moment's notice.": *Tacoma Daily News*, January 9, 1892

196.... scheming butler, and even a duel.: *Boston Herald*, May 31, 1892

196.... the heroine's mortgaged homestead.: *Tacoma Daily News*, January 11, 1892

196.... and drew a packed house.: *Boston Globe*, December 14, 1926

196.... a small pair of dumbbells and Indian clubs,: *Morning Olympian*, June 27, 1891

CHAPTER NINE: THE FINAL ROUND

197.... stumble off the train for breakfast.: *Rocky Mountain News*, February 8, 1892

197.... coined Sullivan an "actor-pugilist,": *Saginaw News*, January 26, 1891

198.... fighting, not foot racing," he asserted.: *Boston Herald*, March 6, 1892

198.... to cover the sizable side bet.: *Boston Globe*, September 3, 1978

198.... to sign the articles of agreement.: *New York Herald*, March 16, 1892

199.... addendum—"except Mr. Mitchell.": *Once a Week*, May 10, 1892

199.... a prizefighter, he flew into a rage.: Sullivan and Sargent, *Life and Reminiscences*, 277

199.... Baltimore Orioles, and St. Louis Cardinals.: Myler, *Gentleman Jim*, 18

199.... subject themselves to a surefire whipping.: Myler, *Gentleman Jim*, 16

199.... for striking one of the brothers: Myler, *Gentleman Jim*, 10–11

200.... mauled around by a lot of drunks.": Corbett, *The Roar of the Crowd*, 172

200.... like a divinity student than a prize fighter.": *Boston Herald*, February 26, 1933

200.... animal force and a thinking brain.": *Boston Globe*, September 9, 1892

200.... to pay out one night in Milwaukee.: Myler, *Gentleman Jim*, 50

200.... John L. had been too bitter.: *Boston Globe*, September 3, 1978

201.... training a championship fighter.: *Trenton Evening Times*, May 29, 1892

201.... fellow is a haircut and a shave,": *Fight Stories*, Spring 1940

201.... his hooks, crosses, and leads.: *Boston Herald*, August 8, 1920

201.... at a local ice cream parlor.: Corbett, *The Roar of the Crowd*, 178–80

201.... weights in his trouser pockets.: Corbett, *The Roar of the Crowd*, 182–83

202.... retreat for New York's Tammany Hall bosses.: *New York Times*, July 16, 1894

202.... used as a Native American canoe portage.: *New York Times*, July 6, 1921

202.... USS *Ohio*, guarded the inn's entrance.: *New York Times*, July 6, 1921

202.... rheumatism in his knees and feet,: Donovan, *The Roosevelt That I Know*, 164

202.... to just Vichy water and soda,: *Once a Week*, June 7, 1892

202.... Bass Ale flowed freely.: *National Police Gazette*, July 4, 1925

203.... more living than me? Nobody!": *Literary Digest*, January 12, 1929

203. . . . visited Sullivan at his training ground: *New York Tribune*, August 13, 1892

203. . . . several thousand Harvard students and athletes.: Sullivan and Sargent, *Life and Reminiscences*, 283

203. . . . respiratory apparatus is his weak point vitally.": Sullivan and Sargent, *Life and Reminiscences*, 292

204. . . . beside the Bible without fear,": *Sport*, March 1950

204. . . . the future heavyweight champion "Jack" Dempsey.: Jack Dempsey, *Dempsey* (New York: Harper & Row, 1977), 7–8

204. . . . broke his training camp on August 29.: *Boston Globe*, August 29, 1892

204. . . . Maybe it won't last two rounds.": *National Police Gazette*, September 17, 1892

204. . . . sculpted by Augustus Saint-Gaudens.: Edwin G. Burrows and Mike Wallace, *Gotham: A History of New York City to 1898* (New York: Oxford University Press, 1999), 1147

205. . . . sparred three rounds with Daly.: *National Police Gazette*, September 17, 1892

205. . . . and old acquaintance Frank Moran.: *Plain Dealer*, September 2, 1892

205. . . . agility of a decade ago had decayed.: *Harper's Weekly*, December 3, 1910

205. . . . handle the special dispatches from ringside: Myler, *Gentleman Jim*, 57–58

206. . . . pandemic would reach American shores any day.: *Cincinnati Post*, September 5, 1892

206. . . . a glimpse of Sullivan inside his car.: *New York Herald*, September 3, 1892

206. . . . and then don't care a damn.": *New York Herald*, September 3, 1892

207. . . . cars on the other side of Chattanooga.: *Daily Picayune*, September 4, 1892

207. . . . fearful of being infected by malaria: *Wilkes-Barre Times*, September 3, 1892

207. . . . even his own bed aboard the train,: *Boston Globe*, September 9, 1892

207. . . . leave Charlotte early the next morning,: *State*, September 5, 1892

207. . . . and stowed away in a sleeping car,: *Plain Dealer*, September 6, 1892

207. . . . into the St. Charles Hotel the next day.: *Cincinnati Post*, September 5, 1892

207. . . . first time at the Young Men's Gymnastic Club,: *Boston Globe*, February 18, 1910

207. . . . gained nine pounds since leaving Long Island,: *Cincinnati Post*, September 5, 1892

207. . . . the morning before the battle,: *Boston Globe*, September 7, 1952

207. . . . The saloons and gambling houses: *Ring*, July 1935

208. . . . wore buttons proclaiming their allegiance.: *Cincinnati Post*, September 5, 1892

208. . . . workouts at the Southern Athletic Club.: *Fight Stories*, October 1928.

208. . . . but I don't think he'll win a round.": *Boston Globe*, February 17, 1933

208. . . . lick him without mussing my hair.": *Boston Herald*, December 15, 1929

208. . . . a swimming pool, and a gymnasium.: Melissa Haley, "Storm of Blows," *Common-Place*, January 2003

209. . . . law that still prohibited prizefights,: Dale A. Somers, *The Rise of Sports in New Orleans: 1850–1900* (Baton Rouge: Louisiana State University Press, 1972), 178

209. . . . just a block from the Mississippi River.: *Boston Herald*, August 7, 1978

209. . . . Dixon's demonstration of skill and fitness.: *Fight Stories*, Spring 1940

210. . . . of superiority," reported the *New York Herald*.: *New York Herald*, September 8, 1892

210. . . . witnessed a boxing match in New Orleans.: Haley, "Storm of Blows"

210. . . . and refreshed after a short nap,: *Daily Picayune*, September 8, 1892

210. . . . entourage, which now included McAuliffe.: *The Life of John L. Sullivan*, 93

210. . . . chewed on a quilled toothpick,: *Kate Field's Washington*, September 14, 1892

210. . . . of the cheers of his loyal people.": *Harper's Weekly*, December 3, 1910

210. . . . that was an impossible request.: *The Life of John L. Sullivan*, 93

210. . . . drifted through the downtown streets.: Haley, "Storm of Blows"

210. . . . of thirsty and hungry fight fans.: *The Life of John L. Sullivan*, 92–94

210. . . . carriage approached the Olympic Club.: *Harper's Weekly*, December 3, 1910

211. . . . doesn't jump the rope before that time.": *Kate Field's Washington*, September 14, 1892

211.... that he would not kill Corbett.: Inglis, *Champions Off Guard*, 89

211.... it will be done with one punch!".": Corbett, *The Roar of the Crowd*, 190–91

211.... Corbett's entourage trailed behind.: *Boston Globe*, September 8, 1892

211.... an unfathomable one hundred dollars.: *Boston Globe*, September 3, 1978

211.... Sixty bright bulbs: Haley, "Storm of Blows"

211.... in the arena's murky outer reaches.: *Harper's Weekly*, December 3, 1910

211.... a priest gave Corbett a blessing,: *Daily Picayune*, September 8, 1892

211–212.... whenever a prominent person arrived.: *Boston Globe*, February 19, 1910

212.... "the deadliest shot in the South.": *Boston Globe*, November 7, 1993

212.... only black men in an ocean of white faces.: *Boston Herald*, September 8, 1892

212.... soda water sold by the vendors.: *Harper's Weekly*, December 3, 1910

212.... in their hind pockets for quick nips.: *Boston Herald*, September 8, 1892

212.... to allow the heavens to peer in.: *Daily Picayune*, September 8, 1892

212.... scrambled to engage the makeshift roof.: *Boston Globe*, September 8, 1892

212.... cloudburst that delivered welcome relief: *Boston Herald*, September 8, 1892

212.... and Dixon the two previous nights.: *The Life of John L. Sullivan*, 94

212.... who had injured his ankle walking,: *The Life of John L. Sullivan*, 94

212.... tights, green socks, and black boots: *Boston Globe*, September 3, 1978

213.... from the bottom of the Mississippi River.: *Harper's Weekly*, December 3, 1910

213.... boxed Peter Burns in a preliminary match.: Haley, "Storm of Blows"

213.... the champion look him dead in the eye.: Corbett, *The Roar of the Crowd*, 194–95

213.... Delaney to "explode with laughter.": *Harper's Weekly*, December 3, 1910

214.... connecting by an eighth of an inch.: Corbett, *The Roar of the Crowd*, 197

214.... that of a fan in the row behind.: *Boston Globe*, April 1, 1904

214.... Corbett slid back to the middle of the ring: Corbett, *The Roar of the Crowd*, 197

214.... champion for the rest of the round.: *Boston Globe*, February 19, 1910

214.... and still be out of Sullivan's reach.: *Harper's Weekly*, December 3, 1910

214.... should corner him later in the bout.: Corbett, *The Roar of the Crowd*, 197

214.... to escape the charging brawler.: *Kate Field's Washington*, September 14, 1892

214.... to his opponent to land a big blow,: *Boston Globe*, February 19, 1910

215.... "Wait a while! You'll see a fight.": Corbett, *The Roar of the Crowd*, 198

215.... Corbett had yet to land a solid punch,: *Daily Picayune*, September 8, 1892

215.... like a "ballet master": *Harper's Weekly*, December 3, 1910

215.... power to the champion's face.: *Harper's Weekly*, December 3, 1910

215.... and swung their coats in the air.: Corbett, *The Roar of the Crowd*, 199

215.... he always possessed a knockout wallop.: *Boston Globe*, February 19, 1910

215.... slowness and majesty of an iceberg.": *Boston Globe*, September 19, 1892

215.... fight like a man!" Corbett only laughed.: *Boston Globe*, February 19, 1910

216.... rivulets trickling down his chest.: *Boston Globe*, September 9, 1892

216.... champion's blood slathered both fighters.: *Kate Field's Washington*, September 14, 1892

216.... and blowing to regain his lost breath.": *Boston Globe*, September 9, 1892

216.... to land that knockout punch.: *Boston Globe*, February 19, 1910

216.... even if it prolonged the bout.: Corbett, *The Roar of the Crowd*, 199

216.... to the face as the crowd roared.: *Kate Field's Washington*, September 14, 1892

216.... thought was the inevitable end.: *National Police Gazette*, September 24, 1892

216.... as the storm of blows washed over him.: *State*, February 4, 1906

216.... returned to the corner groggy,: *Boston Globe*, February 19, 1910

216.... delivered three quick punches to the stomach.: *Boston Globe*, February 19, 1910

217.... and sent John L. to the ropes.: *Harper's Weekly*, December 3, 1910

217.... He dropped in a heap.: *Kate Field's Washington*, September 14, 1892

217.... feel himself plummeting into the water.: *National Police Gazette*, September 24, 1892

217.... a torrent of water filling his ears.: *Boston Globe*, February 21, 1910

217.... "uproar like Niagara tumbling over the cliffs": Corbett, *The Roar of the Crowd*, 201

217.... sensational single episode in the history of American sport.": *Boston Globe*, February 17, 1933

217.... vowed to beat up Corbett to avenge their hero.: *Boston Globe*, September 7, 1942

217.... "They're both damned liars.": *New York Times*, February 10, 1918

218.... lost $30,000 on John L.: *New York Times*, June 12, 1912

218.... borrowed train fare just to return to New York.: Myler, *Gentleman Jim*, 65–66

218.... at the downtown Quincy House hotel.: *Boston Record American*, February 5, 1963

218.... his friend did not make the wager.: Inglis, *Champions Off Guard*, 89

218.... fighter, at least he was the champion.: *Boston Globe*, September 9, 1892

218.... cow owned by his mother, Mrs. O'Leary.: *Chicago History*, Winter 1976-1977

219.... death was buried on the fourth page.: *Boston Globe*, September 8, 1892

219.... oil painting of Sullivan hanging outside.: *Daily Picayune*, September 8, 1892

219.... printing presses, in their ink-stained hands.: *Boston Globe*, September 9, 1892

219.... do it?" McAuliffe broke the truth.: *Boston Globe*, February 19, 1910

220.... now that he was down and out.": Corbett, *The Roar of the Crowd*, 201

220.... ropes on the opposite side of the ring.: *Boston Globe*, September 9, 1892

220.... until he felt one of the posts for support.: *Harper's Weekly*, December 3, 1910

220.... with one of her own people.": *Daily Picayune*, September 8, 1892

220.... sixteen hundred people feted the new champion.: *Daily Picayune*, September 8, 1892

220.... he had brought with him from Asbury Park.: *Boston Globe*, September 9, 1892

221.... What'll become of me?": *Boston Globe*, September 9, 1892

CHAPTER TEN: "I'M STILL JOHN L. SULLIVAN—AIN'T THAT RIGHT?"

222.... ring without expecting to win.: *Boston Herald*, June 23, 1895

223.... along his triumphant journey,: *Boston Herald*, September 12, 1892

223.... military to develop through physical training.: Donald J. Mrozek, *Sport and American Mentality, 1880–1910* (Knoxville: University of Tennessee Press, 1983), 56

223.... not the same man I examined this afternoon.": *New York Times*, February 23, 1893

223.... as usual, had been tampered with.: *New York Times*, February 23, 1893

223.... I was beaten by a good man.": *Boston Herald*, September 26, 1892

224.... engaged in such mismanaged training.: *Boston Herald*, September 26, 1892

224.... "looked like mourners at a funeral.": *New York Times*, September 12, 1892

224.... reception he would receive from his subjects,: *New York Times*, September 12, 1892

224.... handshakes, encouraging words,: *New York Times*, September 12, 1892

224.... "the greatest champion yet known.": *Boston Globe*, September 12, 1892

224.... smile that had been absent for days.: *Boston Globe*, September 12, 1892

224.... Ain't I John L. Sullivan yet?": *Boston Herald*, September 12, 1892

224.... three thousand fans in attendance: *New York Times*, September 13, 1892

224.... that rained down from the galleries.: *New York Times*, September 13, 1892

224.... that had consistently greeted Sullivan.: *New York Times*, September 13, 1892

225.... well-wishers to his waiting carriage.: *Boston Herald*, February 26, 1933

225.... "romantic four-act drama.": *Boston Herald*, May 8, 1893

225.... "Three cheers for Sullivan!": *New York Times*, September 13, 1892

225.... "a solid mass of pushing, jostling humanity": *National Police Gazette*, October 8, 1892

225.... six dollars for a reserved seat, prowled for prey.: *New York Times*, September 18, 1892

225.... lingered outside just to be near history.: *National Police Gazette*, October 8, 1892

226. . . . the croquet champion of the world": *New York Times,* September 18, 1892
226. . . . with a dignity befitting his nickname.: *National Police Gazette,* October 8, 1892
226. . . . like Sullivan's mighty bass. "Louder!": *National Police Gazette,* October 8, 1892
226. . . . "gloves as big as feather pillows.": *New York Times,* September 18, 1892
226. . . . Corbett to prove his bite remained,: *Boston Globe,* September 19, 1892
226. . . . how easy they could hit each other,": *New York Times,* September 18, 1892
226. . . . taking half of the benefit's box office.: *Boston Globe,* September 19, 1892
226. . . . deeper adulation of his public.: *National Police Gazette,* October 8, 1892
227. . . . on stage after the first act.: *National Police Gazette,* October 8, 1892
227. . . . floral horseshoe and three encores.: *National Police Gazette,* October 8, 1892
227. . . . and punctuated the play with a knockout.: *Boston Globe,* May 9, 1893
227. . . . "inferior" support when they forgot their lines.: *Boston Herald,* September 20, 1892
227. . . . certainly a remarkable success.": *Boston Globe,* September 27, 1892
227–228. . . . chugging under the Berkeley Street Bridge.: *Boston Herald,* September 26, 1892
228. . . . chased behind for almost a mile.: *Boston Globe,* September 26, 1892
228. . . . from seeping into the aisles.: *Boston Globe,* October 3, 1892
228. . . . more than $2,000.: *Boston Globe,* October 3, 1892
228. . . . himself dressed as Captain Harcourt.: *National Police Gazette,* October 22, 1892
228. . . . "was so ludicrous that the audience hissed.": *Boston Herald,* October 8, 1892
228. . . . before John L. could be handcuffed.: *Boston Herald,* November 17, 1892
229. . . . his unsteady gait to "bad corns.": *Patriot,* November 17, 1892
229. . . . show-business entrepreneur at heart.: Myler, *Gentleman Jim,* 47
229. . . . hundreds of extras posing as spectators.: Myler, *Gentleman Jim,* 70–71, 83
229. . . . *Honest Hearts and Willing Hands,*" wrote one.: Myler, *Gentleman Jim,* 72
229. . . . John L. has none of the three.": *Bedford Monthly,* October 1892
229. . . . "I've got no excuses to make.": *New York Times,* September 12, 1892
229. . . . his defeat to the "rapid life": *New York Times,* February 28, 1893
229. . . . out at New Orleans," he told reporters: *New York Times,* March 1, 1893
229. . . . to knock out an ordinary man.": *New York Times,* March 1, 1893
229. . . . could have beaten me the night I fought.": *Boston Globe,* October 23, 1894
230. . . . can't take that away from me, can they?": Theodore Dreiser, *A Book About Myself* (New York: Boni and Liveright, 1922), 150
230. . . . and knocked him unconscious.: *Boston Herald,* January 10, 1894
230. . . . several times before she retaliated.: *Irish Times,* January 11, 1894
230. . . . by a bottle on his right cheek.: *Boston Herald,* June 10, 1894
230. . . . that Lizotte only had one arm.: *New York Times,* May 15, 1893
231. . . . went back in to choke the man.: *Boston Journal,* May 15, 1893
231. . . . had known that he had only one hand.": *Boston Globe,* May 16, 1893
231. . . . and a Boston justice of the peace,: *Boston Globe,* May 22, 1893
231. . . . corroborated the story,: *Boston Journal,* May 16, 1893
231. . . . he appeared on stage that night.: *New York Times,* May 17, 1893
231. . . . hand that grasped Sullivan's windpipe.": *Boston Herald,* May 20, 1893
231. . . . air where he sped away in a carriage.: *Boston Globe,* August 14, 1893
231. . . . his prized photos and scrapbooks.: *Boston Globe,* February 8, 1895
231. . . . extinguish the flames with a mat: *Plain Dealer,* April 22, 1895
231. . . . burning himself in the process.: *National Police Gazette,* May 11, 1895
232. . . . passed away hours later at City Hospital.: *Boston Journal,* April 22, 1895
232. . . . of which their owner may be proud.": *Plain Dealer,* April 22, 1895
232. . . . in a railway station in Zanesville, Ohio.: *Plain Dealer,* November 22, 1894
232. . . . dispatches say he is not even drunk.": *Omaha World Herald,* December 2, 1894
232. . . . mustache were nearly all gray.: *Boston Herald,* September 25, 1894

232. . . . developed from a small scratch.: *Boston Globe,* January 7, 1893

232. . . . training Sullivan for the Jake Kilrain title bout.: *National Police Gazette,* September 30, 1893

232. . . . and drowned in Long Island Sound.: *Boston Herald,* November 9, 1893

232. . . . Sullivan "the picture of health,": *Boston Herald,* May 19, 1894

232–233. . . . victims of the Great Roxbury Fire,: *Boston Herald,* May 20, 1894

233. . . . neighborhood he once roamed as child.: *New York Times,* May 16, 1894

233. . . . returning to their corners puffing away.: *Boston Globe,* May 22, 1894

233. . . . at his West Orange, New Jersey, laboratory.: *Boston Herald,* September 8, 1894

233. . . . actor to ever perform under contract,: Robert Niemi, *History in the Media: Film and Television* (Santa Barbara: ABC-CLIO, 2006), 190

233. . . . before retiring to the eighteen-acre farm: *Boston Herald,* September 25, 1894

233. . . . purchased near Greenfield, Massachusetts.: *Boston Globe,* October 23, 1894

233. . . . expand into breeding cows and sheep.: *Boston Globe,* October 23, 1894

233. . . . from the pen of Edmund E. Price.: *Boston Globe,* October 23, 1894

233. . . . costume to fight with Dan Dwyer,: *Philadelphia Inquirer,* October 14, 1894

234. . . . caused cast members to quit the production.: *Bay City Times–Press,* January 5, 1895

234. . . . and insisted he was "attending strictly to business.": *Florida Times–Union,* June 23, 1996

234. . . . receipts from that night's performance.: *Philadelphia Inquirer,* February 23, 1895

234. . . . Sullivan lodged in fine hotels,: *Philadelphia Inquirer,* February 23, 1895

234. . . . his two large wardrobe trunks.: *New York Times,* February 24, 1895

234. . . . had come to an inglorious close indeed.": *National Police Gazette,* March 16, 1895

234. . . . auctioned off for one hundred dollars,: *Boston Journal,* May 7, 1895

234. . . . called Sullivan a "mutton head.": *National Police Gazette,* April 6, 1895

234. . . . was the man Sullivan really wanted to face.: *Boston Globe,* June 9, 1895

235. . . . to do likewise." Corbett obeyed.: *Boston Herald,* June 28, 1895

235. . . . a punch every now and then.: *Boston Herald,* June 28, 1895

235. . . . and I am no friends of his.": *Boston Herald,* October 15, 1895

235. . . . printing bills for *The Man from Boston.*: *New York Times,* June 28, 1895

235. . . . deputy sheriff could not serve papers.: *New York Times,* June 28, 1895

235. . . . inside the saloons of the South End.: Curley, *I'd Do It Again,* 42

236. . . . only surviving blood relative.: *Irish World,* August 17, 1895

236. . . . fueled Sullivan's alcoholic binges: *Boston Herald,* September 3, 1895

236. . . . spar in a three-round exhibition: *Daily Inter Ocean,* December 11, 1895

236. . . . benefit of his badly winded fighter.: *Morning Star,* December 31, 1895

236. . . . at forty miles per hour at the time.: *Boston Globe,* January 30, 1896

236. . . . facedown in a muddy ditch,: *Illinois State Register,* January 30, 1896

236. . . . "he would clean out the train.": *Boston Globe,* January 30, 1896

237. . . . taking the stage that night.: *Boston Herald,* January 30, 1896

237. . . . by the name of Maggie Lee.": *Illinois State Register,* February 23, 1896

237. . . . during five performances a week: *Denver Post,* June 16, 1896

237. . . . and a merry one is my motto,": *Boston Journal,* March 6, 1896

237. . . . and can get some good out of it?": *Boston Globe,* May 6, 1896

237. . . . Lannan ran the Fairhaven Hotel.: William M. Bergan, *Old Nantasket* (North Quincy, MA: The Christopher Publishing House, 1969), 147

237. . . . for the theatrical and sporting crowd: *Boston Globe,* February 8, 1969

237. . . . blocks from his South End birthplace.: *Boston Globe,* August 1, 1896

237. . . . thirty-seven-year-old "grand old man": *Boston Herald,* September 1, 1896

237. . . . fold over the waistband of his trunks.": *Boston Herald,* September 1, 1896

238. . . . Sullivan could barely move.: *Boston Herald,* September 1, 1896

238. . . . common-law wife of John L. Sullivan.": *New York Times,* September 7, 1896

238. . . . money to cover the expenses.: *New York Times,* September 9, 1896

238. . . . property of Sullivan's to satisfy it.: *Boston Journal,* December 22, 1896

238. . . . fortune he had earned in the ring.: *Boston Herald,* December 23, 1896

238. . . . the creditors the following month.: *Boston Journal,* January 16, 1897

238. . . . a sensation when he was champion.: *Boston Herald,* February 19, 1897

238. . . . a public challenge to the winner.: *New York Times,* March 13, 1897

238–239. . . . who still thronged to see him.: Inglis, *Champions Off Guard,* 98

239. . . . will be represented there," he vowed.: John L. Sullivan letter to Joseph Eakins, February 8, 1897

239. . . . not been taking care of himself.": *Boston Globe,* March 18, 1897

239. . . . and theater owner Frank Dunn,: *New York Times,* August 20, 1897

239. . . . hard pounds of fighting flesh.": *Boston Globe,* March 26, 1897

239. . . . Few took Sullivan seriously,: *Boston Herald,* April 15, 1897

239. . . . Allen for the heavyweight championship.: *Boston Globe,* March 6, 1897

239. . . . right hand," reported one Boston paper.: *Boston Herald,* April 15, 1897

239. . . . defeat Corbett first before bothering him.: *Boston Herald,* April 22, 1897

240. . . . stand-ins for Corbett and Fitzsimmons.: *Boston Herald,* May 16, 1897

240. . . . Fitzsimmons crossed in Buffalo in early June,: *New York Times,* June 11, 1897

240. . . . at his White Plains, New York, health farm.: *Boston Globe,* June 26, 1897

240. . . . hadn't given up trying to fight Fitzsimmons,: *Boston Globe,* July 6, 1897

240. . . . at England's Henley Royal Regatta,: *Boston Globe,* August 4, 1897

241. . . . be "independent and honest.": *Boston Journal,* December 4, 1897

241. . . . declared one Boston newspaper.: *Boston Journal,* August 20, 1897

241. . . . in the fall of 1897 approaching: *Boston Journal,* August 20, 1897

241. . . . called it "a pretty cheap joke": *Boston Herald,* August 23, 1897

241. . . . used "as a theatrical billboard.": *Boston Herald,* September 5, 1897

241. . . . chose to stay out of the race.: *New York Times,* December 5, 1897

241. . . . clad in a "natty outing costume": *Boston Herald,* September 14, 1897

241. . . . *A Trip Across the Ocean,* that opened the show.: *Boston Herald,* April 3, 1898

241. . . . with his trainer, Ed B. White,: *Boston Herald,* April 5, 1898

241. . . . much of a stretch for the old gladiator.: *Boston Herald,* April 3, 1898

241. . . . Dunn protested their room charge.: *Boston Herald,* September 5, 1897

241. . . . before the melee was broken up.: *Boston Globe,* September 8, 1897

241. . . . $1,000 civil suit brought by the driver.: *Boston Herald,* September 9, 1897

242. . . . "administer physical chastisement.": *Boston Globe,* October 4, 1897

242. . . . the easy decision and lit into Dunn.: *Boston Globe,* October 4, 1897

242. . . . debts owed to his now-former manager.: *Boston Journal,* October 15, 1897

242. . . . a box for them all at his show.": *Boston Journal,* June 8, 1898

242. . . . fights that took place in 1812.": *Boston Journal,* December 4, 1897

243. . . . hearty cheers that greeted Sullivan.: *New York Times,* March 26, 1898

243. . . . she could lick a postage stamp.": *New York Times,* March 26, 1898

243. . . . owed his manager, William H. Sherwood.: John L. Sullivan agreement with William H. Sherwood, January 7, 1898

243. . . . unpaid wages from various theatrical: *Boston Journal,* June 8, 1898

243. . . . performances.: *Boston Globe,* January 16, 1898

243. . . . bottle and good cigar with me.": John L. Sullivan letter to Frank McElroy, November 26, 1899

243. . . . courtroom that he was "broke.": *Boston Herald,* December 21, 1899

CHAPTER ELEVEN: UNDILUTED SULLIVAN

244. . . . prohibited hours, including on Sundays.: *New York Times*, May 18, 1900

244. . . . municipalities in the ensuing years.: *Boston Globe*, October 7, 1900

244. . . . from a stray broken wire.": *Boston Globe*, December 16, 1899

244. . . . reigning heavyweight champion James Jeffries,: *Boston Globe*, August 30, 1900

245. . . . between Thirty-Fifth and Thirty-Sixth Streets.: *New York Times*, July 27, 1899

245. . . . a small garden with a portable canopy.: *National Police Gazette*, August 26, 1899

245. . . . couple blocks south on Sixth Avenue,: *New York Times*, May 18, 1900

245. . . . five cents' worth of lard in a paper sack.": *Boston Globe*, March 30, 1900

245. . . . street fight a few weeks before.: *Boston Globe*, October 12, 1899

245. . . . Sullivan's name lit up the Great White Way,: *New York Times*, May 16, 1900

246. . . . and Thomas Allen the chief owner.: *Boston Globe*, May 23, 1900

246. . . . Jefferson Market Courthouse jail for assault,: *Boston Journal*, June 29, 1900

246. . . . Allen refused to give him the belt,: *New York Times*, July 21, 1900

246. . . . tied up in litigation for months.: *New York Times*, December 21, 1900

246. . . . on Forty-Second Street near Sixth Avenue.: *Boston Globe*, August 12, 1900

246. . . . It took 120 stitches,: *National Police Gazette*, December 29, 1900

246. . . . flat on his back for five weeks: *Cato Citizen*, January 26, 1901

246. . . . don't want any more ever again.": *Boston Globe*, December 2, 1900

246. . . . "off the water wagon with a splash,": *National Police Gazette*, December 29, 1900

246. . . . ever comes around to my place.": Herbert Asbury, *Carry Nation* (New York: A.A. Knopf, 1929), 242

246. . . . although it had recently closed.: *Boston Globe*, August 29, 1901

247. . . . shutter in John L.'s upstairs room slowly open.: *New York Times*, August 29, 1901

247. . . . he couldn't master the soft sell.: *Boston Globe*, February 26, 1901

247. . . . named Little Gem won by a nose.: *National Police Gazette*, October 5, 1901

247. . . . if he attempted to throw a single punch.: *Boston Globe*, December 6, 1901

247. . . . Sullivan was too vigorous with his whip.: *Boston Globe*, January 12, 1930

248. . . . all the ice to make highballs,: *Boston Globe*, August 23, 1908

248. . . . his own gin fizzes and Manhattans.: *Boston Globe*, January 26, 1902

248. . . . with instructions to buy a new one.: *Boston Globe*, January 31, 1902

248. . . . 1902, and the company disbanded.: *New York Times*, February 14, 1902

248. . . . sketch teams, comedians, dancers, jugglers,: *Boston Globe*, December 9, 1902

248. . . . black-face comedian Lew Hawkins: *Boston Globe*, December 9, 1902

248. . . . and Clara Adams,: *Boston Herald*, December 7, 1902

248. . . . delivering soliloquies elicited snickers: *Boston Herald*, December 7, 1902

248. . . . got the better of the tussle,: *Boston Globe*, December 9, 1902

248. . . . in the United States for a single monologue act.: *Boston Herald*, November 2, 1902

249. . . . and never let go as, in rapid-fire sentences,: *National Police Gazette*, May 27, 1905

249. . . . and told disjointed Irish stories.: *Boston Herald*, January 10, 1909

249. . . . performance of "undiluted Sullivan": *Boston Globe*, December 9, 1902

249. . . . four-stanza ode, "A Toast to Woman.": *National Police Gazette*, May 27, 1905

249. . . . his residence as the Vanderbilt Hotel: *New York Times*, November 29, 1902

249. . . . by the United States District Court in New York: *New York Times*, December 5, 1902

249. . . . of only sixty dollars in apparel.: *New York Times*, November 29, 1902

249. . . . from bankruptcy in February,: *New York Times*, February 10, 1903

249. . . . $250 for penning Sullivan's monologue.: *Boston Herald*, December 9, 1902

249. . . . of sight on a hot day at Coney Island,": *New York World*, July 1, 1903

249. . . . second-hand jewelry dealer on the Bowery.: *Boston Globe*, November 25, 1903

249 (fn). . . . in a safety deposit box,: *Boston Globe*, May 7, 1925

249 (fn).... United States Mint in Philadelphia in 1926.: *Boston Globe,* April 4, 1926
    250.... yours truly, John L. Sullivan": Malcolm Wallace Bingay, *Of Me I Sing* (Indianapolis: Bobbs-Merrill Co., 1949), 80
    250.... drunker than a fiddler's bitch.": Bingay, *Of Me I Sing,* 81
    250.... and heard scuffling and cursing.: Bingay, *Of Me I Sing,* 81
    250.... he was thoroughly inebriated.: *Detroit Free Press,* December 17, 1902
    250.... happenings in local vaudeville history,": *Detroit Free Press,* December 17, 1902
    250.... picked up John L. and carried him out.: *Denver Post,* December 23, 1902
    250.... had whipped Sullivan into submission,: *New York Times,* February 5, 1933
    250.... ended up with a raise and promotion.: Bingay, *Of Me I Sing,* 80–82
    250.... along with a kettle of coffee.: *Denver Post,* December 23, 1902
    250.... the spree guaranteed sold-out audiences.: *Denver Post,* December 23, 1902
    250.... fellows do," and asked for forgiveness.: *Detroit Free Press,* December 19, 1902
    251.... 1904, after four months on the road,: *Boston Herald,* April 10, 1904
    251.... germs poisoned the optic nerves.": *National Police Gazette,* April 9, 1904
    251.... at his sister's home in Roxbury: *Boston Globe,* March 21, 1904
    251.... included old foe Charley Mitchell: *Boston Herald,* April 10, 1904
    251.... seemed to separate the gladiators,: *Boston Globe,* April 1, 1904
    251.... made him appear even more elderly.: *Boston Herald,* April 10, 1904
    251.... as eating and drinking to me,": *Boston Globe,* April 1, 1904
    251.... "Tell them that I'm not dead yet,": *Boston Globe,* April 20, 1904
    251.... John L. is counted out for good.'": *Boston Globe,* April 20, 1904
    251.... for a benefit fund for Sullivan.: *Boston Globe,* April 2, 1904
    252.... trickling from beneath his goggles.: *Boston Globe,* April 29, 1904
    252.... Huntington Avenue Grounds to Sullivan's benefit fund.: *New York Times,* May 3, 1904
    252.... landed in the umpire's bare hands.: *Boston Herald,* May 3, 1904
    252.... Dudley Street elevated railway terminal.: *Boston Herald,* August 11, 1904
    252.... for drunkenness and ten dollars for profanity.: *Boston Herald,* August 12, 1904
    252.... contacted Sullivan with an enticing proposition: *Boston Herald,* September 7, 1904
    252.... drinking it is concerned, at any rate.": *Boston Herald,* September 7, 1904
    252.... with that fellow around," he grumbled.: *Boston Globe,* September 12, 1904
    253.... being crushed by his admirers.: *Massachusetts Ploughman and New England Journal of Agriculture,* September 17, 1904
    253.... you want?" awaited slack-jawed gawkers.: *Denver Post,* October 16, 1904
    253.... temperance lecture in East St. Louis.: *Denver Post,* October 17, 1904
    253.... he couldn't be found for days.: *St. Louis Republic,* October 13, 1904
    253.... for the railroad ticket back to St. Louis.: *Salt Lake Telegram,* February 7, 1905
    253.... after another drunken spree.: *Grand Rapids Press,* February 9, 1905
    253.... knockdown I ever got," he whispered hoarsely.: *Boston Journal,* February 8, 1905
    253.... headlines that Sullivan was dying.: *Plain Dealer,* February 8, 1905
    253.... ready to "wallop that dude," he said.: *St. Louis Republic,* February 11, 1905
    253.... old age, or else he was drunk.": *Salt Lake Telegram,* February 14, 1905
    254.... I wish the poor old fellow.": *St. Louis Republic,* February 11, 1905
    254.... made it just that more laughable.: *St. Louis Republic,* February 11, 1905
    254.... unfurled his legendary scowl.: *National Police Gazette,* October 7, 1905
    254.... Sullivan's ghastly transformation.: *St. Louis Republic,* September 11, 1904

Chapter Twelve: The Fight of His Life

    255.... Sullivan scrambled for a replacement.: *National Police Gazette,* March 18, 1905
    255.... just hours before the fight: *Grand Rapids Herald,* March 2, 1905

255.... looked like a mismatch.: *National Police Gazette,* March 18, 1905
255.... popped McCormick in the face: *Boston Globe,* March 2, 1905
255.... John L. had the better of it at round's end.: *National Police Gazette,* March 18, 1905
255.... to his corner bruised and concerned.: *Boston Globe,* March 2, 1905
255.... left and a right to the body.: *Boston Globe,* March 2, 1905
256.... dropped McCormick cold to the floor.: *National Police Gazette,* March 18, 1905
256.... Unconscious for ten minutes,: *Grand Rapids Herald,* March 2, 1905
256.... and congratulate the old champion.: *National Police Gazette,* March 18, 1905
256.... "top-notchers" for eight or ten rounds.: *Boston Globe,* March 2, 1905
256.... pages of the *Grand Rapids Herald,*: *Grand Rapids Herald,* March 2, 1905
256.... a big spread on the bout,: *National Police Gazette,* March 18, 1905
256.... knockout made front-page news.: *Boston Globe,* March 2, 1905
256.... who still brawled in their forties.: *Boston Globe,* March 3, 1905
256.... caption read "the real fight.": *Boston Journal,* March 3, 1905
256.... lick any son-of-a-bitch in America.: *Plain Dealer,* October 6, 1912
256.... didn't know than any other American,": *Boston Globe,* August 8, 1915
257.... he ordered either a glass of ale: *New York Sun,* May 28, 1910
257.... or a bottle of champagne.: *Literary Digest,* February 23, 1918
257.... ring challenge, felt depressed.: *New York Tribune,* February 3, 1918
257.... to never take another drink.: *Plain Dealer,* October 6, 1912
257.... to be a good fellow," he said.: *Plain Dealer,* October 6, 1912
257.... puzzled even his closest friends.: *Boston Globe,* August 8, 1918
257.... never experienced the feeling again.": *Plain Dealer,* October 6, 1912
258.... bare-knuckle London Prize Ring Rules.: *Boston Globe,* December 27, 1908
258.... Tacoma, Washington, in September 1905.: *National Police Gazette,* June 3, 1905
258.... sprints between midnight and sunrise.: *Port Townsend Daily Leader,* June 7, 1905
258.... ploy to sell theater tickets.: *Port Townsend Daily Leader,* May 5, 1905
258.... since his ring career began.": *Port Townsend Daily Leader,* June 6, 1905
258.... and there wouldn't be half the damage done.": *Boston Globe,* July 14, 1907
258.... if they hung out over here.": *Boston Globe,* June 14, 1908
258.... Corbett—"a ladylike fighter": *Boston Globe,* June 21, 1908
259.... intramural lightweight championship.: John J. Miller, *The Big Scrum: How Teddy Roosevelt Saved Football* (New York: HarperCollins, 2011), 53–54
259.... I don't care how short it is.": Edmund Morris, *The Rise of Theodore Roosevelt* (New York: Coward, McCann & Geoghegan, 1979), 108–9
259.... during the Spanish-American War.: Theresa Runstedtler, *Jack Johnson, Rebel Sojourner: Boxing in the Shadow of the Global Color Line* (Berkeley: University of California Press, 2012), 33
259.... nearly blind in his left eye.: *New York Times,* October 22, 1917
259.... a frequent dinnertime topic with guests,: *Boston Herald,* March 5, 1924
259.... fighter as ever stepped in the ring,": Theodore Roosevelt letter to John L. Sullivan, August 26, 1915
259.... family business rather than fisticuffs.: *Evening Star,* May 10, 1907
259.... skinned a block," John L. quipped.: *New York Times,* May 9, 1907
260.... put both in your pocket.": Theodore Roosevelt, *Theodore Roosevelt, an Autobiography* (New York: Charles Scribner's Sons, 1922), 44
260.... leave of absence by three days.: *New York Times,* May 17, 1907
260.... low. He took to music!": Roosevelt, *Theodore Roosevelt,* 44
260.... his full term of four years.: *New York Times,* May 17, 1907
260.... discharged serviceman to active duty.: *Evening Star,* May 17, 1907
260.... carrying with him on safari to Africa: Theodore Roosevelt letter to John L. Sullivan, May 2, 1913

260. . . . jump," Roosevelt assured John L.: Theodore Roosevelt letter to John L. Sullivan, May 2, 1913

261. . . . part of *A Trip Across the Ocean*.: *Syracuse Herald*, July 20, 1923

261. . . . the boxing news of the day: *Boston Journal*, May 23, 1908

261. . . . warning of the evils of alcohol.: *National Police Gazette*, May 27, 1905

261. . . . Kilrain in a three-round exhibition.: Eric L. Flom, *Silent Film Stars on the Stages of Seattle: A History of Performances by Hollywood Notables* (Jefferson, NC: McFarland & Co., 2009), 163

261. . . . circuit as a sparring partner.: *Boston Herald*, February 4, 1908

261. . . . trading blows with gloves.: *Salt Lake Telegram*, August 19, 1907

261. . . . been seen in Seattle for years.": Flom, *Silent Film Stars*, 163

261. . . . Kilrain filled theaters from pit to dome.: *Boston Journal*, May 23, 1908

261. . . . to attend "strictly to business.": John L. Sullivan letter to unknown recipient, 1905

261. . . . in 163 consecutive weeks.: *Boston Journal*, May 23, 1908

261. . . . lecturer, and temperance talker.": *Boston Globe*, July 12, 1908

261. . . . grown to $40,000.: *Boston Journal*, March 16, 1907

261–262. . . . during his bar-prowling days,: Rev. R. E. Lyons letter to John L. Sullivan, November 14, 1907

262. . . . to listen to their anecdotes.: *Boston Globe*, August 8, 1908

262. . . . this country than George Washington,": *National Police Gazette*, October 7, 1905

262. . . . Sullivan than Darwin or Tolstoi.": Ernest Thompson Seton, *Boy Scouts of America: A Handbook of Woodcraft, Scouting, and Life-Craft* (New York: Doubleday, Page & Co., 1910), 4

262. . . . Hot Springs, Arkansas, for a respite.": *Boston Journal*, November 17, 1908

262. . . . best to fulfill that assessment.: *Boston Globe*, February 15, 1910

262. . . . over three hundred pounds.: *Boston Globe*, June 16, 1907

262. . . . stimulate blood flow to his scalp.: *Boston Globe*, February 15, 1910

263. . . . recalled Annie Livingston instead.: *Boston Globe*, July 13, 1908

263. . . . she fell in love with John L.: *Boston Globe*, July 12, 1908

263. . . . for an uncontested divorce: *Boston Globe*, December 13, 1908

263. . . . more and more like Bismarck.": *Boston Globe*, July 12, 1908

263. . . . the previous two and a half years.: *Grand Forks Herald*, December 11, 1908

263. . . . her affections to the clergyman.": *Illinois State Register*, December 11, 1908

263. . . . and shunned domestic responsibilities.": *Illinois State Register*, December 11, 1908

263. . . . a time to draw the line.": *Grand Forks Herald*, December 11, 1908

264. . . . "It's all a rank outrage.": *Boston Globe*, December 13, 1908

264. . . . watch "Honey Fitz" take his oath.: *Boston Herald*, February 8, 1910

264. . . . among the political dignitaries.: *Boston Globe*, February 8, 1910

264. . . . around that of Fitzgerald,: *Boston Globe*, February 8, 1910

264. . . . on the front page of the *Boston Globe*.: *Boston Globe*, February 8, 1910

265. . . . typecast Kate in that role,: *Evening News*, May 26, 1916

265. . . . because of his methods of life": *Boston Herald*, February 8, 1910

265. . . . blindness at his sister's house in 1904.: *Poughkeepsie Journal*, February 8, 1910

265. . . . the gray shade of her hair.: *Boston Globe*, February 8, 1910

265. . . . closest acquaintances, knew of his plans.: *Boston Globe*, February 8, 1910

265. . . . to trouble themselves by sending me any presents,": *Irish Independent*, February 16, 1910

265. . . . divorce proceedings in Cook County.: *Boston Journal*, February 9, 1910

265. . . . and turned "mollycoddle.": *Boston Globe*, February 9, 1910

266. . . . as with the wedding itself.: *Boston Globe*, February 8, 1910

266. . . . affectionate glance at his new bride.: *Boston Herald*, February 8, 1910

266. . . . *Ivernia* sailed out of Boston Harbor.: *Boston Globe*, February 9, 1910

266. . . . Queenstown, Ireland, on February 16, 1910,: UK Incoming Passenger Lists, 1878–1960
266. . . . or Abbeydorney," he confessed.: *Kerry Weekly Reporter & Commercial Advertiser*, February 26, 1910
266. . . . for themselves in the civilized world,: *Kerry Sentinel*, February 23, 1910
266. . . . by his first cousin, Eugene.: Kathleen Barrett e-mail, January 3, 2013
267. . . . at the Prince of Wales Hotel: *Westmeath Independent*, February 26, 1910
267. . . . Irish origin and local connection.: *Irish-American Weekly*, March 12, 1910
267. . . . public house to shake Sullivan's hand.: Interview with James Galvin of Athlone provided by Gearoid O'Brien, Westmeath County Library Service, undated
267. . . . before leaving for Dublin,: *Westmeath Independent*, February 26, 1910
267. . . . Twice nightly: *Irish Independent*, February 24, 1910
267. . . . since then," noted the *Irish Independent*.: *Irish Independent*, March 1, 1910
267. . . . glimpse a passing John L. in Glasgow.: *Glasgow Herald*, June 24, 2000
267. . . . various theaters around London.: *New York Times*, May 1, 1910
267. . . . Sullivan was performing in Manchester.: *New York Sun*, May 28, 1910
268. . . . whipped individually and collectively?": *Detroit Free Press*, January 1, 1909
268. . . . $75,000 to make the match.: *Boston Globe*, January 21, 1909
268. . . . white man is king of them all.": Nevada Historical Society, Docent Council, *Early Reno* (Charleston, SC: Arcadia Publishing, 2011), 120
268. . . . to get into fighting form.: *Kerry Weekly Reporter & Commercial Advertiser*, February 26, 1910
268. . . . such a man as Johnson before him.": *Irish Independent*, February 27, 1910
268. . . . a n----- beat a white man.": *Westmeath Independent*, February 26, 1910
268. . . . win," he told *Times* readers.: *New York Times*, April 17, 1910
268. . . . condition that he'd "whip": *Boston Globe*, May 28, 1910
268. . . . and bite his ears off.": *Omaha Daily Bee*, June 3, 1910
269. . . . thoughts into readable prose.: *New York Times*, April 17, 1910
269 (fn). . . . for yours truly, John L.": *New York Times*, June 15, 1910
269. . . . majesty of the Canadian Rockies.: *New York Times*, June 15, 1910
269. . . . Saskatchewan," "Ashland, Oregon.": *New York Times*, June 20, 1910
269. . . . the title bout from his state.: *New York Times*, June 15, 1910
270. . . . the brutality of prizefighting.: *New York Times*, June 23, 1910
270. . . . "husky piece of humanity.": *Boston Herald*, June 22, 1910
270. . . . colored race," wrote Booker T. Washington.: Geoffrey C. Ward, *Unforgivable Blackness: The Rise and Fall of Jack Johnson* (New York, A.A. Knopf, 2004), 308
270. . . . But I always refused.": *New York Times*, May 1, 1910
270. . . . the workouts he required.: *Boston Globe*, May 28, 1910
270. . . . receive a hostile welcome,: *Boston Globe*, June 24, 1910
270. . . . rat at a suffragette meeting,": *Boston Globe*, June 24, 1910
272. . . . somebody called him on it.": *Boston Globe*, June 24, 1910
272. . . . for the second time in his life.: *Boston Globe*, June 24, 1910
272. . . . Rickard tried to defuse the story,: *New York Times*, June 25, 1910
272. . . . photographers and film crews.: *New York Times*, June 26, 1910
273. . . . specially constructed outdoor arena.: *New York Times*, July 5, 1910
273. . . . I just feel it, and that's all.": *New York Times*, July 4, 1910
273. . . . Jack McAuliffe, and Sam Langford.: *New York Times*, July 5, 1910
273. . . . could have six years ago.": *New York Times*, July 5, 1910
273. . . . ain't now, though," Johnson said.: *Ebony*, February 2005
274. . . . emanating from the twenty thousand.: *Boston Herald*, July 5, 1910
274. . . . said they never come back.": *New York Times*, July 5, 1910
274. . . . hundreds, most of them African-American.: Ward, *Unforgivable Blackness*, 217

CHAPTER THIRTEEN: FROM GLORY TO GUTTER TO GOD

275. . . . community of fifty-five hundred people: Porter Sargent, *A Handbook of New England: An Annual Publication* (Boston: Porter E. Sargent, 1916), 5050

275. . . . twenty miles south of Boston.: *Boston Herald,* July 31, 1911

275. . . . acres of woods and meadows: *New York Times,* July 17, 1911

275. . . . known as the "Thicket.": *Boston Herald,* July 17, 1911

275. . . . with two private islands.: *Boston Globe,* August 13, 1911

275. . . . south of the bright red farmhouse: *Boston Journal,* July 23, 1911

275. . . . dating back to the War of 1812.: Martha G. Campbell, John Galluzzo, and Donald Cann, *Remembering Old Abington: The Collected Writings of Martha Campbell* (Charleston, SC: History Press, 2008), 87

275. . . . Boston in a matter of weeks.: *Trenton Evening Times,* July 10, 1912

276. . . . Kate tended to flower beds.: *Boston Globe,* August 8, 1918

276. . . . large trees shading the farmhouse.: *Boston Globe,* April 15, 1915

276. . . . be found in all New England.": *Boston Globe,* August 13, 1911

276. . . . country roads of Plymouth County.: *Boston Journal,* October 24, 1911

276. . . . and visit the post office.: *Boston Globe,* February 19, 1960

276. . . . a friendly wave in return.: *Boston Globe,* August 13, 1911

276. . . . prayer book in his vest pocket.: *Boston Globe,* April 20, 1913

276. . . . until I die," he pledged.: *San Diego Union,* September 14, 1913

276. . . . happiest years of John's life.: *Boston Globe,* April 20, 1918

276. . . . where his mother was born.: *Boston Globe,* August 13, 1911

276. . . . make the heart of an Irishman glad.": *Augusta Chronicle,* November 10, 1912

276. . . . his gripping tales of adventure.: *Boston Globe,* August 13, 1911

276. . . . scattered on his trips into town: *Boston Herald,* February 3, 1918

277. . . . volunteering as a visiting nurse,: *Boston Globe,* May 26, 1916

277. . . . a pelican devouring a fish.: *New York Tribune,* February 3, 1918

277. . . . of the United States Fat Men's Club.: *New York Times,* January 1, 1912

277. . . . "Farmer John": *Boston Journal,* January 5, 1912

277. . . . horses, turkeys, and milk cows.: *Boston Journal,* July 12, 1913

277. . . . Irish setters, and bull terriers.: John L. Sullivan letter to unknown recipient, May 23, 1913

277. . . . him along," the former champion said.: *Rockland Independent,* February 8, 1918

277. . . . nicknamed "Young John L.".: *Boston Globe,* February 24, 1918

277. . . . without kids?" John L. asked a reporter.: *Boston Globe,* August 8, 1915

277. . . . theatrical tours of the country,: *Boston Globe,* August 13, 1911

277. . . . to "pick up a little sugar.": *Boston Globe,* January 29, 1913

278. . . . my courage has forsook me.": John L. Sullivan letter to James Callahan, February 10, 1916

278. . . . John Barleycorn," he told a magazine reporter.: *Outlook,* October 27, 1915

278. . . . consumed by self-aggrandizement.: *Plain Dealer,* October 6, 1912

278. . . . won't need any prohibition laws.": *New York Times,* August 2, 1915

278. . . . they will manufacture it," he said.: John L. Sullivan letter to George A. Rosett, June 24, 1915

278. . . . given a spot on the program.: *Boston Globe,* July 10, 1915

278. . . . business manager, D'Arcy O'Connor: *Fourth Estate,* February 23, 1918

279. . . . for temperance, John L. Sullivan.": *Boston Globe,* July 7, 1915

279. . . . Let us call it quits.": *New York Times,* July 10, 1915

279. . . . reflected the arc of his life.: *Fourth Estate,* February 23, 1918

279. . . . "From Glory to Gutter to God.": *New York Times,* August 2, 1915

279. . . . the scheduled ten-round bout,: *New York Tribune,* February 3, 1918

280. . . . ever sobbed in a ring," Humphreys said.: *Collier's,* July 21, 1928

SOURCES

280. . . . the happiest moment of his life.: *New York Times*, February 3, 1918
280. . . . light forcing the eye to Sullivan.: *New York Times*, January 7, 1945
280. . . . family plot at Mount Calvary Cemetery.: *Evening News*, May 26, 1916
280. . . . to Kate's grave every other week,: *Boston Globe*, February 19, 1960
280. . . . at the same time every night.: *Brockton Enterprise*, January 31, 1988
280. . . . occasional bouts of rheumatism.: *Boston Globe*, August 8, 1915
280. . . . electric massage over his heart.: *New York Tribune*, February 4, 1918
280. . . . with him and William Kelly.: *Boston Herald*, February 3, 1918
281. . . . "wealthy squire," Sullivan was far from it.: *New York Times*, February 3, 1918
281. . . . little interest in the venture.: "John L. Sullivan Motion Picture Co.," Clarence W. Rowley Papers Relating to Buffalo Bill and John L. Sullivan, Yale Collection of Western Americana, Beinecke Rare Book and Manuscript Library, New Haven, CT, undated
281. . . . is not an American at all.": *Boston Journal*, October 13, 1915
282. . . . hero of San Juan Hill led him.: *Boston Globe*, April 22, 1917
282. . . . America the Kaiser is afraid of,": *New York Times*, May 12, 1917
282. . . . fight of democracy," he told the crowd.: *Boston Globe*, May 15, 1917
282. . . . men under Roosevelt's direction.: *Boston Globe*, May 15, 1917
282. . . . crop of potatoes at Donelee-Ross Farm.: *Rockland Independent*, February 8, 1918
282. . . . baseball game at Fenway Park,: *Boston Globe*, August 14, 1917
283. . . . against a pantheon of baseball legends.: *Boston Globe*, September 28, 1917
283. . . . with ambulances," Sullivan once wrote.: *Boston Globe*, October 4, 1908
283. . . . voters returned him to City Hall.: Curley, *I'd Do It Again*, 139
283. . . . just been at rally or a massacre.: Curley, *I'd Do It Again*, 139
284. . . . took the loss harder than he did,: *Boston Globe*, May 22, 1957
284. . . . manly way than has John L. Sullivan,": *Boston Herald*, December 6, 1917
284. . . . A to Z, from soda to hock.": *Boston Globe*, February 3, 1918
284. . . . embargoes only sharpened the bite.: *Boston Globe*, February 2, 1918
284. . . . toes without bending his knees.: *Boston Herald*, February 3, 1918
284. . . . before bothering about a will.": *Boston Globe*, February 9, 1918
284. . . . plans to meet friends in Boston.: *Boston Globe*, February 3, 1918
285. . . . ten-minute address in the center ring.: *The Fourth Estate*, February 23, 1918
285. . . . it was too late. At 11:45 a.m.,: John L. Sullivan death certificate
285. . . . and neighbor George Harris at his bedside.: *Boston Herald*, February 3, 1918; *Boston Globe*, February 3, 1918
285. . . . "came as a bolt from a clear sky.": *Boston Herald*, February 3, 1918
285. . . . "fatty degeneration of heart": John L. Sullivan death certificate
285. . . . than to suffer with a lingering illness.": *New York Times*, March 31, 1893
285. . . . to room whining for the "Big Fellow.": *Boston Herald*, February 3, 1918
286. . . . undertaker Timothy J. Mahoney.: *Boston Globe*, February 7, 1918
286. . . . brought to his sister's Roxbury house,: *Boston Globe*, February 4, 1918
286. . . . superstar, but as their "pal.": *New York Sun*, February 4, 1918
286. . . . tales of princes and presidents,: *Boston Globe*, February 6, 1918
286. . . . early morning until well after midnight.: *Boston Herald*, February 6, 1918
286. . . . nameplate with his name engraved.: *Boston Herald*, February 5, 1918
286. . . . looked "natural in death.": *Boston Globe*, February 4, 1918
287. . . . a constant vigil at her brother's side: *Literary Digest*, May 19, 1928
287. . . . roses, and floral horseshoes.: *New York Sun*, February 6, 1918
287. . . . silent face," reported one observer.: *New York World*, February 7, 1918
287. . . . battle under the Mississippi sun.: *Boston Herald*, February 6, 1918
287. . . . couldn't make it to Boston.: *Boston Globe*, February 5, 1918
287. . . . and I mourn his death.": *Boston Herald*, February 5, 1918

287. . . . from arriving from upstate New York.: *Boston Globe,* February 6, 1918

287. . . . passing was a "great blow,": *Boston Globe,* February 3, 1918

287. . . . New York that he couldn't break.: *Boston Herald,* February 7, 1918

287. . . . only surviving relative, Annie.: *Springfield Republican,* February 8, 1918

287. . . . to his personal friends years ago,: *New York World,* February 8, 1918

287. . . . grass caught in the spikes.: *Literary Digest,* May 19, 1928

287. . . . savings account, a Liberty bond,: *New York World,* February 8, 1918

287. . . . for $3,500: *Boston Globe,* April 30, 1919

287. . . . totaled $3,624.71.: *Watertown Daily Times,* July 5, 1919

288. . . . stores, office buildings, and factories.: *Boston Globe,* February 6, 1918

288. . . . at St. Paul's Catholic Church.: *New York World,* February 7, 1918

288. . . . to sprinkle for packs of children.: *Philadelphia Inquirer,* February 7, 1918

288. . . . the hearse to the front door.: *Boston Globe,* February 7, 1918

288. . . . Curley, Rowley, and Billy Hogarty: Curley, *I'd Do It Again,* 42

288. . . . casket, was among the ushers.: *New York Sun,* February 6, 1918

288. . . . wish him "good luck.": *New York World,* February 7, 1918

288. . . . of Abington's St. Bridget's Church,: *Boston Herald,* February 7, 1918

288. . . . celebrated mass.: *Illinois State Journal,* February 7, 1918

289. . . . citizens of the commonwealth.: *Philadelphia Inquirer,* February 7, 1918

289. . . . the mourners trudged behind.: *Illinois State Journal,* February 7, 1918

289. . . . red trucks draped in black crape,: *Literary Digest,* May 19, 1928

289. . . . ice proved too much for most.: *Philadelphia Inquirer,* February 7, 1918

289. . . . hats between their frozen fingers.: *Boston Herald,* February 7, 1918

289. . . . his victory over the bottle.: *Philadelphia Inquirer,* February 7, 1918

289. . . . coffin into the rock-hard ground,: *Boston Herald,* February 7, 1918

289. . . . carve his resting place with dynamite.: *Literary Digest,* May 19, 1928

BIBLIOGRAPHY

BOOKS

Adelman, Melvin L. *A Sporting Time: New York City and the Rise of Modern Athletics*. Urbana: University of Illinois Press, 1986.

Andrews, T. S. *Ring Battles of Centuries and Sporting Almanac*. Milwaukee: Tom Andrews Record Book Co., 1924.

Asbury, Herbert. *Carry Nation*. New York: A.A. Knopf, 1929.

———. *The Gangs of New York: An Informal History of the Underworld*. New York, London: Thunder's Mouth Press, 2000.

Barrett, James R. *The Irish Way: Becoming American in the Multiethnic City*. New York: Penguin Press, 2012.

Bergan, William M. *Old Nantasket*. North Quincy, MA: The Christopher Publishing House, 1969.

Bingay, Malcolm Wallace. *Of Me I Sing*. Indianapolis: Bobbs-Merrill Co., 1949.

Bordman, Gerald Martin. *The American Musical Theatre: A Chronicle*. New York: Oxford University Press, 1978.

Buel, James Williams. *Mysteries and Miseries of America's Great Cities*. St. Louis: Historical Publishing Co., 1883.

Burrowes, John. *Irish: The Remarkable Saga of a Nation and a City*. Edinburgh: Mainstream Publishing, 2003.

Burrows, Edwin G., and Mike Wallace. *Gotham: A History of New York City to 1898*. New York: Oxford University Press, 1999.

Caldwell, Mark. *New York Night: The Mystique and Its History*. New York: Scribner, 2005.

Campbell, Martha G., John Galluzzo, and Donald Cann. *Remembering Old Abington: The Collected Writings of Martha Campbell*. Charleston, SC: History Press, 2008.

Carlson, Oliver. *Brisbane: A Candid Biography*. New York: Stackpole Sons, 1937.

Carnegie, Andrew. *Triumphant Democracy or Fifty Years' March of the Republic*. New York: Charles Scribner's Sons, 1886.

Collins, Gail. *Scorpion Tongues: Gossip, Celebrity, and American Politics*. New York: William Morrow, 1998.

A Comparative View of the Census of Ireland in 1841–1851. London: House of Commons, 1852.

Coogan, Tim Pat. *The Famine Plot: England's Role in Ireland's Greatest Tragedy*. New York: Palgrave Macmillan, 2012.

Corbett, James J. *The Roar of the Crowd: The True Tale of the Rise and Fall of a Champion*. New York: G.P. Putnam's Sons, 1925.

Crowley, John, William J. Smyth, Michael Murphy, and Charlie Roche. *Atlas of the Great Irish Famine*. New York: New York University Press, 2012.

Cullen, James Bernard. *The Story of the Irish in Boston: Together with Biographical Sketches of Representative Men and Noted Women*. Boston: James B. Cullen & Co., 1889.

Curley, James Michael. *I'd Do It Again: A Record of All My Uproarious Years*. Englewood Cliffs, NJ: Prentice-Hall, 1957.

Dash, Mike. *Satan's Circus: Murder, Vice, Police Corruption, and New York's Trial of the Century*. New York: Crown Publishers, 2007.

DeArment, Robert K. *Bat Masterson: The Man and the Legend.* Norman: University of Oklahoma Press, 1979.

Defenders and Offenders. New York: D. Buchner & Co., 1888.

Dempsey, Jack. *Dempsey.* New York: Harper & Row, 1977.

Donovan, Mike. *The Roosevelt That I Know: Ten Years of Boxing with the President—And Other Memories of Famous Fighting Men.* New York: B.W. Dodge & Co., 1909.

Dreiser, Theodore. *A Book About Myself.* New York: Boni and Liveright, 1922.

Dulles, Foster Rhea. *America Learns to Play: A History of Popular Recreation, 1607–1940.* New York: D. Appleton-Century Co., 1940.

Durso, Joseph. *Madison Square Garden: 100 Years of History.* New York: Simon and Schuster, 1979.

Edwards, Billy. *Gladiators of the Prize Ring.* Chicago: The Athletic Publishing Co., 1895.

———. *The Portrait Gallery of Pugilists of America and Their Contemporaries.* Philadelphia: Pugilistic Publishing Co., 1894.

Flom, Eric L. *Silent Film Stars on the Stages of Seattle: A History of Performances by Hollywood Notables.* Jefferson, NC: McFarland & Co., 2009.

Franceschina, John Charles. *Harry B. Smith: Dean of American Librettists.* New York: Routledge, 2003.

Geer, Alpheus. *Mike Donovan: The Making of a Man.* New York: Moffat, Yard & Co., 1918.

The Gentleman's Companion, New York City in 1870.

Gildea, William. *The Longest Fight: In the Ring with Joe Gans, Boxing's First African-American Champion.* New York: Farrar, Straus and Giroux, 2012.

Gilfoyle, Timothy J. *City of Eros: New York City, Prostitution, and the Commercialization of Sex, 1790–1920.* New York: W.W. Norton & Co., 1992.

Gorn, Elliott J. *The Manly Art: Bare-Knuckle Prize Fighting in America.* Ithaca, NY: Cornell University Press, 1986.

Green, Thomas A., ed. *Martial Arts of the World: An Encyclopedia, Volume Two, R–Z.* Santa Barbara, CA: ABC-CLIO, 2001.

Gribben, Arthur, ed. *The Great Famine and the Irish Diaspora in America.* Amherst: University of Massachusetts Press, 1999.

Handlin, Oscar. *Boston's Immigrants, 1790–1880: A Study in Acculturation.* Cambridge, MA: Belknap Press of Harvard University Press, 1959.

Harding, William E. *Life and Battles of Jake Kilrain, Champion Pugilist of the World.* New York: Richard K. Fox Publishing Co., 1888.

History of Allegany County, N.Y. New York: F.W. Beers and Co., 1879.

Inglis, William. *Champions Off Guard.* New York: The Vanguard Press, 1932.

John L. Sullivan, Champion Pugilist of the World. New York: Richard K. Fox Publishing Co., 1882.

Kelly, John. *The Graves Are Walking: The Great Famine and the Saga of the Irish People.* New York: Henry Holt and Co., 2012.

Lang, Arne K. *Prizefighting: An American History.* Jefferson, NC: McFarland & Co., 2008.

Lardner, Rex, and Alan Bodian. *The Legendary Champions.* New York: American Heritage Press, 1972.

Laxton, Edward. *The Famine Ships: The Irish Exodus to America.* New York: Henry Holt, 1997.

Leary, John J., Jr. *Talks with T. R.* Boston and New York: Houghton Mifflin Co., 1919.

Lee, J. J., and Marion R. Casey, eds. *Making the Irish American: History and Heritage of the Irish in the United States.* New York: New York University Press, 2006.

Lewis, Lloyd, and Henry Justin Smith. *Oscar Wilde Discovers America: 1882.* New York: Harcourt, Brace and Co., 1936.

The Life and Battles of Jack Johnson, Champion Pugilist of the World. New York: Richard K. Fox Publishing Co., 1912.

The Life and Battles of James J. Corbett, Champion Pugilist of the World. New York: Richard K. Fox Publishing Co., 1892.

The Life of John L. Sullivan. New York: Richard K. Fox Publishing Co., 1892.

Lynch, Bohun. *Knuckles and Gloves*. London: W. Collins Sons & Co. 1922.

Marti, Jose. *The America of Jose Marti: Selected Writings*. New York: Noonday Press, 1954.

McCullough, David. *The Great Bridge: The Epic Story of the Building of the Brooklyn Bridge*. New York: Simon and Schuster, 1972.

———. *The Johnstown Flood*. New York: Simon and Schuster, 1968.

Merrill, Arch. *A River Ramble: Saga of the Genesee Valley*. Rochester, NY: L. Heindl & Son, 1943.

Midgley, R. L. *Boston Sights; Or Hand-Book for Visitors*. Boston: A. Williams and Company, 1865.

Miles, Kathryn. *All Standing: The Remarkable Story of the* Jeanie Johnston, *The Legendary Irish Famine Ship*. New York: Free Press, 2013.

Miller, John J. *The Big Scrum: How Teddy Roosevelt Saved Football*. New York: HarperCollins, 2011.

The Modern Gladiator: Being an Account of the Exploits and Experience of the World's Greatest Fighter, John Lawrence Sullivan. St. Louis: Athletic Publishing Co., 1889.

Morell, Parker. *Diamond Jim: The Life and Times of James Buchanan Brady*. New York: Simon and Schuster, 1934.

Morris, Edmund. *The Rise of Theodore Roosevelt*. New York: Coward, McCann & Geoghegan, 1979.

Morris, Lloyd R. *Incredible New York: High Life and Low Life of the Last Hundred Years*. New York: Random House, 1951.

Mrozek, Donald J. *Sport and American Mentality, 1880–1910*. Knoxville: University of Tennessee Press, 1983.

Myler, Patrick. *Gentleman Jim Corbett: The Truth Behind a Boxing Legend*. London: Robson Books, 1998.

Naughton, W. W. *Kings of the Queensberry Realm*. Chicago: The Continental Publishing Co., 1902.

Nevada Historical Society, Docent Council. *Early Reno*. Charleston, SC: Arcadia Publishing, 2011.

Niemi, Robert. *History in the Media: Film and Television*. Santa Barbara, CA: ABC-CLIO, 2006.

O'Connor, Thomas H. *Boston Catholics: A History of the Church and Its People*. Boston: Northeastern University Press, 1998.

———. *The Boston Irish: A Political History*. Boston: Northeastern University Press, 1995.

O'Hara, Barratt. *From Figg to Johnson*. Chicago, The Blossom Book Bourse, 1909.

O'Reilly, John Boyle. *Ethics of Boxing and Manly Sport*. Boston: Ticknor and Co., 1888.

Odell, George Clinton Densmore. *Annals of the New York Stage, Volumes 12–13*. New York: Columbia University Press, 1940.

The Picayune's Guide to New Orleans. New Orleans: The Picayune, 1903.

Power, Jerome W. *The Boston Strong Boy*. US Work Projects Administration, Federal Writers' Project (Folklore Project, Life Histories, 1936–39); Manuscript Division, Library of Congress, 1937.

Puleo, Stephen. *A City So Grand: The Rise of an American Metropolis, Boston 1850–1900*. Boston: Beacon Press, 2010.

Quinlin, Michael. *Irish Boston: A Lively Look at Boston's Colorful Irish Past*. Guilford, CT: Globe Pequot Press, 2004.

Records and Proceedings of the Senate Committee Appointed to Investigate the Police Department of the City of New York. Albany: State of New York, 1895.

Reel, Guy. *The* National Police Gazette *and the Making of the Modern American Man, 1879–1906*. New York: Palgrave Macmillan, 2006.

Report on Transportation Business in the United States at the Eleventh Census 1890. Washington, DC: Government Printing Office, 1895.

Reports of Cases Decided by the Supreme Court of Mississippi, at the October Term, 1889, and April Term, 1890, Vol. 67. Philadelphia: T. & J.W. Johnson & Co., 1890.

Riess, Steven A. *City Games: The Evolution of American Urban Society and the Rise of Sports*. Urbana: University of Illinois Press, 1989.

Robertson, Patrick. *Robertson's Book of Firsts: Who Did What for the First Time*. New York: Bloomsbury, 2011.

Roosevelt, Theodore. *Theodore Roosevelt, an Autobiography.* New York: Charles Scribner's Sons, 1922.

Runstedtler, Theresa. *Jack Johnson, Rebel Sojourner: Boxing in the Shadow of the Global Color Line.* Berkeley: University of California Press, 2012.

Russell, Don. *The Lives and Legends of Buffalo Bill.* Norman: University of Oklahoma Press, 1960.

Ryan, Dennis P. *Beyond the Ballot Box: A Social History of the Boston Irish, 1845–1917.* Rutherford, NJ: Fairleigh Dickinson University Press, 1983.

Sachsman, David B., S. Kittrell Rushing, and Roy Morris, eds. *Seeking a Voice: Images of Race and Gender in the 19th Century Press.* West Lafayette, IN: Purdue University Press, 2009.

Sammons, Jeffrey T. *Beyond the Ring: The Role of Boxing in American Society.* Urbana: University of Illinois Press, 1988.

Sansing, David G. *The University of Mississippi: A Sesquicentennial History.* Jackson: University Press of Mississippi, 1999.

Sante, Luc. *Low Life: Lures and Snares of Old New York.* New York: Farrar Straus Giroux, 1991.

Sargent, Porter. *A Handbook of New England: An Annual Publication.* Boston: Porter E. Sargent, 1916.

Schaffer, Julia. *The Washington Monument.* New York: Chelsea Clubhouse, 2010.

Schorow, Stephanie. *Drinking Boston: A History of the City and Its Spirits.* Wellesley, MA: Union Park Press, 2012.

Seton, Ernest Thompson. *Boy Scouts of America: A Handbook of Woodcraft, Scouting, and Life-Craft.* New York: Doubleday, Page & Co., 1910.

Smith, Gene, and Jayne Barry Smith. *The* National Police Gazette. New York: Simon and Schuster, 1972.

Somers, Dale A. *The Rise of Sports in New Orleans: 1850–1900.* Baton Rouge: Louisiana State University Press, 1972.

Stott, Richard Briggs. *Jolly Fellows: Male Milieus in Nineteenth-Century America.* Baltimore: Johns Hopkins University Press, 2009.

Stratmann, Linda. *The Marquess of Queensberry: Wilde's Nemesis.* New Haven, CT: Yale University Press, 2013.

Sullivan, Dean A. *Early Innings: A Documentary History of Baseball, 1825–1908.* Lincoln: University of Nebraska Press, 1995.

Sullivan, John L., and Dudley A. Sargent. *Life and Reminiscences of a Nineteenth-Century Gladiator.* Boston: Jas. A. Hearn & Co., 1892.

Sweester, Moses Foster, and Simeon Ford. *How to Know New York City.* Boston: Rand Avery Co., 1887.

Van Every, Edward. *Muldoon: The Solid Man of Sport.* New York: Frederick A. Stokes Co., 1929.

———. *Sins of New York: As "Exposed" by the* Police Gazette. New York: Frederick A. Stokes Co., 1930.

Vrabel, Jim. *When in Boston: A Time Line and Almanac.* Boston: Northeastern University Press, 2004.

Walling, George Washington. *Recollections of a New York Chief of Police.* New York: Caxton Book Concern, 1887.

Walsh, James Patrick, *Michael Mooney and the Leadville Irish: Respectability and Resistance at 10,200 Feet, 1875–1900.* University of Colorado Dissertation, 2010.

Ward, Geoffrey C. *Unforgivable Blackness: The Rise and Fall of Jack Johnson.* New York: A.A. Knopf, 2004.

Zacks, Richard. *Island of Vice: Theodore Roosevelt's Quest to Clean Up Sin-Loving New York.* New York: Anchor Books, 2012.

NEWSPAPERS AND PERIODICALS

Aberdeen Daily News, 1888–1889
Albuquerque Morning Democrat, 1886
Argus, 1891
Augusta Chronicle, 1912
Australian Town and Country Journal, 1891
Baltimore Sun, 1883, 1885, 1889, 1904
Baseball Magazine, 1909
Bay City Times-Press, 1895
Bedford Monthly, 1892
Belfast News-Letter, 1887
Boston Evening Transcript, 1858
Boston Globe, 1879–1920, 1925–1926, 1930, 1932–1933, 1942, 1952, 1957, 1960, 1966, 1969, 1978, 2010
Boston Herald, 1881–1920, 1924, 1929, 1933, 1978, 1989
Boston Journal, 1882–1888, 1893–1898, 1900, 1903, 1905–1915
Boston Record American, 1963
Boston Traveler, 1853
Boxing Illustrated, 1964
Boxing News, 2010
Brockton Enterprise, 1988
Brooklyn Daily Eagle, 1885–1886, 1888
Cato Citizen, 1901
Charlotte Observer, 1905
Chicago Herald, 1891
Chicago History, 1976–1977
Chicago Tribune, 1881–1882
Christian Examiner, 1858
Christian Union, 1887–1889
Cincinnati Commercial Tribune, 1880–1882, 1887
Cincinnati Daily Gazette, 1880–1882
Cincinnati Post, 1883, 1892, 1997, 2006
Clarion Ledger, 1889
Cleveland Leader, 1885, 1891
Collier's, 1928, 1930
Columbus Enquirer-Sun, 1888
Cosmopolitan, 1906
Critic-Record, 1882, 1886
Daily British Colonist, 1884
Daily Inter Ocean, 1881–1882, 1888–1889, 1892, 1895
Daily Mail, 2010
Daily Picayune, 1881–1885, 1889, 1891–1892, 1897–1898
Daily Register, 1884
Denver Post, 1896, 1902, 1904, 1907, 1910
Detroit Free Press, 1902, 1909
Duluth Daily News, 1888
Duluth News-Tribune, 1906
Ebony, 2005
Elkhart Daily Review, 1885

Evansville Courier and Press, 1891
Evening News, 1887, 1916, 1918
Evening Star, 1888–1889, 1907
Facts, 1883
Fight Stories, 1928, 1940, 1947
Fourth Estate, 1918
Freeman's Journal and Daily Commercial Advertiser, 1887–1888
Glasgow Herald, 2000
Grand Forks Herald, 1888, 1908
Grand Rapids Herald, 1905
Grand Rapids Press, 1905
Guardian, 1999
Harper's Weekly, 1910
Hattiesburg American, 1938, 1970
Haverhill Bulletin, 1888
Huddersfield Daily Chronicle, 1887
Illinois State Journal, 1918
Illinois State Register, 1896, 1908
Independent, 1888–1889
Investor's Business Daily, 2000
Irish-American Weekly, 1884, 1892, 1910
Irish Independent, 1910
Irish Times, 1887–1889, 1894
Irish World, 1895
Jackson Daily Citizen, 1885
Kalamazoo Gazette, 1895
Kansas City Star, 1922
Kansas City Times, 1886
Kate Field's Washington, 1892
Kerry Sentinel, 1910
Kerry Weekly Reporter & Commercial Advertiser, 1910
Liberator, 1846
Literary Digest, 1918, 1928–1929
Lockport Union-Sun & Journal, 2010
Los Angeles Sentinel, 1992, 1999
Macon Telegraph, 1884
Manchester Guardian, 1887
Massachusetts Ploughman and New England Journal of Agriculture, 1904
Milwaukee Journal, 1888
Montgomery Advertiser, 1918
Morning Herald, 1889
Morning Olympian, 1892
Morning Post, 1887
Morning Star, 1895
Muskegon Chronicle, 1883
National Police Gazette, 1880–1895, 1899–1905, 1925
New Hampshire Sentinel, 1884
New Haven Register, 1883
New Orleans Item, 1891

New Orleans Times, 1874
New York Clipper, 1881–1882
New York Evangelist, 1889
New York Herald, 1880–1892
New York Illustrated News, 1889
New York Sun, 1881–1882, 1887–1888, 1910, 1917
New York Telegraph, 1918
New York Times, 1855, 1882–1914, 1917–1918, 1921–1922, 1933, 1937–1938, 1945
New York Tribune, 1881-1882, 1884, 1889, 1892, 1918
New York World, 1889, 1903, 1918
Observer, 1888
Omaha Daily Bee, 1910
Omaha World Herald, 1894
Once a Week, 1892
Open Court, 1888
Oregonian, 1889, 1905
Outing, 1903
Outlook, 1915
Pall Mall Gazette, 1887
Patriot, 1892
Pearson's Magazine, 1912
Pelham Sun, 1931
Penny Illustrated Paper and Illustrated Times, 1887
Philadelphia Inquirer, 1883, 1889–1890, 1894–1895, 1918
Plain Dealer, 1883–1884, 1888, 1890, 1892, 1894–1895, 1912, 1989
Port Townsend Daily Leader, 1905
Post-Standard, 2012
Poughkeepsie Journal, 1910
Providence Journal, 1956, 1981
Repository, 1889
Reynold's Newspaper, 1887
Richmond Times Dispatch, 1927
Ring, 1932, 1935, 1994
Riverside Independent Enterprise, 1901
Rockland Independent, 1918
Rocky Mountain News, 1883, 1890, 1892
Sacramento Daily Recorder, 1888
Saginaw News, 1888–1889, 1891
St. Albans Daily Messenger, 1891
St. Louis Republic, 1888–1889, 1904–1905
St. Paul Globe, 1882, 1889
Salt Lake Herald, 1890
Salt Lake Telegram, 1905, 1907
San Antonio Express, 1905
San Diego Union, 1913
San Francisco Bulletin, 1884, 1891
San Francisco Call, 1890
San Francisco Chronicle, 1884, 1891
San Francisco Examiner, 1888

Sheffield & Rotherham Independent, 1887
South Australian Register, 1891
Sport, 1950
Sporting Life, 1909
Sports Illustrated, 1963
Springfield Republican, 1888, 1890, 1918, 1925
State, 1892, 1905–1906
Syracuse Herald, 1923
Tacoma Daily News, 1892
Times-Democrat, 1889
Times of London, 1887
Trenton Evening Times, 1890, 1892, 1912
Trenton State Gazette, 1881
Truth, 1883
Wall Street Journal, 1889
Watertown Daily Times, 1919
Weekly Auburnian, 1886
Weekly Irish Times, 1888, 1890
Weekly Journal Miner, 1891
Westmeath Independent, 1910
Wheeling Register, 1888–1890, 1896
Wilkes-Barre Times, 1892
Worcester Daily Spy, 1889
York Herald, 1887–1888
Zion's Herald, 1887–1888

JOURNAL ARTICLES

Anderson, Jack, "A Champion in Ireland: The Visit of John L. Sullivan," *The CBZ Journal*, May 2002, www.cyberboxingzone.com/boxing/w0502-js.htm.
Gilfoyle, Timothy J., "Barnum's Brothel: P.T.'s 'Last Great Humbug,'" *Journal of the History of Sexuality*, September 2009, 486–513.
Haley, Melissa, "Storm of Blows," *Common-Place*, January 2003, www.common-place.org/vol-03/no-02/haley.
Klein, Alexander, "Personal Income of US States: Estimates for the Period 1880–1910," *Warwick Economic Research Papers*, no. 916, Department of Economics, University of Warwick, 2009.
Paxton, Bill, "Bouts on Barges," *International Boxing Research Organization Journal*, December 2009, 5–22.
Weir, Robert, "Take Me Out to the Brawl Game," *Historical Journal of Massachusetts*, Spring 2009, 29–47.

ONLINE SOURCES

Allegany County Historical Society web site, www.alleganyhistory.org
Ancestry.com, www.ancestry.com
University of Missouri–Kansas City Law School, Lynchings: By Year and Race, http://law2.umkc.edu/faculty/projects/ftrials/shipp/lynchingyear.html

DATABASES

Boston Passenger and Crew Lists, 1820–1943
Griffith's Valuation

LETTERS

Jake Kilrain letter to Johnny Murphy, January 23, 1888
Theodore Roosevelt letter to Henry Cabot Lodge, August 28, 1889
John L. Sullivan letter to Joseph Eakins, February 8, 1897
John L. Sullivan agreement with William H. Sherwood, January 7, 1898
John L. Sullivan letter to Frank McElroy, November 26, 1899
John L. Sullivan letter to unknown recipient, 1905
Rev. R. E. Lyons letter to John L. Sullivan, November 14, 1907
Theodore Roosevelt letter to John L. Sullivan, May 2, 1913
John L. Sullivan letter to unknown recipient, May 23, 1913
John L. Sullivan letter to George A. Rosett, June 24, 1915
Theodore Roosevelt letter to John L. Sullivan, August 26, 1915
John L. Sullivan letter to James Callahan, February 10, 1916

UNDATED SOURCES

Interview with James Galvin of Athlone provided by Gearoid O'Brien, Westmeath County Library
  Service, undated
"John L. Sullivan Motion Picture Co.," Clarence W. Rowley Papers Relating to Buffalo Bill and
  John L. Sullivan, Yale Collection of Western Americana, Beinecke Rare Book and Manuscript
  Library, New Haven, CT, undated
Daniel M. Daniel, "Sullivan-Mitchell Aroused Rancors," unknown publication, 1944
Private scrapbook of newspaper articles, Joe Lannan
Transcript of testimony of T. R. White from prizefighting trial of John L. Sullivan, Sullivan-Kilrain
  Fight Collection, McCain Library and Archives, Hattiesburg, MS, undated
"When John L. Hid in Southern Swamp to Avoid Militia," John Lawrence Sullivan Papers, John J.
  Burns Library, Boston, undated

Index

About the Author

Christopher Klein is a history and travel writer and the author of two previous books—*Discovering the Boston Harbor Islands* and *The Die-Hard Sports Fan's Guide to Boston*. A frequent contributor to the *Boston Globe* and History.com, he has also written for the *New York Times*, *National Geographic Traveler*, *Harvard Magazine*, *Red Sox Magazine*, ESPN.com, Smithsonian.com, and AmericanHeritage.com. He lives in Andover, Massachusetts, with his wife and two children. Visit his website at christopherklein.com.